Scotland's leading educational publishers

National 3/4
APPLICATIONS OF MATHEMATICS

STUDENT BOOK

Craig Lowther • Mary Lucas
Judith Walker • Alysoun Wilson

N3/4 APPLICATIONS OF MATHEMATICS STUDENT BOOK

© 2018 Leckie & Leckie Ltd

001/08012018

10 9 8 7 6 5 4 3 2 1

ISBN 9780008242381

Published by
Leckie & Leckie Ltd
An imprint of HarperCollinsPublishers
Westerhill Road, Bishopbriggs, Glasgow, G64 2QT
T: 0844 576 8126   F: 0844 576 8131
leckieandleckie@harpercollins.co.uk
www.leckieandleckie.co.uk

Commissioning editor: Gillian Bowman
Managing editor: Craig Balfour

Special thanks to
Project One Publishing Solutions (project management and editorial)
Jouve India (layout and illustration)
Jess White (proofreading)
Ronald Gaffin (answer checking)
Rachel Hamar (answer checking)

A CIP Catalogue record for this book is available from the British Library.

Acknowledgements

P28 Yellow jumper © Lucy Liu / Shutterstock.com; Jeans © vetroff / Shutterstock.com; Shrub 1 © Reload Design / Shutterstock.com; Shrub 2 © Wilm Ihlenfeld / Shutterstock.com; P52, 53, 54, 55, 57, 58, 59, 78, 88, 90 Contains public sector information licensed under the Open Government Licence v3.0; P117 Timetable © Scotrail; P123 Timetable © Calmac; P165 Bridge © YuriFineart / Shutterstock.com; P173 Ferris wheel © Vitalliy / Shutterstock.com; P222 Flower © Dobroslawa Szulc / Shutterstock.com; P255 Dog © Grisha Bruev / Shutterstock.com

Whilst every effort has been made to trace the copyright holders, in cases where this has been unsuccessful, or if any have inadvertently been overlooked, the Publishers would gladly receive any information enabling them to rectify any error or omission at the first opportunity.

Printed in Italy by Grafica Veneta S.p.A

Answers

Answers to all Exercise questions, Activities involving numerical calculations and Case studies are provided online at:

www.leckieandleckie.co.uk/page/Resources

Introduction

About this book

This book provides a resource to practise and assess your understanding of the mathematical skills and knowledge covered by the National 3 and National 4 Applications of Mathematics qualifications. There is a separate chapter for each of the skills specified in the SQA course: Numeracy, Financial, Statistical, Measurement, Geometric and Graphical data and probability skills. In addition, numerical skills, such as addition, subtraction, multiplication, division and rounding, are integral to every section of the book to provide you with contextualised practise of Numeracy skills. This book also contains a number of case studies to help you prepare for assessment at National 4 level and chapter review questions for assessment at National 3 and 4.

Most of the chapters use the same features to help you progress. You will find a range of worked examples to show you how to tackle problems, and an extensive set of exercises to help you develop the whole range of skills, knowledge and understanding required for assessment at National 3 and National 4.

You should not work through the book from start to finish. Your teacher will choose a range of topics throughout the school year and teach them in the order they think works best for you and your class, so you will use different parts of the book at different times of the year.

National 3 and National 4

The book covers the requirements of both the National 3 and National 4 Applications of Mathematics qualifications. To help you navigate your way through the book, National 3 content appears first in each chapter and exercise, and National 4 topics are highlighted like this, with a coloured N4 tag and light tint over the text:

N4 **Savings and interest rates**

For short-term savings and small amounts of money, you could put it in a money jar and keep it at home where it is easily available at any time.

If you are studying N3 Applications of Mathematics, you don't need to read the N4 sections, and if you are studying N4 Applications of Mathematics, you should already know what is in the N3 sections and you can use them for revision.

Features

Chapter title
The chapter title shows the skills covered in the chapter.

7 Using statistical information presented in different diagrams

This chapter will show you how to:

Each chapter opens with a list of topics covered in the chapter and tells you what you should be able to do once you have worked your way to the end.

N4

This chapter will show you how to:

- calculate and use the perimeter of a 2D shape
- investigate a situation involving perimeter
- calculate and use the perimeter of a composite shape
- calculate and use the circumference of a circle.

You should already know:

After the list of topics covered in the chapter, there is a list of topics you should already know before you start the chapter. Some of these topics will have been covered before in maths, and others will depend on having worked through different chapters in the book.

You should already know:

- how to use standard metric units of length
- the properties of regular 2D shapes
- that perimeter is the distance around the edge of a 2D shape.

Example

Each new topic is demonstrated with at least one worked Example, which shows how to tackle the questions in the Exercise that follows. Each Example breaks down the question and solution down into steps so that you can see what calculations are involved, what kind of rearrangements are needed, and how to work out the best way of answering the question. Most Examples also include comments which help to explain the process or offer helpful tips or reminders.

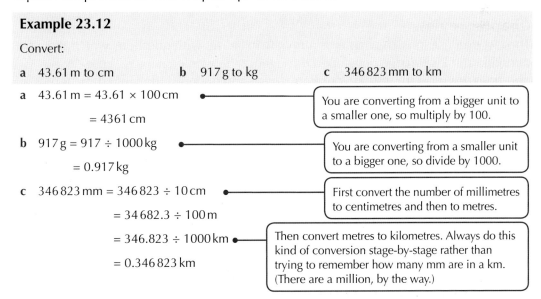

Example 23.12

Convert:

a 43.61 m to cm **b** 917 g to kg **c** 346 823 mm to km

a 43.61 m = 43.61 × 100 cm
　　　= 4361 cm
> You are converting from a bigger unit to a smaller one, so multiply by 100.

b 917 g = 917 ÷ 1000 kg
　　　= 0.917 kg
> You are converting from a smaller unit to a bigger one, so divide by 1000.

c 346 823 mm = 346 823 ÷ 10 cm
　　　= 34 682.3 ÷ 100 m
> First convert the number of millimetres to centimetres and then to metres.

　　　= 346.823 ÷ 1000 km
　　　= 0.346 823 km
> Then convert metres to kilometres. Always do this kind of conversion stage-by-stage rather than trying to remember how many mm are in a km. (There are a million, by the way.)

Exercise

The most important parts of the book are the Exercises. The questions in the Exercises are carefully graded in difficulty, so you should be developing your skills as you work through an Exercise. If you find the questions difficult, look back at the Example for ideas on what to do. Use Key questions, marked with a star ★, to assess how confident you feel about a topic. Questions which require reasoning skills are marked with a cog icon ⚙.

A calculator icon ▦ is used to indicate when a calculator is required or allowed for a particular Exercise or question. A non-calculator icon Ⓐ is used to indicate when a calculator should **not** be used for an Exercise or question, because the topic being learned is an arithmetic or a mental calculation method.

Activity

Activities are placed after the last Exercise in a chapter. These enable individual, small-group or whole class activities to further investigate topics in the chapter.

GO! Activity

You are going to organise a party for your friends and will need to buy all the food and drink. There will be 20 people at the party including yourself.

You are going to do your shopping online.

Write out a list of food and drink you want to buy and find out their prices.

To make the most of your money, you should look for the best buys where they are available.

For example, are multi-packs of crisps better value than single packets?

Is cola sold in bottles better value than cola sold in cans?

Create a summary of the amount and cost of each item you will buy, and the total cost for the party. You can display this as a list or in a poster.

Hint

Where appropriate, Hints are given in the text, Examples and Exercises to help give extra support.

> ⚠ Sketch each composite shape and draw a line to show the different shapes. Then work out any missing lengths.

Chapter review

The last exercise in each chapter is a review exercise, with questions which draw on the skills and knowledge developed throughout the whole chapter. These review questions are ideal for testing your knowledge and understanding of all the topics in the chapter.

Chapter review

1   Kieran is a plumber. He works a basic week of 40 hours.

   His basic pay is £14.50 per hour.

   a   How much is Kieran's basic pay each week?

N4

   Last week, Kieran worked for 44 hours.

   His overtime rate is time and a half.

   b   How many hours overtime did Kieran work?

   c   Calculate Kieran's overtime pay.

   d   How much was Kieran's gross pay last week?

   Last week, Kieran paid £94.94 income tax, £83.21 National Insurance and £33.35 pension.

   e   What were Kieran's total deductions last week?

   f   What was Kieran's net pay last week?

End-of-chapter summary

Each chapter closes with a summary of learning statements showing what you should be able to do when you have completed the chapter. The summary identifies the Key questions for each learning statement. You can use the End-of-chapter summary and the Key questions to check that you have a good understanding of the topics in the chapter.

> • I can calculate the probability of an event.
>   ★ Exercise 29A Q5, Q6
>
> • I can compare probabilities. ★ Exercise 29B Q3
>
> **N4** • I can use relative frequencies to predict the number of times an event will happen. ★ Exercise 29C Q3

End-of-unit case study

Each unit closes with case study material written for the N4 course. These case studies focus on skills from a number of the chapters within the unit and throughout the whole book. Working through the case studies will help you learn how to apply a range of different topics.

N4

Case studies

Stan's garden

This case study focuses on the following skills:

• working with units of measurement **(Ch. 11)**

• calculating the area of a 2D shape **(Ch. 15)**.

Answers

Answers to all Exercise questions and Activities involving numerical calculations are provided online at:
www.leckieandleckie.co.uk/page/Resources

Preparing a budget

This chapter will show you how to:

N4

- use a budget for personal use
- use a budget to plan an event
- balance income and expenditure.

You should already know:

- how to add, subtract, multiply and divide sums of money
- how to work out profit and loss.

Budgeting and planning for personal use

A budget is a financial plan which helps you to make better decisions about what you can afford to spend. A budget balances the money you have coming in (**income**) and the money you spend (**expenditure**).

There are a number of things to think about when planning a budget:

- how much money do you have to start off with
- how much money do you need for essential costs
- how much money do you want for non-essential spending?

What is your income?

Think about your income. This is the money you have coming in. This could include pocket money, wages from a part-time job, money earned for doing household chores and savings.

People with jobs usually have to pay income tax and National Insurance contributions, before they receive their wages. Take-home pay is the amount that you receive, after income tax, National Insurance and any other monies have been deducted. Take-home pay is known as **net pay**.

Net pay = gross pay − deductions

Budgeting should be based on regular money coming in and going out. Try to plan your budget regularly, either every week or every month.

What is your expenditure?

Think about your expenditure. This is what you pay for with the money you spend. Expenditure can be split into things you **need** and things you **want** to have.

The table shows David's monthly expenditure.

The things David **needs** to pay for are rent, gas and electricity, council tax, food and travel costs (to get to work). These are his **essential** costs.

The things David **wants** to pay for are TV/phone/internet, clothes and entertainment. These are his **non-essential** costs.

David has included savings in his budget so that he can buy a treat or a holiday, or to pay for an unexpected bill. He could also choose to spend less on non-essential items in order to save more.

Monthly expenditure	£
Rent	525
Gas/electricity	95
Council tax	103
TV/phone/internet	54
Food	130
Bus fares	72
Clothes	40
Entertainment	180
Savings	150
Total	**1349**

Example 1.1

Ryan wants to buy a television for his bedroom. To help plan his budget, he keeps a record of his weekly income and expenditure.

Day	Income		Expenditure			
Monday	pocket money	£35	bus fare	£2.20	lunch	£1.75
Tuesday			bus fare	£2.20	lunch	£1.75
Wednesday			bus fare	£2.20	lunch	£1.75
Thursday	football coaching	£8	bus fare	£2.20	lunch	£1.75
Friday			bus fare	£2.20	lunch	£1.75
Saturday	gardening	£12	snacks	£1.20	magazine	£2.00
Sunday	helping neighbour	£10	cinema	£7.35	snacks	£3.40

a Calculate Ryan's weekly income and weekly expenditure.

b What is the most that Ryan can save each week?

The television Ryan wants to buy costs £450. He has savings of £199.60.

c How much more will Ryan need to save?

d How many weeks will it take him to save this amount?

a Weekly income = £35 + £8 + £12 + £10 = £65
   Add up all the money Ryan receives during the week.

   Weekly expenditure
   = (5 × £2.20) + (5 × £1.75)
   + £1.20 + £2 + £7.35
   + £3.40 = £33.70
   Add up all the money Ryan spends during the week. Group the bus fares and lunches together and add on the rest of the items. Alternatively, add up the amount that Ryan spends each day, then add up the daily amounts to get the weekly total.

b The most that Ryan can save each week
   = £65 − £33.70 = £31.30
   Calculate the difference between the weekly income and the weekly expenditure.

c Ryan needs to save £450 − £199.60 = £250.40
   Calculate the difference between the cost of the television and Ryan's savings.

d £250.40 ÷ £31.30 = 8

   It will take 8 weeks
   Divide the amount that Ryan needs to save by the amount that he can save each week.

Example 1.2

Alison's net pay is £1585.80 per month.

The table shows Alison's monthly expenditure.

Alison is saving to go on a holiday in 9 months' time.

The total cost for her holiday is £1285 including spending money.

a   What is Alison's total monthly expenditure?

Expenditure	£
Rent	610
Gas/electricity	102
Council tax	108
TV/phone/internet	63
Food	142
Travel	164
Clothes	60
Entertainment	180
Savings	?

b   How much can she save each month?

c   Will Alison be able to save enough money for her holiday?

a   Total monthly expenditure
    = £610 + £102 + £108 + £63 + £142
    + £164 + £60 + £180
    = £1429

> Add up the cost of all the items that Alison has to pay for each month.

b   Alison can save £1585.80 − £1429 = £156.80

> Calculate the difference between Alison's net pay and her monthly expenditure to find out how much money she has left. This is the amount she would be able to save each month.

c   In 9 months, Alison can save 9 × £156.80
    = £1411.20

    £1411.20 is more than £1285,
    so she will have enough money.

> Multiply the number of months that Alison is saving for, by the amount that she can save each month.

Exercise 1A

1   The table shows Matthew's weekly budget.

Income		Expenditure	
Pocket money	£18	Mobile phone top up	£5.00
Sunday paper round wages	£6	Running club	£2.25
		Juice and snacks	£3.50
		Savings	£5.00

a   What is Matthew's total income and total expenditure each week?

b   How much money does Matthew have to spend if he stays within his budget?

★ 2   Sarah is going out with friends to the theatre and for a meal.

She has a budget of £50.

The theatre ticket costs £22.50.

Ice cream and juice at the interval costs £4.95.

Her bus fare costs £2.80 return.

How much money will she have for her meal?

3　Hannah is a secondary school student. The table shows her weekly income and expenditure.

Income		Expenditure	
Pocket money	£25	Mobile phone top up	£10.00
Paper round wages	£16	Swimming	£3.00
		Juice and snacks	£5.00
		Bus pass	£4.50

a　Calculate Hannah's total weekly income.

b　Calculate Hannah's total weekly expenditure.

c　How much money does Hannah have left over each week?

d　One week, Hannah decides to spend all her spare money.

She wants to choose from this list.

T-shirt	£5.50
Music download	£10.00
Cinema ticket	£7.20
Jeans	£18.00
Leggings	£6.75
DVD set	£16.00

She only wants one of each item.

She could buy a t-shirt and a music download.

What other ways could Hannah spend her spare money?

4　Julie is at college.

The table shows her weekly income and expenditure.

Income		Expenditure	
Allowance from parents	£30	Entertainment	£24
Part-time evening and weekend job	£76	Clothing	£12
		Mobile phone	£10
		Bus fares	£15

a　Calculate Julie's weekly income.

b　Calculate Julie's weekly expenditure.

c　How much money does Julie have left over each week?

She wants to buy a new laptop, which costs £405.

d　How many weeks will it take Julie to save enough money to buy the laptop?

5   Peter is an apprentice electrician.

He takes home a net pay of £788 per month.

The table shows his monthly expenditure.

How much does Peter spend on entertainment each month? (Assume he does not save any money.)

Monthly expenditure	£
Rent to parents	200
Car loan	160
Petrol	130
Car insurance	68
Entertainment	?
Clothes	50
Mobile phone	40
Total	788

★ 6   Peter would like to move in with friends who live nearer to his work.

The table shows what his monthly expenditure will be if he moves.

Can Peter afford to spend the same amount on entertainment each month as when he was living with his parents?

Monthly expenditure	£
Share of rent	210
Share of gas/electricity	35
Share of council tax	50
Food	125
Car loan	160
Petrol	100
Car insurance	68
Mobile phone	40

N4
Using a budget to plan an event

When planning an event, such as going on holiday or organising a school fayre, you need to think about:

- how much money you have to start off with

- how much money you need

- how you are going to raise the money you need.

You should also plan what to do if you do not have enough money.

How much money do you have to start off with?
If you are planning an event, you need to think about the money you already have, and the money you need to pay for the event. If you are planning a holiday, you may have some savings already. If this is not enough to pay for everything, you will need to budget weekly or monthly to have enough to pay for the holiday.

If you are planning a fundraising or social event, you may not have any money to start with. In this case, you need to work out the costs and numbers of tickets you need to sell to cover the costs of the event and to raise the money you want to end up with.

How much money do you need?
You should consider all costs and always allow for some extra spending.

If you are planning a holiday, make sure you include enough spending money.

If you are organising a fundraising event, make sure the cost per ticket covers your spending. Allow for fewer people than you expect to attend, in case you do not sell all the tickets.

N4

How are you going to raise the money you need?

If you are planning a fundraising event, such as a school fayre, you may not have any money to start with. As there will be some expenses in preparation for the event, you will need access to some money. Your school should be able to provide some funds in advance, which can then be paid back after the event.

If you are planning a holiday, you should set aside money each week or month. You will need to work out how much to save and how long it will take you to do this.

What do you do if you do not have enough money?

Preparing a budget will tell you if you will have enough money for the event. If you find you will not have enough, you need to find ways of cutting down on costs. Make sure the most important things are budgeted for. Decide if there are costs that you can reduce or do without.

If you are planning a holiday, you could stay somewhere cheaper or cut back on spending money.

If you are organising a fundraising or social event, you may need to:

- change the venue
- increase the cost of tickets
- spend less on food and drink per person.

Profit and loss

When buying and selling goods, or tickets for an event, you can make a **profit** or **loss**, depending on the amount you pay or receive.

You make a **profit** if you sell something for more money than you paid for it.

You make a **loss** if you sell something for less money than you paid for it.

If you are organising an event, you will want to make a profit to raise funds. Deciding how much you ask people to pay – for example, for tickets – depends on your expenses. You will need to carefully plan your budget to make sure that your income exceeds your expenditure.

Example 1.3

Jay is planning a holiday to Portugal. The holiday costs £437.

Jay wants to take £275 spending money.

a What is the total cost of the holiday, including spending money?

Jay has 8 months to save up for her holiday.

b How much will she need to save each month?

a Total cost = £437 + £275 = £712 ●————— Add together the cost of the holiday and the spending money that Jay wants to take.

b £712 ÷ 8 = £89 ●————— Divide the total cost of the holiday by the number of months Jay has to save.

Jay will need to save £89 per month.

N4

Example 1.4

Mr and Mrs Cheyne and their 2 children are planning a holiday to Florida.

They will take 2 pieces of luggage between them.

The table shows the costs.

Price per adult	£659
Price per child	£495
Price per item of luggage	£22

a What is the total cost of the holiday?

Mr and Mrs Cheyne are able to save £168 every month.

b How many months will it take them to save for their holiday?

a $(2 \times £659) + (2 \times £495) + (2 \times £22) = £2352$

2 adults = 2 × £659 = £1318,
2 children = 2 × £495 = £990,
2 pieces of luggage = 2 × £22 = £44.
Add together all of these amounts to get the total cost of the holiday.

b $£2352 \div £168 = 14$
It will take 14 months.

Divide the total cost of holiday by the amount that Mr and Mrs Cheyne are able to save per month.

Example 1.5

Longview Academy organised a beetle drive to raise money for school funds.

They budgeted for 200 people.

They sold 184 tickets, which cost £4 each. The price of the ticket included tea, coffee and biscuits.

They sold 5 books of raffle tickets. This raised £50 per book.

a What was the total income at the beetle drive?

The table shows the items bought by the Academy.

b What was the total expenditure for the beetle drive?

c How much profit was made for school funds?

Beetle drive games	£72.48
Raffle tickets	£7.25
Tea	£6.50
Coffee	£8.20
Milk and sugar	£5.90
Biscuits	£14.85
Raffle prizes	£100.00
Prizes for winners and losers	£20.84

a Total income = $(184 \times £4) + (5 \times £50) = £986$

Add together the cost of the 184 tickets sold at £4 each and the money raised from selling 5 raffle ticket books at £50 each to get the total income.

b Total expenditure
= £72.48 + £7.25 + £6.50 + £8.20 + £5.90
+ £14.85 + £100 + £20.84 = £236.02

Add up the cost of all the items bought to find the total expenditure.

c Profit = £986 − £236.02 = £749.98

Calculate the difference between the total income and the total expenditure to find out the amount of profit made.

N4

Example 1.6

Ben and Abigail are planning for their daughter's wedding.

This table shows a list of their expenses.

Item	Cost
Wedding dress	£495.50
Wedding cake	£350.00
Meal for 70 guests	£2026.50
Photographer	£800.00

a   What are the total wedding costs for Ben and Abigail?

Ben and Abigail can afford to save £200 per month. The wedding is in 18 months' time.

b   If they save £200 every month, will they have enough money to pay these costs?

a   Total costs = £495.50 + £350
                 + £2026.50 + £800
           = £3672

> Add up the cost of all the expenses that Ben and Abigail expect to pay.

b   Total saved = £200 × 18 = £3600

> Multiply the amount that Ben and Abigail are able to save per month by the number of months to work out how much they will have altogether.

No, Ben and Abigail will not have enough money if they save £200 per month. They will be short by £72.

> They will need to reduce their costs by looking for cheaper options – perhaps a different menu for the meal would be less expensive, or they could work out if they can save any more money.

Exercise 1B

1   Jack and Ayesha are planning a city break holiday in Prague.

The holiday costs £848.

They want to take £450 spending money.

a   What is the total cost of the holiday, including spending money?

Jack and Ayesha want to save up for the holiday in 12 months.

b   Between them, how much will they need to save each month?

2   Mr and Mrs Sinclair and their 3 teenage children are planning a holiday in Gran Canaria.

Each person is charged the same amount. The total holiday will cost £2045.

a   How much is the cost per person?

Mr and Mrs Sinclair want to take £500 spending money for themselves.

b   How much money will Mr and Mrs Sinclair need to cover the cost of the holiday?

N4

Over the next 52 weeks, the teenagers are saving up their own spending money.

Jasmine	£2.90 per week
Paula	£2.40 per week
Ben	£2.15 per week

c   How much spending money will they each manage to save?

N4 ★ 3 Mr and Mrs Asiz and their son are planning a holiday to Morocco.

They will each take a piece of luggage. The table shows the costs of the holiday.

Price per adult	£679.00
Price per child	£405.50
Price per item of luggage	£18.00

a   What is the total cost of the holiday?

Mr and Mrs Asiz are able to save £245 every month.

b   How many months will it take them to save for their holiday?

Their son is saving his own money each month, for his spending money.

He gets £20 pocket money per month.

He also has £36 left from his birthday money.

c   How much spending money will he be able to take on holiday?

> ⚠ See your answer from part **b** for the number of months.

★ 4 Primary 7 pupils at the local school are planning to sell ice creams at their sports day.

They have budgeted for 300 ice creams. The table shows the expenses.

30 tubs of ice cream	£3 each
30 packs of cones (10 per pack)	£1.50 per pack
5 ice cream scoops	£3 each

a   What will be the total expenditure?

The pupils will charge 75p per ice cream cone.

b   If they sell all 300 ice cream cones, what will be the total income?

c   If they sell all 300 ice cream cones, how much profit will they make?

d   What is the least amount of ice cream cones that need to be sold in order to break even? (**Break even** means there is no profit or loss.)

5   Ian and May are planning for their son's wedding.

This table shows a list of their expenses.

Item	Cost
Groom's outfit	£320
Hire of venue for wedding reception	£950
Evening entertainment	£1200
Wedding cars	£300
Flowers	£550

a   What are the total wedding costs for Ian and May?

The wedding is in 16 months' time.

b   How much will Ian and May have to save each month to be able to afford these costs?

Ian and May have £440 in savings which they want to put towards their wedding costs.

c   How much will Ian and May now have to save each month to be able to afford these costs?

N4 ★ 6 A village youth club organised a bingo night to raise money towards the cost of repairs to the community hall.

They budgeted for 150 people.

They sold all the tickets, which cost £8 each. This included tea, coffee and cakes.

They also sold 2 books of raffle tickets. This raised £100 per book.

a What was the total income at the bingo night?

The table shows the items bought by the youth club.

Bingo cards	£30.00
Bingo cage, balls and check board	£30.00
Raffle tickets	£2.90
Tea	£4.88
Coffee	£6.15
Milk and sugar	£4.45
Cakes (ingredients – homemade)	£48.00
Raffle prizes	£75.00
Bingo prizes (money)	£200.00

b What was the total expenditure for the bingo?

c How much profit was made for the community hall repairs fund?

7 Fairfield Academy put on a school show. It was a sell-out for all three nights.

The maximum audience allowed each night is 250.

The table shows the numbers of tickets sold each night.

Day	Adult	Child
Wednesday	180	70
Thursday	175	75
Friday	148	102

a Over the three nights:

   i how many adult tickets were sold?

   ii how many child tickets were sold?

Adult tickets cost £6 each and child tickets cost £4 each.

b What was the total income from all the ticket sales?

The table shows the expenditure.

Hire of school hall	£90
Materials for props and scenery	£400
Costumes	£325
Sound and lighting equipment	£600
Printing (tickets and advertising)	£32

c What was the total expenditure?

d How much profit was made?

e If the school show had to be cancelled on Thursday and Friday, how much profit or loss would they have made?

GO! Activity

For the next week, record your own personal budget in a table, such as the one shown here.

Income		Expenditure	
Pocket money	£?	Juice and snacks	£?
Paid work	£?	Bus fares	£?
Gift	£?	Magazines	£?
		Entertainment (music downloads, online games)	£?
		Leisure (going out with friends, sports)	£?
		Other (clothes, mobile phone)	£?
Total			

How much are you saving?

Think about ways you could cut down on any of your expenditure to save up for something special, such as spending money for a family holiday.

GO! Activity

Your school is planning a 7-day watersports trip to Spain for 40 pupils and staff.

The cost of the trip should include:

- breakfast, lunch and dinner each day

- all travelling expenses

- cost of all instructors and watersports equipment hire.

The cost of the trip will not include:

- extra juice and snacks

- spending money.

Research the costs of a 7-day watersports trip to Spain for school groups.

Calculate how much the school should charge per person.

Chapter review

1   Michelle is a shop assistant.
    She takes home a net pay of £946 per month.

    She lives with her parents.

    The table shows her monthly expenditure.

    a   Calculate Michelle's monthly expenditure.

    b   How much money does Michelle have left over each month?

Monthly expenditure	£
Rent and bills to parents	400
Bus fares	72
Gym membership	35
Entertainment	200
Mobile phone	40
Clothes	50
Other	85

   Michelle is saving up for a holiday which costs £340. She also wants to take £250 spending money on holiday.

    c   What is the total amount that Michelle will need to save for her holiday?

    d   If Michelle's expenditure stays the same, how many months will it take for her to save enough for her holiday?

2   Evan works in an office.

His take-home pay is £1122 per month.

He shares a flat with two friends.

The table shows his monthly expenditure.

Monthly expenditure	£
Share of rent	225
Share of gas/electricity	40
Share of council tax	53
Share of TV package	15
Food	160
Bus fares	72
Entertainment	250
Clothes	70
Mobile phone	55
Sports club membership	40

a   Calculate Evan's monthly expenditure.

Evan wants to learn to play the guitar. He has seen a guitar he would like to buy. This guitar costs £160.

b   Can Evan afford to buy the guitar with the money he has left over at the end of the month? Give a reason for your answer.

3   Mr Shand is an engineer whose net pay is £1895 per month.

Mrs Shand works part-time and takes home £728 each month.

a   What is the total income for Mr and Mrs Shand?

Mr and Mrs Shand's monthly expenditure is £2467.

b   How much money do Mr and Mrs Shand have left over at the end of each month?

N4

Mr and Mrs Shand and their child are going on holiday to Tenerife. They will take 1 piece of luggage between them.

The table shows the costs.

Price per adult	£340
Price per child	£208
Price per item of luggage	£24

c   What is the total cost of the holiday?

d   How long will it take Mr and Mrs Shand to save up for the cost of the holiday?

N4

4   To raise funds for a local charity, Hillview Community Centre organised a coffee morning, which also included an indoor table sale.

The community centre has £200 available to buy the items needed for the coffee morning.

The table shows the cost of the items they want to buy.

Item	Cost
Tea	£6.50
Coffee	£8.75
Milk	£5.20
Sugar	£1.10
Diluting juice	£2.20
Cakes and biscuits	£120.00
Raffle tickets	£4.50
Raffle prizes	£60.00

a   Does the community centre have enough money available to buy all of these items? If not, suggest how they can stay in their budget.

The table shows the money raised by the community centre.

Item	Amount raised per item	Total amount raised
3 books of raffle tickets	£50 per raffle book	?
Fee for 12 tables	£10 per table	?
126 entry tickets for coffee morning	£4 per ticket	?
	TOTAL	?

b   Copy and complete the table to find the amount of money raised by the community centre.

c   Assuming the community centre stayed within their budget for the expenditure, how much money did they raise for the local charity?

- I can use a budget for personal use.
  ★ Exercise 1A Q2, Q6

N4
- I can use a budget to plan an event.
  ★ Exercise 1B Q3, Q6

- I can balance income and expenditure.
  ★ Exercise 1B Q4

2 Factors affecting income

This chapter will show you how to:

- investigate factors affecting income
- **N4** investigate factors affecting income, such as commissions and bonuses
- investigate factors affecting deductions
- **N4** investigate factors affecting deductions, such as National Insurance.

You should already know:

- how to add, subtract, multiply and divide sums of money
- how to calculate the percentage of a quantity
- how to calculate simple fractions of a quantity.

Income

Income is the money you have coming in every week or month. This could be from a job, a work pension, or government benefits and allowances.

Wages and salary

People with jobs are paid a **wage** or a **salary**.

A **wage** is usually paid at an hourly rate. The more hours you work, the more you earn. Wages are usually paid every week or every month.

N4 If you work more than the basic number of hours per week (usually 35–40 hours), you are paid **overtime**. The hourly rate for overtime is usually higher than the basic hourly rate.

A **salary** is the amount you earn each year (annually). This is divided equally between the twelve months of the year. Salaries are usually paid every month.

Basic pay is the amount you earn for working your normal basic number of hours each week.

N4 **Gross pay** is the amount you are paid by your employer. It is the total amount of your basic pay and any overtime, bonuses or commission that you earn.

Extra money can be earned with a **bonus** or **commission**.

A **bonus** is an extra payment, such as a Christmas bonus or for work well done.

Commission is paid to sales people as a percentage of their sales, to encourage them to sell more.

A **pay rise** is an increase in your wages or salary. This is usually negotiated and agreed annually, by employers and staff. Pay rises are usually paid as a percentage of the current wage or salary.

Government benefits and allowances

The government pays a range of benefits and allowances. These are paid to people:

- who have children
- who are on a low wage
- who are sick
- who are without a job
- who are disabled
- who are retired.

Example 2.1

Alastair works as a salesman in a furniture store. He earns £7.60 per hour and works a 25-hour week.

a What is Alastair's basic pay?

Alastair also receives £58 each week in benefits to top up his wages.

b What is Alastair's total weekly income?

N4

Last week Alastair got a bonus of £30 for meeting his sales target.

c What was his weekly income last week?

a 25 × £7.60 = £190 ●————
> Multiply the number of hours that Alastair works by the amount he earns each hour to find his basic pay.

b £190 + £58 = £248 ●————
> Add Alastair's basic pay to the benefits he receives to find his total weekly income.

N4

c £248 + £30 = £278 ●————
> Add Alastair's total weekly income to the bonus he received to calculate his weekly income last week.

Example 2.2

Mairi is a nurse. Her annual salary is £23 700.

a What is her monthly pay?

b Next month she will get a 1% pay rise.

   i How much will she now earn each month?

   ii How much will her new annual salary be?

a £23 700 ÷ 12 = £1975 ●————
> Divide Mairi's annual salary by 12 (number of months in a year) to find her monthly pay.

b i Increase each month:

$$\frac{1}{100} \times £1975 = £19.75$$
> Reminder: 1% is equivalent to $\frac{1}{100}$ as a fraction.

New monthly pay
= £1975 + £19.75
= £1994.75
> Add Mairi's monthly salary to her monthly pay increase to find her new monthly pay.

   ii New annual salary
= 12 × £1994.75
= £23 937
> Multiply Mairi's new monthly pay by the number of months in a year to find her new annual salary.

Example 2.3

Fatima works in a supermarket. Her basic pay is £7.20 per hour for a 38-hour week.

a How much does Fatima earn each week?

N4

Last week she worked 5 hours overtime on Saturday at time and a half.

> Overtime at time and a half means $1\frac{1}{2}$ (1.5) hours' pay for 1 hour's work.

She also worked 4 hours overtime on Sunday at double time.

> Overtime at double time means 2 hours' pay for 1 hour's work.

b How much did Fatima earn on:

   i Saturday?

   ii Sunday?

c What was Fatima's gross pay last week?

a $38 \times £7.20 = £273.60$

N4

b i $£7.20 \times 1.5 = £10.80$

   $£10.80 \times 5 = £54$

> Multiply the basic hourly rate by 1.5 to find the hourly overtime rate at time and a half. Then multiply by the number of overtime hours worked at time and a half to find the total amount paid.

   ii $£7.20 \times 2 = £14.40$

   $£14.40 \times 4 = £57.60$

> Multiply the basic hourly rate by 2 to find the hourly overtime rate at double time. Then multiply by the number of overtime hours worked at double time to find the total amount paid.

c $£273.60 + £54 + £57.60 = £385.20$

> Add the basic pay to all the overtime paid to find the gross pay.

Exercise 2A

1 Liam is a chef. He earns £8.85 per hour for a 40-hour week.
   How much does Liam earn each week?

★ 2 Emily is a part-time hairdresser. She earns £8.20 per hour for a 28-hour week.
   a How much does Emily earn each week?
   Emily receives £46.70 in benefits each week.
   b How much is her weekly income?

3 Hannah is a solicitor. Her annual salary is £35 844.
   How much does Hannah earn each month?

4 Karen is an electrician. She earns £11.28 per hour for a 37-hour week.
   a How much does Karen earn each week?

N4

Last week, Karen did 4 hours overtime on Saturday at double time.
   b How much overtime pay did Karen receive?
   c How much did Karen earn last week, in total?

N4

★ 5   Molly works as a hotel receptionist. She earns £7.92 per hour for a 38-hour week.

Sometimes Molly is asked to work overtime and is paid at time and a half.

Last week Molly worked for 43 hours.

a   How many hours overtime did Molly work?

b   How much was Molly's basic pay?

c   How much was Molly paid for overtime?

d   What was Molly's gross pay last week?

> ⚠ Find the difference between the number of hours that Molly worked last week and her basic hours.

6   Callum is a hospital porter. He works a basic 39-hour week and is paid £8.16 per hour. Overtime is paid at double time.

a   How much is Callum's basic weekly pay?

In one week, Callum worked for 45 hours.

b   What was his overtime pay?

c   What was Callum's gross pay?

The following week, Callum's overtime pay was £48.96.

d   How many hours did he work overtime?

Deductions

Deductions are amounts of money taken off your wages or salary by your employer. These are taken from your wages or salary before you receive them.

The main deductions are **income tax**, **National Insurance** and **pension contributions**.

Income tax and **National Insurance** are paid to the government. They are used to help pay for things like education, the National Health Service, law and order, roads, pensions and benefits etc.

Pension contributions are payments towards the pension scheme set up by your employer. This ensures you have regular income when you retire.

If you are in employment, your **payslip** shows all of your earnings and deductions. The amount you receive is called your **net pay** (gross pay minus the deductions).

Net pay = gross pay – deductions

Example 2.4

Mairi is a nurse. Here is a summary of her monthly payslip.

Gross pay	£1975.00
Deductions	£228.33
Net pay	?

Calculate Mairi's net pay.

Net pay = £1975.00 – £228.33 = £1746.67 ●————[Net pay = gross pay – deductions]

Example 2.5

Fatima works in a supermarket. This is her payslip for last week. Some information is missing.

Employee: Fatima Ahmed		Week ending: 10.2.17	
Basic pay £273.60	Overtime £111.60	Bonus £0.00	Gross pay: ?
Income tax £38.58	National Insurance £34.67	Pension £19.26	Deductions: ?
			Net pay: ?

Work out the:

a gross pay

b deductions

c net pay.

a Gross pay = £273.60 + £111.60
        = £385.20

> Add all of Fatima's income:
> basic pay + overtime + bonus = gross pay.

b Deductions = £38.58 + £34.67 +£19.26
        = £92.51

> Add all of Fatima's deductions:
> income tax + National Insurance + pension
> = deductions.

c Net pay = £385.20 – £92.51
        = £292.69

> Net pay = gross pay – deductions

Exercise 2B

★ 1 Hannah is a solicitor. This is a short version of her payslip for last month. Calculate Hannah's net pay.

Gross pay	£2987.00
Deductions	£838.04
Net pay	?

2 Lianne is a chef. This is a short version of his payslip for last week.

   a What were Lianne's deductions?

Gross pay	£354.00
Deductions	?
Net pay	£273.38

> Gross pay – deductions = net pay
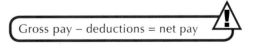

   b If Lianne earns the same amount every week, how much will she take home in 1 year?

3 Mark is a joiner. His weekly gross pay is £425.80. His total deductions were £113.63. How much was Mark's net pay?

4 Molly works as a hotel receptionist. Last week her net pay was £276.88.

   If the deductions were £83.48, how much was Molly's gross pay?

5   Emily is a hairdresser. This is her payslip for last week. Some information is missing.

Name: E. Shepherd		Week number: 37	
Basic pay £229.60	Overtime 0.00	Bonus £30	Gross pay: ?
Income tax £7.53	National Insurance £6.51	Pension £11.48	Deductions: ?
			Net pay: ?

Calculate Emily's:

a   gross pay

b   deductions

c   net pay.

N4   ★ 6   Alastair works as a salesman in a furniture store. He is paid weekly.

Use Alastair's payslip to calculate his net pay for the week.

Mr A. Jones	Pay period 21
Payments	*Deductions*
Basic pay: £288.80 Overtime: £145.62 Commission: £72.81	Income tax: £48.42 National Insurance: £45.78 Pension: £21.72
Gross pay:	**Deductions:**
Net pay:	

7   Matthew is an electrician. Here is his payslip for last week. There has been a printing error.

Write up a new payslip for Matthew with the payments and deductions in the correct place. Recalculate his net pay.

Mr M. Adamson	Week ending 31.7.17
Payments	*Deductions*
Income tax: £63.06 Overtime: £145.62	Basic pay: £417.36 National Insurance: £58.27 Pension: £25.38
Gross pay: £153.30	**Deductions:** £501.01
Net pay: £360.89	

8   Callum is a hospital porter. This is his payslip for last week. Some of the information has been left out.

Copy and fully complete Callum's payslip.

C. MacDonald	Week number 3	
Payments	*Deductions*	
Basic pay: £318.24 Overtime: £ ?	Income tax: £44.77 National Insurance: £ ? Pension: £15.91	
Gross pay: £ ?	**Deductions:** £104.51	**Net pay:** £311.65

Activity

This activity combines the work you have done in Chapters 1 and 2.

From the provided list, choose a job – perhaps the job you would like to do when you are older. The annual salary and annual deductions are included in the list.

Job title	Annual salary	Annual deductions
Office manager	£27 100	£7775.04
Personal trainer	£19 150	£3287.16
Secretary	£18 694	£3072.00
Maintenance engineer	£29 852	£9061.92
Physiotherapist	£33 525	£10 680.96
Sous chef in a restaurant	£23 345	£6235.92
Catering assistant	£15 224	£2655.00
Hairdresser	£20 224	£4854.96
Mechanic	£24 150	£6636.60
Social worker	£26 420	£7605.00
Call centre operator	£14 720	£2480.16
Nursery nurse	£22 335	£5783.04

a From your chosen job, divide the annual salary and annual deductions by 12 to find the gross monthly pay and deductions.

b Calculate your net monthly income.

c Now consider your monthly expenditure. This table shows some representative amounts for essentials.

Rent/mortgage	£680
Gas/electricity	£89
Council tax	£138
Food	£150
Travel (to get to work)	£120

d How much money do you have left over each month?

e Decide how you will spend the rest of your income. Will this include any savings?

Chapter review

1   Kieran is a plumber. He works a basic week of 40 hours.

   His basic pay is £14.50 per hour.

   a   How much is Kieran's basic pay each week?

N4

   Last week, Kieran worked for 44 hours.

   His overtime rate is time and a half.

   b   How many hours overtime did Kieran work?

   c   Calculate Kieran's overtime pay.

   d   How much was Kieran's gross pay last week?

   Last week, Kieran paid £94.94 income tax, £83.21 National Insurance and £33.35 pension.

   e   What were Kieran's total deductions last week?

   f   What was Kieran's net pay last week?

2   Jack is a car salesman. His basic annual salary is £14 250.

   a   How much is Jack's basic salary each month?

N4

   Jack also earns 0.5% commission for the value of every car he sells.

   Last month, Jack sold cars worth £196 500.

   b   How much commission did Jack earn?

   c   Calculate Jack's gross pay last month.

   d   Copy and complete Jack's pay slip for last month.

Jack Sinclair	April	
Payments	*Deductions*	
Basic pay: ?	Income tax:	£267.33
Commission: ?	National Insurance:	£238.70
	Pension:	?
Gross pay: ?	**Deductions:**	£647.08
Net pay: ?		

3   Amanda works part time. She is paid an hourly rate of £7.90 for a 25-hour week.

   a   How much does Amanda earn each week?

   Amanda pays £9.88 per week towards her pension.

   b   What is Amanda's net pay?

   Amanda also gets £72.35 in benefits each week to top up her wages.

   c   How much is Amanda's weekly income?

N4

4   Laura works as a paramedic. She earns £2142 each month.

a   What is Laura's annual salary?

b   Copy and complete Laura's payslip.

Laura James	March	
Payments	*Deductions*	
Basic pay: £2142	Income tax: ? National Insurance: £235.62 Pension: £139.23	
Gross pay: £2142	**Deductions:** ?	
Net pay: £1505.42		

Laura will be getting a 1.5% pay rise from next month.

c   What will Laura's new annual salary be?

d   How much will Laura's gross pay be each month?

This is Laura's payslip for next month.

Laura James	April	
Payments	*Deductions*	
Basic pay: ?	Income tax: £268.16 National Insurance: £239.15 Pension: £141.32	
Gross pay: ?	**Deductions:** £648.63	
Net pay: ?		

e   How much more will Laura's net pay be in April, compared to March?

- I can investigate factors affecting income.
  ★ Exercise 2A Q2

N4
- I can investigate factors affecting income, such as commissions and bonuses.
  ★ Excercise 2A Q5

- I can investigate factors affecting deductions.
  ★ Exercise 2B Q1

N4
- I can investigate factors affecting deductions, such as National Insurance.
  ★ Excercise 2B Q6

3 Determining the best deal, given two pieces of information

This chapter will show you how to:

- compare two products, given two pieces of information on each
- compare at least three products, given two pieces of information on each.

N4

You should already know:

- how to add, subtract, multiply and divide sums of money
- how to calculate the percentage of a quantity
- how to calculate simple fractions of a quantity
- how to interpret data from a table.

Determining the best deal

It is always a good idea to shop around to get the best value for money. You should compare the size and cost of products, taking account of the amount you need.

For example, when buying food with a 'use by' date, the largest pack may not be the best value if you end up having to throw some of it away.

Offers, such as 'buy one get one free', are often good value. However, you should still check that they offer the best deal.

When buying a service such as a mobile phone contract, you should compare providers and check what is included.

If you can work out the best deal you will be able to make good decisions and save money when buying products and services.

Example 3.1

Scott wants to buy some new trainers.

Sports4U have a pair he likes, which costs £39.50.

The same pair usually costs £42.80 at Sport100. This month they have a 10% discount on all their trainers.

In which shop are the trainers cheaper?

10% of £42.80 = $\dfrac{10}{100} \times 42.80 = £4.28$

> Calculate the discount at Sport 100.
> Find 10% of the usual price.
> Remember 10% is equivalent to $\dfrac{10}{100}$

Sale price trainers at Sport100 cost
£42.80 − £4.28 = £38.52

> Subtract the discount from the original price to find the cost of the trainers at Sport100.

£38.52 is less than £39.50 so the trainers are cheaper at Sport100.

> Compare the prices at both shops and state your conclusion.

Example 3.2

At the supermarket, bottles of shampoo are available in three sizes and prices.

      Regular size: 350 ml costs £2.24

      Special offer: 400 ml costs £2.50

      Extra large size: 750 ml costs £4.65

Is the special offer the best buy? Give a reason for your answer.

350 ml bottle: 224p ÷ 350 ml = 0.64p per ml

400 ml bottle: 250p ÷ 400 ml = 0.625p per ml

750 ml bottle: 465p ÷ 750 ml = 0.62p per ml

> Change the price to pence by multiplying by 100. Divide the price (in pence) by the number of millilitres (ml) in the bottle. This compares the cost per ml. The lowest cost per ml gives the best value.

The special offer is **not** the best buy. 0.62p is less than 0.625p and 0.64p per ml, so the 750 ml bottle of shampoo is the best buy.

> Compare the prices per ml of each bottle and state your conclusion.

N4

Example 3.3

Jacqui has seen a new coffee table that she wants to buy.

She would like it to be delivered.

The table shows the charges at three shops.

Furniture4U	Tables'n'chairs	FurnitureCare
£221 including VAT	£172.75 plus 20% VAT	£210 including VAT
Free delivery	£15 delivery	5% delivery

Which shop gives the best option for Jacqui?

> Value added tax (VAT) is a tax added to most goods and services. 20% of the price is added on – this is what customers pay.

Furniture4U

Total cost = £221

> The cost of the table includes VAT and delivery. No further calculations are required.

Tables'n'chairs

$VAT = \frac{20}{100} \times £172.75 = £34.55$

> Calculate the VAT. Find 20% of the cost. 20% is equivalent to $\frac{20}{100}$

Total cost = £172.75 + £34.55 + £15

           = £222.30

> Total cost = cost of table + VAT + delivery charge.

(continued)

N4

FurnitureCare

Delivery = $\frac{5}{100}$ × £210 = £10.50 ●————[Calculate the delivery charge. Find 5% of the cost of the table. 5% is equivalent to $\frac{5}{100}$]

Total cost at FurnitureCare = £210 + £10.50 ●————[Total cost = cost of table + delivery charge. There is no additional charge for VAT as this is included.]
                            = £220.50

The lowest cost is £220.50 at FurnitureCare, so this is the best option for Jacqui. ●————[Compare the prices charged by each shop and state your conclusion.]

Example 3.4

Mr and Mrs Cheyne and their 2 children are planning a holiday to Florida.

They will take 2 pieces of luggage between them.

The table shows the information provided from three travel companies.

Which travel company would give the best value for the Cheyne family?

Give a reason for your answer.

		Price
Travel4U	Per adult	£659
	Per child	£495
	Luggage per piece	£22
Florida Travel	Per adult	£610
	Per child	10% off adult price
	Luggage per piece	£18
HolidayPlus	Per adult	£695
	Per child	£625
	Luggage per piece	Included
	Special offer: 12% discount	

Travel4U

2 adults = 2 × £659 = £1318 ●————[Calculate the cost for 2 adults.]

2 children = 2 × £495 = £990 ●————[Calculate the cost for 2 children.]

2 pieces of luggage = 2 × £22 = £44 ●————[Calculate the cost for 2 pieces of luggage.]

Total cost of Travel4U = £1318 + £990 + £44 = £2352 ●[Total cost = cost for adults + cost for children + cost of luggage.]

Florida Travel

Discount per child = $\frac{10}{100}$ × £610 = £61 ●————[Calculate the discount per child. Find 10% of the cost of an adult. 10% is equivalent to $\frac{10}{100}$]

Cost per child = £610 – £61 = £549 ●————

[Subtract the discount from the adult price to find the cost of the child price.]

2 adults = 2 × £610 = £1220

2 children = 2 × £549 = £1098

2 pieces of luggage = 2 × £18 = £36

Total cost of Florida Travel = £1220 + £1098 + £36 = £2354

[Total cost = cost for adults + cost for children + cost of luggage.]

N4 **HolidayPlus**

2 adults = 2 × £695 = £1390

2 children = 2 × £625 = £1250

2 pieces of luggage = 2 × £0 = £0

Total cost of HolidayPlus = £1390 + £1250 + £0 = £2640

> Total cost = cost for adults + cost for children + cost of luggage.

Discount = $\frac{12}{100}$ × £2640 = £316.80

> Calculate the discount. Find 12% of the total cost of the holiday. 12% is equivalent to $\frac{12}{100}$

Cost of HolidayPlus, with the 12% discount = £2640 − £316.80 = £2323.20

> Subtract the discount from the cost of the holiday to find the total amount to be paid.

The lowest total cost is £2323.20 at HolidayPlus, so this is the best choice.

> Compare the prices charged by each travel company and state your conclusion.

Exercise 3A

1 Sasha is a student and needs to buy 5 folders.

In one shop, single folders are sold for 95p each.

The shop also has a special offer: buy 5 folders for £4.60.

a Which is the better deal for Sasha?

b How much will she save if she chooses the best deal?

2 Rachael is starting a course of 12 driving lessons.

Her instructor charges £28 per lesson.

He also offers a package of 12 lessons for £315.

How much will Rachael save if she buys the package of 12 lessons?

3 Beth wants to buy some perfume for her mother's birthday.

A bottle of Blueflower costs £15.95.

A bottle of Whiteflower normally costs £20.60.

This week, there is a 25% discount on Whiteflower perfume.

Beth wants to buy the cheaper bottle of perfume.

Which one should she buy?

★ 4 Beth has seen a shirt she would like to buy for her father's birthday.

In Shirts'n'suits, the shirt costs £18.99.

In Clothes4U, the shirt is normally on sale for £21.80, but now has 15% taken off this price.

Which shop offers the better deal for Beth?

Give a reason for your answer.

5   Ross and Emma want to buy a new front door for their house. They have seen one that they like.

Windows4U have this door for £667.95.

Windows'n'doors have the same door for £730.25.

This week Windows'n'doors have a sale – 8% off all their stock.

At which company is the front door cheaper?

6   At the local shop, bottles of cola are on sale in two different sizes.

The 2 litre bottle costs £1.79.

The 1.5 litre bottle costs £1.38.

Which bottle gives the better value?

Give a reason for your answer.

7   Clothes4U has an end of season sale. All items are $\frac{1}{3}$ off the normal price.

Work out these sale prices.

a    b

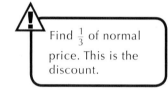
Find $\frac{1}{3}$ of normal price. This is the discount.

£18.99

£25.50

★ 8   The local garden centre has a promotion for their shrubs.

They are all marked at $\frac{1}{4}$ off the usual price.

How much will these shrubs now cost?

a    b

£8.92

£17.76

9   At the greengrocers, bags of potatoes can be bought in three sizes.

10 kg costs £11.25.

2.5 kg costs £2.80.

1.5 kg costs £1.80.

By calculating the cost per kg, work out which bag of potatoes gives the best value.

N4   10   In a supermarket, a single chocolate bar costs 54 pence.

A multi-pack of 5 chocolate bars costs £2.25.

The supermarket also has a special offer – buy 2 single chocolate bars, get a third one free.

Is the multi-pack the best buy? Give a reason for your answer.

N4

11 At the same supermarket, apple juice can be bought in cartons of different sizes.

　　A 1-litre carton costs 84p.

　　A pack of 4 1-litre cartons costs £2.88.

　　A pack of 3 220 ml cartons costs 66p.

By calculating the cost (in pence) per ml, work out which is the best buy.

> Remember 1 litre = 1000 ml.
> Multiply the number of litres by 1000 to change litres to millilitres. ⚠

12 Lights'n'lamps have a deal on light bulbs.

- Pack of 3 light bulbs for £9.90.
- Pack of 5 light bulbs for £14.95.
- Buy one get one free on packs of 2 light bulbs, with a pack price of £6.96.

a Which pack has the cheapest price for a single light bulb?

b What is the difference between the least and most expensive single light bulbs in the packs?

13 Jacqui has seen a new bed that she would like to buy and to be delivered.

The table shows the charges at three shops.

Furniture4U	Beds'n'beds	FurnitureCare
£452 including VAT	£347.50 plus 20% VAT	£420 including VAT
Free delivery	£15 delivery	5% delivery

Which shop gives the best option for Jacqui?

> See Example 3.3 for a reminder on how to solve this kind of problem. ⚠

★ 14 Mr and Mrs Alexander and their 3 children are planning a holiday to Spain.

They will take 1 piece of luggage each.

The table shows the information provided from three different travel companies.

		Prices
Travel4U	Per adult	£474
	Per child	15% off adult price
	Luggage per piece	£29
Spanish Travel	Per adult	£502
	Per child	£358
	Luggage per piece	£22
HolidayPlus	Per adult	£535
	Per child	£490
	Luggage per piece	Included
	Special offer: 10% discount	

Which travel company would give the best value for the Alexander family?

Give a reason for your answer.

N4

15 Jasmine is shopping for groceries and has the choice of different sizes for each food product.

For each item, she wants to buy the size which gives the best value.

This table shows the cost of the different sizes for each food product that Jasmine wants to buy.

Food product	Small	Medium	Large
Chicken breasts	485 g for £3.78	630 g for £3.98	1 kg for £6.15
Potatoes	1.5 kg for £1.80	2.5 kg for £2.80	10 kg for £11.25
Sprouts	250 g for £0.80	500 g for £1.00	1 kg for £1.08
Onions	4 for 89p	6 for £1.30	10 for £1.99
Milk	2 pints for £0.86	4 pints for £1.23	6 pints for £1.45
Ice cream	900 ml for £1.00	1.8 litres for £2.16	2 litres for £2.65

a By calculating the cost (in pence) per gram for the chicken breasts, find which size gives the best value.

> ⚠ 1 kg = 1000 g. Multiply the number of kilograms by 1000 to change kilograms to grams.

b By calculating the cost (in pence) per millilitre for the ice cream, find which size gives the best value.

c Calculate which size gives the best value, for the rest of the items in Jasmine's shopping list.

> ⚠ 1 litre = 1000 ml. Multiply the number of litres by 1000 to change litres to ml.

d If Jasmine buys all the items which give the best value, how much will her groceries cost?

16 Jack and Abbie are looking for a new bedroom carpet.

The room is a rectangle, measuring 4 m by 3.5 m.

They have seen three carpets that they like and want to choose the cheapest one.

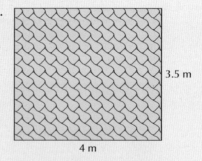

3.5 m

4 m

The table shows the cost of these carpets.

Carpet 1	Cut from roll 4 m by 3.5 m	£12.50 per m²
Carpet 2	End of roll piece 4 m by 3.8 m	£180
Carpet 3	End of roll piece 4 m by 3.9 m	Normally £12.50 per m² Discount of 10%

Which carpet should Jack and Abbie buy?

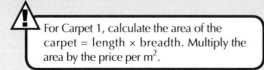

> ⚠ For Carpet 1, calculate the area of the carpet = length × breadth. Multiply the area by the price per m².

Activity

You are going to organise a party for your friends and will need to buy all the food and drink. There will be 20 people at the party including yourself.

You are going to do your shopping online.

Write out a list of food and drink you want to buy and find out their prices.

To make the most of your money, you should look for the best buys where they are available.

For example, are multi-packs of crisps better value than single packets?

Is cola sold in bottles better value than cola sold in cans?

Create a summary of the amount and cost of each item you will buy, and the total cost for the party. You can display this as a list or in a poster.

Chapter review

1　At the local supermarket, the same brand of ice cream is sold in two different sized tubs:

　　1 litre for £2.20.

　　1.5 litres for £2.99.

　a　Which tub gives the better value?

　This week, the supermarket also has a special offer on, for this brand of ice cream:

　　Buy a 1-litre tub and get a second one for $\frac{1}{2}$ price.

　Karen wants to buy 3 litres of this brand of ice cream.

　b　How many tubs of each size should she buy to get the best deal?

2　Mr and Mrs Rennie and their 2 children (aged 3 years and 8 years) want to visit Edinburgh for the day.

　The table shows the cost of public transport to Edinburgh from where they live.

Transport	Adult fare	Child fare	
		Under 5 years	5–15 years
Train	£12.70 return	Free	$\frac{1}{2}$ of adult price
Bus	£12.70 return	Under 2: free 2–4 years: $\frac{1}{2}$ of adult price	£4.50 each way

　a　How much will it cost the Rennie family to travel to Edinburgh by train?

　b　What will it cost if the Rennie family travel by bus to Edinburgh?

　Mr Rennie reckons the cost of driving to Edinburgh would be £14 and the parking fees would be £18.

　c　Which will be the cheapest way for the Rennie family to visit Edinburgh: by train, bus or car? Give a reason for your answer.

N4

3 Eryn wants to buy some perfume.

A bottle of Stardust costs £22.50.

A bottle of Angeldust costs £26.20.

A bottle of Moondust costs £21.60.

This week, there is a 25% discount on Angeldust and 10% discount on all other perfumes.

a Calculate the price of each of the perfumes, with the discount applied.

Eryn likes all of these perfumes.

b Which one should she buy to get the best deal? Give a reason for your answer.

4 Mr and Mrs White and their 4 children are on holiday in north-east Scotland and want to visit some castles and other heritage properties.

The table shows the entrance fees.

	Castles	Other heritage properties
Adult	£12.50	£10.50
2 adult family	£29.50	£24.50
Single adult family	£23.00	£18.00
Concession	£9.00	£7.50

a How much will it cost the White family to visit a castle?

b What will the White family pay in total to visit 1 castle and 2 heritage properties?

Mrs White did some research and found that they could buy a family membership card for £114.60.

This membership card would give them free entry to all castles and other heritage properties that they wanted to visit.

c What is the minimum number of castles they would need to visit to make it worthwhile buying a family membership card?

- I can compare two products, given two pieces of information on each. ★ Exercise 3A Q4, Q8   ○ ○ ◯

N4
- I can compare at least three products, given two pieces of information on each. ★ Exercise 3A Q14, Q16   ○ ○ ◯

4 Converting between currencies

This chapter will show you how to:

N4

- convert between two different currencies and compare costs.

You should already know:

- how to add, subtract, multiply and divide sums of money
- how to calculate the percentage of a quantity
- how to round numbers to two decimal places
- how to interpret data from a table.

N4

Converting between currencies

In Scotland, we use **pounds sterling** (£) as our currency. When you are travelling abroad, you need to have money in the currency of the country you are visiting.

Most countries around the world have their own currency. In Europe, a large group of countries, known as the eurozone, use the **euro**. The countries in the eurozone are Belgium, Germany, Ireland, Spain, France, Italy, Luxembourg, Netherlands, Austria, Portugal, Finland, Greece, Slovenia, Cyprus, Malta, Slovakia and Estonia. If you go on holiday to any of these countries, you can use the same currency.

You can change your pounds sterling for the currency you want at banks, Post Offices, travel agents and online agencies. You may be charged a fee, also known as **commission**, to do this.

The amount of currency you can buy for each pound is called the **exchange rate**. Information boards at ports and airports which display exchange rates often show the exchange rates to more than 2 decimal places, but you will only use 2 decimal places in this chapter.

Exchange rates change daily because they are influenced by the world's money markets.

Exchange rate calculations

To exchange pounds sterling (£) into a foreign currency:

> **Amount of pounds sterling × exchange rate**

To exchange foreign currency into pounds sterling (£):

> **Amount of foreign currency ÷ exchange rate**

You are working with money so all calculations must be rounded to 2 decimal places.

N4

Example 4.1

Ian and Jane are going on holiday to the USA. For their spending money, they change £1200 into US dollars ($) at their local bank.

The exchange rate is £1 = $1.25, plus 1% commission.

a How many US dollars do they get?

While they are in the USA they spend $1180. When they return to the UK they go to the Post Office to exchange their remaining money back to pounds sterling.

The exchange rate is £1 = $1.32, plus a fee of £2.50.

b How much money will they get?

a $\frac{1}{100} \times £1200 = £12$

> Calculate the commission. Find 1% of the number of pounds to be changed. 1% is equivalent to $\frac{1}{100}$

£1200 − £12 = £1188

> Subtract the commission from £1200 to find the amount to be changed into dollars.

£1188 × 1.25 = $1485

Ian and Jane will get $1485.

> Multiply the number of pounds they have by the exchange rate to work out how many dollars they will receive.

b $1485 − $1180 = $305

> Subtract the amount they have spent from the amount of dollars they started with to work out how much they have left to change back to pounds sterling.

$305 ÷ 1.32 = £231.06

> Divide the number of dollars they have by the exchange rate to work out how many pounds they will receive. You are working with money, so round your answer to 2 decimal places.

£231.06 − £2.50 = £228.56

> The Post Office charges a fee of £2.50. Subtract this fee after exchanging their money back to pounds.

Ian and Jane will get £228.56.

Example 4.2

Sandra is planning a clothes shopping trip to France.

She has looked online and has seen a pair of designer jeans for £186 in the UK.

The same pair costs €210 in France.

The exchange rate is £1 = €1.18 euros.

How much money will Sandra save by buying the jeans in France? Give your answer in euros.

£186 × 1.18 = €219.48

> Convert the cost of the jeans in the UK into euros. Multiply the cost in pounds by the exchange rate. You can then compare the prices of the jeans in the same currency.

€219.48 − €210 = €9.48

Sandra will save €9.48 by buying the jeans in France.

> Calculate the difference, in euros, between the prices in the UK and in France, to find out how much Sandra will save by buying the jeans in France.

N4 **Exercise 4A**

For all questions in this exercise use this table of exchange rates, unless otherwise stated.

Country	Currency and exchange rate
Australia	£1 = 1.63 Australian dollars (AUD)
Bulgaria	£1 = 2.31 Bulgarian lev (BGN)
Canada	£1 = 1.64 Canadian dollars (C$)
China	£1 = 8.60 Chinese yuan (CNY)
Czech Republic	£1 = 31.95 Czech koruna (CZK)
European countries in eurozone	£1 = 1.18 euros (€)
India	£1 = 83.44 Indian rupees (INR)
Japan	£1 = 140.55 Japanese yen (JPY)
Malaysia	£1 = 5.56 Malaysian ringgit (MYR)
Norway	£1 = 10.45 Norwegian krone (NOK)
South Africa	£1 = 16.23 South African rand (ZAR)
Switzerland	£1 = 1.26 Swiss francs (CHF)
United Arab Emirates	£1 = 4.60 UAE dirham (AED)
USA	£1 = 1.25 American dollars ($)

1   Convert £50 to each currency, giving your answers to 2 decimal places.

    a   Euros   b   US dollars   c   Australian dollars

    d   Bulgarian lev   e   Japanese yen   f   Indian rupees

2   Convert 200 of each currency to pounds. Round your answers to 2 decimal places.

    a   Canadian dollars   b   Norwegian krone   c   South African rand

    d   Czech koruna   e   UAE dirham   f   Swiss francs

3   The prices of the same item in two different countries are shown. Compare the prices.
    In which country is the item cheaper?

    a   China = 300 CNY   Malaysia = 160 MYR

    b   Australia = 60 AUD   Canada = 65 C$

    c   India = 1500 INR   United Arab Emirates = 80 AED

    d   USA = $70   Switzerland = 60 CHF

    e   France = €200   USA = $240

> ⚠️ Exchange these currencies to compare the cost in pounds.

4   Adam is travelling to Germany and has £8000 to take with him, which he exchanges for euros.

    While he is in Germany, he spends €7986 and then returns to Scotland.

    He exchanges the rest of his euros back to pounds at a rate of £1 = €1.24.

    How much money does he now have in pounds?

5   A camera costs £484 in the UK.

    If the same camera costs €575 in France, is it cheaper or more expensive to buy the camera in France?

N4

6 The diagrams show four cars on sale. Put the cars in order, with the most expensive first.

£12 500   62 475 Malaysian ringgit

51 020 euros   1 749 850 Japanese yen

★ 7 A bicycle costs £355 in the UK.

The same bicycle costs 780 lev in Bulgaria.

How much cheaper is it to buy the bicycle in Bulgaria?

Give your answer in Bulgarian lev.

⚙ 8 Colin and Tricia are going on a safari holiday to South Africa and take £900 spending money. They change this into South African rand at their local bank and pay a fee of £15.

a How many South African rand do they get?

While they are on safari they spend 14 000 rand. When they return to the UK they go to the bank to exchange their remaining money back to pounds sterling.

They can only change multiples of 10 rand, but will not have to pay a fee.

The exchange rate is £1 = 16.62 rand.

b How much money will they get?

★ 9 Mr and Mrs Ipsen and their 2 children are travelling from Norway to Scotland for a holiday.

Mr Ipsen would like to take his children on a steam train trip.

To budget for this trip, he finds the prices charged by the steam train company.

The table shows the prices for these train journeys.

Train journey	Child price	Adult price
Fort William–Mallaig	£20	£35
Inverness–Kyle of Lochalsh	£18	£52
Aviemore–Granton-on-Spey	£10	£25

How much will it cost the Ipsen family to go on the steam train from Fort William to Mallaig? Give your answer in Norwegian krone.

★ 10 Matthew and Emma are going on holiday to Canada and want to take £1250 spending money. They change this into Canadian dollars at their local bank and pay 1% commission.

a How many Canadian dollars do they get?

Whilst in Canada they spend C$1885. When they return to the UK they go to the Post Office to exchange their remaining money back to pounds sterling.

The exchange rate is £1 = C$1.71, plus a fee of £2.50.

b How much money will they get?

N4

11 Mr and Mrs White and their 4 children are on holiday in Paris, France.

The children are 15, 13, 10 and 8 years old.

They plan a day out to climb the Eiffel Tower.

The table shows the prices charged to climb the Eiffel Tower.

	Adults	12–18 years	4–11 years
Lift ticket to 2nd floor	€16.25	€13.80	€8.30
Lift ticket to top	€24.50	€22.00	€16.75
Stairs ticket to 2nd floor	€8.20	€6.45	€5.90

The White family want to take the lift to the top. How much will this cost in pounds?

12 Andrew went on a business trip to Italy and had to hire a car. This cost £255 for the week he was there.

a How many euros did Andrew have to pay to hire the car?

On his day off, Andrew went shopping and bought some perfume for his girlfriend.

He paid €65 for this.

The same perfume was on sale for £56.20 in the UK.

b In which country was the perfume cheaper? Explain your answer.

13 Elizabeth and some friends are on holiday in Japan. They want to visit the Tokyo Skytree. There are two observation decks, which give views across the whole of the city.

The table shows the prices charged to visit the Tokyo Skytree.

Skytree Tembo observation deck (350 metres)	2000 Japanese yen
Skytree Tembo Galleria observation deck (450 metres)	1000 Japanese yen

Elizabeth and her friends would like to visit both the 350 metres and the 450 metres observation decks. They have budgeted £20 each for this.

Will they have enough money? Give a reason for your answer.

14 Stevie is going for a city break to Prague in the Czech Republic. He has up to £350 to change into Czech koruna.

The bank will only exchange money for 50 koruna notes but do not charge any fees.

a What is the maximum number of 50 koruna notes that Stevie can get?

b How much will this cost?

15 Jack is travelling home from his holiday and buys some food and drink on the plane. The table shows the prices of the items available on the plane.

He buys a cheese and ham sandwich, a cake, a coffee and a bottle of water.

He pays part of the cost in euros to use up the last €10.20 of his spending money.

He pays the rest in pounds.

How much does Jack need to pay in pounds?

Price list	
Cheese and ham sandwich	£3.80
Cake	£1.95
Chocolate bar	£1.35
Coffee	£2.60
Tea	£2.40
Orange juice	£2.40
Bottle of water	£1.80

N4 ★ **16** Thomas and John have saved up £5000 spending money for a 6-week holiday travelling around Australia.

In the UK, they exchange their money at the bank and pay a fee of £15.

a How many Australian dollars do they receive?

The table show how they expect to spend their money.

Food	£650
Car rental	£720
Accommodation (in youth hostels)	£2050
Internal flights	£450
Souvenirs and entertainment	£500
Extras	£615

b What will these expenses cost them in Australia?

The car that Thomas and John have rented breaks down. They get it repaired at a nearby garage. The bill comes to 720.45 AUD. This has to be paid for out of the budget they set aside for extras.

c In pounds, how much is now left to spend on extras?

Thomas and John keep within their budget and spend a total of 7560.20 AUD during their holiday.

When they return to the UK, they go to the bank to exchange the remaining Australian dollars to pounds. The exchange rate is £1 = 1.71 AUD, plus 1% commission.

d How much money do they get back?

GO! Activity

You and your family are going on a 7-night holiday. You are trying to decide between:

- a sightseeing tour in New York, USA, which could include going up the Empire State Building

- a skiing trip in Bansko, Bulgaria.

Research the activities available in each location. You should consider the costs in the currency of the country you are visiting.

Create a budget for each holiday before making a decision on which one to book.

⚠ See Chapter 1 for more about how to create a budget.

Think about:

- exchange rates and fees for changing currencies

- exchange rates – what do activities cost in pounds?

- entrance fees to places of interest

- cost of ski lift passes

- other spending money required.

N4   **Chapter review**

1.   Keith and Jenny are going on holiday to China. For their spending money, they change £1500 into Chinese yuan (CNY) at their local bank.

   The exchange rate is £1 = 8.71 CNY, plus 1% commission.

   a   How many Chinese yuan do they get?

   Keith and Jenny want to visit the Terracotta Army. They make an online booking in advance for a day tour. The cost is £71.80 per person.

   b   In Chinese yuan, how much will the Terracotta Army tour cost in total?

   If Keith and Jenny had paid for the Terracotta Army tour on the day, it would have cost them 1350 CNY.

   c   In pounds, how much money did Keith and Jenny save by buying their tickets in advance?

   While they are in China Keith and Jenny spend 11 500 CNY altogether. When they return to the UK they go back to the bank to exchange their remaining money back to pounds sterling.

   The exchange rate is £1 = 8.92 CNY, plus a fee of £3.00.

   d   How much money will they get back?

2.   Mr and Mrs Brown and their 3 children are on holiday in Sydney, Australia. They want to take £6000 spending money. They change this into Australian dollars (AUD) at their local bank.

   The exchange rate is £1 = 1.67 AUD.

   a   How many Australian dollars do they receive?

   While they are in Sydney they want to climb the Harbour Bridge.

   The table shows the prices charged to climb the bridge.

Time of day	Adult		Child	
	Weekday	Weekend	Weekday	Weekend
Night	358 AUD	378 AUD	248 AUD	268 AUD
Day	293 AUD	308 AUD	193 AUD	208 AUD
Twilight	253 AUD	268 AUD	173 AUD	188 AUD
Dawn	378 AUD	378 AUD	268 AUD	268 AUD

   They decide to do the daytime climb on a weekday.

   b   What will be the total cost for the family to climb the bridge, in pounds?

3.   While they are in Australia, the Brown family go shopping. Mrs Brown sees a designer purse she would like, which costs 200 AUD.

   When she checks online, Mrs Brown finds she can buy the same purse in the UK for £115.

   In which country should Mrs Brown buy the purse? Give a reason for your answer.

N4

4   Jeremia and Mariha live in Cape Town, South Africa. They give guided tours for groups of tourists at weekends.

They do not charge a fee, but accept tips from each group.

The table shows the amount they received from each tourist group and the exchange rate for each of the countries.

Tourists' country	Amount received	Exchange rate
UK	£5.50	£1 = 17.24 rand
Japan	852.50 JPY	1 JPY = 0.12 rand
USA	$7.00	$1 = 13.30 rand
Netherlands	€9.70	€1 = 14.50 rand
Brazil	40.50 BRL	1 BRL = 4.20 rand
Australia	9.20 AUD	1 AUD = 10.05 rand
South Africa	55.00 rand	

a   Which group of tourists gave the biggest tip?

b   What was the difference between the biggest and smallest tips?

• I can convert between two different currencies and compare costs. ★ Exercise 4A Q7, Q9, Q10, Q16   ○ ○ ⬭

5 Savings and borrowing

This chapter will show you how to:

- develop a savings plan
- investigate the impact of interest rates on savings

N4
- investigate the impact of interest rates on loans and credit agreements.

You should already know:

- how to add, subtract, multiply and divide sums of money
- how to calculate the percentage of a quantity
- how to round numbers to two decimal places
- how to interpret data from a table.

Developing a savings plan

Savings is the money you put aside each week or month if you have any left over after your everyday spending. You can keep your savings in a money jar at home, or use a bank or building society account.

You can save for something specific, such as a holiday, new clothes or a new games console. By making regular savings, you will be able to afford something you cannot buy at the moment.

Developing a savings plan helps you to manage your money and gives you a goal to look forward to.

If you know how much you need to save, you can decide:

- how long you want to save for – this tells you how much you need to save each week or month.

- how much you can save each week or month – this tells you how long it will take to have enough money for the item you would like to buy.

Example 5.1

Jemma is going to a family wedding and wants to buy a new dress. She has seen one that she likes, which costs £180.

Jemma wants to save up £180 in 5 months.

a How much does she need to save each month?

Jemma has been saving £12 per month to buy a wedding present.

b How much has she saved in 4 months?

a £180 ÷ 5 = £36 ●────────

> Divide the cost of the wedding dress by the number of months that Jemma wants to save to calculate how much she needs to save each month.

Jemma will need to save £36 per month.

b 12 × 4 = £48 ●────────

> Multiply the amount she has saved each month by the number of months that she has been saving.

Jemma has saved £48 for the wedding present in 4 months.

Exercise 5A

1   Hannah is going on holiday and wants to buy some new clothes. She expects to spend £200.

Hannah wants to save up £200 in 8 months.

   a   How much does she need to save each month?

Hannah has been saving £6 per month to buy new shoes for her holiday.

   b   How much has she saved in 6 months?

2   Liam would like to buy a new mobile phone. He has seen one that he likes, which costs £229.50.

Liam wants to save £229.50 in 9 months.

How much does he need to save each month?

★   3   Darren has been saving £21 per month towards a new games console.

   a   How much has he saved in 7 months?

The games console he would like to buy costs £231.

   b   How much more money does Darren need to save?

   c   How many more months will it take Darren to save enough to buy the games console?

4   Niall wants to buy a new laptop. He has seen one that he likes, which costs £448.

Niall is able to save £28 per month.

How many months will it take him to save £448?

★   5   Jessica is saving up to go on a Mediterranean cruise, which costs £526.

Jessica has already saved £274.

   a   How much more does she still need to save?

Jessica can afford to save £28 per month.

   b   How many months will it take her to save the rest of the money that she needs for the cruise?

N4   Savings and interest rates

For short-term savings and small amounts of money, you could put it in a money jar and keep it at home where it is easily available at any time.

For longer-term savings and larger amounts of money, it is better to put your money into a **savings account** at a bank or building society. A savings account pays **interest** on your money. Interest is paid to you because the bank or building society uses your money for other purposes. This is calculated as a percentage of the amount in the account.

The **interest rate** you receive depends on the type of savings account you have. For quick access to your savings, the rate of interest is usually low. Higher rates of interest are paid if you are prepared to leave your savings in the account for longer periods of time. Interest rates are expressed as a percentage.

N4

Example 5.2

Dave has won £5000 in a prize draw and wants to pay it into a savings account for 1 year. He looks at two different savings accounts.

Bank4U
Interest rate of **1.5%** per year.

AnyBank
Interest rate of 1.8% per year
Annual fee of £12

In which bank should Dave invest his money?

Bank4U 1.5% of £5000 $= \dfrac{1.5}{100} \times 5000$
$= £75$

> Calculate the annual interest paid by Bank4U. Find 1.5% of the amount he wants to pay into the account.
> 1.5% is equivalent to $\dfrac{1.5}{100}$

Bank4U pays £75 interest.

AnyBank 1.8% of £5000 $= \dfrac{1.8}{100} \times 5000$
$= £90$

> Calculate the annual interest paid by AnyBank. Find 1.8% of the amount he wants to pay into the account.
> 1.8% is equivalent to $\dfrac{1.8}{100}$

£90 − £12 = £78

> Subtract the annual fee from the amount of interest.

AnyBank pays £78 interest once the fee has been subtracted.

Dave should invest his money at AnyBank because he will receive £3 more than at Bank4U.

> Compare the amounts paid by each bank and state your conclusion.

Exercise 5B

1 Marion has won £2000 in a prize draw and wants to pay it into a savings account for 1 year.

Bank 4U
Interest rate of **1.25%** per year

Any Bank
Interest rate of 1.44% per year
Annual fee of £4

In which bank should Marion invest her money?

2 Jenny has sold one of her paintings for £3000 and wants to pay this money into a savings account.

Bank Online
Interest rate of 2.15% per year
Annual fee of £12

SCOTLAND WIDE
Interest rate of 2.12% per year
Annual fee of £8

a How much interest will Jenny receive from Bank Online after 1 year?

b How much interest will Jenny receive from Scotland Wide after 1 year?

c Which bank will pay more interest to Jenny?

N4 ★ 3 Kenneth has inherited £10 000 and wants to put it into a savings account for 1 year.

Bank Online Interest rate of 2.15% per year Annual fee of £12	**SCOTLAND WIDE** Interest rate of 2.12% per year Annual fee of £8

Kenneth thinks he will earn more with BankOnline because they pay a higher rate of interest. Is he right? Give a reason for your answer.

4 James and Amy are going to work abroad for a year. They have sold their flat and want to leave this money in a savings account.

They have considered saving their money with either BankOnline or ScotBank, but are undecided about the better deal.

Bank Online Interest rate of 2.15% per year Annual fee of £12	**SCOTBANK** Interest rate of 2.13% per year

a Which savings account seems to give the better deal? Give a reason for your answer.

James and Amy have £46 500 left from the sale of their flat.

b How much interest would they receive from each bank?

c Which bank gives the better deal?

d If they decide to save their money with the bank which gives the better deal, how much would they have in their account at the end of the year?

5 Carol wants to put £2700 into a savings account.

This table shows the interest rates paid by the Aberdon Building Society.

Amount invested	Interest rate
Up to £1000	0.75%
Over £1000 up to £5000	1.2%
Over £5000 up to £20 000	1.65%
Over £20 000	2.18%

a What interest rate will Carol receive if she saves her money with the Aberdon Building Society?

b How much interest will she receive after 1 year?

c How much will she have in her account at the end of the year?

6 Jonathon and Alex are comparing their different savings accounts.

Jonathon has invested £5680 and receives 2.4% interest per year.

Alex has invested £5250 and receives 2.6% interest per year.

Who receives more interest? Give a reason for your answer.

N4   ## Loans and credit agreements

If you want to buy something for more money than you can save, you may need to borrow money from a financial institution such as a bank or building society. This is known as taking out a **loan**. If you take out a loan, you will have to sign a **credit agreement**.

A credit agreement is a legal contract which tells you the terms and conditions of the loan. A **repayment plan** tells you the interest charged and the period of the loan.

It is important that you understand the conditions of a credit agreement:

- the **amount to be repaid** each month, on a given date (the **instalments**)
- the **number of months** of the loan
- the **interest** due on the loan
- the consequences of failure to make payments, which could include legal action against you.

If you plan to take out a loan, it is always a good idea to shop around for the best deal.

Example 5.3

Bill and Rebecca want to buy a new car, which costs £12 500.

They will get £4800 for trading in their current car and need a loan to pay the balance.

> The balance is the difference between the total cost of the new car and what they get from trading in their current car.

The maximum they can afford to repay each month is £220.

Their bank offers two different repayment options at an interest rate of 7.2% per year.

Repayment plan	Loan term
Option 1	3 years (36 months)
Option 2	5 years (60 months)

Which option should Bill and Rebecca choose?

How much will they have to repay each month?

Amount of loan = £12 500 − £4800 = £7700

> Calculate the difference between the cost of the car and the amount they receive for trading in their current car.

$$7.2\% \text{ of } £7700 = \frac{7.2}{100} \times £7700$$
$$= £554.40$$

> Work out the annual interest on the loan. Find 7.2% of the amount that Bill and Rebecca will borrow.
> 7.2% is equivalent to $\frac{7.2}{100}$

Option 1

Interest due for 3 years = 3 × £554.40
$$= £1663.20$$

> Calculate the total interest. Multiply the amount of interest for 1 year by the number of years of the loan.

Total loan due = £7700 + £1663.20
$$= £9363.20$$

> Add the amount of the loan and the interest due to find the total amount to be repaid.

Amount due per month = £9363.20 ÷ 36
$$= £260.09$$

> Calculate the monthly repayments. Divide the total loan by the number of months of the loan. You are working with money so round your answer to 2 decimal places.

(continued)

N4

Option 2

Interest due for 5 years = 5 × £554.40

Calculate the total interest. Multiply the amount of interest for 1 year by the number of years of the loan.

= £2772.00

Total loan due = £7700 + £2772.00

Add the amount of the loan and the interest due to find the total amount to be repaid.

= £10 472.00

Amount due per month = £10 472.00 ÷ 60

= £174.54

Calculate the monthly repayments. Divide the total loan by the number of months of the loan. You are working with money so round your answer to 2 decimal places.

Bill and Rebecca will need to take option 2, taking the loan out over 5 years and will repay £174.54 per month.

Compare the cost of the monthly repayments for option 1 and option 2 with the maximum amount they can afford to pay. State which option they will have to choose.

Example 5.4

John and Hollie are planning to buy some new furniture for their living room and need to take out a loan of £1600 from their bank.

⚠ The annual interest rate is the amount of interest received in 1 year.

They can choose from one of these loan payment options.

Repayment plan	Annual interest rate	Loan term
Option 1	7.4%	9 months
Option 2	6.8%	6 months

a   How much is the monthly repayment for each of these options?

b   Which option should John and Hollie choose? Give a reason for your answer.

a   **Option 1**

$\frac{7.4}{100} \times 1600 = £118.40$

Work out the annual interest on the loan. Find 7.4% of the amount they will borrow. 7.4% is equivalent to $\frac{7.4}{100}$

Interest due for 9 months = $\frac{9}{12} \times £118.40$

= £88.80

Calculate the interest due for a fraction of the year. The fraction is the number of months of the loan divided by the number of months in a year.

Total loan due = £1600 + £88.80

= £1688.80

Calculate the total amount to be repaid. Add the amount of the loan and the interest due.

Amount due per month = £1688.80 ÷ 9

= £187.65

Calculate the monthly repayments. Divide the total loan by the number of months of the loan. You are working with money so round your answer to 2 decimal places.

N4

Option 2

$\frac{6.8}{100} \times 1600 = £108.80$

Interest due for 6 months $= \frac{6}{12} \times £108.80$

$\qquad\qquad = £54.40$

Total loan due $= £1600 + £54.40$

$\qquad\qquad = £1654.40$

Amount due per month $= £1654.40 \div 6$

$\qquad\qquad = £275.74$

> Work out the annual interest on the loan. Find 6.8% of the amount borrowed. 6.8% is equivalent to $\frac{6.8}{100}$

> Calculate the interest due for a fraction of the year. The fraction is the number of months of the loan divided by the number of months in a year.

> Calculate the total amount to be repaid. Add the loan and the interest due.

> Calculate the monthly repayments. Divide the total amount of the loan by the number of months of the loan. You are working with money so round your answer to 2 decimal places.

b   If John and Hollie choose option 1, they will pay less per month but it will take them longer to repay the loan.

If John and Hollie choose option 2, they will pay less interest for the whole loan and will repay it in less time.

Exercise 5C

1   Sophia needs £4000 as a deposit to buy a flat.

The table shows three different loan options.

Monthly repayment	Loan term
£131.12 per month	3 years
£100.24 per month	4 years
£81.67 per month	5 years

a   What is the total cost of each of these loans?

b   How much interest is charged for each of these loans?

c   If Sophia is able to pay the loan in 3 years, would this be the cheapest option?

2   Elizabeth wants to buy a new car, which costs £7800.

She will get £3600 for trading in her current car. She needs a loan to pay the balance.

The maximum she can afford to repay each month is £200.

Her bank offers two different repayment options at an interest rate of 6.8% per year.

Repayment plan	Loan term
Option 1	2 years (24 months)
Option 2	3 years (36 months)

> See Example 5.3 for a reminder on how to solve this kind of problem.

a   Which option should Elizabeth choose?

b   How much will she have to repay each month?

N4

3 Ross wants to buy some new furniture for his bedroom. He needs to take out a loan of £1200 from his bank.

He can choose from one of these loan payment options.

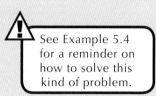

See Example 5.4 for a reminder on how to solve this kind of problem.

Repayment plan	Annual interest rate	Loan term
Option 1	7.1%	9 months
Option 2	7.6%	12 months

a How much is the monthly repayment for each of these options?

Ross can afford to pay £145 per month.

b Ross wants to pay for the loan as quickly as possible. Which option should he choose?

4 Jack wants to visit his relatives in New Zealand. He asks his bank for a £2000 loan.

This table shows the interest rates charged by the bank.

Amount borrowed	Interest rate
Up to £500	11.4%
£500 up to £999.99	8.9%
£1000 up to £1999.99	8.2%
£2000 up to £4999.99	7.1%
Over £5000	6.3%

a What interest rate will Jack be charged to borrow £2000?

Jack wants to repay this loan in 18 months.

b How much interest will he have to pay?

c What is the total cost of the loan?

d How much will Jack's monthly repayments cost?

★ **5** Sara is setting up her own small business and needs a loan to get started. She wants to borrow £7500 from the same bank that Jack uses in Question 4.

a What interest rate will Sara have to pay for a £7500 loan?

Sara wants to repay the loan in 3 years.

b How much will Sara's monthly repayments cost?

★ **6** Mr and Mrs McKenzie need to have their flat roof replaced because it is leaking. They will have to take out a loan of £6480 to pay for this work.

The maximum they can afford to repay is £220 per month.

The table shows the loan options that they could choose from.

Loan provider	Loan terms and conditions
Bank4U	6.8% interest per year for 30 months
ScotlandWide	6.1% interest per year for 2 years
BankOnline	£220 per month for 29 months and a final payment of £100

Mr and Mrs McKenzie want to repay the loan as early as possible.

Which of these loans would be the best option for them?

Give a reason for your answer.

N4

🔵 Activity

Use the internet, newspapers and magazines to research types of savings accounts and loans.

- Where can you open a savings account?
- What types of saving accounts are available?
- What are the advantages and disadvantages of different types of savings accounts?
- Where can you get a loan?
- What types of loans are available?
- What are the advantages and disadvantages of different types of loans?
- Why is there a difference between the interest rates paid to savers and those charged to borrowers?

Chapter review

1   Liam and Chloe are saving up to pay for a new kitchen in their flat. The kitchen will cost £7000, including installation.

A year ago, they invested £5000 in a savings account, which pays an annual interest rate of 1.5%.

a   How much money is now in their savings account?

b   If they use this money to help pay for the new kitchen, how much more do they need to save?

Liam and Chloe can afford to save £220 each month.

c   How many more months will it take them to have enough money to pay for a new kitchen?

N4

2   Adrian has invested £7500 in a savings account with the Scotview Building Society.

This table shows the interest rates paid by the Scotview Building Society.

Amount invested	Interest rate
Up to £1000	0.50%
Over £1000 up to £10 000	0.95%
Over £10 000 up to £20 000	1.20%
Over £20 000	1.85%

a   What interest rate does Adrian receive?

b   How much interest does he receive at the end of the year?

c   How much will he have in his account at the end of the year?

Adrian wants to buy a caravan. He has seen one he likes which costs £14 000.

He will use his savings and take out a loan to pay the rest.

d   How much will Adrian need to borrow?

(continued)

N4

Adrian can afford up to £275 per month to repay a loan and wants to do this as quickly as possible.

The table shows the loan options that he could choose from.

Loan provider	Loan terms and conditions
ScotlandWide	5.9% interest per year for 30 months
Bank4U	6.3% interest per year for 2 years
BankOnline	£270 per month for 24 months

   e   Work out the total cost of the loan for each of these banks.

   f   Which of these loans would be the best option for Adrian? Give a reason for your answer.

3   Gillian has been saving £30 each month to pay for the service and MOT on her car later in the year.

   a   How much has she saved in the 8 months up to the time the car is due to go into the garage?

When she has the service and MOT done on her car, the mechanic tells her that she will need further work completed. The total bill comes to £638.

   b   How much money does Gillian still need to pay the bill?

Gillian will need to take out a short-term loan so that she can pay the garage.

She borrows £400 and agrees to repay this over 6 months.

The interest rate is 64%.

   c   How much interest will Gillian pay for a 6-month loan?

   d   What is the total cost of the loan?

   e   How much will Gillian have to repay each month?

4   Stephanie is going on a long holiday to Australia and New Zealand which costs £12 000. She has paid a deposit of £2000.

For the last 8 months, Stephanie has invested £10 000 in a savings account which pays an annual interest rate of 0.5%.

   a   How much interest would Stephanie get if she closed her account after 8 months?

   b   How much interest would Stephanie get if she waited to the end of the year before she closed her account?

Stephanie decides to close her account after 8 months, so that she can pay the outstanding balance of her holiday.

   c   How much interest will she lose by doing this?

•   I can develop a savings plan. ★ Exercise 5A Q3, Q5   ◯◯◯

N4

•   I can investigate the impact of interest rates on savings. ★ Exercise 5B Q3   ◯◯◯

•   I can investigate the impact of interest rates on loans and credit agreements. ★ Exercise 5C Q5, Q6   ◯◯◯

Using statistics to investigate risk

This chapter will show you how to:

N4
- investigate the meaning of lifestyle statistics.

You should already know:

N4
- how to convert between fractions, decimal fractions and percentages
- how to calculate simple probabilities
- how to use probability to make decisions
- how to interpret data from a table.

N4 ## Lifestyle statistics

Lifestyle describes the way that we live and the choices that we make. Our behaviours, attitudes, interests, opinions and values are all important aspects which determine our own lifestyles.

Lifestyle diseases are diseases that are linked to the way that we choose to live. Smoking, alcohol and drug abuse, lack of physical exercise and unhealthy eating are all lifestyle choices that can lead to disease and ill health. Typical health problems related to lifestyle choices include obesity, high blood pressure, heart disease and some cancers.

When making choices about our lifestyle, we need to be aware of the long-term risks to our health.

Lifestyle statistics are collected and analysed by government departments and private companies. Their findings can help us to make informed choices about what we do. For example, the lower life expectancy of smokers compared to non-smokers has been known for many years. The risks associated with smoking are highlighted by the health warnings printed on tobacco products.

Probability and risk

In everyday life we all make choices about the things that we do. These are usually based on our own experiences and the experiences of friends and family. If we also understand the chance or **probability** of the outcome of our choices then we can make informed decisions.

$$\text{Probability of an event happening} = \frac{\text{number of ways the event can happen}}{\text{total number of possible outcomes}}$$

Risk is the possibility that our choice of action may result in an unwanted outcome. People take risks in everyday activities such as taking part in sports, driving a car, buying lottery tickets and investing money in savings accounts. We can determine the risks of taking part in these activities by using the statistics of past events or of known factors. This is known as **risk assessment**.

We use probability to work out the chance that taking a risk will be worth it. The higher the probability of a successful outcome, the more likely that the risk will pay off. For a low probability, the risk is likely to result in an unsuccessful outcome.

For example, the probability of winning the lottery is very low – buying a ticket is likely to result in the loss of the money paid for the ticket.

N4

Example 6.1

The Scottish School Adolescent Lifestyle and Substance Use Survey (SALSUS) 2015 asked 15-year-old pupils about drinking alcohol. The survey questioned 25 000 pupils.

This information summarises the most common consequences for those drinking alcohol.

Out of a sample of 25 000 pupils:

- 8057 said they vomited after drinking alcohol
- 7636 said they got into an argument
- 6519 said they sent a text or email they wished they hadn't
- 7750 said they did something and later regretted it.

(Source: NHS National Services Scotland)

a Work out the probability that 15-year-old pupils did something that they later regretted after drinking alcohol.

The pupils were also asked if it is OK to try alcohol or try getting drunk.

This information summarises their opinions.

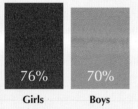

76%	70%
Girls	Boys

It's OK to try alcohol

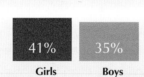

41%	35%
Girls	Boys

It's OK to get drunk

(Source: NHS National Services Scotland)

b What do the results show about the opinions of boys and girls?

a Probability $= \dfrac{7750}{25000} = \dfrac{31}{100}$ or 0.31

> The total number of possible outcomes is the number of people who answered the question. Give your answer as either a simplified fraction or a decimal fraction.

b For both questions, girls were more likely than boys to agree. Although about $\frac{3}{4}$ of pupils thought it was OK to try alcohol, less than $\frac{1}{2}$ of them thought it was OK to get drunk.

N4

Example 6.2

People who buy lottery tickets hope to win the top prize.

The table shows the probability of winning the jackpot for these lotteries.

Name of lottery	Probability of winning jackpot	Jackpot prize
UK lotto	1 in 45 million	Usually over £1 000 000. Depends on ticket sales and number of winners
Euromillions	1 in 116.5 million	Usually well over £1 000 000. Depends on ticket sales and number of winners
Irish lotto	1 in 10.7 million	Usually over £1 000 000. Depends on ticket sales and number of winners
Health lottery	1 in 2.1 million	Maximum £100 000
Thunderball	1 in 8 million	Fixed £500 000

a   Which lottery has the best probability of winning the jackpot?

b   Which lottery has the least probability of winning the jackpot?

a   Health lottery ●————— You would only need 2.1 million different tickets to win this jackpot.

b   Euromillions ●————— You would need 116.5 million different tickets to win this jackpot.

Exercise 6A

1   The SALSUS 2015 survey asked 13-year old and 15-year-old pupils about drinking alcohol.

This graph shows the trends in drinking alcohol in the week immediately before the census. The data is shown for boys and girls aged 13 and 15.

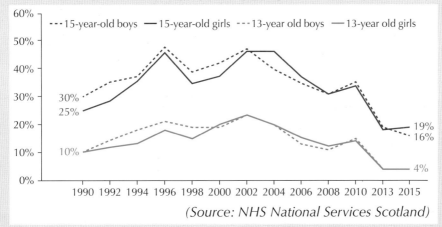

(Source: NHS National Services Scotland)

a   Describe the trend in drinking alcohol for 13-year-olds.

b   In general, are 15-year-old boys or girls more likely to drink alcohol?

c   During which periods were 15-year-old girls more likely to drink alcohol?

d   In which years did an equal number of 13-year-old boys and girls say they drink alcohol?

N4 ★ 2 People who buy lottery tickets hope to win the top prize, where the chance of success is extremely low. However, the chances of them winning any prize is much better.

The table shows the probability of winning any prize, the jackpot and the smallest prize that can be won for these lotteries.

Name of lottery	Probability of winning any prize	Jackpot prize	Smallest prize
UK lotto	1 in 9.3	Usually over £1 000 000. Depends on ticket sales and number of winners	Free ticket worth £2
Euromillions	1 in 13	Usually well over £1 000 000. Depends on ticket sales and number of winners	About £3
Irish lotto	1 in 42	Usually over £1 000 000. Depends on ticket sales and number of winners	£2
Health lottery	1 in 108	Maximum £100 000	£10
Thunderball	1 in 13	Fixed £500 000	£3

a Which lottery has the best probability of winning any prize?

b Which lottery pays the best value smallest prize?

c Why might some people choose not to buy a ticket with the lottery that pays the best value smallest prize?

d Using the probabilities shown in the table, how many £1 Thunderball tickets would you need to buy to win a prize?

e Using the probabilities shown in the table, could you buy enough £1 Thunderball tickets to break even?

3 The Department for Transport publishes reports on the numbers of road accident casualties in Great Britain. The graph shows the results for 2015.

This graph shows the casualties by:

- severity – fatal, serious, slight, all

- road type – built-up, non built-up, motorway.

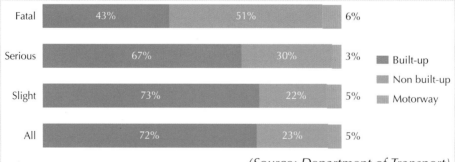

(Source: Department of Transport)

a Which road type has the most accidents?

b Why do you think this is?

c Which road type would you choose for a short journey, to reduce the risk of an accident resulting in a serious casualty?

d Motorways have the lowest probability of an accident casualty. What reasons could account for this?

N4

4 The SALSUS 2013 survey asked 13-year-old and 15-year-old pupils about their opinions on smoking and its effects.

The graph shows attitudes towards smoking (per cent agreeing/strongly agreeing with statement), for both age groups combined, by smoking status.

> ⚠ For example, the top row shows that 93% of regular smokers agree that smoking can cause lung cancer and 97% of non-smokers agree that smoking can cause lung cancer.

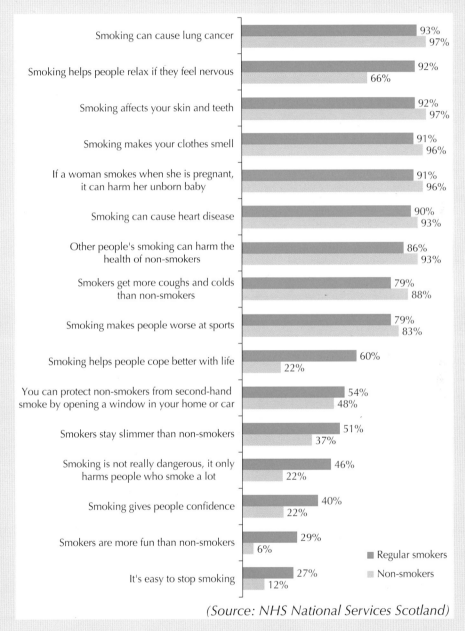

Statement	Regular smokers	Non-smokers
Smoking can cause lung cancer	93%	97%
Smoking helps people relax if they feel nervous	92%	66%
Smoking affects your skin and teeth	92%	97%
Smoking makes your clothes smell	91%	96%
If a woman smokes when she is pregnant, it can harm her unborn baby	91%	96%
Smoking can cause heart disease	90%	93%
Other people's smoking can harm the health of non-smokers	86%	93%
Smokers get more coughs and colds than non-smokers	79%	88%
Smoking makes people worse at sports	79%	83%
Smoking helps people cope better with life	60%	22%
You can protect non-smokers from second-hand smoke by opening a window in your home or car	54%	48%
Smokers stay slimmer than non-smokers	51%	37%
Smoking is not really dangerous, it only harms people who smoke a lot	46%	22%
Smoking gives people confidence	40%	22%
Smokers are more fun than non-smokers	29%	6%
It's easy to stop smoking	27%	12%

(Source: NHS National Services Scotland)

a For which statement is the greatest difference in opinion between regular smokers and non-smokers?

b For which statement is the least difference in opinion between regular smokers and non-smokers?

c What serious health risks are both regular smokers and non-smokers concerned about?

d Which statements do you agree with?

N4

5   Jake and Ellie want to visit London for a few days. They have researched the monthly temperatures there before choosing when to go.

This table shows the monthly temperatures in London.

Month	Normal average temperature (°C)
January	5.9
February	6.0
March	8.0
April	9.9
May	13.3
June	16.2
July	18.6
August	18.6
September	15.9
October	12.4
November	8.7
December	6.9

a   What is the probability that the month Jake and Ellie choose will be hotter than 14°C?

b   If they want to visit London when the temperature is at least 16°C, which months do they have to choose from?

c   Jake and Ellie would prefer to go to London before the schools are on their summer holidays. In which month should they book their holiday?

★ 6   The government publishes statistics on life expectancy of smokers and non-smokers. This includes this information:

Every cigarette smoked reduces life by about 10 minutes.

a   Use this statistic to calculate by how many hours a woman is likely to reduce her life if she smokes 18 cigarettes each day, for 1 week.

b   This woman chooses to smoke 18 cigarettes per day, for 1 year. By how many hours is she likely to reduce her life? How many days is this? 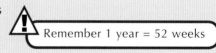 Remember 1 year = 52 weeks

c   She continues to smoke the same amount of cigarettes each day for 20 years, before she decides to quit. By how many days is she likely to reduce her life?

The average life expectancy of a woman in the UK is about 83 years.

In the UK, about 50% of long-term smokers live past 70 years old.

d   Is this woman likely to be one of these 50%? 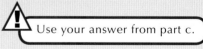 Use your answer from part c.

🔵 Activity

The Department for Work and Pensions is concerned that 12 million people are heading towards retirement without a decent pension. Being out of work for long periods of time is a major contributor to this.

The pie chart shows the numbers of people working and not working for people between the ages of 50 and the state pension age. (The state pension age is the age at which the government will start paying a pension.) The chart shows that there are different reasons why people might not be working – they might be unemployed, looking after family, already retired, or ill or disabled.

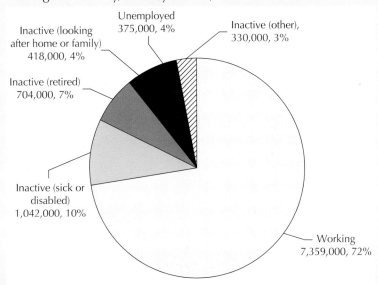

Unemployed 375,000, 4%

Inactive (other), 330,000, 3%

Inactive (looking after home or family) 418,000, 4%

Inactive (retired) 704,000, 7%

Inactive (sick or disabled) 1,042,000, 10%

Working 7,359,000, 72%

(*Source: Labour Force Survey Four Quarter Average 2013Q1–2013Q4*)

More than $\frac{1}{4}$ of these people are not in paid employment and are likely to have an income which is inadequate for them to maintain their living standards into retirement.

Investigate the impact of an inadequate retirement income after state pension age.

Make suggestions on how people can improve their financial position in retirement.

Consider what steps you might need to take in the long term to ensure that you have an adequate income when you retire.

N4 **Chapter review**

1 The Scottish Health Survey 2013 collected information about the length of time since adults last visited the dentist.

The table shows this information.

Length of time since last visit to dentist	2009	2011	2013
Less than 1 year ago	69%	70%	74%
1 year up to 2 years ago	10%	11%	10%
2 years up to 5 years ago	8%	7%	7%
More than 5 years ago	12%	11%	10%
Never	1%	1%	0%
Number in survey	*2578*	*2477*	*2367*

(*Source: Scottish Health Survey, Scottish Government, December 2014*)

a How many adults visited the dentist more than 5 years ago in 2009?

b From the three surveys, what is the probability of choosing an adult in 2013? Give your answer as a fraction in its simplest form.

c What is the probability that an adult chosen from the 2011 survey visited the dentist less than 2 years ago?

d What is the trend for adults who last visited the dentist less than 1 year ago?

2 The Scottish Health Survey looked in more detail about the length of time since adults last visited the dentist in 2013.

The table shows the information by age group.

Time frame	Age group (in years)						
	16–24	25–34	35–44	45–54	55–64	65–74	75 and over
Less than 1 year ago	81%	76%	75%	80%	75%	66%	51%
1 year up to 2 years ago	13%	12%	12%	9%	7%	7%	5%
2 years up to 5 years ago	3%	8%	6%	5%	6%	10%	10%
More than 5 years ago	3%	3%	7%	6%	12%	17%	32%
Never	0%	1%	0%	0%	0%	0%	2%
Number in survey	*320*	*367*	*388*	*436*	*364*	*278*	*215*

(*Source: Scottish Health Survey, Scottish Government, December 2014*)

a How many 16–24-year-olds last visited the dentist at least 2 years ago?

b Which time frame has a gradually decreasing trend in the number of adults last visiting the dentist?

c Which time frame has a gradually increasing trend in the number of adults last visiting the dentist?

d What is the probability that an adult chosen from the survey was aged 45–64? Give your answer as a decimal fraction, rounded to 2 decimal places.

e Which age group is least likely to go to the dentist? Why do you think this is the case?

N4 3 The Scottish Health Survey collects information on the percentages of overweight and obese men and women in Scotland. The graph shows this information over the period from 1995 to 2013.

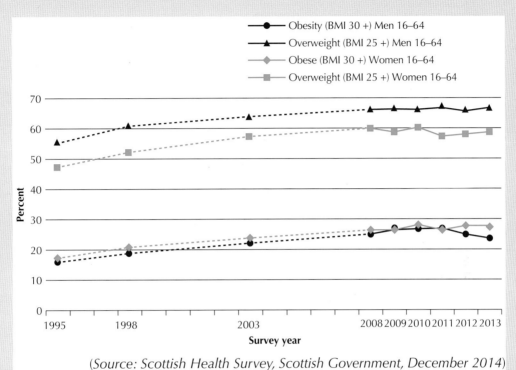

(*Source: Scottish Health Survey, Scottish Government, December 2014*)

a What is the overall trend for obese and overweight adults over the whole period?

b Between which years was there a decrease in the percentage of obese and overweight women?

c In which years was the percentage of obese women the same as the percentage of obese men?

N4

4   The table shows the numbers and percentages for overweight men and women illustrated in the line graphs shown in Question 3.

Year	1995	1998	2003	2008	2009	2010	2011	2012	2013
Number of men	3303	3110	2368	1822	2107	2020	2092	1381	1399
Percentage of men	55.6%	61.0%	64.0%	66.3%	66.2%	66.1%	67.1%	66.0%	66.7%
Number of women	4005	3783	2908	2293	2678	2553	2596	1676	1783
Percentage of women	47.2%	52.2%	57.3%	59.6%	58.4%	60.3%	57.1%	57.7%	58.6%

a   What were the total numbers of men and the total numbers of women surveyed from 1995 to 2013?

b   Out of the women surveyed over the period from 1995 to 2013, what is the probability that a women chosen was surveyed in either 2010 or 2011? Give your answer as a fraction.

c   Out of all the adults surveyed, what is the probability that an adult chosen was surveyed before the year 2000? Give your answer as a decimal fraction, rounded to 3 decimal places.

d   In which year was the greatest difference between the percentage of overweight men and women?

- I can investigate the meaning of lifestyle statistics.
  ★ Exercise 6A Q2, Q6

7 Using statistical information presented in different diagrams

This chapter will show you how to:

- organise and represent data in frequency tables, pictograms, bar graphs and line graphs
- read and interpret data presented in frequency tables, pictograms, bar graphs and line graphs

N4
- organise, represent, read and interpret data in pie charts and stem and leaf diagrams.

You should already know:

- how to calculate fractions and percentages of a quantity
- how to express an amount as a fraction of the total
- how to construct data displays correctly using coordinate grids, labels and titles where necessary.

Organising and representing data

Data is used in everyday life and is organised in ways which make it more easily understandable.

Discrete data can be counted and is often organised into a **frequency table**. For example, the shoe sizes of pupils in a class is discrete data because shoes only come in a fixed number of sizes, such as 35, 36, 37 and so on.

The data given in a frequency table can be represented in graphical form such as bar graphs, pictograms or pie charts. These pictures make it easier to understand and interpret the main features of the data.

Continuous data can take any value in a range. For example, the change in temperature of a hospital patient over a 24-hour period is continuous data, because temperature can take any value.

Continuous data should be represented in a line graph, where it is possible to read information between values along the axes.

Graphs can be drawn by hand or using suitable software apps (such as spreadsheet apps).

Key features of frequency tables and graphs
Frequency tables and graphs must be accurate and must show the data correctly. You must also ensure that the **key features** of each type of graph are included.

Frequency tables
This table shows the data for the numbers of pupils travelling to school using different types of transport.

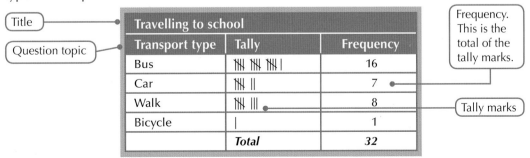

Travelling to school		
Transport type	**Tally**	**Frequency**
Bus	~~IIII~~ ~~IIII~~ ~~IIII~~ I	16
Car	~~IIII~~ II	7
Walk	~~IIII~~ III	8
Bicycle	I	1
	Total	*32*

Title

Question topic

Frequency. This is the total of the tally marks.

Tally marks

Pictogram

The pictogram below uses pictures to represent the numbers of pizzas sold by different members of staff in a fast food restaurant. The pictogram must include a key, to show what the picture represents. The picture chosen to represent the data must be able to clearly show a fraction.

In this pictogram, the key shows that

- 1 whole picture represents 4 pizzas

- $\frac{3}{4}$ of the picture represents 3 pizzas

- $\frac{1}{2}$ of the picture represents 2 pizzas

- $\frac{1}{4}$ of the picture represents 1 pizza.

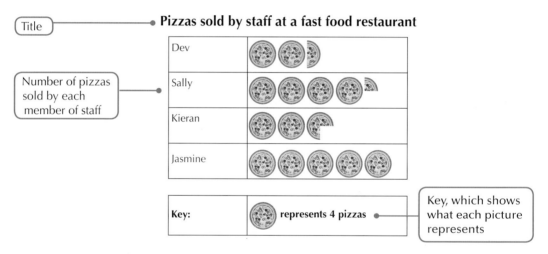

Title → **Pizzas sold by staff at a fast food restaurant**

Number of pizzas sold by each member of staff

Key, which shows what each picture represents

Bar graphs

This bar graph uses the height of the vertical bars to show the numbers of hours Marcus worked each week over a period of 6 weeks.

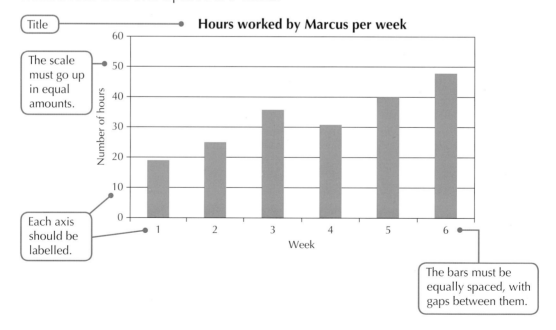

Title → **Hours worked by Marcus per week**

The scale must go up in equal amounts.

Each axis should be labelled.

The bars must be equally spaced, with gaps between them.

Line graphs

This line graph shows the maximum daily temperature recorded at a weather station.
The daily data points are shown with crosses. The daily data points are joined by a line.

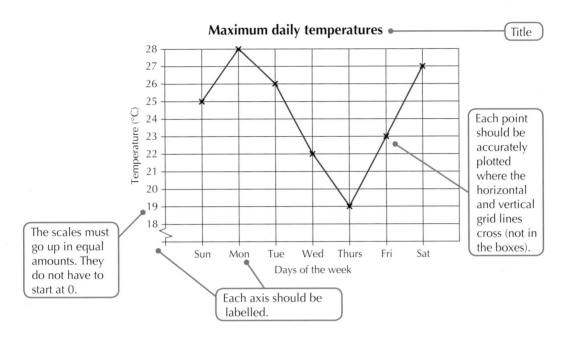

Pie charts

N4

This pie chart shows the proportions of time spent by a group of pupils on different activities.

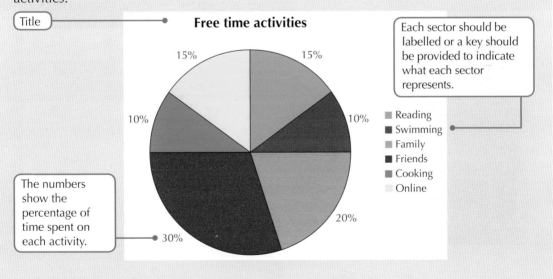

N4

Stem and leaf diagrams

This stem and leaf diagram shows the average speed of cars recorded as they pass along a road. This is an **unordered** stem and leaf diagram. This is a good way to initially transfer data, by reading along the rows or down the columns in the order that it is presented. The numbers can then be ordered, from smallest to biggest.

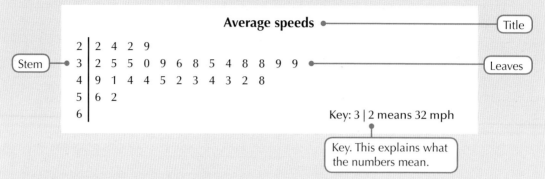

Average speeds ● ————————————— Title

Stem ● ━

2	2 4 2 9
3	2 5 5 0 9 6 8 5 4 8 8 9 9	● ————————————— Leaves
4	9 1 4 4 5 2 3 4 3 2 8
5	6 2
6	

Key: 3 | 2 means 32 mph

Key. This explains what the numbers mean.

This is the **ordered** stem and leaf diagram using the data above. The numbers in each row are ordered, from smallest to biggest.

Average speeds

2	2 2 4 9
3	0 2 4 5 5 5 6 8 8 8 9 9 9
4	1 2 2 3 3 4 4 4 5 8 9
5	2 6
6	

Key: 3 | 2 means 32 mph

	Good for ...	Make sure you ...
Frequency table	collecting and organising data	add up your tally marks correctly to give the correct total
Pictogram	showing a simple picture of totals	include a key to show how many items each picture represents
Bar graph	Discrete data; showing totals of quantities	put labels on the horizontal and vertical axes
Line graph	showing how one thing varies as another changes	put labels on the horizontal and vertical axes and plot the points accurately
Pie chart	showing proportions	convert the quantities to angles properly
Stem and leaf diagram	collecting and organising data	include a key to explain what the numbers mean.

N4

Discrete data is data that must have a specific value, e.g. shoe sizes or flavours of crisps.

Continuous data is data that can take any value within a range, e.g. measurements of length.

Example 7.1

The table shows the results of a survey asking S1 pupils about how they travelled to school.

Bus	Car	Bus	Bus	Car	Bus	Walk	Walk
Walk	Bus	Bus	Walk	Bus	Car	Bus	Bus
Bus	Car	Car	Bus	Car	Bus	Walk	Walk
Bicycle	Bus	Bus	Walk	Bus	Walk	Car	Bus

a   Make a frequency table to show this data.

b   Construct a bar graph to display this data.

c   How many more pupils walk to school compared to those travelling by bicycle?

d   What was the most common way this group of pupils travelled to school?

a

List the types of transport in the left-hand column (**Transport type**).

Create a table with three columns.

Travelling to school

Transport type	Tally	Frequency
Bus	𝚰𝚰𝚰 𝚰𝚰𝚰 𝚰𝚰𝚰	16
Car	𝚰𝚰𝚰 ‖	7
Walk	𝚰𝚰𝚰 ‖‖	8
Bicycle		1
	Total	**32**

In the middle column (**Tally**), use a tally mark for each item in the data table beside the type of transport listed.

In the right-hand column (**Frequency**), write the total amount of tally marks for each type of transport.

Add the frequency for each type of transport to find the total. Make sure your total matches your original data. The total shows the number of pupils surveyed.

b

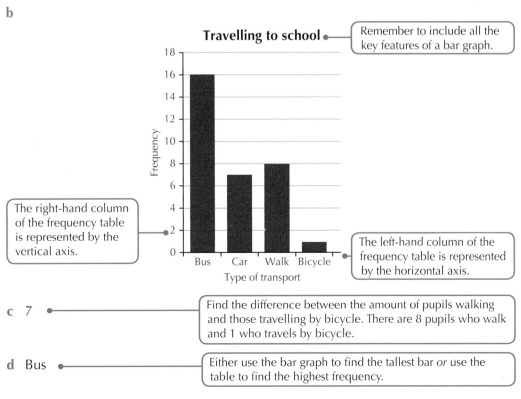

Travelling to school

Remember to include all the key features of a bar graph.

The right-hand column of the frequency table is represented by the vertical axis.

The left-hand column of the frequency table is represented by the horizontal axis.

c   7

Find the difference between the amount of pupils walking and those travelling by bicycle. There are 8 pupils who walk and 1 who travels by bicycle.

d   Bus

Either use the bar graph to find the tallest bar *or* use the table to find the highest frequency.

Example 7.2

A bakery sells cupcakes every day.

The table shows the numbers they sold each day one week.

Monday	Tuesday	Wednesday	Thursday	Friday	Saturday	Sunday
30	15	24	21	42	60	57

a   Construct a pictogram to display this data. Use a single diagram like this to represent 6 cupcakes.

b   How many cupcakes did the bakery sell last week?

a

This pictogram reads horizontally.

The top row of the table is represented by the left-hand column.

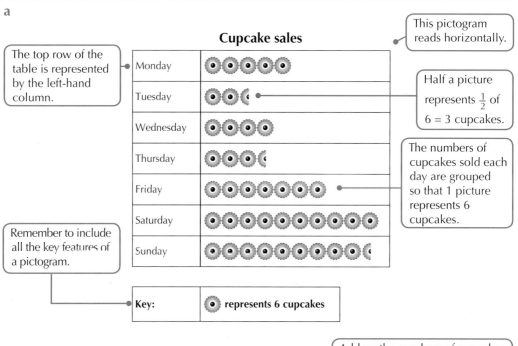

Half a picture represents $\frac{1}{2}$ of 6 = 3 cupcakes.

The numbers of cupcakes sold each day are grouped so that 1 picture represents 6 cupcakes.

Remember to include all the key features of a pictogram.

b   30 + 15 + 24 + 21 + 42 + 60 + 57 = 249 cupcakes

Add up the numbers of cupcakes sold each day to find the total number of cupcakes the bakery sold last week.

Example 7.3

The temperature of a hospital patient was taken every 2 hours during the course of one day.

The table shows the recorded temperatures.

Time	6 am	8 am	10 am	12 noon	2 pm	4 pm	6 pm	8 pm	10 pm
Temperature (°F)	99.2	99.4	99.2	99.1	99.1	98.9	98.7	98.6	98.6

a   Construct a line graph to display this data.

b   At what time was the patient's temperature at its highest?

c   What was the difference between the patient's highest and lowest temperatures?

d   Use your graph to estimate the patient's temperature at 3 pm.

a

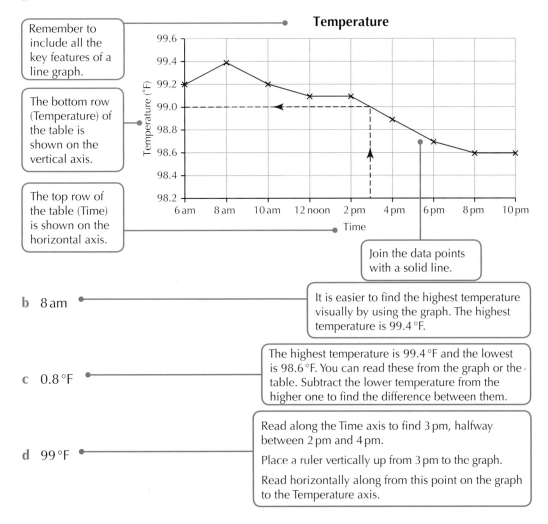

Remember to include all the key features of a line graph.

The bottom row (Temperature) of the table is shown on the vertical axis.

The top row of the table (Time) is shown on the horizontal axis.

Join the data points with a solid line.

b   8 am

It is easier to find the highest temperature visually by using the graph. The highest temperature is 99.4 °F.

c   0.8 °F

The highest temperature is 99.4 °F and the lowest is 98.6 °F. You can read these from the graph or the table. Subtract the lower temperature from the higher one to find the difference between them.

d   99 °F

Read along the Time axis to find 3 pm, halfway between 2 pm and 4 pm.

Place a ruler vertically up from 3 pm to the graph.

Read horizontally along from this point on the graph to the Temperature axis.

N4

Example 7.4

The school charities committee asked pupils and staff which organisations they wanted to raise money for.

This table shows the results of the survey.

Twinned school in Africa	Premature baby unit	Children's cancer charity	Local rotary club	School funds
20%	25%	30%	10%	?%

a What percentage of pupils and staff chose school funds?

The data is shown on a pie chart which has been split into 20 sectors.

b What percentage does each sector represent?

c Construct a pie chart to display this data.

d What fraction of pupils and staff chose twinned school in Africa?

a $20 + 25 + 30 + 10 = 85\%$

  $100 - 85 = 15\%$ •———

> The total of all the percentages add to 100. To find the percentage of the results allocated to school funds, add all the given percentages and subtract this total from 100%.

b $100 \div 20 = 5\%$ •———

> Divide the total percentage of the pie chart by the number of sectors in the pie chart, to find the percentage represented by each sector.

c

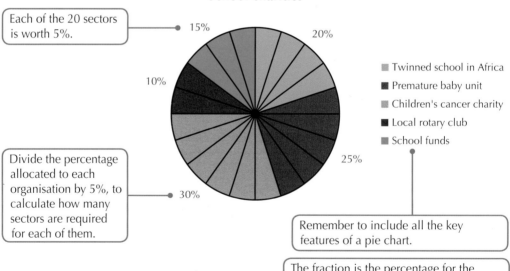

School charities

> Each of the 20 sectors is worth 5%.

> Divide the percentage allocated to each organisation by 5%, to calculate how many sectors are required for each of them.

■ Twinned school in Africa
■ Premature baby unit
■ Children's cancer charity
■ Local rotary club
■ School funds

> Remember to include all the key features of a pie chart.

> The fraction is the percentage for the option chosen out of 100, which is the total percentage of the full circle. Where possible, simplify the fraction.

d $\frac{20}{100}$ or $\frac{1}{5}$ •———

N4

Example 7.5

The table shows the average monthly temperatures (°C) in Cyprus.

Jan	Feb	Mar	Apr	May	Jun	Jul	Aug	Sept	Oct	Nov	Dec
16	17	19	23	26	29	32	33	30	27	22	18

a   Illustrate this information in an **ordered** stem and leaf diagram.

The table shows the average monthly temperatures (°C) in the UK.

Jan	Feb	Mar	Apr	May	Jun	Jul	Aug	Sept	Oct	Nov	Dec
5	6	7	10	12	16	18	18	15	13	9	6

b   Compare the average temperatures in Cyprus and the UK in a back-to-back stem and leaf diagram.

a

```
1 | 6  7  9  8
2 | 3  6  9  7  2
3 | 2  3  0
```

This is an unordered stem and leaf diagram. The information has been recorded in the order it is presented in the table.

Average monthly temperatures in Cyprus

```
1 | 6  7  8  9
2 | 2  3  6  7  9
3 | 0  2  3
```

Key: 2 | 6 means 26°C

The unordered stem and leaf diagram has now been ordered. The numbers in each row are listed from smallest to biggest. A title and key have also been added.

b

Average monthly temperatures in the UK and Cyprus

The UK data has been added to the left-hand side of the Cyprus stem and leaf diagram.

Each side of the stem is labelled – UK and Cyprus – to identify the data set they refer to.

	UK							Cyprus	
	9 7 6 6 5	**0**						
8 8 6 5 3 2 0	**1**	6 7 8 9						
	2	2 3 6 7 9						
	3	0 2 3						

On the left-hand side the numbers in each row are ordered in reverse, with the smallest amount nearest to the stem.

Key: 6 | 1 means 16°C   Key: 1 | 6 means 16°C

Exercise 7A

1   The table shows the results of a survey asking S3 pupils about their favourite music.

Rock	Pop	Hip hop	Rap	Heavy metal	Techno
Pop	Rock	Indie	Techno	Reggae	Hip hop
Hip hop	Rock	Pop	Rock	Heavy metal	Rap
Techno	Heavy metal	Rap	Indie	Rock	Reggae
Reggae	Rap	Techno	Rock	Pop	Techno

a   Copy and complete the frequency table.

b   What fraction of the pupils preferred techno music?

Type of music	Tally	Frequency
Rock		
Pop		
Hip hop		
Rap		
Reggae		
Heavy metal		
Techno		
Indie		
	Total	

★ 2   A supermarket wanted to promote their sales of yogurts. They asked customers which flavours they preferred. The table shows the results of the survey.

Strawberry	Cherry	Plain	Lemon	Strawberry	Mango
Toffee	Strawberry	Raspberry	Banana	Plain	Cherry
Vanilla	Plain	Vanilla	Plain	Blueberry	Vanilla
Banana	Mango	Cherry	Raspberry	Plain	Strawberry
Blueberry	Strawberry	Lemon	Cherry	Toffee	Vanilla
Strawberry	Blueberry	Banana	Strawberry	Raspberry	Raspberry
Lemon	Cherry	Strawberry	Mango	Strawberry	Banana
Plain	Raspberry	Lemon	Strawberry	Banana	Cherry

a   Put this data into a frequency table.

b   Construct a bar graph to display this data.

c   How many more customers preferred cherry to blueberry?

d   What was the most preferred yogurt flavour?

3   The table shows the number of ice creams a shop sold in a week.

Mon	Tues	Wed	Thurs	Fri	Sat	Sun
8	18	12	6	18	20	24

a   Construct a pictogram to display this data. Use a single ice cream cone to represent 4 ice creams.

b   How many ice creams did the shop sell during the week?

★ 4 An S1 class is collecting bottles for recycling. The pictogram shows the bottles that one pupil has collected.

If the pupil collected 54 bottles in total,

what does 🍾 represent?

Bottles for recycling

Clear	🍾🍾🍾🍾🍾
Green	🍾🍾🍾
Brown	🍾🍾🍾🍾🍾🍾🍾

5 The table shows the average monthly rainfall (cm) in Glasgow.

Jan	Feb	Mar	Apr	May	Jun	Jul	Aug	Sept	Oct	Nov	Dec
11	8.5	7	6.5	6	7	9.5	9	10	12	11	13

a Construct a line graph to display this data.

b In which month was the average rainfall at its highest?

c What was the difference between the highest and lowest monthly rainfall amounts?

★ 6 The table shows the numbers of customers in a local shop, over the course of a day.

9 am	10 am	11 am	12 noon	1 pm	2 pm	3 pm	4 pm	5 pm	6 pm
7	9	15	13	22	16	17	14	8	3

a Construct a line graph to display this data.

b When was the shop at its busiest?

c Why do you think it had most customers at this time?

N4 7 The table shows the average weekly amount of pocket money received by a class of 15-year-olds.

£30 or more	£20 to £29.99	£10 to £19.99	£5 to £9.99	£0 to £4.99
30%	25%	20%	20%	5%

a Copy or trace the template and construct a pie chart to display this data.

⚠️ The template can be split into 20 sectors. Each sector represents 5%. To find the number of sectors for each category, divide the percentage by 5. For example 20% is shown with 20 ÷ 5 = 4 sectors.

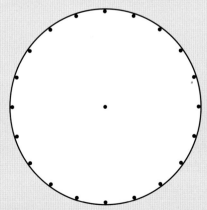

b What fraction of the 15-year-olds received £20 to £29.99?

N4

★ 8 There were 84 000 people at the Rugby World Cup final:

- 46 200 of them supported New Zealand

- 25 200 of them supported Australia

- 8400 of them did not have a preference

- the rest of the people were rugby officials and other staff.

Trace the template in Question 7 and construct a pie chart to display this data.

9 A local community group organised a 5 km fun run to raise money for charity.
The table shows the finishing times (minutes) for some of those taking part.

13	28	15	20	23	16	37	18	19	25
21	17	19	22	34	28	33	19	23	26

Illustrate this information in an ordered stem and leaf diagram.

★ 10 A hospital checked the waiting times for patients in one of its clinics.
The table shows the waiting times (minutes) recorded.

20	22	18	16	31	9	18	23
11	16	25	20	7	15	21	32

a Illustrate this information in an **ordered** stem and leaf diagram.

The hospital reviewed its working practice to reduce waiting times in the clinic.

The table shows the waiting times (minutes) recorded a few months later.

11	15	23	8	25	7	10	22
9	17	21	19	14	13	15	20

b Compare the waiting times before and after the review in working practice in a back-to-back stem and leaf diagram.

c Has the hospital succeeded in reducing the overall waiting times in the clinic? Give a reason for your answer.

Reading and interpreting data

Charts, graphs and tables are used to show data and information in many situations in real life. It is important that you are able to read and interpret the data, to help you draw conclusions and make decisions.

Reading data gives you the facts presented in the graphs, charts and tables. It is important:

- to accurately read the scales used on the axes in bar graphs and line graphs

- to work out the value of each sector in a pie chart

- to read individual cells in tables to be able to interpret what they mean.

Interpreting data means you are looking for patterns, reasons or explanations which will allow you to draw conclusions. For example, you can identify trends in a line graph which records information at regular intervals over a period of time.

Example 7.6

An apprentice builder was asked to check the amount of hardware left at the job site at the end of each day.

The table shows his records for last week.

	Monday	Tuesday	Wednesday	Thursday	Friday
Packs of nuts	8	11	22	16	14
Packs of bolts	5	8	18	21	15
Packs of nails	17	26	9	44	53
Packs of screws	56	32	61	32	41

a   How many packs of screws were left at the job site on Tuesday?

b   How many more packs of nails were left at the job site on Thursday compared to Wednesday?

c   How many pieces of hardware were left at the job site on Monday?

d   How many more packs of bolts than packs of nuts were left at the job site on Friday?

c Add up all the numbers in the column for Monday, to give the total amount of hardware left that day.

d Read along the row labelled **Packs of bolts** and down the column labelled **Friday**. The cell where they meet tells you the number of packs of bolts left on Friday. Read along the row labelled **Packs of nuts** and down the column labelled **Friday**. The cell where they meet tells you the number of packs of nuts left on Friday. Calculate the difference between these two amounts to tell you how many more packs of bolts than packs of nuts were left on Friday.

	Monday	Tuesday	Wednesday	Thursday	Friday
Packs of nuts	(8)	11	22	16	(14)
Packs of bolts	(5)	8	18	21	(15)
Packs of nails	(17)	26	(9)	(44)	53
Packs of screws	(56)	(32)	61	32	41

a Read along the row labelled **Packs of screws** and down the column labelled **Tuesday**. The cell where they meet tells you the number of packs of screws left on Tuesday.

b Read along the row labelled **Packs of nails** and down the column labelled **Thursday**. The cell where they meet tells you the number of packs of nails left on Thursday. Do the same to find the number of packs of nails left on Wednesday. Calculate the difference between these two amounts to tell you how many more packs of nails were left on Thursday compared to Wednesday.

a   32

b $44 - 9 = 35$

c $8 + 5 + 17 + 56 = 86$

d $15 - 14 = 1$

Example 7.7

The bar graph represents the percentage of the UK population that have a social media profile.

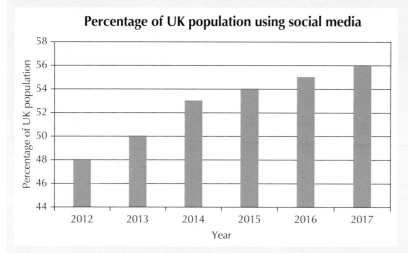

Percentage of UK population using social media

a   In 2017, the estimated population of the UK is 65 500 000 people. How many of these people have a social media profile?

b   In 2014, the population of the UK was 64 150 000 people. How many of these people have a social media profile?

c   Estimate the percentage of people who will have a social media profile in 2020.

a   56% of 65 500 000 = $\dfrac{56}{100}$ × 65 500 000

            = 36 680 000

> The column labelled **2017** shows the proportion of the UK population with a social media profile. Read across from the top of the bar for 2017 to the vertical axis.

b   53% of 64 150 000 = $\dfrac{53}{100}$ × 64 150 000

            = 33 999 500

c   In 2020 the estimated percentage of the UK population with a social media profile will be 59%.

> From 2014 to 2017 the percentage increase has been 1% a year. It is reasonable to estimate the increase for the next 3 years to be the same. It is possible that something could affect this estimate, so the estimate may not be very reliable.

N4

Example 7.8

The amount of daily rainfall at Aberdeen Airport in February 2017 was measured and recorded.

The pie chart represents the data.

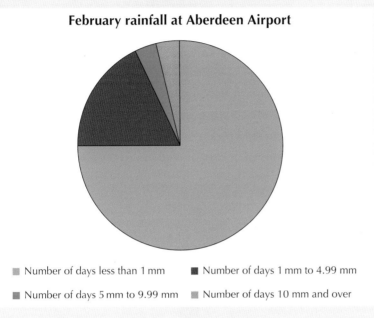

February rainfall at Aberdeen Airport

■ Number of days less than 1 mm   ■ Number of days 1 mm to 4.99 mm

■ Number of days 5 mm to 9.99 mm   ▨ Number of days 10 mm and over

For how many days was the rainfall less than 1 mm?

21 days ●————————

There are 28 days in February 2017. The pie chart has $\frac{3}{4}$ shaded for the number of days when rainfall was less than 1 mm. To work out how many days this is, calculate $\frac{3}{4}$ of 28.

Exercise 7B

1   An oriental fast food take-away has these items on their menu:

- 8 sweet and sour dishes
- 6 spare rib dishes
- 27 chicken dishes
- 16 beef dishes
- 17 king prawn dishes
- 12 roast pork dishes
- 20 rice dishes
- 21 noodle dishes.

a   How many more beef dishes than roast pork dishes are there?

b   Which type of dish has the most choice?

★ 2 Senior pupils are selling flavoured ice cream cones at school to raise money for their expedition trip.

The table shows the record of sales last week.

	Monday	Tuesday	Wednesday	Thursday	Friday
Strawberry	125	118	123	95	107
Chocolate	79	83	75	102	101
Vanilla	141	133	109	121	99
Sundae	53	58	42	63	67

a How many sundae cones were sold on Thursday?

b How many more vanilla cones were sold on Tuesday compared to Friday?

c How many ice cream cones were sold on Wednesday?

d How many more strawberry cones than chocolate cones were sold on Monday?

3 A class of S4 pupils were asked about their favourite type of music.

The bar graph shows the results of the survey.

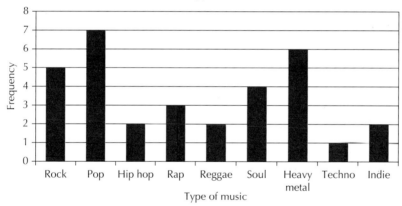

a How many pupils are in the S4 class?

b What fraction prefer either rock or heavy metal?

c Which types of music were equally favourite?

d Why is this discrete data and not continuous data?

4   The line graph shows the UK annual population figures over a 10-year period.

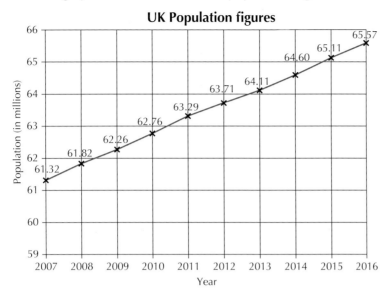

a   Describe the trend of the UK population figures over the 10-year period.

b   What is the difference between the UK population in 2009 and 2014?

c   If the trend in the UK population figures continues in the same way, estimate what the figure will be in 2020.

d   Does this graph represent discrete or continuous data? Give a reason for your answer.

★   5   The line graph shows the monthly sales figures for a local craft shop.

a   What was the total annual sales for the local craft shop?

b   Between which two consecutive months was the greatest difference in monthly sales income?

c   In which months were the income from sales more than 10% of the annual sales?

d   December has the highest sales figures. Why do you think this is the case?

6 The Scottish School Adolescent Lifestyle and Substance Use Survey (SALSUS) 2013 asked 13-year-olds and 15-year-olds where they usually drink alcohol.

This bar graph shows the results of this survey.

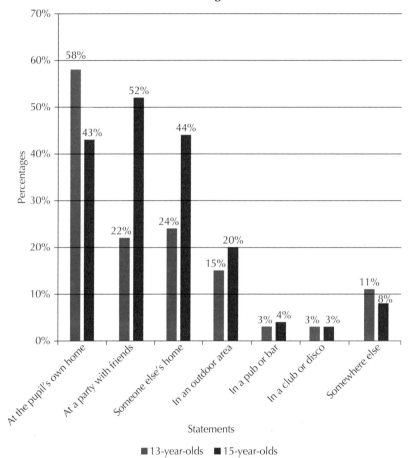

Where teenagers drink alcohol

■ 13-year-olds ■ 15-year-olds

a Which statement has the biggest difference between 13-year-olds and 15-year-olds?

b Comment on the similarities between 13-year-olds and 15-year-olds.

c Comment on the differences between 13-year-olds and 15-year-olds.

N4

7 The government publishes estimates of UK greenhouse gas emissions.

The table shows the annual emissions of road users for the period from 2006 to 2015.

Million tonnes carbon dioxide equivalent (MtCO$_2$e)										
	2006	2007	2008	2009	2010	2011	2012	2013	2014	2015
Passenger cars	76.8	77.1	74.8	72.5	70.2	69.5	69.2	68.0	68.3	69.1
Light duty vehicles	16.3	16.8	16.0	15.8	16.1	16.2	16.4	16.6	17.3	18.0
Buses	4.7	4.8	4.2	4.2	4.3	4.0	3.8	3.8	3.8	3.7
HGVs	20.8	21.0	19.5	18.0	18.6	18.1	18.2	18.3	18.8	19.6
Mopeds and motorcycles	0.7	0.7	0.6	0.6	0.6	0.5	0.5	0.5	0.5	0.5

(*Source: Department for Business, Energy and Industrial Strategy, February 2017*)

N4

a Describe the trend in annual emissions for buses during this 10-year period.

b Calculate the total emissions for these road users in 2014.

c The emissions for light duty vehicles from the period 2005 to 2015 was 181.3 $MtCO_2e$. Use the data in the table to calculate the light duty vehicles emissions in 2005.

8 The bar graph shows the profits made by a mobile phone company in the period 2010 to 2016.

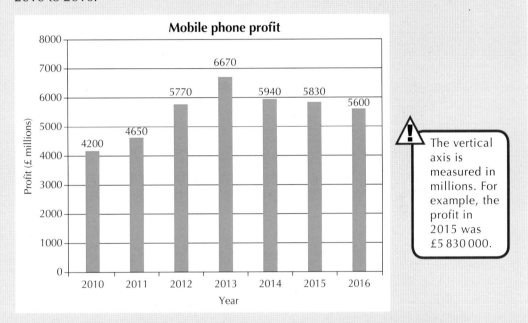

The vertical axis is measured in millions. For example, the profit in 2015 was £5 830 000.

a In which year did the mobile phone company make the largest profit?

b What is the difference between the largest and smallest profits made by the mobile phone company?

c What was the total profit made by the mobile phone company of all the years from 2010 to 2016?

9 A group of holiday makers were asked about their favourite country to visit.

The pie chart shows the top three favourite countries.

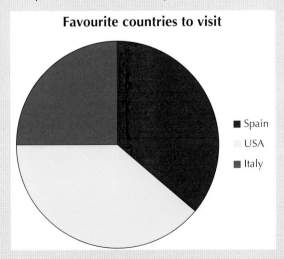

a What percentage chose Italy as their favourite country to visit?

b If 39% chose the USA as their favourite country to visit, what percentage chose Spain?

N4 ★ 10 The pie chart shows the percentage income of an outdoor pursuits company from
go-karting, quad biking, paintballing and mountain biking for the month of July.

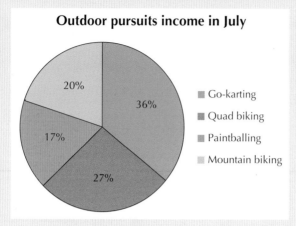

Outdoor pursuits income in July

The total income from mountain biking is £3520 in July.

a   What was the outdoor pursuits company's total income in July?

This pie chart shows their percentage income for the different activities for the month
of September.

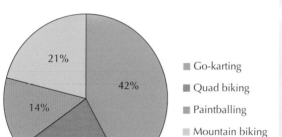

Outdoor pursuits income in September

The outdoor pursuits company's total income in September was £14 350.

b   What was the September income for go-karting?

c   In which month was the income higher for go-karting and by how much?

GO! Activity

Research online to find average temperatures and rainfall in some European cities.

Create appropriate graphs to summarise your findings.

Devise some questions to ask someone else based on your diagrams.

Create a presentation on rainfall in European cities.

Chapter review

1 The Scottish Health Survey published information on the percentage of adults exceeding the guidelines on weekly alcohol consumption from 2008–2013.

The table shows this information.

Survey year	2008	2009	2010	2011	2012	2013
Men	30%	28%	28%	26%	26%	22%
Women	20%	19%	18%	18%	18%	16%

a Using the information in the table, create a line graph to illustrate the percentage of men exceeding the guidelines on weekly alcohol consumption over the period from 2008 to 2013.

b On the same coordinate grid, create a line graph to display the percentage of women exceeding the guidelines on weekly alcohol consumption over the same period.

c Using your graph, describe the trend for the percentage of men exceeding the guidelines on weekly alcohol consumption.

d In which years was the difference between men and women the greatest? What was this difference?

2 The Scottish Health Survey published information on the percentage of adults meeting the recommended daily fruit and vegetable consumption in 2013.

The compound bar graph shows this information for men and women, by age group.

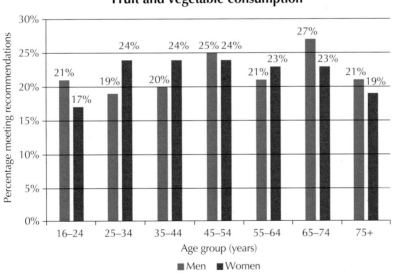

Fruit and vegetable consumption

a Give a reason for displaying this information in a bar graph.

b Which two age groups of women were poorest at meeting the recommended daily fruit and vegetable consumption in 2013?

c Make a comparison between the percentages of men and women meeting the daily recommendations for those who are at least 65 years old.

d Which age group has the least difference in the percentages of men and women meeting the daily recommendations of fruit and vegetable consumption?

e Across all the age groups, are men or women better at meeting the daily recommendations of fruit and vegetable consumption? Give a reason for your answer.

3   The Scottish Health Survey also published information on the percentage of children (aged 2–15 years) eating 5+ portions and no portions of fruit and vegetables per day in 2013.

The table shows this information.

Age group (years)	2–4	5–7	8–10	11–12	13–15
5+ portions	15%	15%	9%	14%	13%
No portions	6%	10%	7%	14%	17%

a   Using the information in the table, create a compound bar graph to illustrate the percentages of children eating 5+ portions and no portions of fruit and vegetables per day in 2013.

b   What is the trend for eating no portions of fruit and vegetables as children get older?

c   What are the similarities and differences between the age groups in the amounts of fruit and vegetables that they eat?

N4

4   The Scottish Health Survey published information on the percentage of adults meeting physical activity guidelines in 2013.

The table shows this information.

Age group (years)	16–24	25–34	35–44	45–54	55–64	65–74	75+
Percentage of adults meeting guidelines	10%	20%	20%	20%	15%	10%	5%

a   Copy or trace the template and construct a pie chart to display this data.

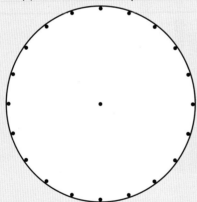

b   What fraction of 35–44-year-old adults met the physical activity guidelines in 2013? Give your answer in its simplest form.

c   Fewer adults aged 75+ met the physical activity guidelines in 2013. Why do you think this was the case?

N4

5 Mr Smith's maths class were given a practice assessment.

The table shows the results, in percentages.

40	34	45	56	21	38	22	25	39	28
44	32	21	38	52	31	60	45	51	42

a Illustrate this information in an **ordered** stem and leaf diagram.

Following the practice assessment, Mr Smith thought the pupils would be able to improve their results following some further class review.

He then gave the pupils a second assessment to see if their marks could be improved.

The table shows these results, in percentages.

76	25	35	41	45	54	62	45	36	38
48	51	60	70	56	39	60	59	57	68

b Compare the assessment results before and after the class review in a back-to-back stem and leaf diagram.

c Did the pupils succeed in improving their assessment results following further revision in class? Give a reason for your answer.

- I can organise and represent data using frequency tables. ★ Exercise 7A Q2
- I can organise and represent data using pictograms. ★ Exercise 7A Q4
- I can organise and represent data using bar graphs. ★ Exercise 7A Q2
- I can organise and represent data using line graphs. ★ Exercise 7A Q6

N4
- I can organise and represent data using pie charts. ★ Exercise 7A Q8
- I can organise and represent data using stem and leaf diagrams. ★ Exercise 7A Q10

- I can read and interpret data using frequency tables. ★ Exercise 7B Q2
- I can read and interpret data using line graphs. ★ Exercise 7B Q5

N4
- I can read and interpret data using pie charts. ★ Exercise 7B Q10

8 Comparing data

This chapter will show you how to:

N4

- compare totals and averages of data sets
- calculate the mean and range of data sets
- compare data sets using mean and range.

You should already know:

- how to add and subtract whole numbers and decimals
- how to divide by a whole number
- how to round numbers to one and two decimal places
- how to interpret data from a table.

Totals and averages

You can find similarities and differences between sets of data by calculating their **totals**. The total amount is found by adding up all the amounts given in the data set. For example, the total cost of a basket of the same items of shopping from two or more supermarkets can be compared, to find out which is cheapest.

You can also find similarities and differences between sets of data by calculating their **averages**. One average (the **mean**) is found by adding up all the amounts given in the data set and dividing the total by the number of items in the data set.

Example 8.1

The table shows the cost of the same 10 items in three different supermarkets.

Item	Supermarket 1	Supermarket 2	Supermarket 3
4 pack yogurts	£1.80	£1.75	£1.99
160 teabags	£3.20	£3.25	£3.20
Loaf of bread	£0.90	£1.35	£1.15
400 g jar coffee	£5.00	£4.75	£4.88
1 kg porridge oats	£2.25	£1.99	£2.00
Tinned soup	£0.99	£0.95	£1.10
350 g cheese	£2.33	£2.20	£2.50
2 litres milk	£1.25	£1.25	£1.25
Washing powder	£3.50	£4.00	£4.72
9 toilet roll pack	£4.45	£4.20	£3.50

a Calculate the total cost of the basket of items at each of the supermarkets to find out which one is the cheapest.

b Find the average cost of 1 kg porridge oats.

c Find the average cost of a loaf of bread, rounding your answer to the nearest penny.

a **Supermarket 1**

£1.80 + £3.20 + £0.90 + £5.00 + £2.25 + £0.99
+ £2.33 + £1.25 + £3.50 + £4.45
= £25.67

> Add up the cost of all the items in the basket for supermarket 1 to find the total cost of the basket.

Supermarket 2

£1.75 + £3.25 + £1.35 + £4.75 + £1.99 + £0.95 + £2.20 + £1.25 + £4.00 + £4.20
= £25.69

Supermarket 3

£1.99 + £3.20 + £1.15 + £4.88 + £2.00 + £1.10 + £2.50 + £1.25 + £4.72 + £3.50
= £26.29

The lowest total is £25.67, so supermarket 1 has the cheapest basket.

> Compare the total costs of all 3 supermarket baskets of items and choose the one with the lowest total. In your conclusion, include a statement which makes the comparison between the prices.

b £2.25 + £1.99 + £2.00 = £6.24

Average $= \dfrac{£6.24}{3} = £2.08$

> Add the costs of 1 kg porridge oats in all 3 supermarkets and divide the total by 3 to find the average cost.

c £0.90 + £1.35 + £1.15 = £3.40

Average $= \dfrac{£3.40}{3} = £1.133\,333\ldots$

> Add the costs of the loaf of bread and divide by 3 to find the average cost.

$= £1.13$ (to the nearest penny)

> Round the answer to 2 decimal places to give an answer to the nearest penny.

Exercise 8A

1 Cara wants to buy some new clothes for her holiday.

The table shows the prices of the same clothes at two different shops.

	Shop 1	Shop 2
T-shirt (1)	£6.49	£6.20
T-shirt (2)	£8.99	£10.50
Dress	£23.99	£21.90
Skirt	£12.25	£12.60
Vest top	£4.99	£4.50
Shorts	£11.50	£10.75
Leggings	£6.99	£5.99
Sandals	£13.75	£15.99

a What is the total cost of the clothes in shop 1?

b What is the total cost of the clothes in shop 2?

c In which shop is the total cost of clothes cheaper, and by how much?

2 A group of pupils were asked how much pocket money they were given each week. The table shows the amounts they receive.

Pupil 1	Pupil 2	Pupil 3	Pupil 4	Pupil 5	Pupil 6	Pupil 7	Pupil 8
£5.00	£7.00	£10.00	£7.50	£5.00	£7.00	£10.00	£12.00

Pupil 9	Pupil 10	Pupil 11	Pupil 12	Pupil 13	Pupil 14	Pupil 15	Pupil 16
£5.00	£7.50	£10.00	£15.00	£7.00	£12.00	£14.00	£7.50

What is the average amount of pocket money received by the pupils?

Give your answer to the nearest penny.

3 The table shows the income from sales at a catering van each day for the last week.

Monday	Tuesday	Wednesday	Thursday	Friday	Saturday	Sunday
£720	£775	£749	£789	£844	£1035	£976

a What was the total income for the catering van last week?

The owner of the catering van keeps a record of the income from sales each week. The table shows this record.

	Mon	Tues	Wed	Thurs	Fri	Sat	Sun
Week 1	£720	£775	£749	£789	£844	£1035	£976
Week 2	£715	£768	£754	£796	£806	£1176	£1052
Week 3	£726	£770	£752	£756	£851	£1088	£958
Week 4	£730	£782	£746	£783	£867	£1245	£1132

b What was the average weekly income?

Give your answer to the nearest penny.

⚠ Find the total income for each week.

c What was the total income on Tuesdays for these 4 weeks?

d How much more was the total income on Saturdays compared to Thursdays?

★ 4 The table shows the cost of the same 10 items in three different supermarkets.

	Supermarket 1	Supermarket 2	Supermarket 3
1 kg apples	£1.80	£2.10	£1.96
Fresh pizza	£3.50	£2.80	£3.65
1 kg long grain rice	£0.95	£0.99	£0.89
Fresh chicken	£6.20	£5.95	£5.80
Cake	£2.35	£2.50	£2.75
Diluting juice	£1.20	£0.99	£1.10
2.5 kg potatoes	£1.75	£2.00	£1.80
Butter	£1.20	£1.28	£1.15
Jar pasta sauce	£1.22	£1.30	£1.00
Pack of bananas	£1.50	£1.30	£1.45

a Calculate the cost of the basket of items at each of the supermarkets to find out which one is the cheapest.

b Find the average cost of 2.5 kg potatoes.

c Find the average cost of a fresh pizza, rounding your answer to the nearest penny.

5 The table shows the number of goals scored by three Scottish football teams for the last 15 games in the season.

	Team 1	Team 2	Team 3
Game 1	2	1	3
Game 2	4	2	1
Game 3	1	3	1
Game 4	1	1	2
Game 5	1	0	1
Game 6	2	2	1
Game 7	2	1	0
Game 8	1	3	1
Game 9	3	0	2
Game 10	1	2	0
Game 11	0	1	0
Game 12	4	3	1
Game 13	2	3	1
Game 14	0	1	1
Game 15	0	2	2

a What was the average number of goals per team? Give your answer to 1 decimal place.

b Which was the best goal scoring team? Give a reason for your answer.

N4 Mean and range

Finding the average is a helpful way of getting an overall picture about a set of data, as you can calculate one value to represent all the data. The mathematical word for an average is the **mean**.

$$\text{Mean} = \frac{\text{total of all the values}}{\text{number of values}}$$

When you calculate a mean, you should always check that your answer is sensible. The mean value must always be somewhere between the smallest and biggest values of the data set.

The mean can be used to compare two or more sets of data. For example, finding the mean cost of a basket of shopping in different supermarkets could influence where you choose to regularly shop.

The **range** of a data set measures the difference between the highest and lowest values in a data set. It is a measure of how spread out the data is. The larger the range, the more variation there is between the values being measured.

Range = biggest value – smallest value

The range can be used to compare the spread of two or more sets of data. For example, finding the range of temperatures in different holiday resorts could influence your choice of destination.

N4

Example 8.3

The Department for Transport collects data on the number of road fatalities by UK region.

The table shows the number of road fatalities in 2014 and 2015.

Region	2014	2015
Scotland	200	162
North West	184	178
West Midlands	156	162
Wales	103	105
South West	184	173
North East	57	62
Yorkshire and the Humber	159	149
East Midlands	169	174
East of England	188	195
London	130	136
South East	246	236

(Source: Department for Transport)

a What was the mean number of road fatalities in the UK in 2014? Give your answer to 1 decimal place.

b What was the difference between the mean number of road fatalities in the UK in 2014 and 2015?

c What was the range of road fatalities in the UK in 2015?

d Make a comment comparing the ranges of road fatalities in 2014 and 2015.

a Mean in 2014 = $\frac{1776}{11}$ = 161.454... = 161.5 (1 d.p.)

> Add up the numbers of road fatalities in all the UK regions for 2014 to find the total of all the values. Divide the total of all the values (1776) by the number of regions (11). Round your answer to 1 decimal place and remember to check the answer is sensible.

b Mean in 2015 = $\frac{1732}{11}$

= 157.454...

= 157.5 (1 d.p.)

Difference between 2014 and 2015

= 161.5 – 157.5 = 4

> Repeat the process in part **a** for 2015. Find the difference by subtracting the smaller mean from the larger one.

c Range in 2015 = 236 – 62 = 174

> The range = biggest value (236) – smallest value (62).

d Range in 2014 = 246 – 57 = 189

There is a greater variation in the numbers of road fatalities in 2014.

> Repeat the process in part **c** for 2014. Compare this value with the one for 2015. You could also say there is a smaller variation in the numbers of road fatalities in 2015.

N4

Exercise 8B

1 a Calculate the mean of the following weights of a group of 10-year-old children. Give your answer to 1 decimal place.

31.4 kg, 28.2 kg, 31.3 kg, 29.6 kg, 33.0 kg, 30.8 kg, 31.2 kg, 29.9 kg, 30.7 kg, 31.1 kg, 28.5 kg, 29.4 kg, 31.4 kg, 31.6 kg, 30.7 kg, 30.3 kg, 32.2 kg, 31.2 kg

b Find the range of the weights of this group of 10-year-old children.

2 a Calculate the mean and range of the following monthly wages of workers in the production section of a factory.

£2400, £2620, £2000, £2000, £1670, £1670, £1670, £1583, £1583, £1583

These are the monthly wages of workers in the despatch section of the factory.

£2500, £2740, £2000, £2000, £1850, £1630, £1630, £1630, £1500, £1500

b Calculate the mean and range of the monthly wages of the workers in the despatch section of the factory.

c Compare the mean monthly wages of the workers in each section of the factory.

d Make a comment comparing the range of monthly wages of the workers in each section of the factory.

> ⚠️ Write a sentence when you are comparing sets of data, which relates to the context of the question.

3 The tables show the average monthly temperatures (in degrees Celsius) and the average number of days it rained, in two holiday resorts in Cyprus, Limassol and Paphos.

Limassol	Jan	Feb	Mar	Apr	May	Jun	Jul	Aug	Sep	Oct	Nov	Dec
Avg. temp (°C)	13	13	14	17	21	24	27	27	25	22	17	14
Avg. max temp (°C)	17	17	18	21	26	29	31	31	29	27	22	18
Avg. min temp (°C)	8	8	9	13	17	20	23	23	21	17	13	9
Avg. rainy days	8	6	6	4	2	0	0	0	0	3	5	6

Paphos	Jan	Feb	Mar	Apr	May	Jun	Jul	Aug	Sep	Oct	Nov	Dec
Avg. temp (°C)	12	12	13	16	20	23	26	26	24	21	17	14
Avg. max temp (°C)	17	17	18	21	24	28	29	30	28	26	22	19
Avg. min temp (°C)	7	7	8	11	14	17	20	21	18	16	12	9
Avg. rainy days	9	7	7	5	2	0	0	0	1	3	6	7

a Calculate the mean for the average maximum temperature for the whole year in both Limassol and Paphos. Give your answers to 1 decimal place.

> ⚠️ Make sure you use the right data. The question asks about the average maximum temperature.

b Calculate the mean for the average rain days for the whole year in both Limassol and Paphos. Give your answers to 1 decimal place.

Janis is considering which of these two resorts to stay in when she goes on holiday to Cyprus. She is not keen on the weather being too hot or wet.

c Using your information on the mean temperature and number of rainy days, advise Janis which resort she should choose to stay at.

N4 ★ 4 The table shows the list of food that a couple bought in the last 4 weeks.

	Week 1	Week 2	Week 3	Week 4
Bread	£1.20	£0.95	£1.10	£1.20
Fruit	£3.20	£2.40	£2.60	£1.95
Vegetables	£2.45	£2.65	£2.70	£2.55
Milk	£1.80	£1.80	£1.80	£1.80
Supermarket	£21.30	£23.24	£26.10	£22.42
Meat	£15.00	£12.95	£10.80	£14.45

What was the mean weekly food bill for the couple? Give your answer to the nearest penny.

★ 5 The Department for Transport keeps records on the number of civilian search and rescue helicopter operations.

The table shows these records for 2016, for each quarter of the year.

Helicopter bases	Jan–Mar	Apr–Jun	Jul–Sept	Oct–Dec
Caernarfon	62	84	142	72
Humberside	42	71	77	71
Inverness	79	85	88	44
Lee-on-Solent	33	47	66	47
Portland	19	33	41	23
Stornoway	18	43	41	16
Sumburgh	25	34	39	24
St Athan	44	68	87	44
Lydd	36	64	79	41
Prestwick	93	93	105	72
Newquay	57	89	99	64

(*Source: Department for Transport*)

a   Calculate the mean number of search and rescue operations for each quarter of 2016. Give your answers to 1 decimal place.

b   Calculate the range of the number of search and rescue operations for each quarter of 2016.

c   Make two comments comparing the numbers of search and rescue operations in January–March and in April–June.

d   Which helicopter base has the least variation in its number of search and rescue operations?

N4 ★ 6 A bookshop wanted to find out about the customers using its instore café.

The table shows the information they collected at short intervals one morning during the week.

Amount spent	Length of stay (minutes)
£4.90	30
£2.85	35
£6.20	20
£3.65	20
£7.15	30
£3.95	40
£5.20	35
£5.45	15
£3.95	25
£5.75	25

a What was the mean and range of the amount spent by the customers during the morning? Round your answers appropriately.

b What was the mean and range of the length of stay of the customers during the morning?

The table shows the information they collected at short intervals during an afternoon of the same week.

Amount spent	Length of stay (minutes)
£5.20	20
£2.50	30
£4.20	30
£5.55	45
£4.90	50
£2.85	40
£6.10	60
£8.20	60
£7.90	55
£6.95	45

c What was the mean and range of the amount spent by the customers during the afternoon? Round your answers appropriately.

d What was the mean and range of the length of stay of the customers during the afternoon?

e Make two comments comparing the amount spent by the customers in the morning and the afternoon.

Activity

The Royal Society for the Protection of Birds (RSPB) asks the public to take part in the annual Big Butterfly Count every summer. This is a survey to find out about the populations of different species of butterflies in the UK.

The table shows the top 16 butterflies and the numbers counted by every 1000 people.

Butterfly species	2012	2013	2014	2015	2016
Meadow brown	2799	1989	1333	1534	1499
Gatekeeper	1324	1729	1838	2139	1245
Ringlet	1283	701	316	552	705
Small white	740	3471	1507	1449	1620
Large white	622	3077	1142	1660	1645
Six spot burnet	479	420	186	188	220
Marbled white	417	193	107	161	247
Green-veined white	245	876	499	288	441
Large skipper	211	214	182	223	214
Small tortoiseshell	200	1111	1454	626	323
Red admiral	199	383	589	420	695
Comma	169	387	265	375	197
Speckled wood	161	241	331	246	269
Common blue	129	246	410	358	155
Small copper	82	122	123	887	60
Peacock	71	2939	2197	855	484

Create your own questions on finding averages from this table, for other pupils to answer.

N4

Extended activity

Exploring other average measures and misleading information

A small company has 12 employees. Their annual salaries are:

£18 996	£18 996	£18 996	£20 040	£20 040	£20 040
£24 000	£24 000	£28 800	£31 440	£32 880	£89 040

The mean annual salary is:

$$\frac{£347\,268}{12} = £28\,939$$

Only 3 employees earn more than the mean annual salary.

This is not the most representative figure for the employees' salaries.

The largest salary is earned by the Managing Director. This is an extreme value compared to the rest of the salaries. Including this value in the calculation gives misleading information about the mean salary of the employees.

If you exclude the Managing Director's salary, the mean annual salary is:

$$\frac{£258\,228}{11} = £23\,475.27$$

This is a much better representative amount of the employees' salaries. 6 employees earn more and 6 employees earn less than this.

The mean is just one way to find an average of a set of data. You can also find the **median** and the **mode** as different averages, to best represent a data set.

The **median** is the **number nearest the middle value** of all the numbers listed in order from smallest to biggest.

If there are an odd number of values, the median is the middle value.

If there are an even number of values, the median is the mean of the two middle values.

To find the median, you need to write the values in numerical order and find the value or values in the middle.

| £18 996 | £18 996 | £18 996 | £20 040 | £20 040 | **£20 040** |
| **£24 000** | £24 000 | £28 800 | £31 440 | £32 880 | £89 040 |

For the employees' salaries above, the median = $\frac{20\,040 + 24\,000}{2} = \frac{44\,040}{2} = £22\,020$

This is a good representative of the data as the majority of the salaries are reasonably close to the median.

The **mode** is the most common value – the one which occurs most often.

If all the values are different, there is no mode.

If two or more values occur most often, they are all said to be the mode.

| **£18 996** | **£18 996** | **£18 996** | **£20 040** | **£20 040** | **£20 040** |
| £24 000 | £24 000 | £28 800 | £31 440 | £32 880 | £89 040 |

For the employees' salaries above, there are two values which occur three times. The mode is both £18 996 and £20 040.

This is not a good representative of the data as these are the two lowest values and all other salaries are greater than these.

The best average measure for the employees' salaries is the median.

Deciding which average measure is the best to use

The table shows the advantages and disadvantages of each of the average measures.

Average	Advantages	Disadvantages
Mean	It takes all of the data into account.	It may not be representative if there are extreme values in the set of data.
Median	It is a better average to use if there are extreme values in the data as it only looks at the middle values.	It could be misleading as it does not look at all the values.
Mode	It is not affected by extreme values.	It could be misleading if it is not near the centre of the set of data. If all the values are different, there is no mode.

N4

For each set of data in Questions 1–4, calculate the mean, median and mode.

Decide which average measure **best** represents the data.

1 House sale prices in an area of Aberdeen for 12 properties were:

   £225 000   £240 000   £240 000   £252 000   £268 245   £298 950

   £322 500   £344 990   £390 000   £395 995   £470 000   £695 750

   What was the average house sale price?

2 The table shows the weekly pocket money for a group of 15 pupils.

Pupil 1	Pupil 2	Pupil 3	Pupil 4	Pupil 5
£5	£5	£5	£5	£5

Pupil 6	Pupil 7	Pupil 8	Pupil 9	Pupil 10
£5	£7.50	£7.50	£10	£10

Pupil 11	Pupil 12	Pupil 13	Pupil 14	Pupil 15
£10	£10	£12	£12	£12

   What was the average amount of weekly pocket money received by pupils?

3 The table shows the daily income of a catering van for a 4-week period.

	Mon	Tues	Wed	Thurs	Fri	Sat	Sun
Week 1	£720	£775	£749	£789	£806	£1035	£976
Week 2	£715	£768	£754	£806	£806	£1176	£1052
Week 3	£726	£770	£752	£756	£851	£1088	£958
Week 4	£730	£782	£746	£783	£867	£1245	£1132

   What is the average income per day for the catering van?

4 The table shows the average monthly temperatures in Glasgow.

January	February	March	April	May	June
3°C	4°C	5.5°C	8°C	10.5°C	13.5°C

July	August	September	October	November	December
15°C	15°C	12.5°C	9.5°C	6°C	4.5°C

   What is the average temperature for the whole year in Glasgow?

5 Use the internet and other media to investigate averages claimed by different people and companies.

   What average do you think they have used – mean, median or mode?

   Have they used the best average measure to represent the data?

   Or is their average measure misleading?

Chapter review

1   The Scottish School Adolescent Lifestyle and Substance Use Survey 2013 published information on regular teenage smokers.

The line graphs show the percentages of 15-year-old boys and girls who were regular smokers from 1990 to 2013.

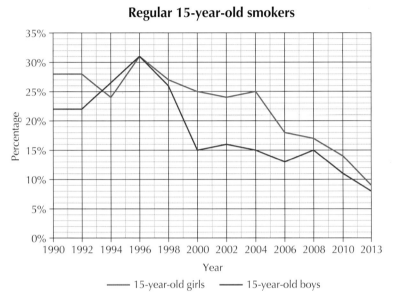

Regular 15-year-old smokers

—— 15-year-old girls   —— 15-year-old boys

a   Calculate the mean percentage per year of 15-year-old girls who were regular smokers.

b   Calculate the mean percentage per year of 15-year-old boys who were regular smokers.

c   Make a comparison between the percentage of 15-year-old girls and boys who were regular smokers.

The line graphs show the percentages of 13-year-old boys and girls who were regular smokers from 1990 to 2013.

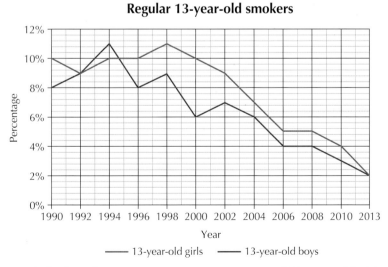

Regular 13-year-old smokers

—— 13-year-old girls   —— 13-year-old boys

e   Calculate the mean percentages per year of 13-year-old girls and boys who were regular smokers.

f   Make a comparison between the percentage of 15-year-old boys and 13-year-old boys who were regular smokers.

N4

2 Senior pupils are selling ice cream cones at school break time to raise money for their expedition trip.

The table shows the record of sales in one week.

	Monday	Tuesday	Wednesday	Thursday	Friday
Strawberry	125	118	123	95	107
Chocolate	79	83	75	102	101
Vanilla	141	133	109	121	99
Sundae	53	58	42	63	67

a For each flavour of ice cream, calculate the mean number sold per day.

b For each day of the week, calculate the mean number of ice creams sold.

c Make a comparison between the mean number of strawberry cones and vanilla cones sold.

d Make a comparison between the mean number of ice cream cones sold on Wednesday and Friday.

e Comment on the range of ice cream cones sold each day.

3 Mrs Davidson's maths class were given a maths assessment.

This stem and leaf diagram summarises their results.

```
2 | 0  1  2  3  6  9
3 | 2  2  7  8  9
4 | 2  4  6  6  7
5 | 3  5  8
6 | 2
7 |
```

Key: 5 | 3   means 53%

a Calculate the mean and range of the assessment marks for Mrs Davidson's class.

Following the assessment, Mrs Davidson thought the pupils would be able to improve their results following some further class review.

She then gave the pupils a second assessment to see if their marks could be improved.

The table shows these results, in percentages.

56	37	41	72	46	60	59	38	47	41
52	44	71	58	62	63	38	55	66	54

b Calculate the mean and range of the marks for Mrs Davidson's class, following the class review and the second assessment.

c Make two comments comparing the assessment marks before and after class review.

N4

4   The bar graph shows the number of ice creams a shop sold in one week.

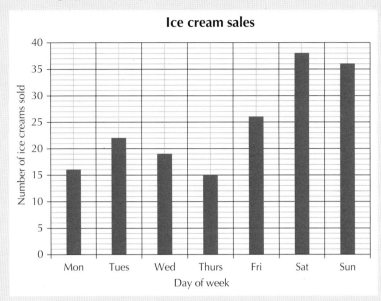

a   Calculate the mean number of ice creams sold each day. Round your answer to 1 decimal place.

b   What is the range of ice creams sold during the week?

The bar graph shows the number of ice creams the shop sold in a different week.

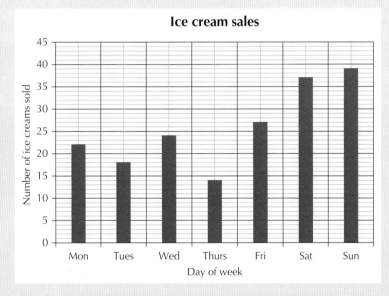

c   Calculate the mean and range for the number of ice creams sold each day. Round your answer to 1 decimal place where appropriate.

d   Make a comment comparing the mean number of ice creams sold in each week.

---

* I can compare totals and averages of data sets.
    ★ Exercise 8A Q4, Q5

N4

* I can calculate the mean and range of data sets.
    ★ Exercise 8B Q4–Q6

* I can compare data sets using mean and range.
    ★ Exercise 8B Q5, Q6

9 Scattergraphs

This chapter will show you how to:

N4

- construct a scattergraph
- draw a best-fitting straight line on a scattergraph.

You should already know:

N4

- how to construct data displays correctly using coordinate grids, labels and titles where necessary
- how to plot points on a coordinate grid
- how to read information from a line graph
- how to interpret data from a table.

N4

Constructing a scattergraph

A **scattergraph** is a visual mathematical diagram which uses coordinates to represent two sets of data. It is usually used to investigate the relationship between the two sets of data.

Scattergraphs are usually created using data given in a table. You need to be able to read and understand tables in order to draw scattergraphs. To create a scattergraph:

- draw a coordinate grid and label the axes
- for each axis, choose a range of values that includes the **minimum** and **maximum** of each set of data
- use the information from the table and plot the points.

Plot the data on the top row of the table on the horizontal axis.

Plot the data on the bottom row of the table on the vertical axis.

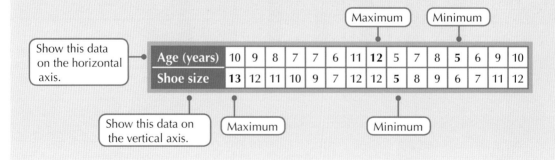

| Age (years) | 10 | 9 | 8 | 7 | 7 | 6 | 11 | 12 | 5 | 7 | 8 | 5 | 6 | 9 | 10 |
| Shoe size | 13 | 12 | 11 | 10 | 9 | 7 | 12 | 12 | 5 | 8 | 9 | 6 | 7 | 11 | 12 |

N4

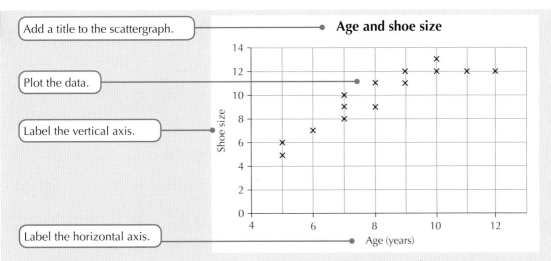

Add a title to the scattergraph.

Plot the data.

Label the vertical axis.

Label the horizontal axis.

Correlation

There are three possible types of relationship or **correlation** between the data on the diagram.

Positive correlation   This scattergraph shows the relationship between shoe size and the age of a child – the older the child, the larger their shoe size. This is **positive correlation**. As one quantity increases, the other quantity also increases.

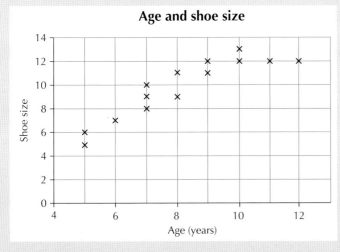

Negative correlation   This scattergraph shows the relationship between the age of a car and its value – the older the car, the lower its value. This is **negative correlation**. As one quantity increases, the other quantity decreases.

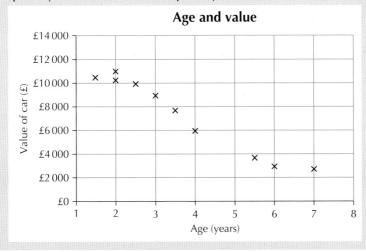

N4 **No correlation** This scattergraph shows there is no relationship between the weight of a parcel and the time taken for it to be delivered. There is **no correlation**. There is no relationship between the two sets of data.

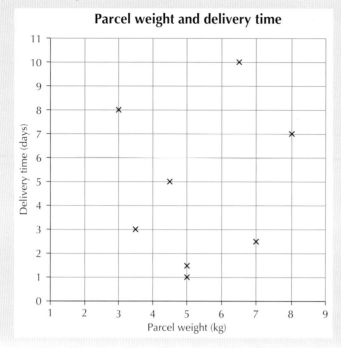

Drawing a best-fitting straight line on a scattergraph

If there is a positive or negative correlation between the two sets of data displayed in a scattergraph, it is possible to draw a straight line through the middle of the scatter points. This straight line is the **line of best fit** or **best-fitting line**.

A line of best fit is used to show a trend. It is not an exact representation of the data. It might pass through some of the data points, or it might pass through none of the data points.

To draw a line of best fit:

- use a transparent ruler (on its edge) to help decide where the line should be drawn

- place the ruler in the same direction and through the middle of the data points

- there should be about an equal number of points above and below the ruler. Some points may be on the line

- try to ensure the points are as close to the ruler as possible

- move the ruler until you are satisfied that you have the best-fitting line before drawing it on your scattergraph.

A best-fitting line is used to estimate or predict values that are not shown directly on the scattergraph.

Interpolation is used where values are **inside** the set of data points.

Extrapolation is used where values are **outside** the set of data points. Care needs to be taken, as this can give misleading results.

The following scattergraph shows the best-fitting straight line for the relationship between age and shoe size. The line goes through the middle of the points. It has a roughly equal number of points above and below it. A best-fitting line does not have to start and finish at the first and last points on a scattergraph.

N4

Example 9.1

The table shows the height and weight of a group of teenagers.

Teenagers	A	B	C	D	E	F	G	H	I	J	K	L
Height (m)	1.60	1.75	1.63	1.68	1.53	1.63	1.62	1.73	1.56	1.77	1.66	1.55
Weight (kg)	47	56	45	50	38	54	51	50	47	57	59	39

a Draw a scattergraph to show the data in the table.

b Draw the best-fitting line on your scattergraph.

c Using the best-fitting line, estimate the weight of a teenager with a height of 1.7 m.

a

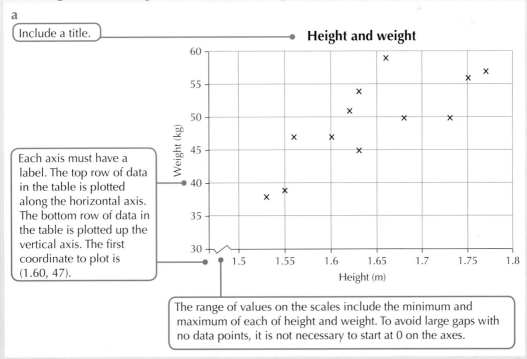

Include a title.

Each axis must have a label. The top row of data in the table is plotted along the horizontal axis. The bottom row of data in the table is plotted up the vertical axis. The first coordinate to plot is (1.60, 47).

The range of values on the scales include the minimum and maximum of each of height and weight. To avoid large gaps with no data points, it is not necessary to start at 0 on the axes.

N4

b

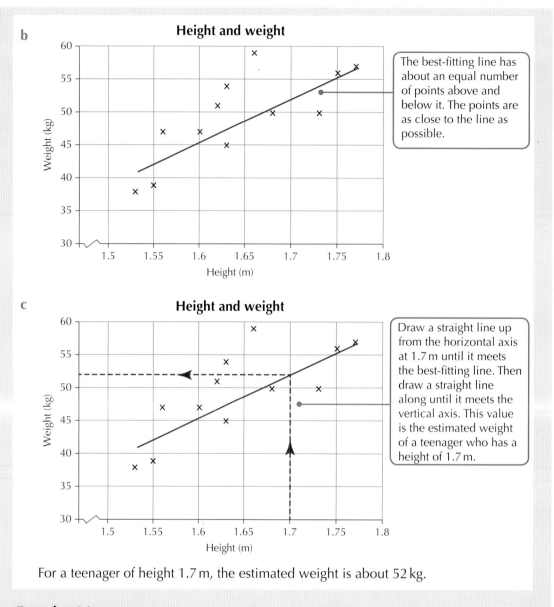

Height and weight

The best-fitting line has about an equal number of points above and below it. The points are as close to the line as possible.

c

Height and weight

Draw a straight line up from the horizontal axis at 1.7 m until it meets the best-fitting line. Then draw a straight line along until it meets the vertical axis. This value is the estimated weight of a teenager who has a height of 1.7 m.

For a teenager of height 1.7 m, the estimated weight is about 52 kg.

Exercise 9A

1   The table shows the age and value of a car.

Age of car (years)	5.5	2	6	3.5	2.5	4	7	1	3	1.5	2
Value of car (£)	3750	10250	3000	7500	10000	6000	2750	12000	9000	10500	11000

   a   Draw a scattergraph to show the data in the table.

   b   Draw the best-fitting line on your scattergraph.

   c   Using the best-fitting line, estimate the value of the car when it is 6 years old.

N4

2   The table shows the grades achieved in an exam compared to the time spent revising, for a group of pupils. Grade 1 is the highest grade that can be scored.

Hours spent revising	8	7	10	4	8	5	1	9	2	6	8	7	4	7	11	3	6
Grade	1	2	1	4	3	5	6	2	6	5	1	4	5	2	1	6	4

a   Draw a scattergraph to show the data in the table.

b   Draw the best-fitting line on your scattergraph.

c   Using the best-fitting line, estimate the grade for a pupil who revised for 8 hours.

3   The table shows the UK population growth since 1992.

Year	Population (millions)
1992	57.58
1994	57.87
1996	58.17
1998	58.49
2000	58.89
2002	59.37
2004	59.99
2006	60.85
2008	61.82
2010	62.76
2012	63.71
2014	64.60
2016	65.57

In this case, **Year** is plotted along the horizontal axis. **Population** is plotted up the vertical axis.

a   Draw a scattergraph to show the data in the table.

b   Draw the best-fitting line on your scattergraph.

c   Using the best-fitting line, estimate the population in 1995.

d   Using the best-fitting line, estimate the year in which the population was about 60 million.

★ 4   The table shows the amount of money spent by businesses on advertising and the value of their sales.

Advertising spend (£'000)	25	30	31	40	38	42	50	50	54
Sales value (£'000)	120	195	200	100	280	140	190	280	180

Advertising spend (£'000)	58	60	61	62	66	68	75	78	100
Sales value (£'000)	175	200	220	280	300	315	610	660	860

a   Draw a scattergraph to show the data in the table.

b   Draw the best-fitting line on your scattergraph.

c   Using the best-fitting line, estimate the value of the sales for a business which spent £80 000 on advertising.

d   Using the best-fitting line, estimate the amount a business would spend on advertising if the value of their sales was £400 000.

N4

5   A catering van sells cups of hot soup. The owner keeps record of the numbers of cups of soup and the daily temperature.

The table shows part of this record.

Temperature (°C)	Hot soup sales
3	110
4	100
7	82
8	80
5	96
11	57
10	72
12	60
13	53
16	39
15	42
18	40
20	21
19	30

a   Draw a scattergraph and line of best fit to show this data.

b   What can you conclude about the temperature and the amount of hot soup sold by the catering van?

c   Using your line of best fit, estimate the number of cups of hot soup sold when the temperature is 9 °C.

★ 6   The Sustainable Energy Authority of Ireland have published information on car engine size and fuel use.

The table shows this information.

Engine size (cc)	Average fuel use (litres per 100 km)
1100	5.01
1200	5.45
1300	5.39
1500	6.03
1700	7.08
1900	7.03
2100	7.87
2300	7.87
2500	8.70

a   Draw a scattergraph and line of best fit to show this data.

b   What can you conclude about the engine size of a car and its average fuel use?

c   Using your line of best fit, estimate the average fuel use for a car engine size of 1000 cc.

N4

7   Sea levels rise as water is added from melting land ice and from the expansion of sea water as it warms. Satellite observations can give very accurate measurements of the rise.

The table shows the rise in sea levels since 1993.

Year	Change in sea levels (mm)
1993	0
1997	10.6
2001	27.6
2005	42.9
2009	51.2
2013	70.8
2017	88.2

(*Source: NASA Global Climate Change, Vital signs of the planet*)

a   Draw a scattergraph and line of best fit to show this data.

b   What is the trend in the change of sea levels since 1993?

c   Using your line of best fit, estimate how much the sea level rose between 1993 and 2008.

d   Using your line of best fit, predict how much the sea level will rise between 1993 and 2020.

GO! Activity

By researching online, investigate pairs of data to find which ones have:

• positive correlation, such as the cost of mobile phone contracts and the amount of data use above the monthly limit.

• negative correlation, such as the cost of heating a house as the temperature outside increases.

Write your own questions on creating scattergraphs and their line of best fit for pairs of data with a relationship. Test these out on pupils in your class.

Explore using technology, such as a spreadsheet software package, to draw scattergraphs and best-fitting lines.

N4 **Chapter review**

1 The table shows the amount of petrol a car uses for different journey lengths.

Distance (km)	20	93	195	42	104	155	75	140	180	168
Petrol used (litres)	3.5	8.9	18.5	4.1	9.5	13.8	7	12.5	16	15.2

a Draw a scattergraph to show the data in the table.

b Draw the best-fitting line on your scattergraph.

c Using the best-fitting line, estimate the amount of petrol the car would use on a journey of 160 km.

d Using the best-fitting line, predict the amount of petrol the car would use on a journey of 210 km.

2 A clothes shop sells scarves in its accessories section. The staff make a note of the outside temperature and record the number of scarves sold.

The table shows this information.

Temperature (°C)	20	17	11	16	5	19	15	9	17	13
Sales of scarves	10	25	66	40	82	17	53	74	30	57

a Draw a scattergraph to show the data in the table.

b Draw the best-fitting line on your scattergraph.

c Describe the relationship between the number of scarves sold and the outside temperature.

c Using the best-fitting line, estimate the outside temperature if the shop sells 50 scarves.

d Using the best-fitting line, estimate the number of scarves sold if the outside temperature is 18 °C.

3 The table shows the average cost of a city break to Barcelona for the last 10 years.

Year	2007	2008	2009	2010	2011	2012	2013	2014	2015	2016
Cost (£)	320	335	355	370	395	420		460	470	490

a Draw a scattergraph to illustrate the data in the table.

b Draw the best-fitting line on your scattergraph.

c Using the best-fitting line, estimate the cost of the Barcelona city break in 2013.

d Using the line of best fit, predict the cost of a city break to Barcelona in 2018.

• I can construct a scattergraph and draw its best-fitting line. ★ Exercise 9A Q4, Q6

N4 # Case studies

Marcia's case study

This case study focuses on the following skills:

- organising and representing data **(Ch. 7)**
- reading and interpreting data **(Ch. 7)**
- comparing data **(Ch. 8).**

Marcia is a patient in Ward 44. Her fluid intake is measured over a 16-hour period.
The table shows the amount of Marcia's fluid intake.

Time	6 am	8 am	10 am	12 noon	2 pm	4 pm	6 pm	8 pm	10 pm
Fluid intake (ml)	400	400	250	250	400	270	400	300	300

1   Represent the data on an appropriate graph.

Marcia's fluid output is also measured over the same 16-hour period.
The line graph shows this information.

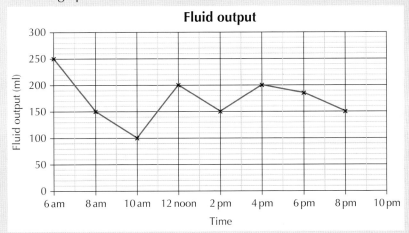

The fluid output for 10 pm has not been recorded. Marcia's total fluid output for this
16-hour period was 1485 ml.

2   **a**   What amount should be recorded at 10 pm?

    b   What was Marcia's mean amount of fluid output for the 16-hour period?

If Marcia's mean fluid intake is double the mean fluid output, the nurses do not need
to continue to measure her fluid intake and output.

3   Will Marcia need to have her fluid intake and output measured again?

| N4 | **Holiday time** |

This case study focuses on the following skills:

- reading and interpreting data (**Ch. 7**)
- converting between currencies (**Ch. 4**)
- using a budget to plan an event (**Ch. 1**).

The Campbell family are planning a holiday to the USA for one week.

The family consists of 2 adults and 3 children, aged 12, 9 and 7 years.

The holiday costs £4155 and they need £1800 spending money.

They can save £525 per month.

1 How many months will it take the Campbell family to save all the money they need for their holiday?

While they are in New York, they visit the Empire State Building.

The table shows the cost of entry to the Main Deck and the Top Deck.

	Main Deck (86th floor) only	Main Deck and Top Deck (102nd floor)
Adult	£27.20	£43.20
Child (6–12 years)	£21.60	£37.60

The exchange rate is £1 = $1.25.

The family decide to visit both the Main Deck and the Top Deck.

2 In US dollars, how much of their spending money will they use visiting the Empire State Building?

Whilst on holiday the Campbell family expect to spend $300 per day on food, drink and activities.

3 Have they brought enough spending money? Give a reason for your answer.

N4 | **Shopping for furniture**

This case study focuses on the following skills:

- calculating income and deductions **(Ch. 2)**
- comparing products to find the best value **(Ch. 3)**
- investigating the impact of interest rates on loans **(Ch. 5)**.

Emma is a newly qualified nurse. This is her partially completed payslip for last month.

Name: E. Miller			Month: 8
Basic pay £1807.67	Overtime ----------	Bonus ----------	Gross pay: £1807.67
Income tax £193.86	National Insurance £152.88	Pension £116.49	Deductions:
			Net pay:

1   Use the information in the payslip to calculate Emma's net pay.

Emma's monthly expenditure is £1180.

2   How much money does Emma have left over each month?

Emma wants to buy a new dining table and chairs set, which costs £1095.

She does not have any savings so she wants to take out a loan. She will repay the loan from the money she has left over each month.

The table shows the payment options offered by the shop selling the set.

Option 1	Option 2	Option 3
No deposit	Deposit = 10% of cost	Deposit = 15% of cost
Interest rate = 1.74%	15 payments @ £67.20	10 payments @ £94.45
12 equal monthly payments		

3   Which option gives Emma the best value for money?

School excursion

> **This case study focuses on the following skills:**
>
> • using a budget to plan an event **(Ch. 1)**
>
> • comparing products to find the best value **(Ch. 3)**
>
> • reading and interpreting data **(Ch. 7)**
>
> • selecting and carrying out calculations involving whole numbers **(Ch. 22)**
>
> • selecting and carrying out calculations involving decimal fractions **(Ch. 23)**.

Mr Watson is planning a day out for his S3 class of 30 pupils. He is considering three different choices.

The table shows information about these choices.

Place	Distance from school	Entrance fee per person
Science exhibition centre	26 miles	£4 per pupil Free for all accompanying teachers
Historic building and museums	34 miles	Educational visit Free for pupils and all accompanying teachers
Country park and exhibition	28 miles	£3 per pupil Free for all accompanying teachers

Mr Watson will hire a bus to take the class. The pupils will have to contribute to the travel costs.

The hire charge for the bus company is £8.25 per mile.

1 What is the total cost to visit:

   a the science exhibition centre

   b the historic buildings and museums

   c the country park and exhibition?

> Remember to double the distance from school for the total distance.

Here is some additional information about the cost of the trip:

• the school will pay £200 of the overall cost

• teachers go free of charge

• each pupil will pay the same amount.

2 How much will each pupil have to pay to go to:

   a the science exhibition centre

   b the historic buildings and museums

   c the country park and exhibition?

   Give your answers to the nearest penny.

Mr Watson wants to get the best deal for his pupils.

3 Where should Mr Watson take his class?

   Give a reason for your answer.

10 Calculate time intervals and solve basic problems in time management

This chapter will show you how to:

- calculate time intervals to manage tasks or activities
- convert between 12-hour time and 24-hour time
- calculate time intervals using 12-hour time and 24-hour time

N4
- calculate time intervals using 12-hour time and 24-hour time including intervals spanning midnight

- read a timetable to plan a journey

N4
- read a timetable to plan a journey spanning midnight
- solve a basic problem in time management

You should already know:

- how to tell the time from a clock face and from a digital clock
- the conversions between seconds, minutes, hours, days, weeks, months and years
- the relationship between digital and analogue time
- the relationship between 12-hour and 24-hour clock times
- how to read, use and create a timetable

N4
- how to use the duration of events to plan real-life events.

Using time

Knowing how to work with times is an essential part of life. You need to know what time it is, and how long it takes to carry out tasks, and how to manage time. In the morning you need to know when to get out of bed in time to have breakfast and get to school on time. You might need to fit this with bus timetables to make sure you have enough time to make sure you are not late. Outside school you might need to know how much time to allow to get to a film or a job, and you need to know when each event finishes.

Calculating the length of time between two events is an important skill in order to manage tasks and activities, both in a work situation and at home.

12-hour time and 24-hour time

In everyday life, we usually use **12-hour time**. We say *It is 11:15 am* or *It is 3:35 pm* or *The maths class is at a quarter past 2*.

In the first example – *It is 11:15 am* – we know the time is in the morning because it uses **am** to show this.

In the second example – *It is 3:35 pm* – we know the time is in the afternoon because it uses **pm** to show this.

The third example – *The maths class is at a quarter past 2* – doesn't use am or pm. So, how do we know it means quarter past 2 at lunchtime, or quarter past 2 in the middle of the night? Without am or pm it is impossible to know.

In conversation, it would probably be obvious which one was meant. You probably wouldn't be going to a maths lesson in the middle of the night!

When it is important to avoid confusion, for example in travel timetables, **24-hour time** is used.

In 12-hour time, times from midnight to midday are shown as **am** times. Times from midday to midnight are shown as **pm** times.

The times midnight and midday are special cases. They are neither am nor pm; am starts immediately after midnight and pm starts straight after midday.

In 24-hour time midnight is 0000 and time then counts on continuously until the following midnight.

Converting between 12-hour and 24-hour time

The 12-hour system uses numbers 1 to 12 for hours with a colon or a full stop between the hours and minutes. From midnight to midday, time is shown with **am** after the minutes, and from midday to midnight, time is shown with **pm** after the minutes.

For example, 5:15 am means 5:15 in the morning. 6:30 pm means 6:30 in the evening.

The 24-hour system uses the numbers 00 to 23 for hours, and is shown with 4 digits. For example, 0340 means 3:40 in the morning. 1330 means 1:30 in the afternoon. You sometimes see 24-hour times with a colon or a full stop between the hours and minutes, but this isn't necessary. For example, 0340 could be written as 03:40 or 03.40.

Example 10.1

a Convert these 12-hour times to 24-hour times:

   i 8:30 am   **ii** 9:15 pm   **iii** 11:00 am

b Convert these 24-hour times to 12-hour times:

   i 0017   **ii** 2246   **iii** 0532

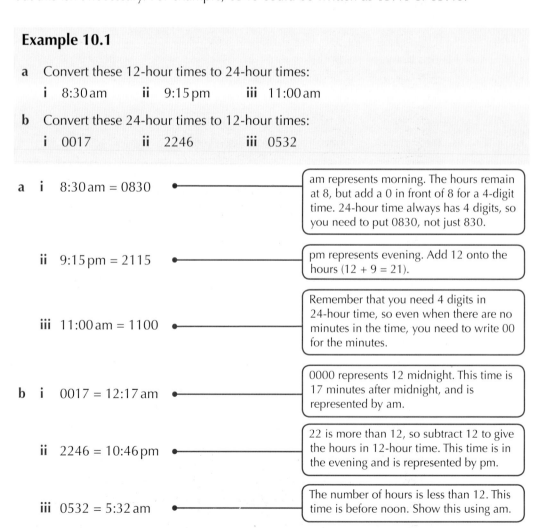

a **i** 8:30 am = 0830

> am represents morning. The hours remain at 8, but add a 0 in front of 8 for a 4-digit time. 24-hour time always has 4 digits, so you need to put 0830, not just 830.

ii 9:15 pm = 2115

> pm represents evening. Add 12 onto the hours (12 + 9 = 21).

iii 11:00 am = 1100

> Remember that you need 4 digits in 24-hour time, so even when there are no minutes in the time, you need to write 00 for the minutes.

b **i** 0017 = 12:17 am

> 0000 represents 12 midnight. This time is 17 minutes after midnight, and is represented by am.

ii 2246 = 10:46 pm

> 22 is more than 12, so subtract 12 to give the hours in 12-hour time. This time is in the evening and is represented by pm.

iii 0532 = 5:32 am

> The number of hours is less than 12. This time is before noon. Show this using am.

Exercise 10A

★ 1 Change each of these 12-hour times into 24-hour times.

    a 10:15 am   **b** 2:45 am   **c** 2:15 pm   **d** 11:50 pm

    e noon   **f** 10 am   **g** 11 pm   **h** 3:25 pm

    i midnight   **j** 12:15 am   **k** 12:15 pm   **l** 6:59 am

★ 2 Change each of the following 24-hour times into 12-hour times.

    a 1130   **b** 0620   **c** 0745   **d** 1345

    e 1535   **f** 1200   **g** 2135   **h** 2359

    i 1940   **j** 0315   **k** 2020   **l** 0000

Time intervals

A time interval is a length of time between a start time and a finish time. It could be the time taken for a school class or a game of football, or it might measure the time you need to wait for a bus.

With 60 seconds in a minute, 60 minutes in an hour and 24 hours in a day, the usual rules of column addition or subtraction to calculate a time interval do not work. To find time intervals you can use a timeline to count on or back.

Example 10.2

Calculate the time interval between:

a 3:45 pm and 7:10 pm

N4   **b** 2110 and 0520

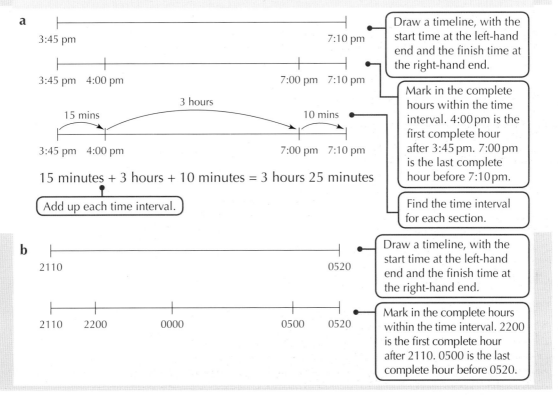

a Draw a timeline, with the start time at the left-hand end and the finish time at the right-hand end.

Mark in the complete hours within the time interval. 4:00 pm is the first complete hour after 3:45 pm. 7:00 pm is the last complete hour before 7:10 pm.

Find the time interval for each section.

15 minutes + 3 hours + 10 minutes = 3 hours 25 minutes

Add up each time interval.

N4 **b** Draw a timeline, with the start time at the left-hand end and the finish time at the right-hand end.

Mark in the complete hours within the time interval. 2200 is the first complete hour after 2110. 0500 is the last complete hour before 0520.

(continued)

N4

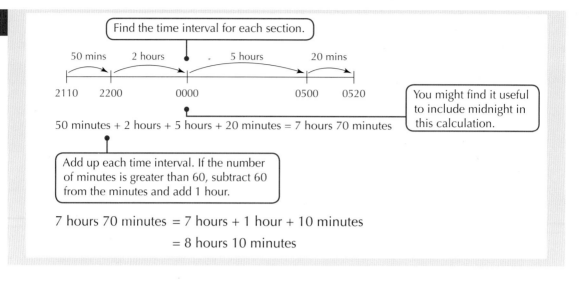

Find the time interval for each section.

50 minutes + 2 hours + 5 hours + 20 minutes = 7 hours 70 minutes

You might find it useful to include midnight in this calculation.

Add up each time interval. If the number of minutes is greater than 60, subtract 60 from the minutes and add 1 hour.

7 hours 70 minutes = 7 hours + 1 hour + 10 minutes

= 8 hours 10 minutes

Example 10.3

A film started at 7:30 pm.

It lasted for 2 hours 10 minutes.

At what time did the film finish?

7 hours + 2 hours = 9 hours

Split the times into hours and minutes. Add the hours, and then add the minutes.

30 minutes + 10 minutes = 40 minutes

The film finished at 9:40 pm.

Combine the numbers of hours and the minutes to find the final time.

Example 10.4

A train left Inverness at 1630 and arrived in Aberdeen at 1940.

How long did the journey last?

1630 = 16 hours and 30 minutes

1940 = 19 hours and 40 minutes

Split the times into hours and minutes.

16 hours + **3 hours** = 19 hours

Count on (add) to find the number of whole hours first.

30 minutes + **10 minutes** = 40 minutes

Count on (add) to find the number of minutes.

The journey took 3 hours and 10 minutes.

Combine the numbers of hours and the minutes to find the total length of the journey.

Example 10.5

James lives in Biggar. He visited his friend Ali who lives in Perth.

He arrived at Ali's house at 3:40 pm.

His journey took him 2 hours and 15 minutes.

At what time did James leave Biggar?

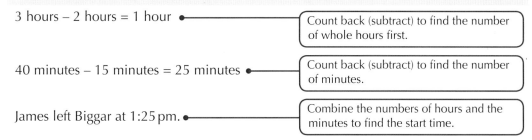

3 hours – 2 hours = 1 hour ●————— Count back (subtract) to find the number of whole hours first.

40 minutes – 15 minutes = 25 minutes ●————— Count back (subtract) to find the number of minutes.

James left Biggar at 1:25 pm. ●————— Combine the numbers of hours and the minutes to find the start time.

Exercise 10B

1   The table shows the start times for a set of events, and the time that each event lasts.
Calculate the finishing time for each event.

	Start time	Event lasts for	Finish time
a	4:30 pm	2 hours 20 minutes	
b	10:25 am	1 hour 15 minutes	
c	1815	3 hours 25 minutes	
d	1545	6 hours 30 minutes	
e	0940	8 hours 50 minutes	
f	11:10 am	7 hours 45 minutes	
g	2250	45 minutes	

2   The table shows how long a set of journeys take and the arrival time for each journey.
Work out the start time for each journey.

	Start time	Journey takes	Arrival time
a		2 hours 15 minutes	10:30 pm
b		3 hours 20 minutes	11:45 am
c		1 hour 35 minutes	1640
d		5 hours 15 minutes	1925
e		2 hours 20 minutes	1:10 pm
f		4 hours 35 minutes	1425
g		55 minutes	2305

3 Calculate the time interval between each pair of times.

a 2:00 am and 3:30 pm   b 4:45 pm and 6:00 pm

c 5:00 pm and 8:30 pm   d 10:40 am and 2:20 pm

e 3:15 am and 5:45 am   f 1335 and 1824

g 0913 and 1236   h 0305 and 1343

★ **4** Jeff and Freda went hillwalking. They set off at 9:45 am and they completed their hike at 3:23 pm.

How long were they hiking for?

5 Hilary left her house in Glasgow at 0815 and arrived at her friend's house in Inverness at 1133.

How long did her journey take?

6 Bernie started to watch a film at 2024 and finished watching it at 2253.

How long was the film?

7 Shaniya starts work at 7:55 am and works for 7 hours 24 minutes.

What time will she finish work?

★ **8** Stuart lives in Aberfeldy. He is going to visit his friend Mo who lives in Glasgow.

Stuart leaves his house at 10:45 am.

Stuart's satnav says that the journey should take 1 hour 55 minutes.

Stuart tells Mo that he should arrive before 1 pm.

Is he correct? Give a reason for your answer.

★ **9** Mel is meeting her friend Steph for a night out.

Mel takes 1 hour 15 minutes to get ready and 50 minutes to travel from her house to where she is meeting Steph.

She is meeting Steph at 2030.

What is the latest time that Mel can start to get ready if she is going to be on time?

N4 ★ **10** Calculate the time interval between each pair of times.

a 10:50 pm and 12:30 am   b 9:45 pm and 2.20 am

c 6:30 pm and 4:10 am   d 8:25 pm and 4:45 pm

e 2214 and 0347   f 1705 and 0224

g 0931 and 0754   h 1021 and 0837

11 Fiona and her friends participated in a 26-mile Moonwalk to raise money for charity. They started walking at 11:30 pm and completed the Moonwalk at 6:47 am.

How long did they take to complete the walk?

★ **12** Gillian and her family took the ferry from Aberdeen to Lerwick. The ferry left Aberdeen at 1912 and arrived in Lerwick at 0736.

How long did the journey take?

N4 ⚙ **13** Philip fell asleep at 10:42 pm and woke up at 6:22 am.

Gordon fell asleep at 2324 and woke up at 0802.

Who was asleep for longer? Give a reason for your answer.

Timetables

A timetable is a chart showing departure and arrival times of public transport, such as buses, trains and aeroplanes. Timetables can also be used to show the start and end times of TV programmes or events at a festival. You might have a timetable at school to show when your classes are, and when the lunch break is.

Timetables can show a lot of information, and can help you to plan your day and be on time.

This timetable shows train times from Inverness to Aberdeen. Travel timetables are often written using the 24-hour clock.

Mondays to Saturdays

		A	B	C	SXD	SO	SX	B	E	A	F	A	G	H	J	A	J	SXA	SOA	SXK	SOL	SXP	SOG	SXD	SOD
Inverness	d	0453	·	0554	·	·	·	·	0709	·	0900	·	1057	·	1246	·	1427	·	·	·	·	1529	1529	·	·
Nairn	d	0508	·	0609	·	·	·	·	0725	·	0916	·	1114	·	1301	·	1442	·	·	·	·	1546	1546	·	·
Forres	d	0519	·	0620	·	·	·	·	0737	·	0927	·	1125	·	1312	·	1453	·	·	·	·	1557	1557	·	·
Elgin	d	0533	·	0634	·	·	·	·	0752	·	0952b	·	1141	·	1330	·	1509	·	·	·	·	1611	1611	·	·
Keith	d	0554	·	0655	·	·	·	·	0813	·	1011	·	1202	·	1349	·	1530	·	·	·	·	1635	1635	·	·
Huntly	d	0609	·	0711	0746	·	·	·	0839	·	1026	·	1216	·	1403	·	1545	·	·	·	·	1650	1650	·	·
Insch	d	0624	·	0729	0802	·	·	·	0857	·	1048c	·	1235	·	1419	·	1603	·	·	·	·	1706	1706	·	·
Inverurie	d	0637	0713	0743	0816	0817	0846	·	0909	1038	1100	1134	1247	1333	1431	1524	1616	·	1638	1647	·	1719	1719	1750	1752
Dyce	d	0651	0726	0759	0830	0830	0859	0907	0921	1050	1113	1146	1302	1348	1443	1538	1630	1639	1653	1705e	1705	1735	1735	1804	1806
Aberdeen	a	0702	0736	0811	0841	0840	0909	0917	0933	1100	1125	1156	1313	1358	1455	1548	1641	1650	1703	1717	1717	1746	1746	1814	1816

		A	G	Q	D	D		D
Inverness	d	·	1714	·	1813	2004	·	2133
Nairn	d	·	1730	·	1828	2020	·	2148
Forres	d	·	1741	·	1839	2031	·	2158
Elgin	d	·	1759e	·	1857	2047a	·	2213
Keith	d	·	1820	·	1919	·	·	2234
Huntly	d	·	1847	·	1942	·	·	2251
Insch	d	·	1902	·	1958	·	·	2306
Inverurie	d	1845	1915	1946	2010	·	2124	2319
Dyce	d	1858	1929	1957	2024	·	2137	2332
Aberdeen	a	1909	1940	2008	2035	·	2148	2343

(Source: Scotrail)

Television guides are similar to timetables. They show a lot of information to help you to plan your evening's viewing.

CHANNEL	◀ 7.00PM	7.30PM	8.00PM	8.30PM	9.00PM ▶
Variety	Best Bakers 7.00PM	Rover 7.30PM	Hijacked 8.00PM		Nightwatch 9.00PM
RED	Framed 7.00PM	Once Upon A Scream 7.30PM		The Other Side 8.30PM	
5pecial	The Savvy Shopper 7.00PM		Runway 8.00PM	Hot Property 8.30PM	
REELtime	Couch Potato 7.00PM	Lost In London 7.30PM			The Casting 9.00PM

Example 10.6

Sam is going from the city centre to visit her Gran's house in the village. The buses run at regular intervals during the day.

Part of the bus timetable is shown below.

Depart City centre	1800	1815	1830					
Arrive Village	1850	1905	1920					

a Copy and complete the timetable to show the departure and arrival times of the next five buses.

b How long does the journey take?

Sam takes the bus which leaves the city centre at 0945.

c What time will she arrive in the village?

a

Depart City centre	1800	1815	1830	**1845**	**1900**	**1915**	**1930**	**1945**
Arrive Village	1850	1905	1920	**1935**	**1950**	**2005**	**2020**	**2035**

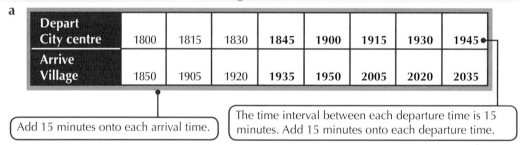

Add 15 minutes onto each arrival time.

The time interval between each departure time is 15 minutes. Add 15 minutes onto each departure time.

b 18 hours – 18 hours = 0 hours ●———— Separate the hours and minutes.

50 minutes – 0 minutes = 50 minutes

Journey time = 50 minutes.

c 9 hours + 0 hours = 9 hours ●———— Separate the hours and minutes.

45 minutes + 50 minutes = 95 minutes ●———— Add the minutes.

95 minutes – 60 minutes = 1 hour 35 minutes ●———— The minutes total is more than 60, so subtract 60 from the total number of minutes to find the number of hours and minutes.

9 hours + 1 hour 35 minutes = 10 hours 35 minutes ●———— Add the total hours and minutes.

= 1035 (or 10:35 pm) ●———— Rewrite the total hours and minutes in 24-hour time.

Example 10.7

The table shows part of the bus timetable for buses from Inverness to Berriedale in the Highlands.

Service X99	Monday to Friday		
Inverness	1240	1430	1745
Alness	1312	1502	1817
Tain (arr)	1330	1520	1835
Tain (dep)	1335	1525	1840
Dornoch	1352	1542	1857
Brora	------	1606	1924
Helmsdale	1435	1625	1940
Berriedale	1450	1635	2000

Use the timetable to answer these questions.

a   What time did the first bus leave Inverness?

b   What time did the second bus reach Tain?

c   Which bus takes the shortest time to go from Inverness to Berriedale?

d   Why is no time given for the first bus at Brora?

Ramesh lives in Tain. He is going to visit his mother who lives in Helmsdale. He needs to be in Helmsdale by 7 pm.

e   What time does the latest bus that he can catch leave Tain?

a   1240

b   1520

c   Bus 1 departs Inverness at 1240, arrives Berriedale 1450.

Journey time = 2 hours 10 minutes.

Bus 2 departs Inverness at 1430, arrives Berriedale 1635.

Journey time = 2 hours 5 minutes.

Bus 3 departs Inverness at 1745, arrives Berriedale 2000.

Journey time = 2 hours 15 minutes.

So Bus 2 takes the shortest time.

d   The first bus doesn't stop at Brora.

e   Bus 1 arrives in Helmsdale at 1435.

Bus 2 arrives in Helmsdale at 1625.

Bus 3 arrives in Helmsdale at 1940.

Ramesh must take the second bus, which leaves Tain at 1525.

> The first column of times tells you about the journey of the first of the three buses. This one leaves Inverness at 1240.

> Arrival (arr) and departure (dep) times to and from Tain are shown. The second bus (the middle column) arrives in Tain at 1520.

> Calculate the journey times for each journey.

> 7 pm is the same as 1900. Bus 3 arrives after 1900, at 1940, which is too late.

Exercise 10C

1 Hannah is going from the city centre to the ice rink by bus. The buses run at regular intervals during the day.

The table shows part of the bus timetable.

Depart City centre	1400	1410	1420					
Arrive Ice rink	1415	1425	1435					

  a Copy and complete the bus timetable to show the departure and arrival times of the next five buses.

  b When will the 1250 bus arrive at the ice rink?

2 William catches the bus from Cherry Tree Lane to the shopping centre to meet his friends. The buses run at regular intervals during the day.

The table shows part of the bus timetable.

Depart Cherry Tree Lane	0900	0908	0916					
Arrive Shopping centre	0935	0943	0951					

  a Copy and complete the bus timetable to show the departure and arrival times of the next five buses.

  b When will the 1332 bus arrive at the shopping centre?

3 John is going from his house to the rugby stadium by tram. The trams run at regular intervals during the day.

The table shows part of the tram timetable.

Depart City centre	1005	1025	1045					
Arrive Rugby stadium	1030	1050	1110					

  a Copy and complete the tram timetable to show the departure and arrival times of the next five trams.

  b John wants to be at the stadium at 2:30 pm. At what time should he catch the tram?

★ 4 Mo is going to meet his friends at the cinema by train. The trains run at regular intervals during the day.

The table shows part of the train timetable.

Depart Pigeon Street	2010	2022	2034					
Arrive Cinema	2035	2047	2059					

  a Copy and complete the train timetable to show the departure and arrival times of the next five trains.

  b Mo arranged to meet his friends at the cinema at 6:30 pm. What is the latest train he can catch to get there on time?

5   The timetable shows train times from Glasgow Central to Edinburgh.

Glasgow Central	0705	0933	1146	1406	1547
Motherwell	0721	0959	1202	1427	1603
Wishaw	0733	1005	1207	1432	1617
Carluke	0739	1011	1213	1442	1628
Carstairs	0749	1021	1222	1452	1637
Haymarket	0829	1050	1249	1519	1705
Edinburgh	0834	1054	1255	1524	1711

a   How long does the 0933 take to travel from Glasgow Central to Edinburgh?

b   How long does the 1406 take to travel from Glasgow Central to Edinburgh?

Greg walks to Wishaw Station and arrives there at 1128.

c   How long does he have to wait for the next train to Edinburgh?

Heather lives in Carluke. She has a job interview in Edinburgh at 3:30 pm. She knows it will take her 10 minutes to walk from the railway station to the interview.

d   What time should she get the train from Carluke to make sure she gets to the interview on time?

6   The timetable shows bus times from Peebles to Biggar.

Peebles High School					15:55	
Peebles Post Office	07:10	08:00	12:00	14:00	16:00	17:20
Lyne Station	07:17	08:07	12:07	14:07	16:07	17:27
Stobo Village Hall	07:23	08:13	12:13	14:13	16:13	17:33
Thaines House	07:30	08:20	12:20	14:20	16:20	17:40
Broughton Primary School	07:35	08:30	12:25	14:25	16:25	17:45
Skirling Village Green	07:45	08:37	12:35	14:35	16:35	17:55
Biggar High Street	07:50	08:45	12:40	14:40	16:40	18:00

a   How long does each bus take to get from Peebles Post Office to Biggar?

b   How long does it take to get from Stobo Village Hall to Skirling Village Green?

Sam goes to school in Peebles and lives in Skirling. He finishes school at 3:45 pm.

c   What is the earliest time that he can get home to Skirling?

Mani lives in Lyne Station. He needs to get to Biggar before 2:30 pm.

d   What is the latest bus that he can catch at Lyne Station?

7 The schedule shows TV programmes on Monday evening.

Channel 1	Channel 2	Channel 3	Channel 4	Channel 5
5:15 pm What's the Point?	5:10 pm Get rid of the rubbish	5:00 pm Catch!	5:15 pm A Way to Dine	5:00 pm News on 5
				5:30 pm Good Pals
6:00 pm News at 6	6:05 pm Genius at Work	6:00 pm News	5:55 pm The Thomsons	5:50 pm Far and Away
6:30 pm Regional News	6:40 pm The American Dream	6:35 pm Folk on a Farm	6:20 pm Chesterfield	6:25 pm Boxing Championship
7:00 pm One Two Three		7:10 pm Jubilation Street	7:00 pm 4 News	
7:30 pm Deadenders	7:35 pm Wartime	7:45 pm Money Money Money		
8:00 pm Paradise	8:00 pm Brainy People	8:15 pm The Funny Show	8:05 pm Celebrity Jungle Sister	8:10 pm Judge Julie

a How long does each programme last?

   i *Genius at Work*   **ii** *Folk on a Farm*

   iii *Boxing Championship*   **iv** *The Thomsons*

   v *Jubilation Street*

Sheila finishes work at 5:45 pm. It takes her 35 minutes to get home.

b Will she get home in time to see *Folk on a Farm*?

Jenny wants to watch *Far and Away* but her mum is already watching *A Way to Dine*.

c How much of *Far and Away* will she miss if she watches all of *A Way to Dine*?

d What is the shortest programme on the schedule?

N4

8 The timetable shows ferry times from Aberdeen to Lerwick.

	Monday	Tuesday	Wednesday	Thursday	Friday
Aberdeen	1705	1935	1720	1910	1810
Scrabster	1915		1930		2020
Stromness	2120		2135		2225
Lerwick	0740	0745	0755	0725	0845

a How long does the Monday ferry take to travel from Aberdeen to Stromness?

b How long does the Tuesday ferry take to travel from Aberdeen to Lerwick?

c How long does the Wednesday ferry take to travel from Scrabster to Lerwick?

d If you travel from Aberdeen to Lerwick, how much shorter is the Thursday crossing than the Friday crossing? Give a reason for your answer.

N4 ★ **9** The timetable shows train and ferry times from Glasgow to Oban, Coll and Tiree.

🚶 🚗 ♿ 🍴 ☕ 🚻 ⓖⓜ ⓡ

COLL & TIREE

TEXT CODE 16

OBAN - COLL - TIREE

Table 16

🚆 🚢 🚢 🚢 🚢 🚢 🚢 🚢 🚢 🚆

Operates 31 March until 23 June and 27 August until 22 October										
DAY	**Glasgow Queen St Depart**	**Oban Depart**	**Coll Arrive**	**Coll Depart**	**Tiree Arrive**	**Tiree Depart**	**Coll Arrive**	**Coll Depart**	**Oban Arrive**	**Glasgow Queen St Arrive**
MON	1820 B	0715	0955	1010	1105	1135	1230	1245	1525	2122
TUE	1037	1500	1740	1755	1850	1920	-	-	2240	-
WED	1821 B	0715 A	0955 A	1010 A	1105 A	1130 A	-	-	-	-
	-	-	-	-	1715 A	1740 A	1835 A	1850 A	2130 A	-
THU	1821 B	0715	0955	1010	1105	1135	1230	1245	1525	2122
FRI	1821 B	0615	-	-	0935	1005	1100	1115	1410	1748
SAT	1821 B	0715	0955	1010	1105	1135	1230	1245	1525	1919
SUN	1821 B	0715	0955	1010	1105	1135	1230	1245	1525	1917
Operates 24 June until 26 August										
DAY	**Glasgow Queen St Depart**	**Oban Depart**	**Coll Arrive**	**Coll Depart**	**Tiree Arrive**	**Tiree Depart**	**Coll Arrive**	**Coll Depart**	**Oban Arrive**	**Glasgow Queen St Arrive**
MON	1820 B	0715	0955	1010	1105	1135	1230	1245	1525	2122
TUE	1037	1500	1740	1755	1850	1920	-	-	2240	-
WED	1821 B	0715 A	0955 A	1010 A	1105 A	1130 A	-	-	-	-
	-	-	-	-	1715 A	1740 A	1835 A	1850 A	2130 A	-
THU	1821 B	0715	0955	1010	1105	1135	1230	1245	1525	2122
FRI	1821 B	0615	-	-	0935	1005	1100	1115	1410	1748
SAT	1821 B	0615	0855	0910	1005	1045	1140	1155	1435	1919
	1037	1515	-	-	1835	1855	1950	2000	2240	-
SUN	1821 B	0715	0955	1010	1105	1135	1230	1245	1525	1917

Code

B Train connection arrives the previous day. Overnight accommodation will be required.

(Source: Calmac)

a What time does the 0715 ferry from Oban on a Monday first reach Coll?

Andy is on holiday in Tiree in July. He wants to take the ferry from Tiree to Coll on Friday.

b What time will the ferry leave Tiree?

Gillian lives in Glasgow. She is going to her son's wedding in Coll. She needs to arrive in Coll on the Tuesday before the wedding.

c Which train should she catch from Glasgow Queen St Station so that she will arrive on time?

d How long will Gillian's journey take her to get from Glasgow to Coll?

e Flynn leaves Tiree on Thursday to return to Glasgow. What time will he arrive at Glasgow Queen St?

f How long was Flynn's journey?

Manor catches a train at Glasgow Queen St Station on Wednesday to go to Tiree.

g When does she arrive in Tiree?

h Is it possible to sail from Oban to Coll on a Friday?

N4 Solve a basic problem in time management

Planning events and activities is an essential skill in everyday life. You will have to manage simple day-to-day events such as getting to work, cooking a meal and organising social activities. You will probably also have to plan bigger events such as holidays, parties or even a wedding.

You have many factors to consider:

- which tasks you need to complete
- the expected length of time for each task
- the order in which you need to complete each task.

Creating a timeline for your event can help you.

Example 10.8

Barry is baking a cake. He writes a list of the tasks and the time each task will take.

Task	Estimated time to complete task
Go to shop to purchase ingredients	45 minutes
Mix ingredients	20 minutes
Cake in oven	25 minutes
Wait for cake to cool	30 minutes
Ice cake	10 minutes

Barry starts his tasks at 2:15 pm.

When will his cake be ready?

Method 1

Add the separate times together.

45 minutes + 20 minutes + 25 minutes + 30 minutes + 10 minutes = 130 minutes

130 minutes = 60 minutes + 60 minutes + 10 minutes

If the total is more than 60 minutes you need to break it down into groups of 60 to calculate the number of hours.

= 2 hours 10 minutes

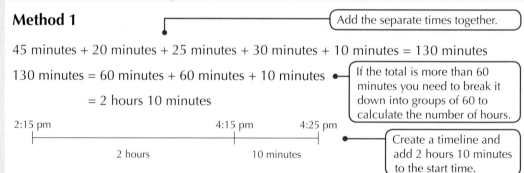

Create a timeline and add 2 hours 10 minutes to the start time.

His cake will be ready at 4:25 pm.

Method 2

Task	Estimated time to complete task	Start time	Finish time
Go to shop to purchase ingredients	45 minutes	2:15 pm	3:00 pm
Mix ingredients	20 minutes	3:00 pm	3:20 pm
Cake in oven	25 minutes	3:20 pm	3:45 pm
Wait for cake to cool	30 minutes	3:45 pm	4:15 pm
Ice cake	10 minutes	4:15 pm	4:25 pm

His cake will be ready at 4:25 pm.

Add each time on individually. The finish time of one task becomes the start time of the next task.

N4   **Exercise 10D**

1   George goes to the gym after work. He estimates the times of the following:

Task	Estimated time to complete task
Getting changed	5 minutes
Treadmill	15 minutes
Cross-trainer	20 minutes
Rowing machine	12 minutes
Weights	15 minutes
Shower and change	10 minutes

If he arrives at the gym at 5:20 pm, what time will he expect to leave?

2   Scott arrives at work and carries out the following tasks:

Task	Estimated time to complete task
Opens mail	20 minutes
Reads and replies to emails	5 minutes
Makes coffee	3 minutes
Attends meeting	1 hour 15 minutes
Answers telephone call	8 minutes

He looks at his watch when he completes all these tasks. It is 9:46 am.

What time did he arrive at work?

3   Shelley is a nurse. She starts work at 10:30 pm. She has to complete a number of tasks before she can take a break. The table shows her estimates for the length of time for each task:

Task	Estimated time to complete task
Check on patients	20 minutes
Check medical orders	45 minutes
Prepare paperwork for the next day's discharge	1 hour 20 minutes
Dispense medicine	50 minutes
Second check on patients	20 minutes

When does she have her break?

4   Melvin takes his family to the zoo. They estimate the length of time it will take to visit their favourite animals:

Animals	Estimated time to visit each animal
Pandas	15 minutes
Penguins	20 minutes
Gibbons	13 minutes
Gorillas	35 minutes
Zebras	25 minutes

If they arrive at the zoo at 10:40 am and see all of these animals before lunch, when do they expect to stop for lunch?

N4

5   Sheona goes into town and has several tasks to do. She estimates the time each task will take:

Task	Estimated time to complete task
Hairdresser's appointment	1 hour 45 minutes
Bank	20 minutes
Nail appointment	35 minutes
Coffee with friend	1 hour 30 minutes
Walk home	25 minutes

   a If her hairdresser's appointment is at 1245, what time is her nail appointment? (Give your answer in 24-hour time.)

   b When will she get home?

★ 6   Henry and Jo spend an evening relaxing. They want to do the following and estimate the length of time for each activity:

Activity	Estimated time to complete task
Make dinner	45 minutes
Eat dinner	20 minutes
Call friend on Skype	15 minutes
Watch film	2 hours 20 minutes
Play on games console	1 hour 30 minutes

If Henry arrives at Jo's house at 2025, what time do they estimate their evening will be finished?

🔵 Activity

Plan a trip abroad by plane. You will need to research the following information:

- how to get to the airport from your house (car, bus, taxi, tram)
- the length of time you need to be at the airport before your flight

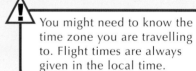

You might need to know the time zone you are travelling to. Flight times are always given in the local time.

- how to get from the airport to your final destination.

What is your total travelling time?

Chapter review

1. Change the following 12-hour times into 24-hour times.

   a 11:30 am   **b** 3:25 pm   **c** 1:45 am   **d** noon

2. Change the following 24-hour times into 12-hour times.

   a 1735   **b** 0650   **c** 2356   **d** 0000

3. The table shows the start and finish times and durations for a set of events. Copy and complete the table.

	Start time	Event lasts for	Finish time
a	3:30 pm	3 hours 10 minutes	
b		1 hour 15 minutes	10:25 am
c	1815		2035
d	1335		1715
e		8 hours 50 minutes	0940
f	12:20 am	2 hours 45 minutes	
g	2250	45 minutes	

4. Henrik started to paint the fence at 1045 and finished painting at 1325.

   How long did it take him to paint the fence?

5. Jane is going to meet her friends at the shops by train. The trains run at regular intervals during the day.

   Part of the train timetable is shown below.

Depart Beach Lane	1110	1118	1126					
Arrive Shopping Centre	1135	1143	1151					

   a Copy and complete the train timetable to show the departure and arrival times of the next five trains.

   Jane arranged to meet her friends at the shopping centre at 12:30 pm.

   b What is the latest train she can catch to get there on time?

6. The school day at Peebles High School starts at 0850 and finishes at 1545.

   The students get a 15-minute break in the morning and 50 minutes for lunch.

   How many hours and minutes do the students at Peebles High School spend in class each day?

7. A train left Thurso at 1632 and arrived in Inverness at 2010.

   How long did the train journey take?

8. A cross-channel ferry from Plymouth in England arrived in Roscoff in France at 2120.

   The journey from Plymouth took 6 hours 30 minutes.

   At what time did the ferry leave Plymouth?

N4

9 Georgie took the overnight bus from Glasgow to London. The bus left Glasgow at 2213 and arrived in London at 0842.

How long did the journey take?

10 Jack is going on holiday and has several tasks to do in town the day before he goes. He estimates the time each task will take:

Task	Estimated time to complete task
Barber's appointment	15 minutes
Collect euros from bank	20 minutes
Buy clothes	1 hour 15 minutes
Meet friend for game of pool	1 hour 30 minutes
Walk home	20 minutes

a If his barber's appointment was at 10:45 am, what time did he arrange to meet his friend? (Give your answer in 24-hour time.)

b When will he expect to get home?

- I can convert between 12-hour time and 24-hour time. ★ Exercise 10A Q1, Q2

- I can calculate time intervals using 12-hour time and 24-hour time. ★ Exercise 10B Q4, Q8, Q9

N4
- I can calculate time intervals using 12-hour time and 24-hour time including intervals spanning midnight. ★ Exercise 10B Q10, Q12

- I can read a timetable to plan a journey. ★ Exercise 10C Q4

N4
- I can read a timetable to plan a journey spanning midnight. ★ Exercise 10C Q9

- I can solve a basic problem in time management. ★ Exercise 10D Q6

11 Units of measurement

This chapter will show you how to:

N4

- select and use appropriate units of measurement
- calculate a quantity based on a related measurement
- investigate the need for tolerance.

You should already know:

- how to estimate length, mass and volume
- how to use standard metric units of measure and convert between related units
- calculate with simple fractions.

Select and use appropriate units of measurement

This chapter explores three forms of measurement: length, weight and volume.

The table shows the conversions between standard metric units.

Length	1 centimetre (cm) = 10 millimetres (mm) 1 metre (m) = 100 centimetres (cm) 1 metre = 1000 millimetres (mm) 1 kilometre (km) = 1000 metres (m)
Volume	1 millilitre (ml) = 1 cubic centimetre (cm^3) 1 litre (l) = 1000 millilitres (ml) 1 cubic metre (m^3) = 1000 litres (l)
Weight (mass)	1 kilogram (kg) = 1000 grams (g) 1 tonne = 1000 kilograms (kg)

To convert from a **smaller** unit to a **larger** unit, **divide** by the given amount using the above table.

To convert from a **larger** unit to a **smaller** unit, **multiply** by the given amount using the above table.

Use these multipliers and dividers to convert between units of length.

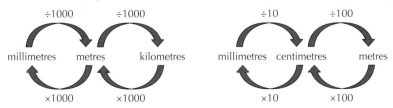

You can use the same method when converting between units of volume and of weight.

Example 11.1

Convert:

a   3.2 m to centimetres

b   42 g into kilograms.

a $3.2 \times 100 = 320$ cm

> Multiply by 100 using the conversion 1 m = 100 cm. You are converting **larger** units to **smaller** units, so there will be more of them.

b $42 \div 1000 = 0.042$ g

> Divide by 1000 using the conversion 1 kg = 1000 g. You are converting **smaller** units to **larger** units, so there will be fewer of them.

Exercise 11A

1   State which metric unit you would use to measure each of these measurements:
    a   the height of your teacher
    b   the distance from your house to the nearest bus stop
    c   the thickness of this textbook
    d   the volume of a mug of coffee
    e   the weight of a loaf of bread
    f   the distance from your house to Edinburgh Castle
    g   the length of a lorry
    h   the weight of a dog.

2   Suggest a measuring instrument you could use to find out the answers in Question 1.

★ **3**   Estimate the approximate metric length, weight or volume of each of these:
    a   the length of this book
    b   the length of the street you live on
    c   the volume of water in a swimming pool
    d   the weight of your front door
    e   the weight of a £2 coin
    f   the volume of water in a bath.

4   Convert each of these lengths into centimetres:
    a   60 mm   **b**   143 mm
    c   3.6 m   **d**   14.25 m

N4
    e   3 m 8 cm   **f**   4.2 km

5 Convert each of these lengths into millimetres:

   a 7 cm   **b** 13.8 cm

   c 31.4 cm   **d** 24 cm 7 mm

N4   **e** 8.3 m   **f** 7 km

6 Convert each of these lengths into kilometres:

   a 6200 m   **b** 13 km 43 m

N4   **c** 41 400 cm

7 Convert each of these weights to kilograms:

   a 5000 g   **b** 3214 g

   c 84 g   **d** 6 tonnes

   e 4.23 tonnes   **f** 13 tonnes 23 kg

8 Convert each of these weights to grams:

   a 5 kg   **b** 6.12 kg

   c 14.5 kg   **d** 3 kg 2 g

N4   **e** 3.5 tonnes   **f** 12 kg 451 g

9 Convert each of these volumes to litres:

   a 4030 ml   **b** 839 ml

   c 14 l 15 ml   **d** 5 l 3 ml

N4   **e** 7.2 m^3 **f** 1236 cm^3

10 A packet of cereal weighs 620 g. A smaller box is $\frac{1}{2}$ the weight of the larger box.

   What is the weight of the smaller box?

11 A packet of cheese weighs 540 g. A smaller packet is $\frac{1}{3}$ the weight of the larger packet.

   What is the weight of the smaller packet?

12 A bar of chocolate weighs 240 g. A smaller bar is $\frac{1}{4}$ the weight of the larger bar.

   What is the weight of the smaller bar?

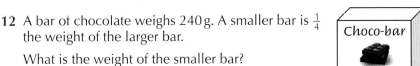
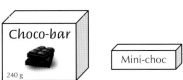

13 The volume of a shoe box is $420\,cm^3$. A larger box is twice the volume of the smaller box.

What is the volume of the larger box?

14 The volume of an oil container is 260 litres. A larger oil container has three times the volume of the smaller container.

What is the volume of the larger oil container?

15 The volume of a swimming pool is $1800\,m^3$. A larger pool has one and a half times the volume of the smaller pool.

What is the volume of the larger swimming pool?

★ **16** Rearrange these lengths, from smallest to largest:

2.4 m   215 cm   2251 mm   2 m 5 cm   231 mm

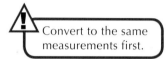

Convert to the same measurements first.

N4   Calculate a quantity based on related measurements

When a measurement is given to you within a problem or story, you need to use the information within the question to solve the problem. As well as using measurements you may need to calculate the cost of an item, or to calculate a quantity.

For example you may need to calculate:

- the number of bottles of juice needed for a party, and the cost of the bottles
- how much paint is needed to paint a room, and the cost of the tins of paint
- the number of eggs needed for a cake recipe and the cost of the eggs.

Example 11.2

A plot of land has an area of $480\,m^2$.

Grass seeds are sold in 10 kg packets. One packet covers an area of $200\,m^2$.

a How many packets do you need to buy to cover the land in grass seeds?

b Each packet costs £38. How much will the grass seeds cost?

a $480 \div 200 = 2.4$, so 3 bags must be purchased

You can only buy a whole bag of seed. If the amount needed is a decimal fraction, you need to round up to the next whole number.

b $3 \times £38 = £114$

To calculate the cost, multiply the number of bags required (3) by the cost of each bag (£38).

N4 **Exercise 11B**

1   Selina wants to put a fence around her back garden. She needs 2 sections of fencing measuring 4.2 m and 1 section measuring 5.7 m.

   a   How much fencing does she need to buy?

   Fencing is sold by the metre. One metre of fence costs £56.

   b   How much will it cost Selina to buy a fence for her back garden?

★ 2   Bruce wants to paint the walls in his living room. He measures the room and finds he has 105 m² of wall to be painted.

   a   One pot of paint covers 16 m². How many pots of paint will he need?

   b   One pot of paint costs £26.50. How much will it cost Bruce to paint his living room?

3   Haidar makes cuboid-shaped candles with a volume of 180 ml each.

   Candle wax is sold in 2-litre blocks.

   a   How many candles can Haidar make out of one block of wax?

   b   If the block of wax costs him £12, and he sells each candle for £5, how much money has he made?   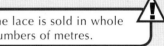 This is the **profit**.

4   A tablecloth is finished with lace around its edge.
   It needs 458 cm of lace.
   Lace is sold at £1.45 per metre.
   How much will the lace cost?

   The lace is sold in whole numbers of metres.

5   **a**   A paperweight is made of bronze. It has a volume of 125 cm³.

      1 cm³ of bronze weighs 8.5 g. What is the weight of the paperweight?

   b   A silver ornament has a volume of 90 cm³. 1 cm³ of silver weighs 10.5 g. What is the weight of the ornament?

   c   Which weighs more, the paperweight or the ornament? Give a reason for your answer.

6   A garden has a length of 30 m. Concrete slabs with length 80 cm are placed in a row along the length of the garden.

   a   How many complete slabs are placed along the length of the garden?

   b   What length of the garden will **not** be covered by a slab?

7   Neil has a 2-litre jug and 6 glasses. Each glass holds 330 ml.

   If he fills the jug with juice, does he have enough juice to fill all 6 glasses?
   Give a reason for your answer.

N4

8 Sonja is sending three presents to her family at Christmas. She weighs the presents she is sending and finds they weigh 324 g, 532 g and 780 g.

The table shows the cost of posting parcels of different weights.

Weight	Up to 250 g	Up to 500 g	Up to 750 g	Up to 1 kg	Up to 1.5 kg	Up to 2 kg
Cost	£1.27	£1.54	£2.09	£2.85	£3.10	£3.35

a Sonja sends the three presents together in one parcel.

  i What is the weight of the parcel?

  ii How much will it cost to send the parcel?

b If she sent each present separately, how much more would it cost her?

Investigate the need for tolerance

When measuring, it is very difficult to be 100% accurate. As a result, manufacturers allow a **tolerance**, which means that measurements close to the correct sizes are allowed if they are within a given range.

For example, a manufacturer may make earphone jacks with a length of 25 mm with a tolerance of 1 mm on either side of this length, meaning that the jack would still fit into the earphone plug.

The tolerance would be written as ±1 mm.

This means that the minimum accepted length would be 25 − 1 = 24 mm, and the maximum accepted length would be 25 + 1 = 26 mm.

The symbol ± means 'plus or minus'.

This is written as (25 ± 1) mm.

Example 11.3

A joiner has to cut a piece of wood (625 ± 2) mm in length.

a Write down the minimum and maximum acceptable sizes.

b If the joiner has cut a piece of wood 628 mm, is it acceptable? Give a reason for your answer.

a Minimum: 625 − 2 = 623 mm

  Maximum: 625 + 2 = 627 mm

b No, as 628 mm is more than 627 mm, which is the maximum acceptable length.

Exercise 11C

1 For each of the following measurements, write down the maximum and minimum acceptable sizes.

a (425 ± 10) g   b (370 ± 15) ml   c (1785 ± 50) kg

d (42.5 ± 0.3) cm   e (31.2 ± 0.6) g   f (412 ± 7.5) m

g (32.3 ± 0.25) °C   h (5.46 ± 0.07) l   i (12.32 ± 0.25) cm

N4 **2** A manufacturer sells shampoo bottles advertised as 350 ml. Which of these bottles would be within a tolerance of (350 ± 3) ml?

a 351 ml   b 347 ml   c 354 ml   d 348 ml

e 345 ml   f 352 ml   g 346 ml   h 350 ml

3 A company sells boxes of drawing pins. A sample of boxes was counted:

83   82   79   77   74   81   82   78

Which of these boxes would be within a tolerance of (80 ± 2)?

4 A sweet manufacturer sells packets of sweets. The number of sweets in a sample of packets was counted:

47   52   49   44   50   48   53   45   46

Which of these packets of sweets would be outside of a tolerance of (48 ± 3)?

★ **5** Fence panels are cut to a length of 127 cm. A sample was measured:

126 cm   127.2 cm   125.8 cm   128.2 cm   127.8 cm   126.4 cm

Which of these panels would be outside of a tolerance of (127 ± 0.5) cm?

6 Nails are made to be 2.54 cm long. A random sample of nails was measured:

2.55 cm   2.53 cm   2.54 cm   2.52 cm   2.44 cm   2.56 cm   2.5 cm

Which of these nails would be outside of a tolerance of (2.54 ± 0.02) cm?

7 A sheet of metal is cut into the shape of a rectangle with a length (123 ± 5) mm and breadth (98 ± 4) mm.

a i   Write down the largest possible length and breadth of the sheet of metal.

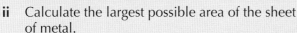

Area of a rectangle = length × breadth

   ii Calculate the largest possible area of the sheet of metal.

b i   Write down the smallest possible length and breadth of the sheet of metal.

   ii Calculate the smallest possible area of the sheet of metal.

c   What is the difference in area between the largest and smallest possible rectangles?

⚙ **8** 5 passengers checked in 1 bag each at the airport. Each bag was weighed separately. The scales at the airport are accurate to ± 500 g. The total weight of the bags came to 97 kg.

a   What is the maximum possible total weight of the bags?

b   What is the minimum possible weight of the bags?

9 A storage box is in the shape of a cuboid and has length (40 ± 0.5) cm, breadth (30 ± 0.5) cm and height (25 ± 0.5) cm.

a i   Write down the largest possible length, breadth and height of the storage box.

Volume of a cuboid = length × breadth × height

   ii Calculate the largest possible volume of the storage box.

b i   Write down the smallest possible length, breadth and height of the storage box.

   ii Calculate the smallest possible volume of the storage box.

c   What is the difference in volume between the largest and smallest possible boxes?

🔵 GO! Activity

1 Research how far you live from school/college.

   How many trips to and from school/college would you need to walk or drive in order to travel 100 km?

2 Measure your weight in kilograms. How many people the same weight as you would be needed for a weight of 1 tonne?

N4 3 A set of scales has a tolerance of ± 0.2 g. If a piece of gold weighs 3.2 g on the scales and gold costs £24.09 per gram, what is the maximum and minimum value of the gold?

Chapter review

1 Convert:

   a 7.3 cm to millimetres   b 4100 cm^3 to litres

N4 c 31 000 g into tonnes

2 Rearrange these lengths, from smallest to largest:

   3.7 m   365 cm   3458 mm   3 m 8 cm   362 mm

3 A packet of rice weighs 978 g. A smaller packet is $\frac{1}{3}$ the weight of the larger packet.

   What is the weight of the smaller packet?

N4 4 Gary wants to varnish the fence in his garden. He has 56 m^2 of fence to be covered.

   a One pot of varnish covers 10 m^2. How many pots of varnish will he need?

   b One pot of varnish costs £6.75. How much will it cost Gary to varnish his fence?

5 A company sells boxes of paper clips. A sample of boxes was counted:

   94   87   88   91   85   90   89   92

   Which of these boxes would be within a tolerance of (90 ± 2)?

• I can select and use appropriate units of measurement. ★ Exercise 11A Q3, Q16

N4 • I can solve problems by calculating a quantity based on a related measurement. ★ Exercise 11B Q2

• I can calculate tolerance and find the maximum and minimum size allowed for an object. ★ Exercise 11C Q5

12 Scale drawings

This chapter will show you how to:

- interpret a simple scale drawing
- construct a scale drawing with a given scale
- interpret map scales
- use maps, plans and scale drawings to solve problems.

You should already know:

- how to give directions for movement
- how to use an 8-point compass for directions and movement
- how to convert one metric unit to another.

Interpret a scale drawing

A **scale drawing** is a drawing of a real object. It is often smaller than the real object but can sometimes be bigger. For example, maps are scale drawings which represent areas of land.

A scale is always given on the drawing. Scales are usually written as:

'length on drawing' to 'actual length'

For example, a scale of 1 cm representing 10 km on a map would be written as:

1 cm to 10 km

If you are asked to use a scale drawing to calculate an actual measurement, follow these steps.

- Measure the length accurately. You are allowed a tolerance of ± 2 mm when measuring a length.

  > For more about tolerance, look back at Chapter 11. ⚠

- Multiply your measurement by the right-hand side of the scale. For example, for a scale of 1 cm to 5 km, multiply the length you measured by 5.

- The units of the actual size required are the same units used in the right-hand side of the scale. For example, for a scale of 1 cm to 5 km, the answer will be written in km.

Example 12.1

Here is the scale drawing of a classroom.

a i Find the actual length of the classroom.

ii Find the actual breadth of the classroom.

b If the actual width of a window in the classroom is 2.4 m, what length represents the window in the scale drawing?

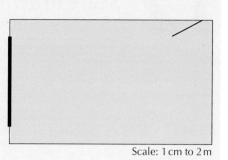

Scale: 1 cm to 2 m

a i Scale length = 5.5 cm

Actual length = 5.5 × 2 = 11 m

> Multiply the scale length by the right-hand side of the scale. The units are the same as the right-hand side of the scale.

ii Scale breadth = 3.3 cm

Actual breadth = 3.3 × 2 = 6.6 m

b Scale width of window = 2.4 ÷ 2 = 1.2 cm

> Divide the actual width by the right-hand side of the scale.

Exercise 12A

1 For each line:

i measure and write down the length of each line

ii work out the length represented by each line.

a _____ 1 cm to 3 m

b _____ 1 cm to 5 m

c _____ 1 cm to 10 m

d _____ 1 cm to 500 m

e _____ 1 cm to 2 km

★ 2 The distance between John and Bob's houses is 4 cm on a map. The scale is 1 cm represents 500 m.

What is the actual distance between their houses?

John's house

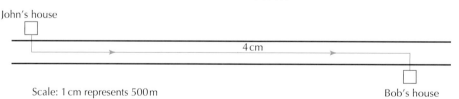

4 cm

Scale: 1 cm represents 500 m

Bob's house

3 The distance between two villages on a map is measured to be 8 cm.

What is the actual distance between the two villages?

Village A

8 cm

Village B

Scale: 1 cm represents 1200 m

4 Sam went for a walk. When he got home, he measured the walk on a map. Using a piece of string, he recorded the walk to be 6.5 cm long on his map. The scale of the map is 1 cm to 800 m.

How far did Sam walk?

5 The diagram shows a scale drawing of a living room.

   a Find the actual
      i length   ii breadth
      of the living room.

   b Find the actual distance between the opposite corners of the living room.

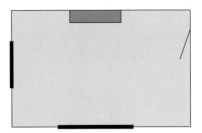

Scale: 1 cm to 1.5 m

6 The map below shows part of the south-east of England.

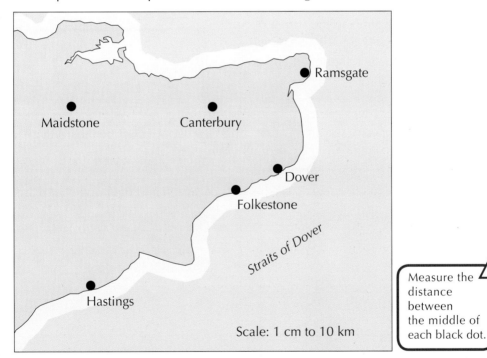

Ramsgate

Maidstone   Canterbury

Dover

Folkestone

Straits of Dover

Measure the distance between the middle of each black dot.

Hastings

Scale: 1 cm to 10 km

   a Find the actual direct distance between:
      i   Maidstone and Canterbury   ii Hastings and Ramsgate
      iii Canterbury and Folkestone   iv Maidstone and Hastings.

   b Why are the distances between each town longer than this if you are driving?

7   The map shows part of Glasgow city centre. It has a scale of 1 cm to 100 m.

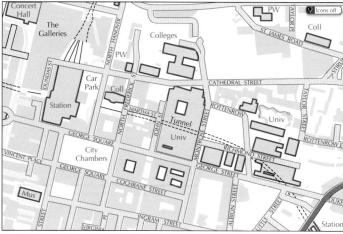

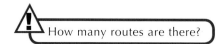

Scale of 1 cm to 100 m

a   Find the actual length of Cochrane Street.

b   Find the actual length of Rottenrow.

c   Find the distance round George Square (all four sides).

d   **i**   Find the distance travelled if you walked from the corner of George Street/Montrose Street to the corner of North Frederick Street/Cathedral Street.

   ii   Which route is shorter and by how much?

How many routes are there?

N4   Map scales

A map scale is often given as a ratio. For example, a scale of 1:10000 means that 1 cm on the map represents an actual distance of 10000 cm.

This is also known as the **representative ratio**.

No units are given in ratio form because the units of the left and right of the ratio are the same.

N4

Example 12.2

The scale on a map is given as 1 : 10 000.

Find the actual distance represented by 4.5 cm on the map.

Scale: 1 : 10 000

1 cm : 10 000 cm ● ———————— (Rewrite your scale with units (cm).)

4.5 cm represents 4.5 × 10 000 ● ———— (Multiply the right-hand side by 4.5.)

     = 45 000 cm

     45 000 ÷ 100 ● ———— (Convert your answer to an appropriate unit, in this case, metres. With bigger ratios, it may be more appropriate to convert to kilometres.)

     = 450 m

Exercise 12B

(Convert the right-hand side of each scale to centimetres.) ⚠

1 Write each of these map scales as a ratio:

   a 1 cm to 2 m   **b** 1 cm to 500 m

   c 1 cm to 10 km   **d** 1 cm to 250 km   **e** 2 cm to 5 km

2 Each line is drawn to the given scale. Write down the length each line represents.

   a ———————————————————————— 1 : 400

   b —————————————————— 1 : 1500

   c ———————————— 1 : 10 000

   d —————————————————— 1 : 25 000

   e ————— 1 : 500 000

★ 3 The distance between Mel and Sam's houses is 6 cm on a map.
     The map ratio is 1 : 25 000.

     What is the actual distance between their houses?

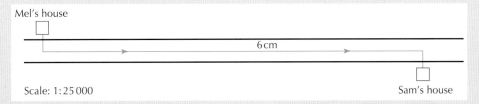

Mel's house

6 cm

Scale: 1 : 25 000   Sam's house

4 The distance between two towns on a map is measured to be 4.7 cm.
     The map ratio is 1 : 150 000.

     What is the actual distance between the two towns?

Town L   Town M
               4.7 cm

               Scale: 1 : 150 000

N4

5   The map shows Edinburgh city centre. The map ratio is 1 : 10 000.

Find the actual distance (as the crow flies) between:

a   the Sheriff Court and Stills Gallery

b   Adam House and Princes Mall

c   How far is it to walk from the corner of Chambers Street and South Bridge to the Edinburgh Dungeon?

6   Janice goes for a bike ride. When she gets home, she measures her ride on a map. Using a piece of string, she records the ride to be 11.8 cm long on her map. The map ratio is 1 : 750 000.

How far did Janice cycle?

7   Two cities are 225 km apart. A map of the area has a ratio of 1 : 3 000 000.

Find the distance between the cities on the map.

Use scale drawings to solve problems

A scale drawing can be used to find missing information.

For example, an engineer may be able to measure an angle from a point on the ground to the top of a building, and measure the distance from the base of a building, then use a scale drawing to find the height of the building.

Scale drawings are used in everyday life. Examples include:

•   construction of buildings, ships and vehicles

•   planning of house extensions or roads

•   drawing of maps

•   making models or replicas of vehicles, buildings or famous landmarks.

N4 To make a scale drawing:

- use the scale to calculate the lengths to be drawn

  > The scale needed for a drawing will be given to you. ⚠

- state the scale in your drawing

- accurately draw and measure all lengths and angles

  > You may find drawing a sketch will help you if no sketch is given in the question. ⚠

- use your drawing to measure the required length (as asked for in the question)

- use your scale to convert the scale length to the actual length (as you have done in Exercises 12A and 12B).

Example 12.3

From a point 50 m from the base of a building, an angle of 35° is made with the top of the building. The triangle illustrates the situation.

a Using a scale of 1 : 500, make a scale drawing of the triangle shown.

b Use your scale drawing to find the actual height of the building.

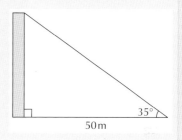

a Scale is 1 : 500

> Interpret the given scale from the representative ratio given.

1 cm to 500 cm or 1 cm to 5 m

Length of base $= \dfrac{50}{5} = 10$ cm

> Calculate the length of the base by dividing by the right-hand side of the scale.

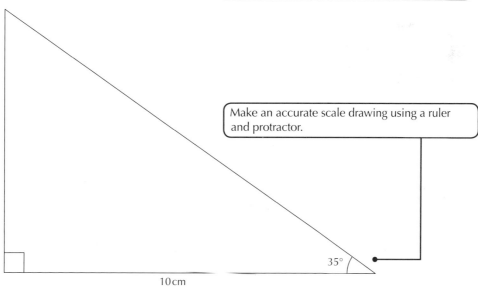

> Make an accurate scale drawing using a ruler and protractor.

b Height of diagram = 7 cm

> Measure the height on the diagram.

$7 \times 5 = 35$

> Multiply the measured height by the right-hand side of the scale.

The building is 35 m tall in real life.

N4   **Exercise 12C**

★ **1**   **a**   Make a scale drawing of this garden.
Use a scale of 1 cm to 2 m.

   b   Use your scale drawing to find the direct
distance from *A* to *B*.

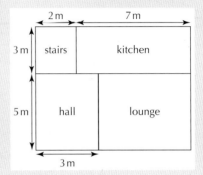

2   **a**   Make a scale drawing of the ground floor
of this house, using a scale of 1 : 150.

   b   Use your scale drawing to find the actual
distance between the opposite corners
of the lounge.

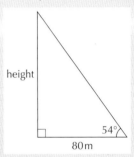

3   From a point 80 m from the base of a tower,
an angle of 54° is made with the top of the tower.
The triangle illustrates the situation.

   a   Make a scale drawing of the triangle.
Use a scale of 1 : 800.

   b   Use your scale drawing to find the height
of the tower.

4   The beams of a roof form an isosceles triangle as shown below.

   a   Make a scale drawing of the roof, using a scale of 1 : 200.

   b   Use your scale drawing to find the height of the roof.

N4 ★ **5** A balloon is 32° from point *A* and 64° from point *B*.

Points *A* and *B* are 450 m apart.

a Make a scale drawing of the diagram. Use a scale of 1 cm to 50 m.

b Use your scale drawing to find the distance between point *A* and the balloon.

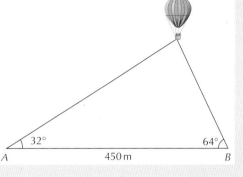

6 The diagram shows a sketch of a car park.

a Using a scale of 1 : 300, make a scale drawing of the car park.

b Use your scale drawing to find the length of AB.

c Use your scale drawing to find the length of the longer diagonal.

Give your answer in metres.

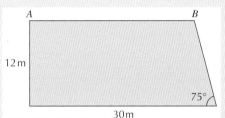

GO! Activity

1 Make a scale drawing of your bedroom, making sure you choose a suitable scale and measure your furniture carefully.

2 Design your own kitchen. You will find dimensions (lengths and breadths) on most kitchen design websites. Use the length and breadth of your own kitchen as a starting point.

Chapter review

1 For each line:

  i measure and write down the length of each line

  ii work out the length represented by each line.

a _____ 1 cm to 4 m

N4 **b** _____ 1 : 25 000

2 The distance from Harriet's house to her school on a map is measured to be 7 cm. The map scale is: 1 cm represents 1500 m.

What is the actual distance between Harriet's house and her school?

N4

3 From a point 60 m from the base of a
monument, an angle of 40° is made with
the top of the monument.

The diagram illustrates the situation.

a Using a scale of 1 cm to 10 m, make
a scale drawing of the diagram.

b Use your scale drawing to find the
height of the monument.

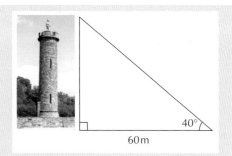

4 A kite is 35° from point A and 62° from point B. Points A and B are 120 m apart.

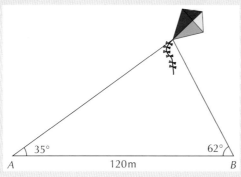

a Make a scale drawing of the above diagram. Use a scale of 1 : 2000.

b Use your scale drawing to find the distance between point A and the kite.

- I can interpret a simple scale drawing.
  ★ Exercise 12A Q2

N4
- I can interpret map scales. ★ Exercise 12B Q3

- I can construct a scale drawing with a given scale.
  ★ Exercise 12C Q1

- I can use maps, plans and scale drawings to solve
  problems. ★ Exercise 12C Q5

13 Directions and navigation

This chapter will show you how to:

N4

- give or follow directions
- use bearings and relate them to compass directions
- use maps, plans and scale drawings to plan a navigation course.

You should already know:

- how to convert between metric units
- how to read and apply scales
- how to give and interpret directions based on moves forward and back, turns and angles.

Give and follow directions

Maps are scale drawings which represent areas of land. You can use maps to give and follow directions. It sometimes helps to turn your map around to follow the correct direction of travel.

Maps can be drawn at different scales to show different sized areas. You can get maps which show just a small part of a town, or which show a whole country or continent. Different types of maps are used for different purposes.

Maps are also drawn with different amounts of detail on them. When you go for a walk in the countryside, you want a map that shows you hills, rivers, lochs, woodland, footpaths and other features which help you find your way.

If you are using a map in a town or city, you want a map that has street names and the names of prominent buildings.

With a bit of practice, you can learn how to 'read' a map, so you can visualise what a map is showing you. This is a useful skill, particularly if you want to go exploring in the countryside, or if you are in a new town and need to find an address, such as a college or a venue for a concert. If you study geography, you will learn to use different types of maps.

The maps used in this section are all **street maps**. These are maps which show features in towns and cities, such as street names, buildings such as libraries, schools, churches, and parks. If you have a smartphone, you might have a maps app which you can use to get round town.

Example 13.1

You have been given the following instructions to get from the school to Joe's house:

- come out of the school and turn left along Anderson Road

- turn left and walk along Cairn Road

- take the second right and go along Ford Lane

- turn a half-turn and walk along Great Scott Street. Joe's house is halfway along Great Scott Street.

a Trace the map and show the route you need to take to reach Joe's house.

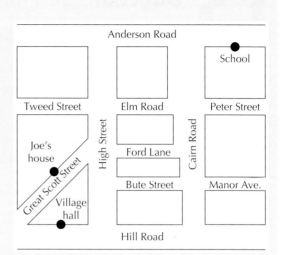

b The map is drawn to a scale of 1 cm to 100 m. Estimate the distance you have to walk.

c Give directions from the village hall to the school.

a

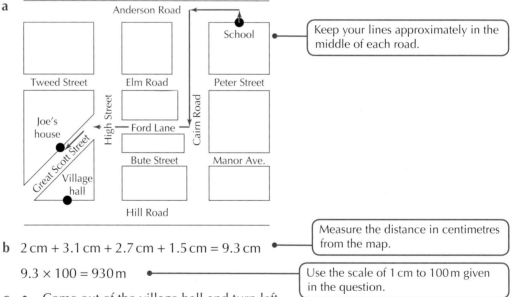

> Keep your lines approximately in the middle of each road.

b 2 cm + 3.1 cm + 2.7 cm + 1.5 cm = 9.3 cm

> Measure the distance in centimetres from the map.

9.3 × 100 = 930 m

> Use the scale of 1 cm to 100 m given in the question.

c
- Come out of the village hall and turn left into Hill Road.

- Take the second left and walk along Cairn Road.

- Walk to the end of Cairn Road and turn right onto Anderson Road. The school is on the right-hand side.

> ⚠ There are often different routes you could take and there may be variations in answers. Select a route which appears the most direct. Turn your book around if it helps you work out directions and turns.

Exercise 13A

★ 1   You have been given the following instructions to get from the library to Annie's house:

- come out of the library and turn left along Hamilton Road

- turn right and walk along MacRae Avenue

- take the second left and walk along Woodend Avenue

- turn right into Dunbar Street followed quickly by a left turn into Grey Street. Annie's house is on the right.

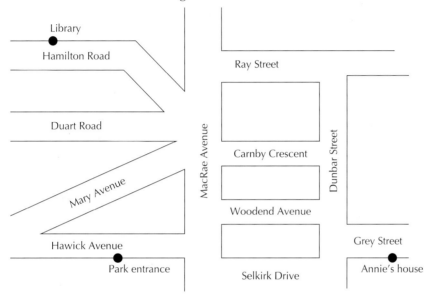

a   Trace the map and show the route you need to take from the library to reach Annie's house.

b   The map is drawn to a scale of 1 cm to 100 m. Estimate the distance you have to walk.

c   Write the directions from the park entrance to the library.

2 You have been given the following instructions to get from the church to Harry's house:

- come out of the church and turn left along Cairnwell Road

- turn left and walk along Rosewell Crescent

- take the first left and walk along Rosewell Drive

- take the first right and walk along Red Avenue. Harry's house is at the end of the street.

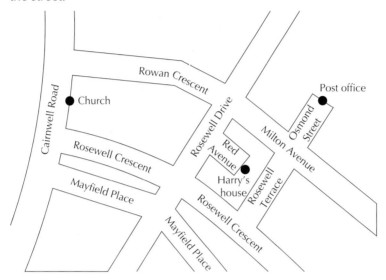

a Trace the map and show the route you need to take from the church to reach Harry's house.

b The map is drawn to a scale of 1 cm to 80 m. Estimate the distance you have to walk.

c Give directions from the post office to the church.

3 You have been given the following directions to get from Granny's house to the dentist:

- come out of Granny's house and turn right along Miller Road
- turn right and walk along Larch Avenue
- turn left and walk along Craig's Road
- turn right and walk along Middlemoor Avenue
- take the first right and walk along Lavender Avenue
- turn right into Heather Avenue. The dentist is on the right at the end of this road.

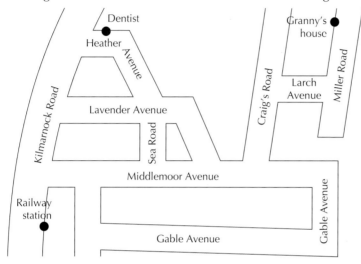

a Trace the map and show the route you need to take to get from Granny's house to reach the dentist.

b The map is drawn to a scale of 1 cm to 50 m. Estimate the distance you have to walk.

c Give directions from the railway station to Granny's house.

4   The map shows part of Inverness.

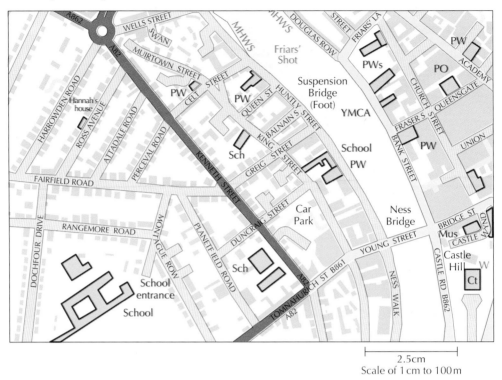

2.5cm
Scale of 1 cm to 100 m

You have been given the following directions to go from the YMCA to Hannah's house:

*   come out of the YMCA and turn left along Bank Street

*   turn right and walk over the Ness Bridge along Young Street

*   take the third right and walk along Kenneth Street

*   take the fifth left and walk along Ross Avenue. Hannah's house is halfway along Ross Avenue on the right.

a   Trace the map and show the route you need to take to get from the YMCA to reach Hannah's house

b   The map is drawn to a scale of 1 cm to 100 m. Estimate the distance you have to walk.

c   Give directions to walk from the entrance of the school to the post office (PO) on Queensgate.

5   The map shows part of Stranraer.

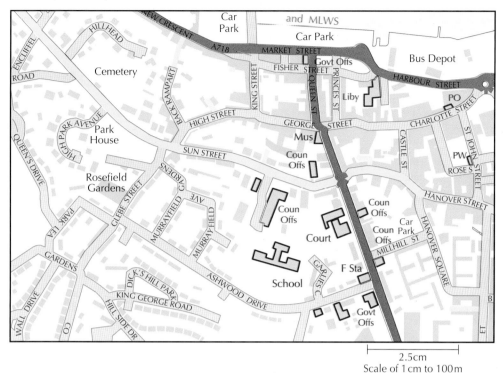

2.5cm
Scale of 1 cm to 100 m

You have been given the following directions to get from the school to the bus depot:

• come out of the school on Garlies Crescent, turn left and walk along Ashwood Drive

• turn left and walk along Queen Street

• take the fourth right and walk along Fisher Street

• turn right and walk along Harbour Street. The bus depot is on the left.

a   Trace the map and show the route you need to take to walk from the school to the bus depot.

b   The map is drawn to a scale of 1 cm to 100 m. Estimate the distance you have to walk.

c   Give directions to walk from Rosefield Gardens to the post office on Charlotte Street.

N4 Bearings

Bearings are a way of measuring an angle on land, at sea and in the air. They are often used for navigating when travelling in a boat or by plane. Orienteering is a popular sport that uses bearings and distances as a challenge to navigate between flags on a course.

Compass points and bearings

Compasses were invented by sailors during the Middle Ages, and show the direction of travel from a point.

Reading clockwise from the top, the four main points on a compass (also called 'cardinal points') are north (N), east (E), south (S) and west (W). There are 360 degrees (symbol °) around a point, so there are 90° between each cardinal point.

Halfway between each cardinal point there are other points:

- north-east (NE)
- south-east (SE)
- south-west (SW)
- north-west (NW).

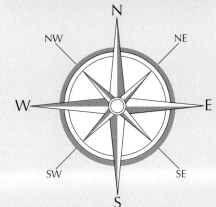

Bearings are measured in degrees, and the angle is measured clockwise from north. Bearings are always given in three digits, so north is read as 000°.

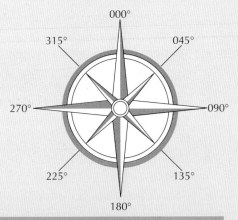

Point	N	NE	E	SE	S	SW	W	NW
Bearing	000°	045°	090°	135°	180°	225°	270°	315°

Measuring and drawing diagrams involving bearings

A bearing is measured:

- from a north line
- clockwise
- with three digits (called a three-figure bearing).

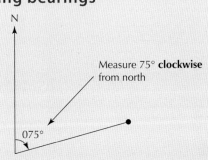

Measure 75° **clockwise** from north

075°

N4

Example 13.2

Find the three-figure bearing: **a** from *A* to *B* **b** to *D* from *C*.

a

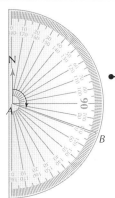

> Measure the angle from the north line reading clockwise. Always put your protractor at the point 'from'.

Bearing from *A* to *B* is 109°.

b Method 1 using a 360° protractor

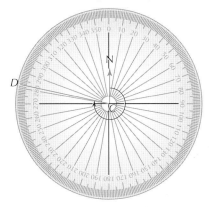

> Use a 360° protractor to measure the angle. Make sure that 0° is placed on the north line and read clockwise round the protractor.

Bearing to *D* from *C* is 282°.

> The bearing **to *D* from *C*** is the same as the bearing **from *C* to *D***. This is different from the bearing **from *D* to *C***. Be careful when reading 'from' and 'to'.

Method 2 using a 180° protractor

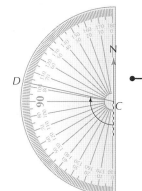

> It helps to extend the north line down. Then, using a 180° protractor, measure the angle from south clockwise and add on 180°, the angle from north to south.

Bearing to *D* from *C* is 180 + 102 = 282°.

N4 **Exercise 13B**

★ **1** Find the three-figure bearing from *A* to *B* in each of the following.

a

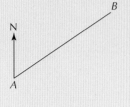

b

c

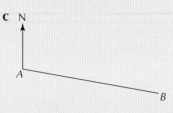

d

2 Find the three-figure bearing to *K* from *G* for each of the following.

a

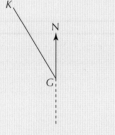

b

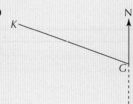

c

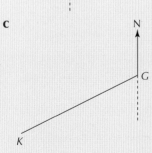

d

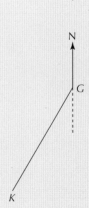

3 Draw a sketch (using a protractor or angle measure) to show:

   a the bearing of 075° from helicopter *A* to airport *B*

   b the bearing of 134° from ship *C* to yacht *D*

   c the bearing of 213° from hill *E* to hill *F*.

N4

4 a i What is the bearing from *B* to *M*?

ii What is the bearing from *M* to *B*?

b i What is the bearing from *H* to *L*?

ii What is the bearing from *L* to *H*?

c How can you find the back bearing if you know the initial bearing?

> A back bearing is the bearing in the opposite direction.

Use scale drawings to plan a navigation course

To make a scale drawing:

- use the scale given to calculate the lengths to be drawn

- accurately draw and measure all lengths and angles

- state the scale in your drawing

- use your drawing to measure any length or bearing asked for in the question.

> This is an extension of the work covered in Chapter 12. You may find it helpful to draw a sketch if no diagram is given in the question as this helps to place the starting point. The scale required for a drawing will be given to you in the question.

N4

Example 13.3

A plane flies 60 km on a bearing of 050°, then turns and changes direction and flies 80 km on a bearing of 125°.

a Using a scale of 1 cm to 10 km, make a scale drawing to represent the plane's journey.

b How far is the plane from its starting point?

c What bearing would it need to **now** fly to get back to its starting point?

a $\dfrac{60}{10} = 6\,\text{cm}$  Find lengths by dividing by the right-hand side of the scale.

$\dfrac{80}{10} = 8\,\text{cm}$

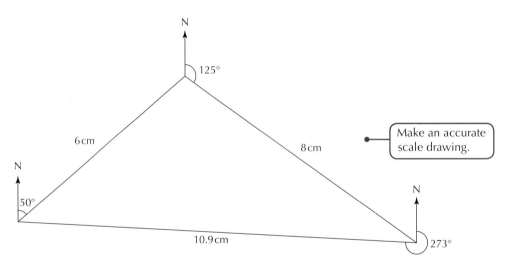

Make an accurate scale drawing.

b On the scale drawing, the third side measures 10.9 cm.

$10.9 \times 10 = 109$

The plane is 109 km from its starting point.

c 273° ● Measure the bearing from the scale drawing.

Exercise 13C

★ **1** A plane flies 120 km on a bearing of 074°, then turns and changes direction and flies 90 km on a bearing of 200°.

a Using a scale of 1 cm to 20 km, make a scale drawing to represent the plane's journey.

b How far is the plane from its starting point?

c What bearing would it need to now fly to get back to its starting point?

N4

2   Heather is taking part in an orienteering course. She is given these instructions:

- start at checkpoint A: 600 m on a bearing of 120°
- checkpoint A to checkpoint B: 800 m on a bearing of 065°
- checkpoint B to checkpoint C: 900 m on a bearing of 155°
- return to start.

a   Using a scale of 1 cm to 100 m, make a scale drawing to represent Heather's journey.

b   What is the bearing and distance from checkpoint C back to the start?

c   What is the total distance Heather must walk to complete the course?

> ⚠ Turn your page around so that your scale drawing is landscape. Start your drawing on the left-hand side of the page, about a quarter of the page from the top.

3   Port *A* is directly north of harbour *B*. They are 4 km apart.
A boat is spotted is on a bearing of 102° from point *A* and 073° from point *B*.

a   Using a scale of 1 : 100 000, make a scale drawing using the above information.

b   How far is the boat from port *A*?

c   How far is the boat from harbour *B*?

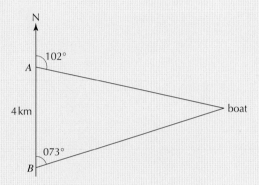

4   Hanna's scout group set off from camp and walked 6.5 km on a bearing of 130°. Johan's group set off from the same camp and walked 4 km on a bearing of 210°.

a   Use a scale of 1 : 50 000 to make a scale drawing showing Hanna and Johan's groups' walks.

b   How far apart are the two groups?

c   What bearing would Johan's group need to walk to join Hanna's group?

5   Village *C* is directly north of town *D*. They are 32 km apart.
A supermarket is to be built which is on a bearing of 252° from village *C* and 305° from town *D*.

a   Using a scale of 1 : 400 000, make a scale drawing using the above information.

b   How far is village *C* from the supermarket?

c   How far is town *D* from the supermarket?

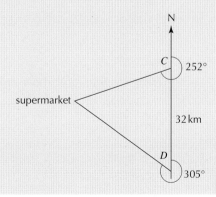

N4

6 A plane flies 90 km on a bearing of 245°, then turns and changes direction and flies 70 km on a bearing of 105°.

   a Using a scale of 1 cm to 10 km, make a scale drawing to represent the plane's journey.

   At the start of the journey, the pilot knew she had enough fuel for a journey of 200 km.

   b Does she have enough fuel left to return to her starting point? Give a reason for your answer.

GO! Activity

Use a map (or online map) to help you to give directions from your house to your school/college. Use the scale of the map to estimate the distance you travel each day.

Chapter review

1 You have been given the following instructions to get from the school to Eric's house:

   • come out of the school and turn right along Kingswood Road

   • turn sharp right and walk along Milton Road

   • take the second left and go along Burns Road

   • walk along Burns Road. Eric's house is the last house on the left.

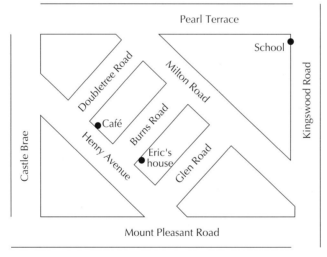

   a Trace the map and show the route you need to take to reach Eric's house.

   b The map is on a scale of 1 cm to 100 m. Estimate the distance you have to walk.

   c Give directions from the school to the café.

N4

2 a Find the bearing of *B* from *A*.

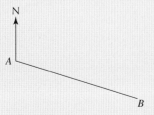

   b Draw a sketch (using a protractor or angle measure) to show the bearing of 305° from port *K* to ship *M*.

N4

3 Lighthouse *C* is directly north of village *D*.
They are 6 km apart.

A raft is spotted which is on a bearing of 115°
from lighthouse *C* and 081° from village *D*.

  a Using a scale of 1 : 100 000, make a scale
    drawing using the above information.

  b How far is the raft from lighthouse *C*?

  c How far is the raft from village *D*?

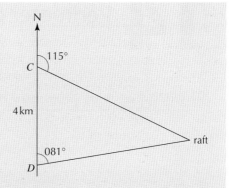

4 Sheona set off from the entrance to a park and walked 450 m on a bearing of 140°.
Jeff set off from the same entrance and walked 750 m on a bearing of 225°.

  a Using a scale of 1 : 10 000, make a scale drawing demonstrating Sheona and
    Jeff's journeys.

  b How far apart are Sheona and Jeff?

  c What bearing would Jeff need to walk to meet Sheona?

- I can follow directions. ★ Exercise 13A Q1a
- I can give directions. ★ Exercise 13A Q1c

N4
- I can use bearings and relate them to compass directions. ★ Exercise 13B Q1
- I can use maps, plans and scale drawings to plan a navigation course. ★ Exercise 13C Q1

14 Perimeter of a 2D shape

This chapter will show you how to:

N4

- calculate and use the perimeter of a 2D shape
- investigate a situation involving perimeter
- calculate and use the perimeter of a composite shape
- calculate and use the circumference of a circle.

You should already know:

- how to use standard metric units of length
- the properties of regular 2D shapes
- that perimeter is the distance around the edge of a 2D shape.

Calculating and using perimeter of a regular 2D shape

The **perimeter** of a 2D shape is the total distance around the shape.

To calculate the perimeter, add the lengths of all the sides together.

Example 14.1

Calculate the perimeter of the triangle.

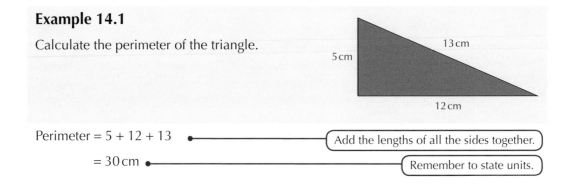

Perimeter = 5 + 12 + 13 ———•—————(Add the lengths of all the sides together.)

= 30 cm •———————————————————————(Remember to state units.)

Metric units of length are used in this chapter (millimetres, centimetres, metres, kilometres).

Perimeter of a rectangle

The perimeter of the rectangle can be calculated as follows:

Perimeter = length + length + breadth + breadth

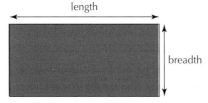

You will be given the measurements of length (longer side) and breadth (shorter side).

Example 14.2

Calculate the perimeter of each shape.

a

8 cm

3 cm

b

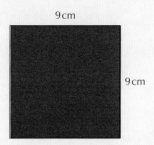

9 cm

9 cm

a Perimeter = 8 + 8 + 3 + 3

= 22 cm

> Add the lengths of all four sides together. Remember that, in a rectangle, the opposite sides have the same length.

b Perimeter = 9 + 9 + 9 + 9

= 36 cm

> This is a square because the length and breadth are the same.

Example 14.3

Jane wants to put a fence around her rectangular flowerbed.

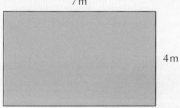

7 m

4 m

a Calculate the length of fencing Jane needs.

N4 Fencing can only be bought in whole metres. One metre of fencing costs £6.

b How much will the fence cost Jane?

a Perimeter = 7 + 7 + 4 + 4

= 22 m

N4 **b** Cost = 22 × 6 = £132

> Multiply your answer to part **a** by the cost of 1 metre.
>
> Make sure your answer has a £ symbol.

Exercise 14A

1. Find the perimeter of these rectangles:

a

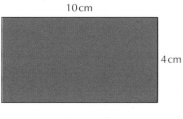

10 cm

4 cm

b

5 mm

13 mm

c

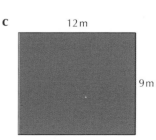

12 m

9 m

2 Find the perimeter of each rectangle by using your ruler to measure the length of each side.

a

b

c

3 Find the perimeter of each shape by using your ruler to measure the length of each side.

a

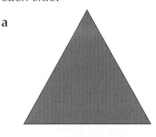

b

c

d

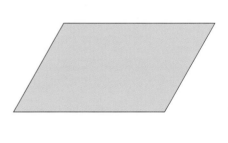

N4

4 Using *P* for perimeter, *l* for length and *b* for breadth, write a formula in letters to represent the perimeter of a rectangle. Give your answer in its simplest form.

⚠️ The formula can be written in two ways. Can you write it in both ways?

5 Iain wants to put a fence around his rectangular chicken pen.

a Calculate the length of fencing needed.

N4

Fencing can only be bought in whole metres. One metre of fencing costs £7.

b How much will the fence cost Iain?

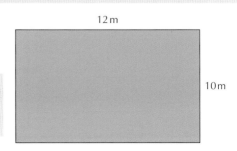

12 m

10 m

★ **6** The diagram shows the floor of a rectangular room.

A skirting board is to be placed around the room (except for the door).

a Calculate the length of skirting board required.

N4 Skirting board can only be bought in whole metres. Skirting board costs £2.50 per metre.

⚙ **b** How much will the skirting board cost?

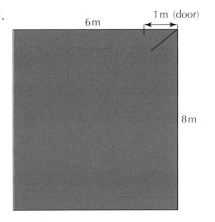

6 m   1 m (door)

8 m

7 A rectangular photograph measures 90 cm by 70 cm.

A frame is to be placed around the photo.

a Calculate the length of frame required.

N4 Framing can only be bought in multiples of 10 cm. A frame costs £3 for every 10 cm.

⚙ **b** How much will the frame cost?

90 cm

70 cm

8 Ali has designed a rectangular stained-glass window.

Ali wants to frame the window.

a Calculate the length of frame needed.

N4 Framing can only be bought in multiples of 10 cm. A frame costs £1.50 for every 10 cm.

⚙ **b** How much will the frame cost Ali?

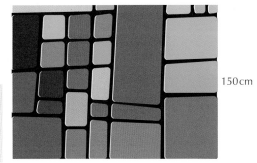

180 cm

150 cm

9 The diagram shows the floor of a rectangular room.

Carpet grippers are to be placed around the room.

a Calculate the length of carpet grippers needed.

N4 Carpet grippers can only be bought in whole metres. Carpet grippers cost £0.80 per metre.

⚙ **b** How much will the carpet grippers cost?

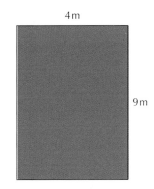

4 m

9 m

N4

10 Hannah is making a rectangular sign for her class's stall at the school fete.

She has 350 cm of coloured edging to put around the perimeter of the sign.

Does she have enough edging? Give a reason for your answer.

N4

Calculating and using perimeter of a composite shape

A **composite 2D shape** is a shape which is made from two or more other shapes including rectangles, squares and triangles.

To calculate the perimeter of a composite shape, you may have to use information given in the question to work out lengths not given directly. The perimeter is the whole distance around the shape, not **only** the lengths initially quoted.

Example 14.4

The shape below is made from two rectangles. Calculate the perimeter of the shape.

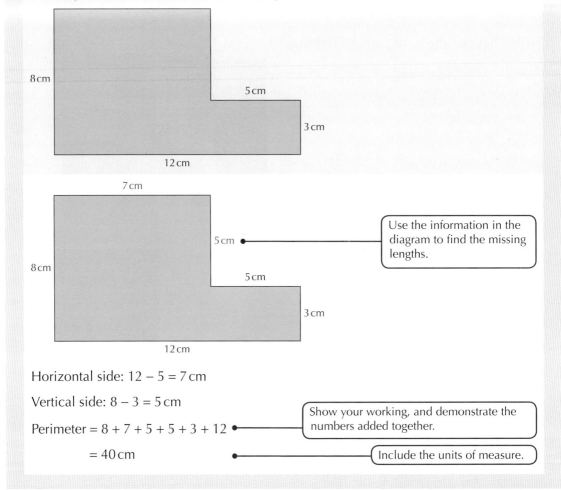

Use the information in the diagram to find the missing lengths.

Horizontal side: 12 − 5 = 7 cm

Vertical side: 8 − 3 = 5 cm

Perimeter = 8 + 7 + 5 + 5 + 3 + 12

= 40 cm

Show your working, and demonstrate the numbers added together.

Include the units of measure.

N4   **Exercise 14B**

1   The following shapes are made from two rectangles.

Work out:
    i   the missing lengths
    ii the perimeter of each composite shape.

a

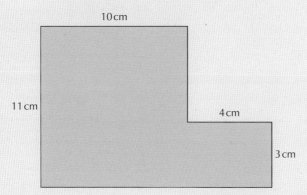

b

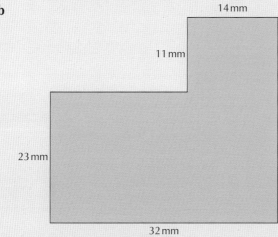

c

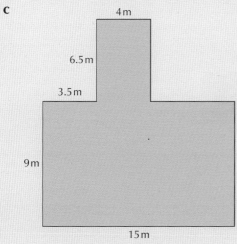

N4

2 Rashid wants to put a fence around his garden, which consists of two rectangles.

a Calculate the length of fencing needed.

Fencing can only be bought in whole metres. One metre of fencing costs £6.50.

b How much will the fence cost Rashid?

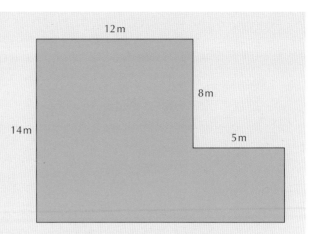

3 The floor plan below shows a room which is made from two rectangles.

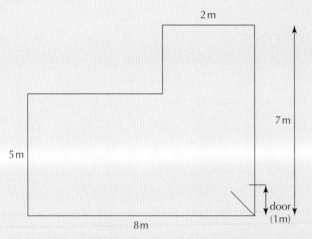

Skirting board is to be placed around the room (except for the door).

a Calculate the length of skirting board required.

Skirting board is bought in whole metres and costs £2.25 per metre.

b How much will the skirting board cost?

4 A patio is made from two rectangles.

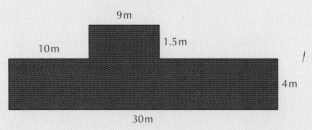

A safety barrier is to be placed around the patio.

a Calculate the length of barrier needed.

Safety barriers can only be bought in whole metres. One metre of barrier costs £11.

b How much will the barrier cost?

N4   **5**   A fireplace-surround is made from three rectangles.

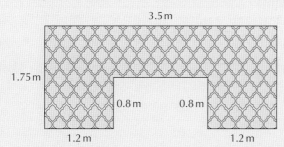

3.5 m

1.75 m

0.8 m   0.8 m

1.2 m   1.2 m

In December, Jack puts fairy lights around all the sides of the fireplace-surround.

If Jack has a string of fairy lights 10 metres long, will this be enough to go around the fireplace-surround? Give a reason for your answer.

6   A room consists of a rectangle and right-angled triangle.

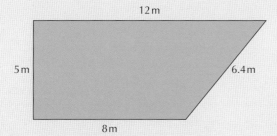

12 m

5 m   6.4 m

8 m

Carpet grippers are to be placed around the room.

a   Calculate the length of carpet grippers needed.

Carpet grippers can only be bought in whole metres.
Carpet grippers cost £0.75 per metre.

b   How much will the carpet grippers cost?

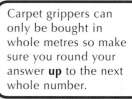

Carpet grippers can only be bought in whole metres so make sure you round your answer **up** to the next whole number.

★ **7**   Joe wants to build a fence around his vegetable patch.

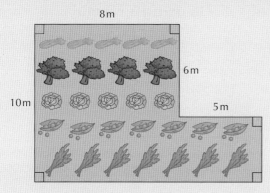

8 m

6 m

10 m   5 m

He buys 45 metres of fence.
Has he bought enough fence for his vegetable patch? Give a reason for your answer.

N4   Calculating and using circumference of a circle

A **circle** is a 2D shape in which all points on its perimeter are the same distance from the centre of the circle.

The perimeter of a circle is called the **circumference**.

The **radius** of a circle is the distance from the centre to the circumference.

The **diameter** of the circle is the distance across the circle passing through the centre.

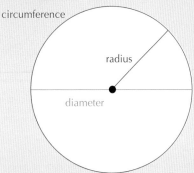

Approximations of π

The circumference of a circle is a little more than three times the length of the diameter. However, this number cannot be accurately written as a fraction or a decimal fraction.

Many ancient civilisations discovered and used their own approximate values, but a more accurate value is a number we now call π (a Greek letter pronounced 'pi').

> ⚠ Activity 2 at the end of the chapter shows how to find the numerical relationship between circumference and diameter.

Using the π button on your calculator, you can see that π has a value of 3.14159...

It is often rounded to 2 decimal places (3.14) to make calculations easier, but it has been calculated to millions of decimal places!

Calculating the circumference of a circle using a formula

To find the circumference, C, of a circle with diameter, d, use this formula:

circumference = π × diameter   or $C = \pi d$

If you are given the radius, r, then use this formula:

circumference = 2 × π × radius   or $C = 2\pi r$

Or you can double the radius (since the diameter is twice the radius) and use $C = \pi d$ as before.

N4

Example 14.5

Find the length of the circumference of each circle, rounding your answer to 1 decimal place.

> ⚠ See Chapter 22 for more on rounding.

a

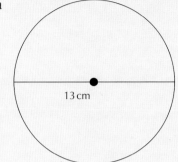

13 cm

b

11 mm

a $C = \pi d$ — Write down the formula you intend to use.

$= \pi \times 13$ — Replace d with 13.

$= 40.8407...$

$= 40.8 \text{ cm} \text{ (1 d.p.)}$ — Round your answer to the number of decimal places given in the question, and remember to state units.

b $C = 2\pi r$

$= 2 \times \pi \times 11$

$= 69.1150...$ — Write down the formula you intend to use.

$= 69.1 \text{ mm} \text{ (1 d.p.)}$ — In part **b**, you could have used the formula $C = \pi d$, replacing 2×11 with 22.

In Example 14.5, instead of using the 𝜋 button, you could have used 3.14.

Exercise 14C

For Questions 1–6, use 𝜋 = 3.14 or use the 𝜋 button on your calculator.

1 Calculate the circumference of each circle. Round each answer to 1 decimal place.

a

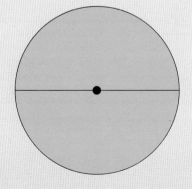

b

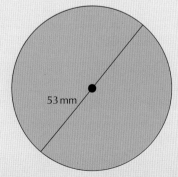

53 mm

N4

c

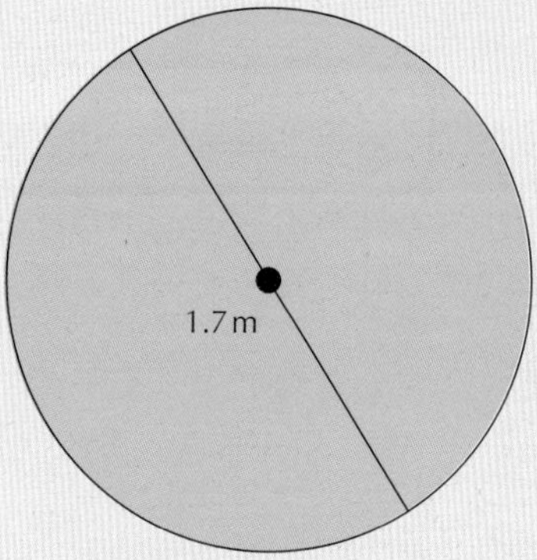

1.7 m

d

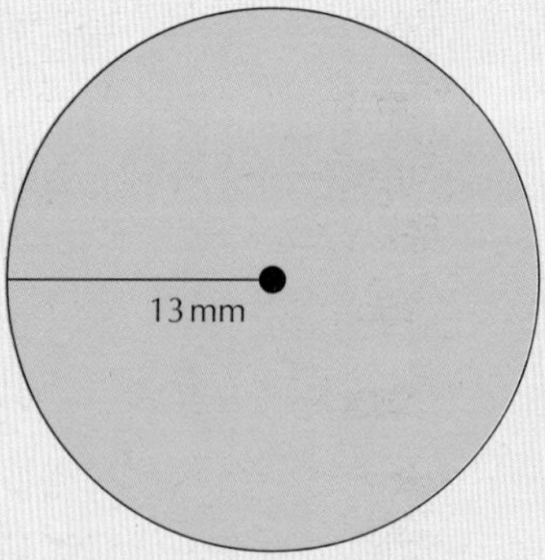

13 mm

e

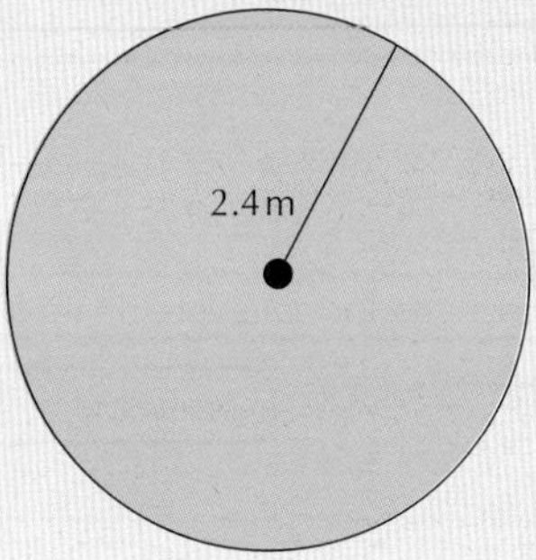

2.4 m

f

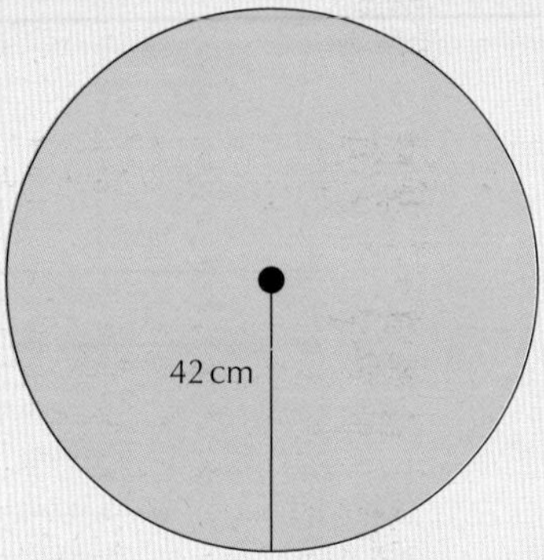

42 cm

2 Find the perimeter of each shape. Round each answer to 2 decimal places.

a

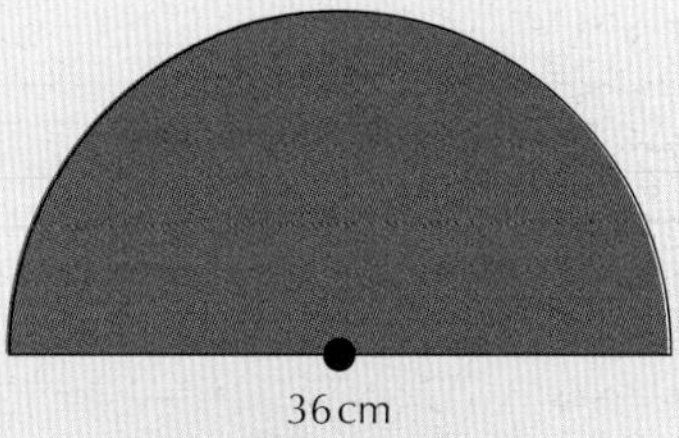

36 cm

⚠️ Find the circumference of a whole circle with diameter 36 cm, then divide by 2 to get the length of the curved part of the shape. Don't forget to add the diameter for your final answer.

b

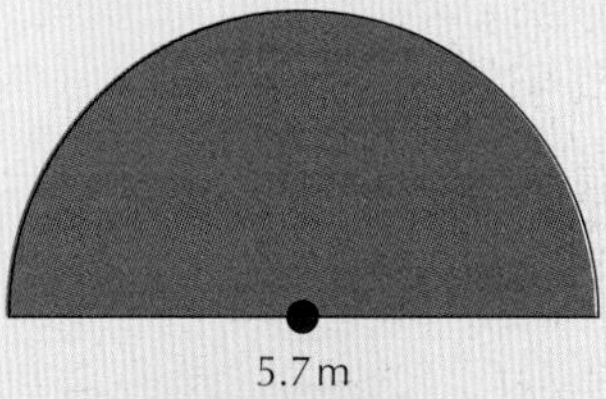

5.7 m

c

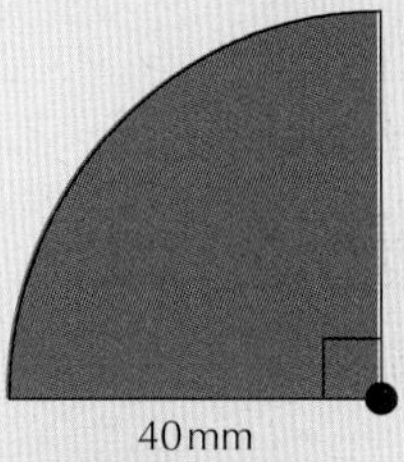

40 mm

⚠️ Find the circumference of a whole circle with radius 40 mm, then divide by 4. Don't forget to add the two radii for your final answer.

d

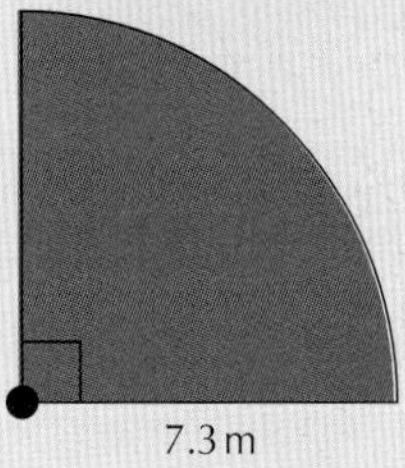

7.3 m

N4

3 A wheel has a diameter of 45 cm.

★ **a** What distance would be travelled in one complete turn? Give your answer to 1 decimal place.

⚙ **b** How many complete turns would the wheel need to make to travel 100 m?

4 The surface of a circular clock has a circumference of 25 cm.

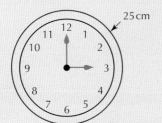

25 cm

Rearrange the formula and use $d = \frac{C}{\pi}$

a Find the diameter of the clock. Give your answer to 1 decimal place.

⚙ **b** Find the radius of the clock. Give your answer to 1 decimal place.

⚙ **5** What is the radius of a trundle wheel with a circumference of 1 metre? Give your answer in centimetres.

⚙ **6** A Ferris wheel has 20 cabins. The wheel has a circumference of 90 metres and each cabin is supported by two iron spokes, each of which is a radius of the circle. What is the length of iron required to make all the spokes? Give your answer to the nearest metre.

GO! **Activity**

1 a Draw as many rectangles as you can with a perimeter of 20 cm.

b For a perimeter of 20 cm, explain the connection between the length and breadth. Are there a limited number of rectangles you can draw if the length and breadth don't have to be whole numbers? Give a reason for your answer.

2 a Find circular objects such as a can of drink, a water bottle, a plate or a glass.

b Measure the diameter and circumference of each object. Use string and a ruler if you do not have a tape measure.

c Calculate $\frac{C}{d}$ for each object and compare it to π. Are your answers close to 3.14?

Chapter review

1 Find the perimeter of each shape.

a

14 cm

31 cm

b

4.7 m   4.7 m

2.8 m

N4

c

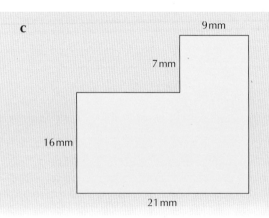

9 mm

7 mm

16 mm

21 mm

d

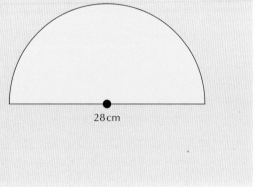

28 cm

2 Elena wants to put a new fence around her rectangular rabbit pen.

  a Calculate the length of fencing needed.

Fencing can only be bought in whole metres. One metre of fencing costs £6.50.

  b How much will the fence cost Elena?

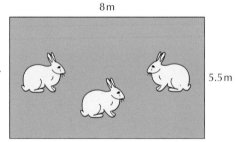

8 m

5.5 m

N4

3 The diagram shows the floor of a room made from two rectangles.

Skirting board is to be placed around the room (except for the door).

  a Calculate the length of skirting board needed.

Skirting board can only be bought in whole metres. Skirting board costs £2.10 per metre.

  b How much will the skirting board cost?

3 m

(1 m) door

6 m

8 m

10 m

4 What is the radius of a wheel with a circumference of 3 metres? Give your answer in centimetres.

N4

- I can calculate and use the perimeter of a regular 2D shape. ★ Exercise 14A Q6

- I can investigate a situation involving perimeter. ★ Exercise 14A Q10

- I can calculate and use the perimeter of a composite shape. ★ Exercise 14B Q7

- I can calculate and use the circumference of a circle. ★ Exercise 14C Q3

15 Area of a 2D shape

This chapter will show you how to:

N4

- calculate the area of a rectangle and square
- calculate the area of a triangle
- calculate the area of a kite, a rhombus, and a parallelogram
- calculate the area of a circle
- calculate the area of a composite shape
- investigate a situation involving area.

You should already know:

- how to use standard metric units of length
- the properties of regular 2D shapes.

Calculating the area of a rectangle and square

The **area** of a shape is the amount of space occupied by the shape.

It is measured in square units.

For example, we can use square millimetres (mm^2), square centimetres (cm^2), square metres (m^2) or square kilometres (km^2).

Counting squares

To find the area of a rectangle or square drawn on squared paper or a grid, you can count the number of smaller squares inside the shape.

Example 15.1

The rectangle is drawn on centimetre squared paper. Work out the area of the rectangle.

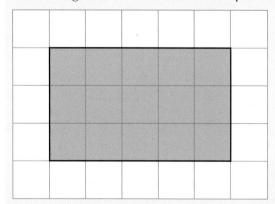

> ⚠ 'Centimetre squared' paper means that the side of each small square measures 1 cm. The area of each small square is $1\,cm^2$.

Area of rectangle = $15\,cm^2$ ●————

> Count the squares inside the shape. Include units in your answer (cm^2).

Example 15.2

The shape is drawn on centimetre squared paper. Estimate the area of the shape.

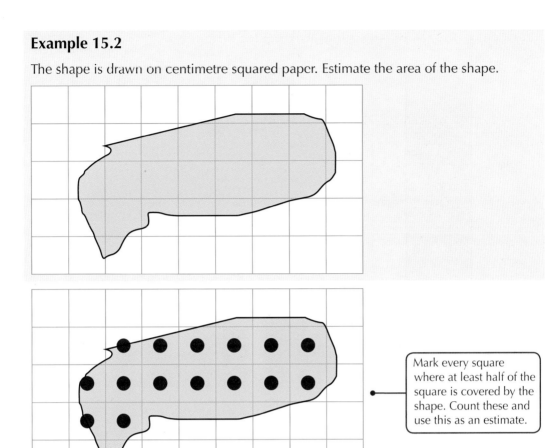

Mark every square where at least half of the square is covered by the shape. Count these and use this as an estimate.

Area is approximately 15 cm^2

Exercise 15A

1   These rectangles are drawn on squared paper. Each small square represents a 1 cm grid square. Count the squares to find the area of each rectangle.

a

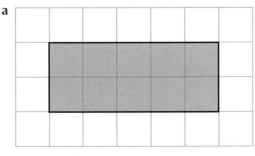

b

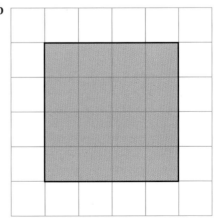

c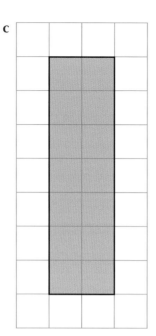

d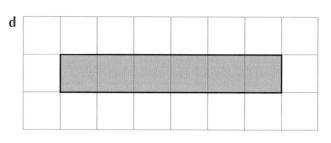

e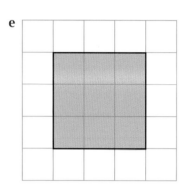

f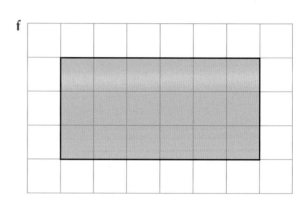

2 These shapes are drawn on squared paper. Each small square represents a 1 cm grid square. Count the squares to find the area of each rectangle.

a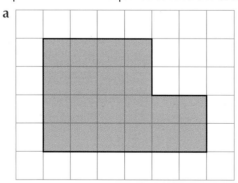

b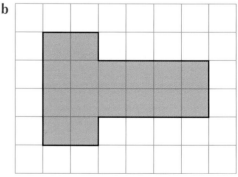

c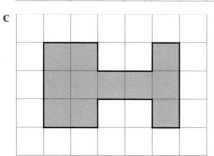

d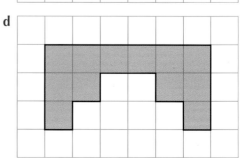

3   These shapes are drawn on squared paper. Each small square represents a 1 cm grid square. Estimate the area of each shape.

a

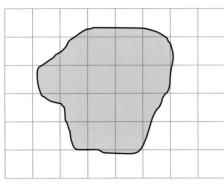

b

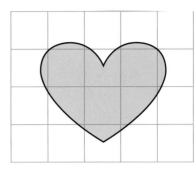

c

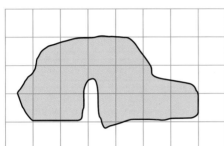

d

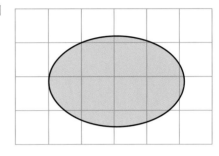

4   a   Look at your answers to Question 1. If you know the length and breadth of a rectangle, how can you calculate the area without having to count squares?

N4   b   Write a formula to represent your answer to part **a**.

> A formula is a rule. In a formula, we usually use one letter to represent one piece of information.

Using a formula

You can calculate the area of a rectangle if you know its length and breadth.

To find the area of a rectangle, use this formula:

area = length × breadth   or $A = lb$

You will be given the measurements of length (longer side) and breadth (shorter side).

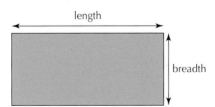

length

breadth

Example 15.3

Calculate the area of each shape.

a

b

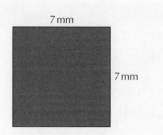

a $A = lb$

$\quad = 9 \times 4$

$\quad = 36\,\text{cm}^2$

> Always start your answer by stating the formula you will use. You could also have written Area = length × breadth.

> Replace l and b with the measurements given, then multiply.

> Include the correct units.

b $A = lb$

$\quad = 7 \times 7$

$\quad = 49\,\text{mm}^2$

> The length and breadth of a square are the same, so you could have written $A = l^2$.

Example 15.4

Flo wants to cover her garden in grass turf.

a Calculate the area of grass turf needed.

Grass turf costs £6 per square metre.

N4

b How much will it cost Flo to cover her garden in grass turf?

a $A = lb$

$\quad = 8 \times 5$

$\quad = 40\,\text{m}^2$

N4

b Cost = 40×6 = £240

> Multiply your answer to part **a** by the cost of 1 square metre. Make sure your answer has a £ symbol.

Exercise 15B

1 Find the area of each rectangle.

a

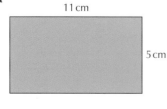

b

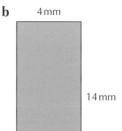

c

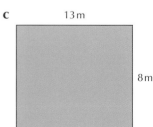

d

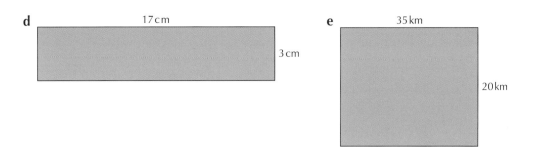

17 cm

3 cm

e

35 km

20 km

★ **2** The diagram shows the floor of a rectangular room.
The carpet in the whole room is to be replaced.

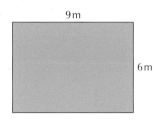

9 m

6 m

  a Calculate the area of new carpet needed.

N4 Carpet costs £18 for every square metre.

  ⚙ **b** How much will the new carpet for the room cost?

3 A rectangular pane of glass needs to be replaced.

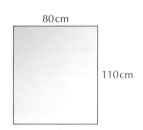

80 cm

110 cm

  a Calculate the area of the pane of glass.

N4 Glass costs 3p for every square centimetre.

  ⚙ **b** How much will the new pane of glass cost?

4 The diagram shows a rectangular playground.
The surface of the whole playground is to be replaced.

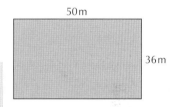

50 m

36 m

  a Calculate the area of the playground.

N4 Resurfacing costs £30 for a square metre.

  ⚙ **b** How much will the new surface cost?

5 Mikel wants to paint one wall of his office blue.
  a Calculate the area of the wall.

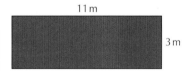

11 m

3 m

N4 Paint costs £1.20 to cover 1 square metre.

  ⚙ **b** How much will it cost Mikel to paint the wall?

6 A rectangular paved patio is shown.
The patio is to be paved with concrete slabs.

  a What is the area of the patio?

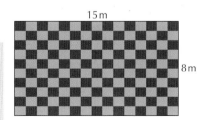

15 m

8 m

N4 Concrete slabs cost £9 for each square metre
of slab.

  ⚙ **b** How much will it cost for the patio to be
paved with concrete slabs?

7 A rectangular sports field needs to be re-turfed.

    a Calculate the area of new grass turf needed.

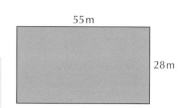

55 m

28 m

N4 Grass turf costs £5.50 per square metre.

    b How much will it cost to re-turf the sports field?

8 A rectangular flag has breadth 1.2 m and an area of 2.76 m².

1.2 m

⚠ Work backwards by dividing the area by the breadth. Rearrange the formula to give $l = A \div b$.

What is the length of the flag?

1.4 m

9 One rectangular panel of a fence is shown. There are 8 identical panels which need to be painted.

    a Calculate the total area which needs to be painted.

One tin of paint covers 10 m² of fence. Each tin costs £11.50.

    b i How many tins of paint need to be bought to cover the fence?

2.5 m

N4   **ii** How much will this cost?

⚠ You can only buy complete tins, so round your answer **up** to the nearest tin to make sure you have enough paint.

N4 ## Calculating the area of a triangle

Any rectangle can be split into two right-angled triangles.

The area of each right-angled triangle is half of the area of the rectangle.

If you draw **any** triangle, you can draw a rectangle surrounding it.

The area of the triangle is half of the area of the surrounding rectangle.

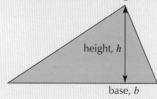

height, h

base, b

N4 To find the area of a triangle, use this formula:

area = $\frac{1}{2}$ of area of surrounding rectangle

or

area = $\frac{1}{2}$ of base × height   or $A = \frac{1}{2}bh$

To find the area of a triangle, you will be given the length of its base, *b*, and the height of the triangle, *h* (sometimes known as the perpendicular or vertical height).

Example 15.5

Calculate the area of each triangle.

a 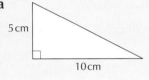   **b** 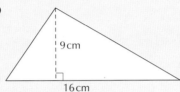   **c**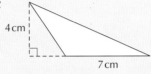

a $A = \frac{1}{2}bh$ ●————————————— State the formula you will use.

$= \frac{1}{2} \times 10 \times 5$ ●————— Substitute the values for *b* and *h*. In a right-angled triangle the height is the same as the length of the side at right angles to the base.

$= \frac{1}{2} \times 50$

$= 25\,\text{cm}^2$ ●————————————— Remember to include the correct units.

b $A = \frac{1}{2}bh$ **c** $A = \frac{1}{2}bh$

$= \frac{1}{2} \times 16 \times 9$ $= \frac{1}{2} \times 7 \times 4$ ●————— Sometimes the height is marked outside the triangle.

$= \frac{1}{2} \times 144$ $= \frac{1}{2} \times 28$

$= 72\,\text{cm}^2$ $= 14\,\text{cm}^2$

Exercise 15C

1 Find the area of each triangle.

a 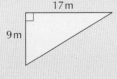   **b**

c 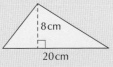   **d**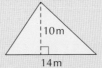

> ⚠ The base is not always given as a horizontal line, and the height is not always given as a vertical line on your page. You may need to turn the textbook round to see the base and height as horizontal and vertical, as shown in the examples above.

183

N4

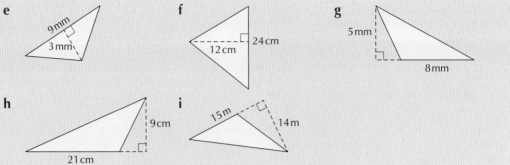

e

f

g

h

i

2   By calculating the area of each triangle, arrange them in order from least to greatest.

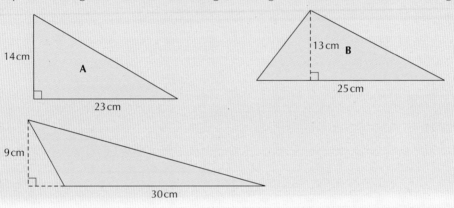

⚙ 3   The triangle shown has an area of 175 cm².

Find the height of the triangle.

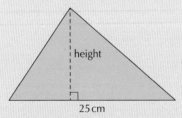

⚠ Work backwards by dividing the area by the base, then multiplying by 2.

⚙ 4   The triangle shown has an area of 12.6 m².

Find the length of the base of the triangle.

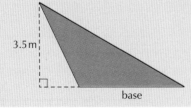

N4

★ **5** Anna's back garden is in the shape of a triangle.

   a What is the area of Anna's garden?

   b She would like to plant grass seeds to grow a new lawn. One packet of grass seed costs £9 and covers 20 m².

      i How many packets does she need to buy?

      ii How much will this cost her?

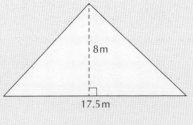

6 A regular hexagon consists of 6 identical triangles with base of length 10 cm and a vertical height of 8.7 cm.

What is the area of the hexagon?

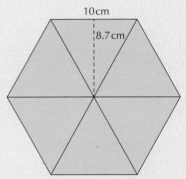

Calculating the area of other quadrilaterals

In this section you will calculate the area of other types of quadrilateral:

* rhombus
* kite
* parallelogram.

The area of a rhombus

A **rhombus** is a quadrilateral (four-sided shape) with:

* four sides of equal length
* two pairs of equal angles
* two lines of symmetry.

If you draw a rhombus, you can draw a rectangle surrounding it.

The area of the rhombus is half of the area of the surrounding rectangle.

To find the area of a rhombus, you use the length of its two diagonals (diagonal 1 and diagonal 2). The diagonals have the same measurements as the length and breadth of the surrounding rectangle. The diagonals of a rhombus meet at right angles.

To find the area of a rhombus use this formula:

   area = $\frac{1}{2}$ of area of surrounding rectangle

or

   area = $\frac{1}{2}$ × diagonal 1 × diagonal 2   or $A = \frac{1}{2}d_1d_2$

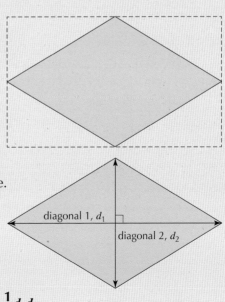

N4

Example 15.6

Calculate the area of this rhombus.

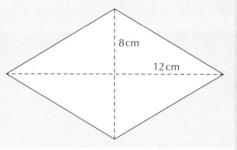

$A = \dfrac{1}{2}d_1d_2$ •———————————————— State the formula you are using.

$= \dfrac{1}{2} \times 12 \times 8$ •———————————— Replace d_1 and d_2 with the values from the diagram.

$= \dfrac{1}{2} \times 96$

$= 48\,\text{cm}^2$ •———————————————— Remember to include the correct units.

The area of a kite

A **kite** is a quadrilateral (four-sided shape) with:

- two pairs of sides of equal lengths
- one pair of equal angles
- one line of symmetry.

If you draw a kite, you can draw a rectangle surrounding it. You can also draw in the diagonals, d_1 and d_2, which meet at right angles.

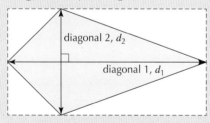

The area of the kite is half of the area of the surrounding rectangle. So it has the same formula as the rhombus:

area $= \dfrac{1}{2}$ **of area of surrounding rectangle**

or

area $= \dfrac{1}{2} \times$ **diagonal 1 $\times$ diagonal 2**　　or　　$A = \dfrac{1}{2}d_1d_2$

N4

Example 15.7

Calculate the area of each kite.

a

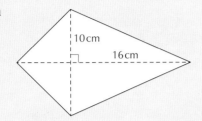

b

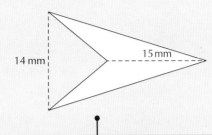

> The shape in part **b** is a V-shaped kite (also known as an inverted kite). It has the same properties as the other type of kite, and you use the same formula to calculate the area.

a $A = \frac{1}{2} d_1 d_2$

$= \frac{1}{2} \times 10 \times 16$

$= \frac{1}{2} \times 160$

$= 80 \, \text{cm}^2$

b $A = \frac{1}{2} d_1 d_2$

$= \frac{1}{2} \times 14 \times 15$

$= \frac{1}{2} \times 210$

$= 105 \, \text{mm}^2$

Exercise 15D

1 Calculate the area of each rhombus.

a

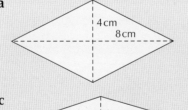

b

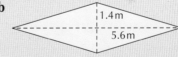

c

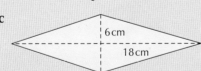

d

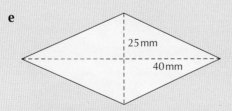

e

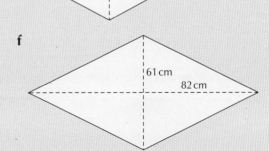

f

N4   **2**   Calculate the area of each kite.

a

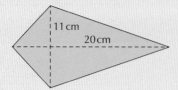
11 cm
20 cm

b

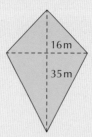
16 m
35 m

c

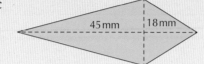
45 mm   18 mm

d

30 mm   12 mm

e

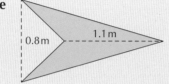
0.8 m   1.1 m

f

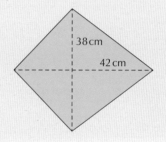
38 cm
42 cm

⚙ **3**   The area of this rhombus is $875\,cm^2$.

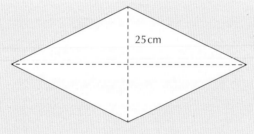
25 cm

⚠ Work backwards by dividing the area by 25 and then multiplying by 2.

Find the length of the longer diagonal.

⚙ **4**   The area of this kite is $3.85\,m^2$.
Find the length of the longer diagonal.

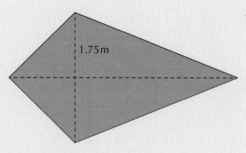
1.75 m

★ **5**   A necklace is to be made using three rhombi of identical sizes.

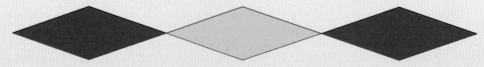

Each rhombus has diagonals measuring 1.8 cm and 0.8 cm.
What is the total area of the three rhombi?

The plural of rhombus is rhombi.

N4 **★ 6** A kite is constructed for flying with diagonals of 95 cm and 84 cm.

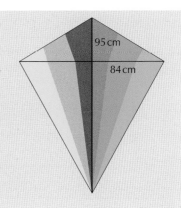

a What is the area of material required for the kite?

The kite is to be made of nylon. 1000 cm² of nylon costs £2.

b How much will the nylon cost for the kite?

The area of a parallelogram

A parallelogram is a quadrilateral (four-sided shape) with:

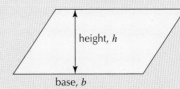

*   opposite sides parallel and of equal length

*   two pairs of equal angles

*   no lines of symmetry.

A parallelogram can be cut up and rearranged to make a rectangle with the same base and vertical height.

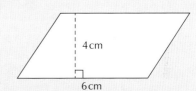

From the diagram, you can see that the area of the parallelogram can be calculated using this formula:

area = base × vertical height   or $A = bh$

Example 15.8

Calculate the area of this parallelogram.

$A = bh$

$\quad = 6 \times 4$

$\quad = 24 \, \text{cm}^2$

Exercise 15E

1 Calculate the area of each parallelogram.

a

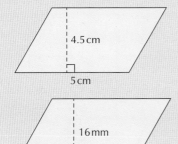

4.5 cm

5 cm

b

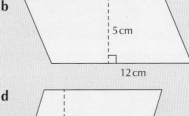

5 cm

12 cm

c

16 mm

25 mm

d

32 m

70 m

N4

e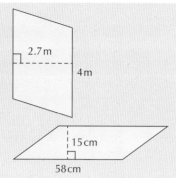

f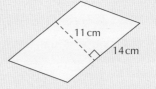

g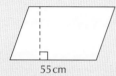

h

⚙ 2 The area of this parallelogram is 1760 cm².

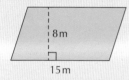

What is the height of the parallelogram?

★ 3 Haika's garden is in the shape of a parallelogram.

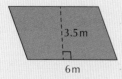

a What is the area of her garden?

⚙ Haika wants to plant grass seeds to grow a new lawn. One packet of grass seed costs £4.25 and covers 10 m².

b i How many packets does Haika need to buy?

ii How much will this cost her?

4 The floor of a room in an art gallery is in the shape of a parallelogram.

a Calculate the area of the carpet.

The carpet in the whole room is to be replaced.

a Calculate the area of the carpet.

Carpet costs £16.50 for every square metre.

⚙ **b** How much will the new carpet cost?

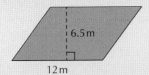

5 A flower bed in a formal garden is in the shape of a parallelogram.

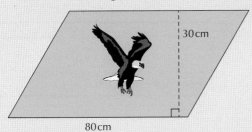

6.5 m

12 m

a Calculate the area of the flower bed.

The gardener is planning to grow special new flowers. Bags of flower seed cost £28 for a square metre.

b How much will the gardener pay to buy enough bags of flower seed to cover the whole flower bed?

6 A company's logo is in the shape of a parallelogram. They want to put up a plastic version of their logo outside their workplace.

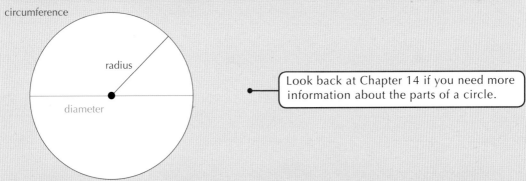

30 cm

80 cm

a Calculate the area of plastic required for the logo.

Plastic costs 50p for every 100 cm^2.

b How much will the logo cost?

Calculating the area of a circle

As seen in Chapter 14, a circle is a 2D shape in which all points on its perimeter are the same distance from the centre of the circle.

circumference

radius

diameter

> Look back at Chapter 14 if you need more information about the parts of a circle.

To calculate the area of a circle, you need to use the same number π as you used in Chapter 14 to calculate the perimeter of a circle. The area is calculated as:

area = π × radius × radius = π × radius^2   or $A = \pi r^2$

Be careful! Sometimes you will be given the diameter of the circle, so you need to be sure you find the radius first. Remember the radius is half the diameter.

N4

Example 15.9

Calculate the area of each circle below, rounding your answer to 1 decimal place.

a

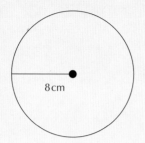

8 cm

b

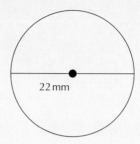

22 mm

a $A = \pi r^2$

$\quad = \pi \times 8^2$

$\quad = 201.0619...$

$\quad = 201.1\,\text{m}^2 \ (1 \text{ d.p.})$

> Round your answer to the number of decimal places stated in the question.

> ⚠ Instead of using the $\boxed{\pi}$ button, you could have used 3.14, which gives an answer of $201.0\,\text{cm}^2$.

b $A = \pi r^2$

$\quad = \pi \times 11^2$

> The diameter is 22 mm, so you need to divide this by 2 to find the length of the radius.

$\quad = 380.1327...$

$\quad = 380.1\,\text{mm}^2$

> Using 3.14 instead of π gives an answer of $379.94\,\text{mm}^2$.

Exercise 15F

1 Calculate the area of each circle. Give your answer to 1 decimal place.

a

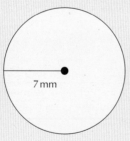

7 mm

b

3.7 m

c

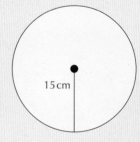

15 cm

d

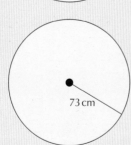

73 cm

e

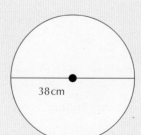

38 cm

f

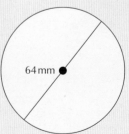

64 mm

N4

2 Calculate the area of each circle. Give your answer to 2 decimal places.

a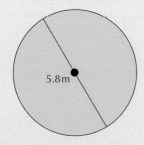

b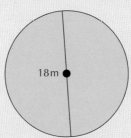

★ **3** A circular rug is to be made with radius 40 cm.

a Calculate the area of the rug. Give your answer correct to the nearest square centimetre.

The rug costs 3p for every square centimetre.

b How much does it cost to make the rug?

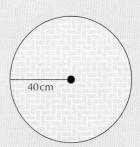

4 Dina is making a coffee table with a circular glass top.

a Calculate the area of glass required for the table top. Round your answer to the nearest 10 square centimetres.

Glass costs 4p for every 10 cm².

b How much will the table top cost Dina?

5 Zharnel is designing a large circular tile to hang on the wall.

a Calculate the area of the tile. Give your answer to the nearest square centimetre.

Tiling costs 3p for every square centimetre.

b How much will it cost to make the tile?

6 A circular grass area is built within a roundabout.

a What is the area of the grass area? Give your answer to the nearest square metre.

The council wants to plant grass seeds to grow new grass. One packet of grass seed costs £3.75 and covers 10 m².

b i How many packets do they need?

ii How much will this cost?

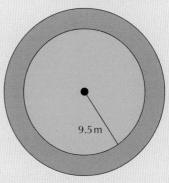

N4 ⚙ 7 The area of a circle is $95\,\text{cm}^2$.
What is the radius of the circle?
Give your answer to 1 decimal place.

⚠ Work backwards. Divide the given area by π (or 3.14), then find the square root of your answer (using the √ button on your calculator).

8 A plastic protractor is in the shape of a semicircle.

It has a diameter of 10 cm.

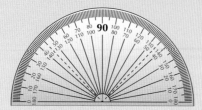

What is its area? Give your answer to 2 decimal places.

9 A pizza has a diameter of 12 cm. It is cut into 4 equal pieces.

What is the area of topping needed for each slice?

Give your answer correct to 2 decimal places.

10 A sign above a shop is in the shape of a semicircle.

The owner decides to repaint the sign.

   a What area needs to be painted? Give your answer to 1 decimal place.

One tin of paint covers $1.5\,\text{m}^2$.

   b How many tins are needed?

One tin of paint costs £2.70.

   c How much does it cost to repaint the sign?

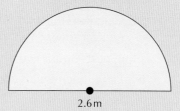
2.6 m

Calculating the area of a composite shape

A **composite 2D shape** is a shape which is made from two or more shapes (as shown in Chapter 14).

To work out the area of a composite shape, calculate the area of each shape and add them together (or subtract if a piece has been removed).

You may have to use the information given in the question to calculate any lengths not given directly.

N4

Example 15.10

Calculate the area of this composite shape.

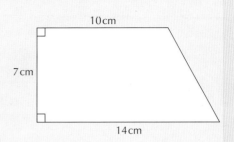

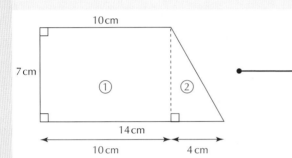

> Work out and mark the two shapes the composite shape is made from.
>
> Use the information in the diagram to work out any missing lengths.
> Base of triangle = 14 − 10 = 4 cm.

Area of rectangle ① = length × breadth

$$= 10 \times 7 = 70 \, \text{cm}^2$$

Area of triangle ② = $\frac{1}{2}$ × base × height

$$= \frac{1}{2} \times 4 \times 7 = 14 \, \text{cm}^2$$

Total area = 70 + 14 = 84 cm^2

> Add the areas together.
> State the correct units.

Example 15.11

This shape is a parallelogram with a hole in the shape of a circle.

Calculate the coloured area.

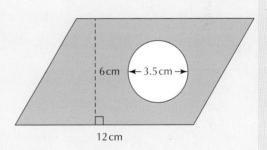

Area of parallelogram = base × height

$$= 12 \times 6 = 72 \, \text{cm}^2$$

Area of circle = πr^2

$$= \pi \times 1.75^2 = 9.6 \, \text{cm}^2$$

> Round your answer to 1 decimal place.

Coloured area = area of parallelogram − area of circle

$$= 72 - 9.6 = 62.4 \, \text{cm}^2$$

> The circle has been removed from the parallelogram, so subtract the area of the circle from the area of the parallelogram. Include the correct units.

N4   **Exercise 15G**

1   Calculate the area of each composite shape using the information given about the shapes each composite shape is made from.

   a   a rectangle and a right-angled triangle

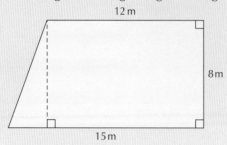

> ⚠️ Sketch each composite shape and draw a line to show the different shapes. Then work out any missing lengths.

   b   a square and a semicircle

   c   a rectangle and two right-angled triangles

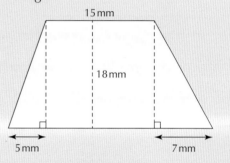

2   Calculate the area of each composite shape.

   a

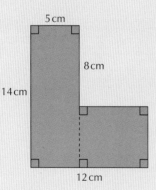

   b

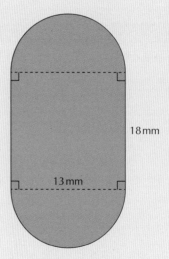

   c

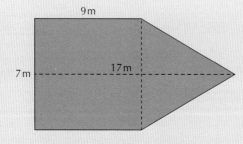

N4 3 Calculate the area of the coloured part of each shape.

a a parallelogram with a rhombus removed

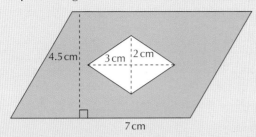

b a kite with a triangle removed

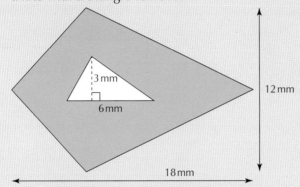

c a semicircle with a parallelogram removed

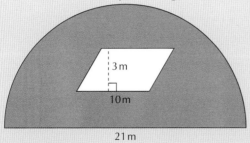

d a rhombus with a circle removed

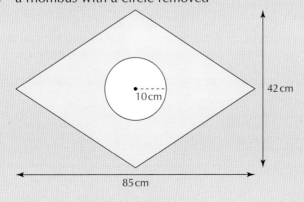

(continued)

N4

e   a rectangle with two identical circles removed

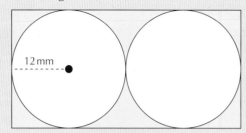

f   a parallelogram with a kite removed

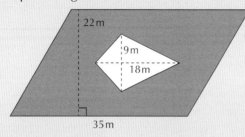

★ **4**   A rectangular wall needs to be painted. It has two windows: one is a rectangle and the other is a circle.

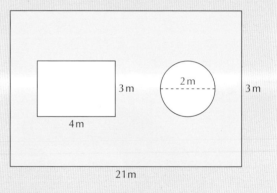

a   What is the area of the wall? Give your answer to 1 decimal place.

One tin of paint covers 8 square metres.

b   If 5 tins are bought, is this enough to paint the wall? Give a reason for your answer.

Each tin of paint costs £4.50.

c   How much will it cost to paint the wall?

GO! Activity

1   A farmer has 60 m of fence. Investigate the length and breadth of a rectangular field, using all the fencing, which would give you the largest area of field.

2   On 1 cm squared paper draw circles with radius 2 cm, 3 cm, 4 cm and 5 cm.

Use the technique on page 177 of counting squares to estimate the area of each circle. Then calculate the area of each using the formula $A = \pi r^2$.

Compare your estimates and calculated answers.

You should find that they are close, and that the bigger the circle the more accurate your estimate is likely to be.

Investigate for larger circles.

Chapter review

1 Find the area of each shape.

a

7 cm

12 cm

b

11 mm

18 mm

c

11 cm

8 cm

15 cm

2 A driveway of a house is in the shape of a rectangle.

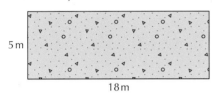

5 m

18 m

a Calculate the area of the driveway.

The surface of the driveway is to be replaced.

Resurfacing costs £26 for a square metre.

b How much will it cost for the driveway to be resurfaced?

3 The area of this rectangle is 54 cm^2. Find the breadth of the rectangle.

breadth

12 cm

N4 **4** **a** The area of this parallelogram is 527 mm². Find the length of the base of the parallelogram.

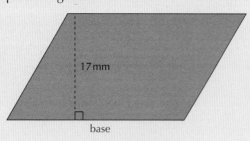

base

b The area of this rhombus is 24.48 m². Find the length of the shorter diagonal.

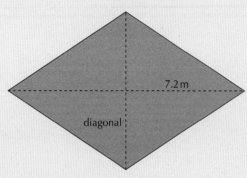

5 Find the area of each shape.

a

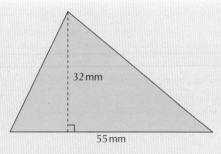

b

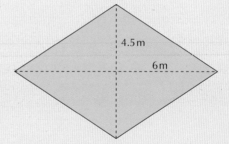

c

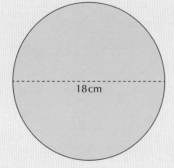

N4

6 A bathroom mirror is in the shape of a triangle.

   a What is the area of the mirror?

   Mirror glass costs 4p per cm².

   b How much does the mirror glass cost?

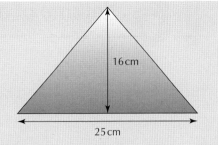

16 cm

25 cm

7 Shauna wants to paint her feature wall in a new colour. The wall is rectangular with a rectangular door and a circular window.

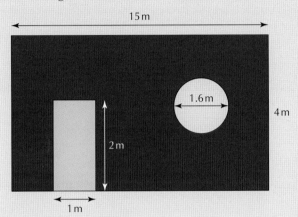

15 m

1.6 m

4 m

2 m

1 m

   a What area of wall needs to be painted? Give your answer to the nearest square metre.

   One tin of paint covers 12 square metres.

   b Shauna buys 4 tins of paint. Has she bought enough to paint the wall? Give a reason for your answer.

   c Each tin of paint costs £4.75. How much will it cost to paint the wall?

- I can calculate the area of a rectangle and square.
  ★ Exercise 15B Q2

N4
- I can calculate the area of a triangle.
  ★ Exercise 15C Q5

- I can calculate the area of a rhombus, a kite and a parallelogram. ★ Exercise 15D Q5, Q6
  ★ Exercise 15E Q3

- I can calculate the area of a circle.
  ★ Exercise 15F Q3

- I can calculate the area of a composite shape.
  ★ Exercise 15G Q4

- I can investigate a situation involving area.
  ★ Exercise 15C Q5 ★ Exercise 15D Q5, Q6
  ★ Exercise 15E Q3 ★ Exercise 15F Q3
  ★ Exercise 15G Q4

16 Volume of a 3D object

This chapter will show you how to:

- calculate and use the volume of a cuboid

N4
- calculate the volume of a prism (including a cylinder)
- investigate a situation involving the volume of a prism.

You should already know:

- how to use a formula to find the area of 2D shapes
- the properties of a cuboid

N4
- the term 'prism' and how to recognise a prism.

The volume of a cuboid

Volume is the amount of space a 3D object occupies.

Volume is measured in cubic units such as cubic centimetres (cm^3), cubic metres (m^3) and cubic millimetres (mm^3).

A cubic centimetre ($1\,cm^3$) is the volume occupied by a cube with side lengths of 1 cm.

1 cm
1 cm
1 cm

A cuboid is a 3D object with six rectangular faces. Its volume can be measured in cubic units.

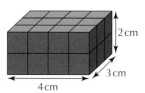
2 cm
3 cm
4 cm

In this cuboid, you can see the top layer has 12 cubes, and there are two layers, so the total volume is 24 cubes.

This volume is calculated by multiplying the length, breadth and height:

$$4 \times 3 \times 2 = 24\,cm^3$$

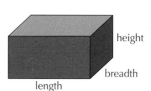
height
breadth
length

To calculate the volume of a cuboid, use this formula:

volume = length × breadth × height   or $V = lbh$

Units of measure

Metric units of volume commonly used are:

- cubic millimetres (mm^3)

- cubic centimetres (cm^3)

- cubic metres (m^3).

The **capacity** of a 3D object is the amount of liquid or gas it can hold. It is usually measured in litres, or in millilitres. These conversions will help you to solve problems involving capacity:

- $1\,cm^3 = 1$ millilitre (ml)

- 1 litre (l) = 1000 ml

- 1000 l = $1\,m^3$

Example 16.1

Find the volume of this cuboid.

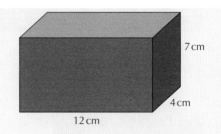

7 cm

4 cm

12 cm

$V = lbh$

$\quad = 12 \times 4 \times 7$ ●————— Substitute the values for length, breadth and height into the formula.

$\quad = 336\,cm^3$ ●————————————————— Include correct units.

Example 16.2

A fish tank is in the shape of a cuboid.

Find the volume of the tank in:

a cm^3 **b** millilitres   **c** litres.

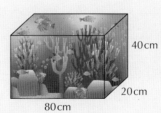

40 cm

20 cm

80 cm

a $V = lbh$

     $= 80 \times 20 \times 40$

     $= 64\,000\,cm^3$

b $64\,000\,cm^3 = 64\,000\,ml$ ●——————————— $1\,cm^3 = 1\,ml$

c $64\,000\,ml \div 1000 = 64\,l$ ●——————— 1000 ml = 1 l so divide your answer in part **b** by 1000.

Exercise 16A

1 Find the volume of each cuboid.

> ⚠ Remember to include the correct units of measure in your answers.

a

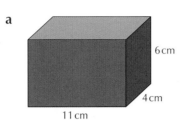

6 cm
4 cm
11 cm

b

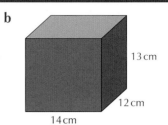

13 cm
12 cm
14 cm

c

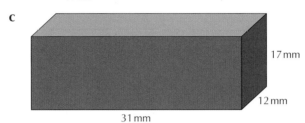

17 mm
12 mm
31 mm

d

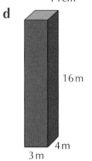

16 m
4 m
3 m

e

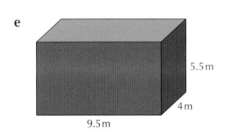

5.5 m
4 m
9.5 m

f

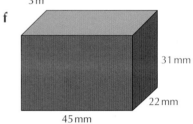

31 mm
22 mm
45 mm

2 Find the volume of each cuboid in:

    i cm³   **ii** millilitres   **iii** litres.

a

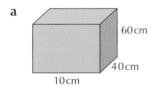

60 cm
40 cm
10 cm

b

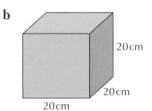

20 cm
20 cm
20 cm

c

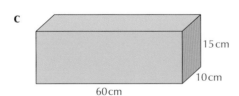

15 cm
10 cm
60 cm

d

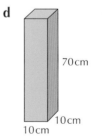

70 cm
10 cm
10 cm

e

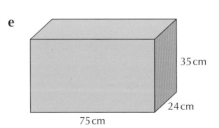

35 cm
24 cm
75 cm

f

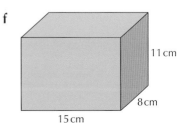

11 cm
8 cm
15 cm

3 A carton of orange juice has dimensions as shown.

    a What is its volume in millilitres?

    b If one glass holds 200 ml, how many glasses can be filled from:

        i one carton

       ii five cartons?

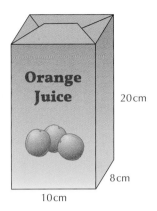

4 Calculate the height of each cuboid using the information given.

    a

$V = 1755\,cm^3$

height

9 cm

15 cm

> Work backwards to find the height. Divide the volume by (length × breadth).

    b

$V = 10\,800\,ml$

height

15 cm

24 cm

    c

$V = 3.2\,litres$

height

10 cm

20 cm

> Change the volume into cm^3 before carrying out the calculation.

5 A swimming pool is in the shape of a cuboid.

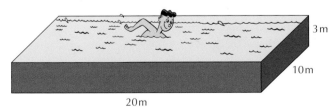

3 m

10 m

20 m

    a Calculate the volume of the swimming pool. Give your answer in cubic metres.

    b Calculate the volume of the swimming pool in litres.

> $1\,m^3 = 1000\,l$

6 a i Calculate the volume of this shoebox.

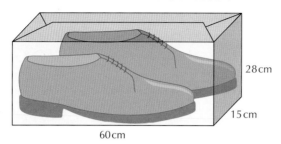

28 cm
15 cm
60 cm

ii What is the volume of a shoebox which has twice the volume?

b i Calculate the volume of this tissue box.

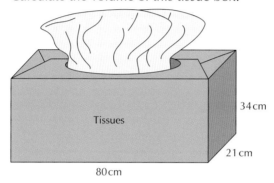

34 cm
21 cm
Tissues
80 cm

ii What is the volume of a tissue box which holds three times the amount of tissues?

c i Calculate the volume of this cotton wool box.

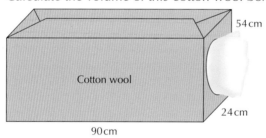

54 cm
Cotton wool
24 cm
90 cm

ii What is the volume of a box which holds four times the amount of cotton wool?

d i Calculate the volume of this box of printer paper.

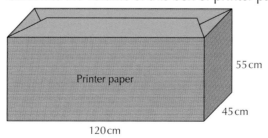

55 cm
Printer paper
45 cm
120 cm

ii What is the volume of a box which holds twice the amount of paper?

★ **7** The diagram shows a water tank.

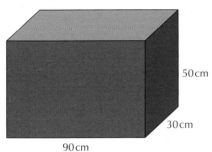

50 cm
30 cm
90 cm

a Calculate its volume in cm^3.

b What is its volume in litres?

A bucket has a capacity of 2.5 litres.

c How many buckets of water would it take to fill the tank?

N4 ## The volume of a prism

A **prism** is a 3D object with the same 2D shape at each end. The same 2D shape is also called the **cross-section** of the prism.

A prism is named using the name of the 2D shape of the cross-section, followed by the word 'prism'.

For example, this is a triangular prism:

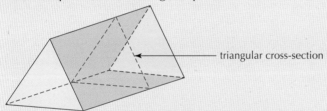

triangular cross-section

And this is a pentagonal prism:

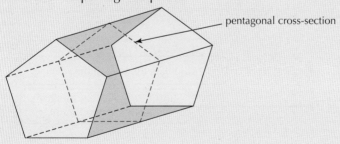

pentagonal cross-section

The volume of any prism can be found by multiplying the area of the cross-section by the length of the prism.

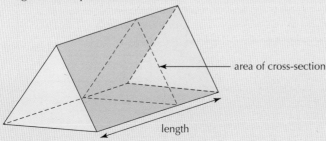

area of cross-section

length

To calculate the volume of a prism, use this formula:

volume = area of cross-section × length   or $V = Al$

N4

Example 16.3

Calculate the volume of this hexagonal prism.

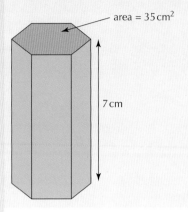

area = 35 cm²

7 cm

$V = Al$

$\quad = 35 \times 7$ ●————— Substitute the values for area and length into formula.

$\quad = 245\ cm^3$ ●————— State the correct units.

Example 16.4

Calculate the volume of this triangular prism.

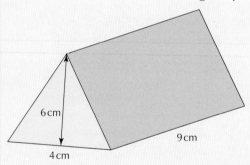

6 cm

9 cm

4 cm

Area of triangular face $= \frac{1}{2}bh$ ●————— First calculate the area of the triangle.

$\qquad = \frac{1}{2} \times 4 \times 6$ ●————— Substitute the values for base and height into the formula.

$\qquad = \frac{1}{2} \times 24$

$\qquad = 12\ cm^2$

$V = Al$ ●————— Use your answer for the area of the triangle, and substitute the length into the formula.

$\quad = 12 \times 9$

$\quad = 108\ cm^3$ ●————— State the correct units.

N4 **Exercise 16B**

1 Find the volume of each prism.

a

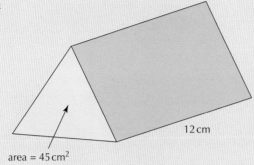

12 cm

area = 45 cm²

b

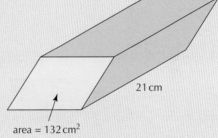

16 mm

area = 78 mm²

c

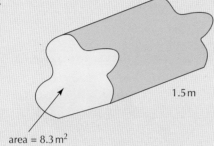

1.5 m

area = 8.3 m²

d

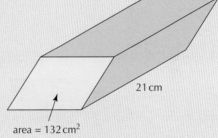

21 cm

area = 132 cm²

e

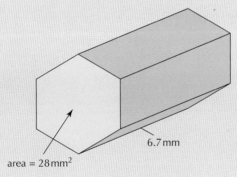

6.7 mm

area = 28 mm²

f

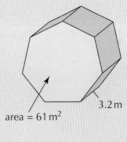

3.2 m

area = 61 m²

2 Calculate the volume of each triangular prism.

a

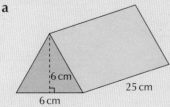

6 cm

6 cm

25 cm

b

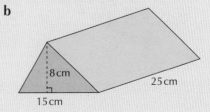

8 cm

15 cm

25 cm

(continued)

N4

c

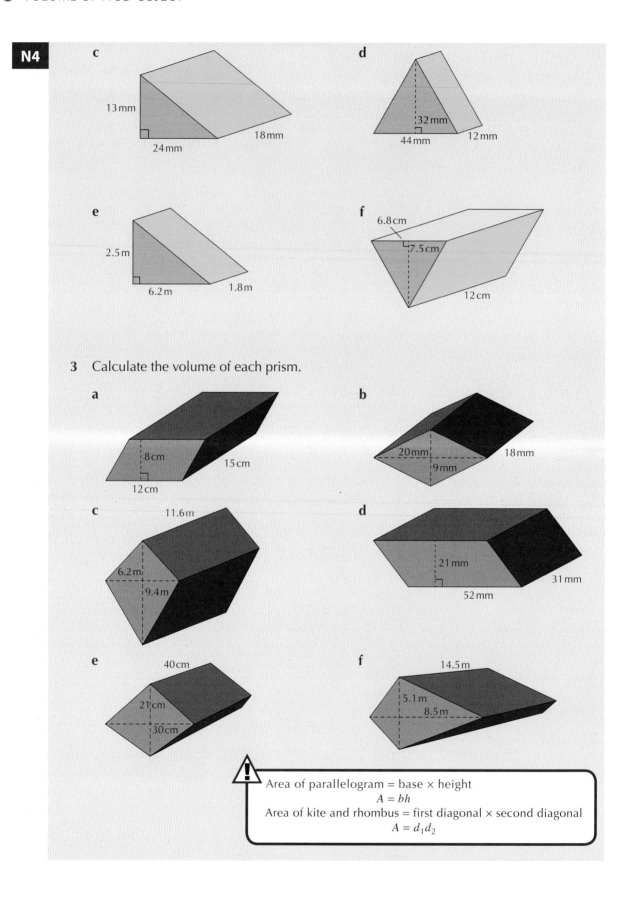

13 mm
24 mm
18 mm

d

32 mm
44 mm
12 mm

e

2.5 m
6.2 m
1.8 m

f

6.8 cm
7.5 cm
12 cm

3 Calculate the volume of each prism.

a

8 cm
15 cm
12 cm

b

20 mm
9 mm
18 mm

c

11.6 m
6.2 m
9.4 m

d

21 mm
52 mm
31 mm

e

40 cm
21 cm
30 cm

f

14.5 m
5.1 m
8.5 m

⚠️ Area of parallelogram = base × height
$A = bh$
Area of kite and rhombus = first diagonal × second diagonal
$A = d_1 d_2$

N4 4 Find the volume of each prism.

a

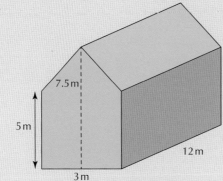

First you need to work out the area of the composite shape of the cross-section. Look at Chapter 15 pages 194–195 to remind you how to calculate the area of a composite shape.

b

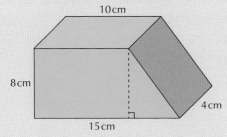

c

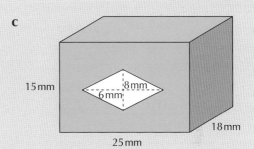

5 Calculate the volume of this door wedge.

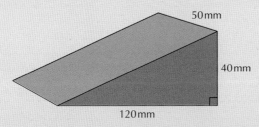

6 A swimming pool is in the shape of a prism.

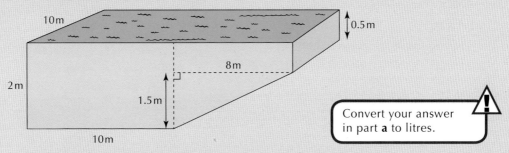

Convert your answer in part **a** to litres.

a Calculate the volume of the swimming pool in cubic metres.

One litre of water weighs 1 kilogram.

b What is the weight of the water in the swimming pool?

N4 ★ 7 Sandra makes candles in the shape of a triangular prism.

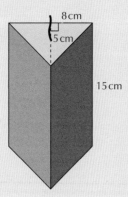

8 cm

5 cm

15 cm

a Calculate the volume of one candle.

She buys wax in 6-litre tubs.

b How many candles can she make out of one tub?

The volume of a cylinder

A **cylinder** is a prism with circular faces and a circular cross-section.

There are two methods you can use to calculate the volume of a cylinder.

radius

length (height)

Method 1

Method 1 uses the same formula that was used to calculate the volume of a prism.

Calculate the area first.

The area A is the area of the circle which forms the ends of the cylinder, and is given by the formula:

$A = \pi r^2$

Then use the formula for the volume of a prism:

$V = Al$

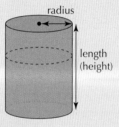

r

A

l

Method 2

Method 2 combines the two formulae in Method 1 into a single formula:

$V = \pi r^2 l$

The length l is often expressed as the height h, so the formula is written as:

$V = \pi r^2 h$

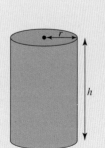

r

h

N4 Example 16.5

Calculate the volume of this cylinder. Give your answer to 1 decimal place.

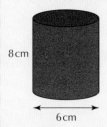

8 cm

6 cm

Method 1

$A = \pi r^2$

$= \pi \times 3^2$ •————

$= 28.274... \text{cm}^2$ •

$V = Al$

$= 28.274... \times 8$

$= 226.2 \text{cm}^3 \ (1 \text{ d.p.})$ •

Remember to use the radius (divide the diameter by 2).

Make sure you don't round to the required accuracy until the end of the answer.

Round to the number of places given in the question and state the correct units. If you used 3.14 instead of using the $\boxed{\pi}$ button, the answer is 226.1cm^3.

Method 2

$V = \pi r^2 h$

$= \pi \times 3^2 \times 8$

$= 226.2 \text{cm}^3$

Exercise 16C

Throughout this exercise, round your answers to 1 decimal place unless otherwise stated.

1   In each of these cylinders, the area of the circular face has been given to you. Calculate the volume of each cylinder.

a   area = 28.27 cm²

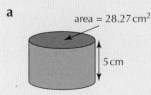

5 cm

b   12 mm

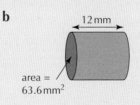

area = 63.6 mm²

c   area = 13.9 m²

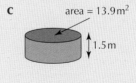

1.5 m

N4

2 Calculate the volume of each cylinder.

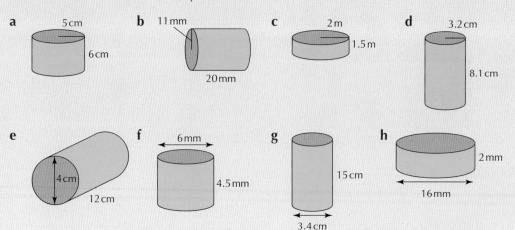

a 5 cm, 6 cm   **b** 11 mm, 20 mm   **c** 2 m, 1.5 m   **d** 3.2 cm, 8.1 cm

e 4 cm, 12 cm   **f** 6 mm, 4.5 mm   **g** 15 cm, 3.4 cm   **h** 2 mm, 16 mm

3 A plastic water pipe of length 450 cm has an outside diameter of 40 cm and an inside diameter of 35 cm.

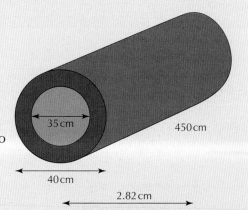

a Calculate the volume of plastic used to make the pipe. Give your answer correct to the nearest thousand cm^3.

b What is the maximum capacity of the pipe? Give your answer in litres, correct to the nearest litre.

★ **4** A coin has a diameter of 2.82 cm and a thickness of 0.21 cm.

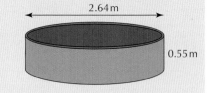

a Calculate the volume of the coin. Give your answer correct to 2 decimal places.

The coin is made of nickel brass.
1 cm^3 of nickel brass weighs 8.4 g.

b Calculate the weight of the coin. Give your answer correct to 2 decimal places.

5 The diagram shows a cylindrical paddling pool.

a Calculate the volume of the paddling pool. Give your answer in m^3 to 2 decimal places.

b If the pool is only half full of water, what is the volume of water in:

   i litres (to the nearest 10 litres)

   ii millilitres (to the nearest 10000 millilitres).

c If one bucket holds 10 litres, how many buckets of water will be needed to fill the paddling pool to half full?

N4

6   An urn for boiling water is in the shape of a cylinder.

50 cm

110 cm

a   Calculate the volume of the urn. Give your answer to the nearest thousand cm³.

b   If one mug of tea holds 240 ml, how many cups of tea can be poured from the full urn?

7   A wooden candle holder is made by drilling a cylindrical hole into a cube as shown in the diagram.

The cube has side length 5 cm and the cylinder has a diameter of 3.8 cm and a height of 5 cm.

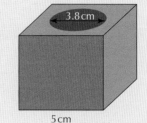

3.8 cm

5 cm

a   Calculate the volume of the original cube.

b   Calculate the volume of the cylindrical hole drilled out.

c   Calculate the volume of wood remaining.

8 a   A cylinder has a capacity of 1 litre.

Its base has an area of 113 cm².

What is its height? Give your answer correct to 2 decimal places.

A cylinder has a capacity of 10 litres.

It has a height of 20 cm.

b   Calculate:

   i   the area of the base

   ii   the radius of the base. Give your answer to 1 decimal place.

Draw a sketch if it helps. Work backwards to find the height. Remember to change litres into cm³.

Work backwards by dividing the capacity by 20. Check that you don't mix units of measure.

Work backwards by dividing by π then taking the square root of your answer.

GO! Activity

1   Find cuboids, prisms and cylinders in your classroom or at home.

Estimate their volume, then measure.

Were your estimates close?

2   The surface area of a shape is the area of all the surfaces added together.

Using cuboids of packaging (for example, cereal boxes or juice cartons), investigate the packaging which gives the largest volume and the smallest surface area.

Think about why manufacturers might want to combine the least surface area with the greatest volume.

Chapter review

1   Calculate the volume of each 3D shape.

a

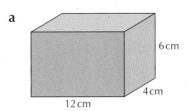

N4

b

c

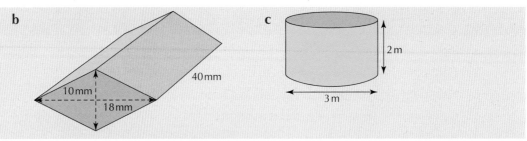

2   A paddling pool is in the shape of a cuboid.

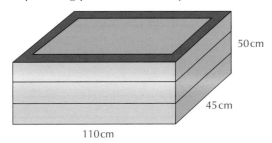

a   Find the volume of the paddling pool in:

   i   cm^3 **ii**   millilitres   **iii**   litres.

b   If the pool is only half full of water, what volume of water is in the pool?
        Give your answer in litres.

N4   3   A water tank is in the shape of a cylinder.

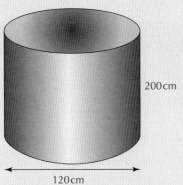

a   Find the volume of the water tank in:

   i   cm^3 (round your answer to the nearest cm^3)

   ii   millilitres   (round your answer to the nearest ml)

   iii   litres   (round to the nearest litre).

A bucket has a volume of 20 litres.

b   How many buckets of water would it take to fill the tank?

N4

4 Chocolate sweets are cylindrical in shape.

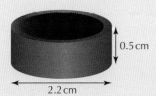

0.5 cm

2.2 cm

a What is the volume of one sweet? Give your answer correct to 1 decimal place.

A larger chocolate block is in the shape of a triangular prism.

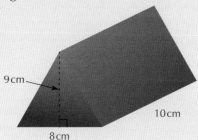

9 cm

10 cm

8 cm

b What is the volume of the chocolate block?

The chocolate block is melted and made into the cylindrical sweets.

c How many sweets can be made from the block of chocolate?

- I can calculate and use the volume of a cuboid.
  ★ Exercise 16A Q7

N4

- I can calculate the volume of a prism (including a cylinder). ★ Exercise 16B Q7 ★ Exercise 16C Q4

- I can investigate a situation involving the volume of a prism. ★ Exercise 16B Q7 ★ Exercise 16C Q4

17 Scale factors

Scale factor

A **scale factor** is a number which multiplies (or scales) a quantity.

A scale factor can be used to enlarge a length or height, an area, or a volume or a mass.

Multiplying a quantity by a number bigger than 1 **enlarges** the quantity, and multiplying a quantity by a number between 0 and 1 **reduces** the quantity.

Example 17.1

The rectangle shown is enlarged by a scale factor of 2. Draw the enlarged rectangle.

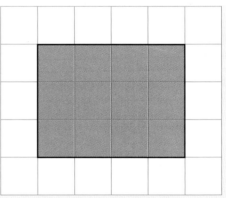

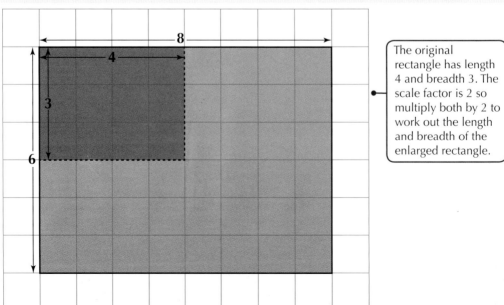

The original rectangle has length 4 and breadth 3. The scale factor is 2 so multiply both by 2 to work out the length and breadth of the enlarged rectangle.

Example 17.2

A shop sells a milk jug in two sizes.

One jug holds 385 ml of milk.

The second jug holds 3 times the amount of milk.

How much milk does the second jug hold?

$385 \times 3 = 1155\,\text{ml}$ •————————

The scale factor is 3 so multiply the first amount by 3. Include units.

Example 17.3

A supermarket sells bags of pasta in two different sizes.

One bag weighs 884 g.

The second bag weighs $\frac{1}{4}$ of the weight of the larger bag.

What is the weight of the smaller bag?

$\frac{1}{4}$ of $884 = 884 \div 4$ •————

Finding a quarter of a quantity means dividing by 4.

$\qquad = 221\,\text{g}$

Exercise 17A

1   A coffee shop sells two sizes of coffee cup. One cup holds 230 ml. The second cup holds twice the volume of the smaller cup.

What is the volume of the larger cup?

2   A company makes two sizes of packets of biscuits. One packet weighs 328 g. The second packet weighs $\frac{1}{2}$ of the weight of the larger bag.

What is the weight of the smaller packet?

3   A small van has a capacity of $5.5 \, \text{m}^3$. A larger van has a capacity 3 times the size of the smaller van.

What is the capacity of the larger van?

4   Jim's garden has an area of $168 \, \text{m}^2$. His granny's garden is $\frac{1}{3}$ the size of Jim's garden.

What is the area of Jim's granny's garden?

5   Shona's phone has a memory of 16 GB. She upgrades her phone, and the new phone has a memory 8 times the size of her old phone.

What is the memory of her new phone?

6   A tree has a height of 14 metres. A second tree is planted nearby and its height is $\frac{1}{4}$ of the height of the larger tree.

What is the height of the second tree?

★ 7   A storage box in the shape of a cuboid has dimensions 30 cm, 40 cm and 50 cm.

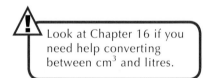
Look at Chapter 16 if you need help converting between cm^3 and litres.

a   What is its volume in cm^3?

b   What is the volume of this box in litres?

A second storage box has a volume twice the size of the first box.

c   What is its volume?

8   A rectangular carpet has dimensions 8 m and 5.5 m.

a   What is the area of the carpet?

A second rectangular carpet has an area $\frac{1}{2}$ the size of the original carpet.

b   What is the area of the new carpet?

9   A taxi driver picks up his first passenger and travels 4.5 miles. The second passenger he picks up travels 3 times the distance of the first passenger.

What distance does the taxi driver drive his second passenger?

10   Freda buys two cabbages. The first one weighs 800 g.

The second weighs $1\frac{1}{2}$ times the weight of the first cabbage.

What is the weight of the second cabbage?

11 A goldfish pond in the shape of a cuboid has dimensions 11 m by 9 m by 2 m.

    a What is the volume of the pond?

    A second goldfish pond has $\frac{2}{3}$ of the volume of the first pond.

    b What is the volume of the second pond?

12 A design engineer makes a model robot as a prototype before making the full-sized robot. The height of the model robot is 41 cm. The full-sized model is to be made $3\frac{1}{2}$ times the height of the model.

    What is the height of the full-sized robot?

13 A mountain in Scotland has a height of 1200 m. A mountain in Asia has a height of 7200 m.

    How many times the height of the Scottish mountain is the Asian mountain?

N4   Scale factor of two similar shapes

Two shapes are described as **similar** if one is a direct enlargement or reduction of the other.

For example, the following rectangles are similar:

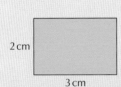
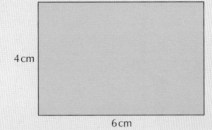

The length and breadth of the second rectangle are twice the length and breadth of the first rectangle. (The rectangle on the left has been enlarged by a scale factor of 2.)

Example 17.4

These rectangles are mathematically similar.

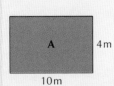
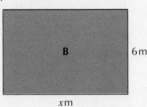

  a Work out the scale factor of enlargement from **A** to **B**.

  b Calculate x, the missing length in **B**.

  a Scale factor $= \dfrac{6}{4} = \dfrac{3}{2}$ (or 1.5)

> Identify the corresponding lengths which are 6 m and 4 m, then make a fraction with these numbers. This is the scale factor.

  b $x = \dfrac{3}{2} \times 10$

      $= 15$ m

> Multiply the scale factor by the length of the side corresponding to x, which is 10 m.
>
> Remember to multiply by the numerator and divide by the denominator.

N4

Using scale factor

To find the scale factor of **enlargement** of two similar shapes:

- identify two corresponding sides and note their lengths

- make a fraction: scale factor = $\dfrac{\text{new length}}{\text{original length}}$

To find the scale factor of **reduction** of two similar shapes:

- identify two corresponding sides and note their lengths

- make a fraction: scale factor = $\dfrac{\text{new length}}{\text{original length}}$

 To check you have used the correct numbers to make your scale factor (SF):
SF > 1 for enlargements and SF < 1 for reductions.

You can use your scale factor to calculate a missing length.

Example 17.5

A print and a postcard of a painting are mathematically similar.

40 cm

24 cm

15 cm

y cm

a Find the scale factor of reduction.

b Find y, the missing length on the postcard.

a Scale factor = $\dfrac{15}{40} = \dfrac{3}{8}$

Identify the corresponding lengths which are 15 cm and 40 cm. Make a fraction with the new length as the numerator. This is a reduction so the scale factor will be less than 1.

b $y = \dfrac{3}{8} \times 24$

$= 9$ cm

Multiply the scale factor by the length of the side corresponding to y, which is 24 cm.

N4

Exercise 17B

1 Each pair of shapes is similar. For each pair:

    i find the scale factor of enlargement

    ii calculate the length of the side labelled with a letter.

a

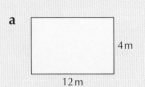 

b

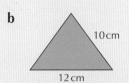 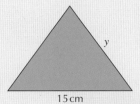

c

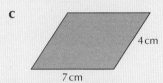 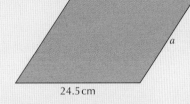

d

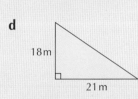 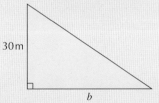

2 Each pair of shapes is similar. For each pair:

    i find the scale factor of reduction

    ii calculate the length of the side labelled with a letter.

a

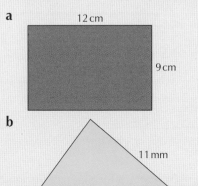 

b

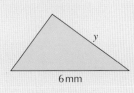

(continued)

N4

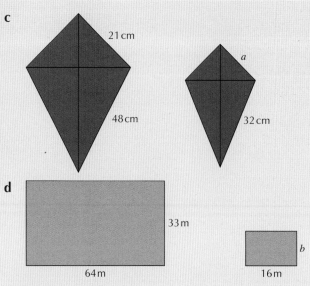

c 21 cm 48 cm a 32 cm

d 33 m 64 m 16 m b

★ **3** The dimensions of a car are shown.

height 127.5 cm

length 420 cm

A toy company makes a model of the car with length 56 cm.

a What is the scale factor of reduction to make the model car?

b What is the height of the model?

★ **4** Blackpool Tower is 158 metres in height. A model of Blackpool Tower is 79 cm tall.

a What is the scale factor of enlargement from the model to the actual tower?

b If one of the lengths of the square base of the model is 5 cm, what is the measurement of the square base of Blackpool Tower in real life?

Make sure that your measurements are in the same units before you calculate scale factor.

5 An 8-metre tree has a shadow of length 3 metres. Ben is standing next to the tree. Ben is 1.6 metres tall.

What is the length of his shadow?

Draw a sketch to help you, and find the scale factor of reduction from the tree's height to Ben's height.

6 A tourist shop in Edinburgh has two models of the Scott Monument.

The larger model has a base of length 16 cm and a height of 30 cm.

The smaller model has a height of 18 cm.

a What is the scale factor of reduction from the larger model to the smaller model?

b What is the length of the base of the smaller model?

N4 **7** The Nagoya TV Tower in Japan is mathematically similar to the Eiffel Tower.

The Eiffel Tower is 300 m tall and the Nagoya Tower is 200 m tall.

   a   **i**   What is the scale factor of enlargement from the Nagoya Tower to the Eiffel Tower?

      ii   What is the scale factor of reduction from the Eiffel Tower to the Nagoya Tower?

   b   If the length of the square base of the Nagoya Tower is 83 m, what is the length of the square base of the Eiffel Tower?

8 Two photos are mathematically similar. One photo's dimensions are 8 cm and 6 cm. A second photograph has one of its dimensions as 12 cm.

 12 cm could be either the length or the breadth of the second photo.

Calculate two possible measurements of the other dimension of the second photo.

9 Cloaks for a school show were found to be too large for some pupils.

The costume designer asked for some cloaks to be reduced by a scale factor of $\frac{4}{5}$.

The original cloaks had a breadth of 50 cm and a height of 1.4 m.

What are the measurements of the new cloaks?

10 A building is planned to fit into a space with length 40 m. However, when the land is purchased, only 35 m in length can be built on. The plans need to be adjusted to produce a building mathematically similar to the original building.

   a   What is the scale factor of reduction from the original building to the new building?

   b   What is the new breadth if the breadth was originally planned to be 34 m?

11 Alishba takes a photograph which measures 6 cm by 4 cm when printed.

4 cm

6 cm

18 cm

28 cm

Alishba would like a direct enlargement of her photograph to fit exactly into a frame she previously bought.

Will an enlargement fit exactly into this frame? Give a reason for your answer.

 **Activity**

1 a Find the area of this rectangle:

2 cm

6 cm

b Enlarge all the sides by a scale factor of 2, and calculate the area of the new rectangle.

c Repeat this for an enlargement of scale factor 3.

d Try for other enlargements and reductions.

What is the connection between the scale factor and enlargement/reduction of the area?

2 a Find the volume of this cuboid:

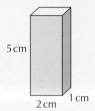

5 cm

2 cm   1 cm

b Enlarge each of the sides by a scale factor of 2, and calculate the volume of the new cuboid.

c Repeat this for an enlargement of scale factor 3.

d Try for other enlargement/reductions.

What is the connection between the scale factor and enlargement/reduction of the volume?

Chapter review

1 A shop sells two sizes of mug. One holds 180 ml of liquid. The second holds twice the amount of liquid.

How much does the second mug hold?

2 A shoe box in the shape of a cuboid has dimensions 20 cm, 30 cm and 15 cm.

a What is its volume in cm^3?

b What is the volume of this box in litres?

A children's shoe box has a volume $\frac{1}{3}$ of the volume of the first box.

c What is its volume?

N4

3   The three ornamental giraffes shown below are mathematically similar. The middle giraffe is 24 cm in height.

a   The largest giraffe is $\frac{5}{3}$ of the height of the middle giraffe. What is its height?

b   The smallest giraffe is $\frac{3}{4}$ of the height of the middle giraffe. What is its height?

4   An architect makes a model of a house. The length of the base of the model is 72 cm and the actual building has a base of 900 cm.

a   What is the scale factor of enlargement?

b   If the height of the model is 28 cm, what is the actual height of the building?

- I can apply a basic scale factor to solve a problem.
  ★ Exercise 17A Q7

N4

- I can calculate the scale factor, given the dimensions of two similar objects. ★ Exercise 17B Q3, Q4

- I can use a scale factor to work out a missing length.
  ★ Exercise 17B Q3, Q4

18 Simple patterns

This chapter will show you how to:

- repeat and continue a pattern involving numbers
- repeat and continue a pattern involving shapes.

You should already know:

- how to add and subtract integers
- how to find missing terms in a sequence and explain the rule.

Number sequences

A set of ordered numbers is a **sequence**. Each number in a sequence is called a **term**.

Each term in a sequence can be found by applying a **rule** to get the next term.

Example 18.1

For the number sequence 2, 4, 6, 8, ...

a write down the rule to find the next term

b find the next three terms.

a 2   4   6   8   Rule: add 2.

$+2$ $+2$ $+2$ ● ───────── *Look at the sequence. If it is **increasing**, calculate the number you need to **add** each time.*

b $8 + 2 = 10$ ●───────── *Add 2 to last term given.*

$10 + 2 = 12$ ●───────── *Add 2 to your new term. Repeat this to find the following terms.*

$12 + 2 = 14$

The next three terms are 10, 12, 14.

Example 18.2

For the number sequence 4, 7, 10, 13, ...

a write down the rule to find the next term

b find the next three terms.

a 4   7   10   13   Rule: add 3.

$+3$ $+3$ $+3$

b $13 + 3 = 16$ ●───────── *Add 3 to last term given.*

$16 + 3 = 19$

$19 + 3 = 22$

The next three terms are 16, 19, 22.

Example 18.3

For the number sequence 60, 55, 50, 45, …

a write down the rule to find the next term

b find the next three terms.

a 60   55   50   45   Rule: subtract 5.

−5   −5   −5   •———— Look at the sequence. If it is **decreasing**, calculate the number you need to **subtract** each time.

b 45 − 5 = 40 •———— Subtract 5 from last term given.

40 − 5 = 35 •———— Subtract 5 from your new term. Repeat this to find the following terms.

35 − 5 = 30

The next three terms are 40, 35, 30.

Exercise 18A

★ **1** For each sequence, describe the rule and find the next three terms in the sequence.

a 1, 3, 5, 7, 9, …	**b** 3, 6, 9, 12, 15, …	**c** 4, 6, 8, 10, 12, …
d 5, 7, 9, 11, …	**e** 11, 14, 17, 20, …	**f** 15, 21, 27, 33, …
g 13, 25, 37, 49, …	**h** 200, 250, 300, 350, …	**i** 54, 75, 96, 117, …
j 19, 17, 15, 13, …	**k** 33, 29, 25, 21, …	**l** 54, 49, 44, 39, …
m 850, 750, 650, 550, …	**n** 76, 63, 50, 37, …	**o** 87, 80, 73, 66, …

2 Use each rule and first term to make the first four terms of a sequence.

a First term: 13. Rule: add 4

b First term: 32. Rule: add 7

c First term: 74. Rule: add 15

d First term: 120. Rule: add 60

e First term: 35. Rule: subtract 6

f First term: 67. Rule: subtract 9

g First term: 96. Rule: subtract 14

h First term: 340. Rule: subtract 70

For part **a**: 13 + 4 = 17
17 + 4 = 21
and so on.

3 Fill in the gaps in these sequences.

a 12, 15, _____, _____, 24, …

b 23, _____, 37, 44, _____, …

c _____, 25, 34, _____, 52, …

d _____, _____, 17, 23, _____, 35, …

e 37, 33, _____, _____, 21, …

f 90, _____, 68, 57, _____, …

g _____, 90, 65, _____, 15, …

h _____, _____, 380, 310, _____, 170, …

Extending a shape pattern

Shape patterns use shapes instead of numbers to create sequences. You might be given a shape pattern of at least three patterns, where either a shape or part of a shape is added each time.

To work out how to extend the sequence, you need to look at the existing pattern and work out what is being added on to the pattern from one picture to the next. You then need to draw the next pattern in the sequence.

Example 18.4

Matches are arranged in a pattern of squares to create a sequence.

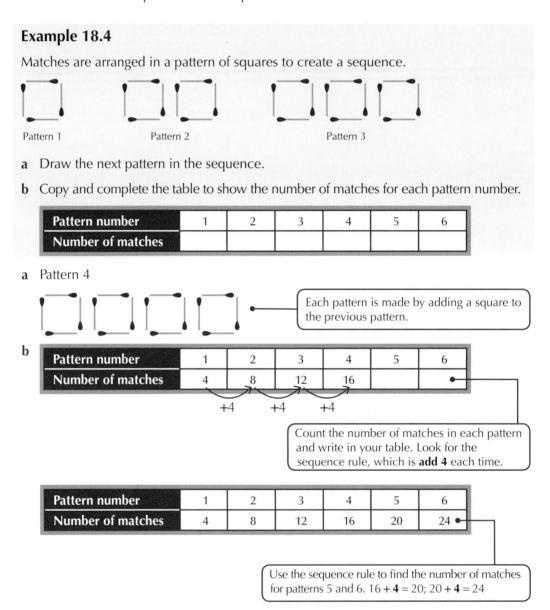

Pattern 1   Pattern 2   Pattern 3

a Draw the next pattern in the sequence.

b Copy and complete the table to show the number of matches for each pattern number.

Pattern number	1	2	3	4	5	6
Number of matches						

a Pattern 4

Each pattern is made by adding a square to the previous pattern.

b

Pattern number	1	2	3	4	5	6
Number of matches	4	8	12	16		

+4   +4   +4

Count the number of matches in each pattern and write in your table. Look for the sequence rule, which is **add 4** each time.

Pattern number	1	2	3	4	5	6
Number of matches	4	8	12	16	20	24

Use the sequence rule to find the number of matches for patterns 5 and 6. $16 + \mathbf{4} = 20$; $20 + \mathbf{4} = 24$

Example 18.5

A pattern of triangles is made with metal rods.

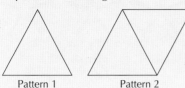

Pattern 1   Pattern 2   Pattern 3

a Draw the next pattern in the sequence.

b Copy and complete the table to show the number of rods for each pattern number.

Pattern number	1	2	3	4	5	6
Number of rods						

a Pattern 4

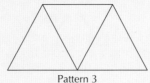

> Each pattern is made by adding two rods to the previous pattern and making a new triangle.

b

Pattern number	1	2	3	4	5	6
Number of rods	3	5	7	9		

+2   +2   +2

> Count the number of rods in each pattern and write in your table.
> Look for the sequence rule, which is **add 2** each time.

Pattern number	1	2	3	4	5	6
Number of rods	3	5	7	9	11	13

> Use the sequence rule to find the number of rods for patterns 5 and 6.
> $9 + 2 = 11$; $11 + 2 = 13$

Exercise 18B

★ **1** A pattern is made with matches.

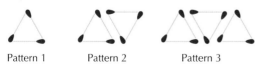

Pattern 1   Pattern 2   Pattern 3

a Draw the next pattern in the sequence.

b Copy and complete the table to show the number of matches for each pattern number.

Pattern number	1	2	3	4	5	6
Number of matches						

2 A pattern is made with pencils.

Pattern 1   Pattern 2   Pattern 3

a Draw the next pattern in the sequence.

b Copy and complete the table to show the number of pencils for each pattern number.

Pattern number	1	2	3	4	5	6
Number of pencils						

3 For each of the sets of patterns of pencils shown below:

    i draw the fourth pattern

    ii copy and complete the table to show the number of pencils for each pattern number.

Pattern number	1	2	3	4	5	6
Number of pencils						

a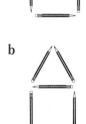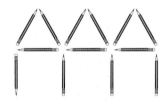

b

c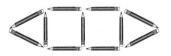

d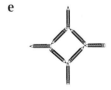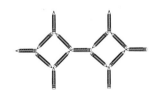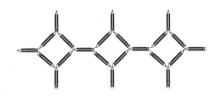

e

★ 4 The diagram shows how chairs can be arranged around different sized tables in a café.

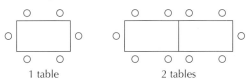 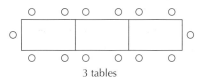

1 table   2 tables   3 tables

a Draw the pattern for 4 tables.

b Copy and complete the table to show the numbers of chairs.

Number of tables	1	2	3	4	5	6
Number of chairs						

5 The diagram shows how chairs are arranged around different sized tables in a conference centre.

 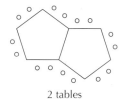 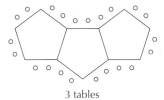

1 table   2 tables   3 tables

a Draw the pattern for 4 tables.

b Copy and complete the table to show the numbers of chairs.

Number of tables	1	2	3	4	5	6
Number of chairs						

6 A fence is constructed with vertical posts and horizontal panels.

 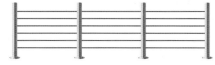

2 posts   3 posts   4 posts

a Draw the pattern for 5 posts.

b Copy and complete the table to show the numbers of panels.

Number of posts	2	3	4	5	6	7
Number of panels						

7   A jewellery designer uses silver rods to make patterns for his jewellery.

Pattern 1   Pattern 2   Pattern 3

a   Draw the fourth pattern.

b   Copy and complete the table to show the number of silver rods.

Pattern number	1	2	3	4	5	6
Number of silver rods						

Activity

1   The Fibonacci sequence is generated by adding the two previous terms in the sequence.

Continue this sequence for the next 15 terms. (You don't need to use different colours!)

$$0 + 1 = 1$$
$$1 + 1 = 2$$
$$2 + 1 = 3$$
$$3 + 2 = 5$$
$$5 + 3 = 8$$

2   The diagram shows Pascal's triangle.

Spot the pattern and see if you can continue the pattern for at least two more rows.

```
          1
       1     1
     1    2    1
   1    3    3    1
 1    4    6    4    1
```

3   Look at this sequence of patterns of dots.

Pattern 1   Pattern 2   Pattern 3

a   Draw the fourth pattern.

b   Copy and complete the table to show the numbers of dots.

Pattern number	1	2	3	4	5	6
Number of dots						

c   Can you explain the rule for this pattern?

d   These numbers are called square numbers. Why do you think they are given this name?

4 Look at this sequence of patterns of dots.

 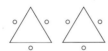 

Pattern 1   Pattern 2   Pattern 3

a Draw the fourth pattern.

b Copy and complete the table to show the numbers of dots.

Pattern number	1	2	3	4	5	6
Number of dots						

c Can you explain the rule for this pattern?

d These numbers are called triangular numbers. Why do you think they are called this?

Chapter review

1 For each sequence, describe the rule and use this to find the next three terms:

a 4, 8, 12, 16, 20, …   b 7, 13, 19, 25, 31, …   c 78, 71, 64, 57, 50, …

2 Fill in the gaps in these sequences.

a 11, 15, _____, _____, 27, …   b 58, _____, 48, 43, _____, …

3 The diagram shows how chairs are arranged round different sized tables in a café.

  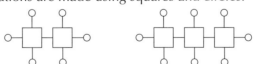

a Draw the fourth pattern.

b Copy and complete the table to show the numbers of chairs.

Number of tables	1	2	3	4	5	6
Number of chairs						

4 Christmas decorations are made using squares and circles:

a Draw the fourth pattern.

b Copy and complete the table to show the numbers of circles.

Number of squares	1	2	3	4	5	6
Number of circles						

- I can repeat and continue a pattern involving numbers. ★ Exercise 18A Q1

- I can repeat and continue a pattern involving shapes. ★ Exercise 18B Q1

19 Carry out container packing

This chapter will show you how to:

N4

- pack items into a container or storage space
- find the most efficient packing solution
- use the first-fit algorithm to carry out container packing.

You should already know:

- how to fit quantities of an item into a given space.

N4

Packing items

Packing items into a box, case or storage space efficiently is an important skill to learn in everyday life. Efficient packing and storing means that you don't use up space unnecessarily. This is essential for businesses: if they can reduce the cost of storage and transport of goods, they can increase their profit.

To store items, you need to know the dimensions of each item to be stored, and the dimensions of the storage space.

Finding the most efficient solution

To find the most efficient solution, you will need to calculate ways of storing items by rotating them in different ways, then compare your answers. The **most efficient** way of packing or storing items is the solution which can store the most items within the same space.

Make sure you show your numerical calculations as part of your conclusion.

Example 19.1

Zain has bought a rack for storing his CDs.

The rack has 7 shelves.

Each shelf measures 60 cm long by 14 cm high.

Each CD measures 12.5 cm by 14 cm by 1 cm (spine width).

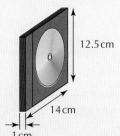

N4

Zain can stack the CDs in two different ways:

horizontally

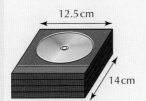

12.5 cm

14 cm

vertically

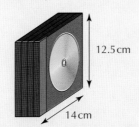

12.5 cm

14 cm

a Work out the maximum number of CDs Zain can put in the CD rack:

   i horizontally   **ii** vertically.

b Explain to Zain how he should stack his CDs so that he can get the most onto the rack.

a **i** When stacked horizontally, the number of CDs in a pile = 14 ÷ 1 = 14

> Each CD is 1 cm in height so 14 CDs can be stored in one pile.

Number of piles in a shelf = 60 ÷ 12.5 = 4.8

> Each shelf is 60 cm wide and a CD is 12.5 cm when laid horizontally.

So 4 piles can be stored on a shelf.

> Always round your answer **down**.

Number of CDs on each shelf = 14 × 4 = 56

Total number of CDs in the rack when stored horizontally = 56 × 7 = 392 CDs

> Multiply the number that can be stored in a pile by the number of piles.

> There are 7 shelves.

ii 14 ÷ 12.5 = 1.12, so 1 CD can be stored vertically

Number of CDs on each shelf = 60 ÷ 1 = 60

> Each shelf is 60 cm wide and a CD is 1 cm when stored vertically.

Total number of CDs in the rack when stored vertically = 60 × 7 = 420 CDs

b It is better to store the CDs vertically. You can store more when arranged vertically (420) than horizontally (392).

> Always use the numbers you have calculated when giving your reason.

N4 **Exercise 19A**

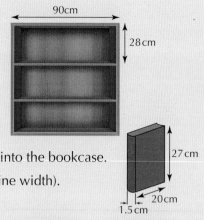

1 Mr Mackay has bought a bookcase for
storing his textbooks.

The bookcase has 3 shelves.
Each shelf measures 90 cm long by 28 cm high.

When the books are stacked on the shelves, the
spines must be visible.

He has a set of identical textbooks he wants to put into the bookcase.

Each book measures 20 cm by 27 cm by 1.5 cm (spine width).

Mr Mackay can stack them in two different ways:

★ **a** Work out the maximum number of books
he can put in the bookcase:

   i horizontally   **ii** vertically.

★ **b** Explain to Mr Mackay how he should stack his books so that
he can get the most onto the bookcase.

2 A cylindrical can of soup has a diameter of 8 cm
and a height of 10 cm.

The soup cans are packed in a cardboard box
with dimensions 32 cm by 24 cm by 21 cm.

a If the cans stay upright, how many can be
stored in the box?

b If the cans can be stored by turned on their
sides, can they be packed more efficiently?
Give a reason for your answer.

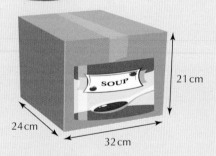

> ⚠ In part **a**, storing a cylinder is equivalent to storing a cuboid
> with breadth the same as the diameter of the cylinder.
> In part **b**, you should find two other options by turning them on
> their sides.

3 Stock cubes are sold in boxes measuring 8 cm by 5 cm by 4 cm.
Each stock cube has sides of length 2 cm.

a What is the maximum number of stock cubes that can be stored in a box?

b What is the volume of unoccupied space in each box?

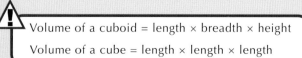

> ⚠ Volume of a cuboid = length × breadth × height
> Volume of a cube = length × length × length

N4

4 The Smiths are moving home and are using a van with storage dimensions 350 cm by 220 cm by 200 cm.

They have identical storage boxes with dimensions 60 cm by 50 cm by 40 cm.

The storage boxes must stay upright with 'This way up' remaining the right way round.

By considering two different ways of storing the boxes, find the maximum number of boxes that can be transported in the van.

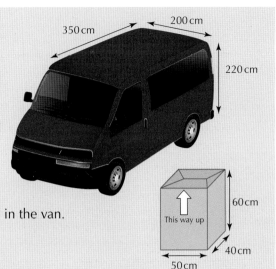

5 Orange juice cartons have the dimensions shown.

The cartons arrive at school packed in a cardboard box with dimensions 36 cm by 27 cm by 22 cm.

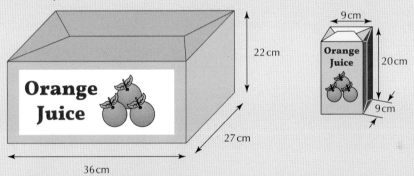

a If the cartons stay upright, how many can be stored in the box?

b If the cartons can be stored turned on their sides, can they be packed more efficiently? Give a reason for your answer.

6 Billy designs jewellery. He puts the pieces in boxes which he then packs into a cuboid-shaped suitcase to make it easier to transport the pieces when he takes them to market.

Each box has the dimensions shown and needs to stay upright so that he can open each lid easily.

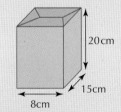

The suitcase has the dimensions shown.

By considering two different ways of storing the boxes, find the maximum number of boxes that Billy can carry in the suitcase.

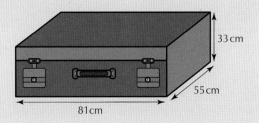

N4

7 Sara is designing a car park. It will have dimensions 80 m by 20 m.

Each car parking space will be 6.6 m by 2.7 m.

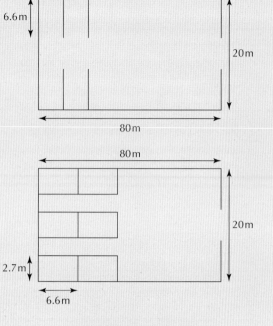

a If she places the spaces vertically against the top and bottom of the long sides, how many spaces can she fit in?

b If she places the spaces horizontally against the top and bottom as well as a middle row, how many spaces can she fit in?

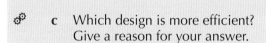

c Which design is more efficient? Give a reason for your answer.

8 John has bought a shelving unit for storing his picture frames.

The shelving unit has 4 shelves. Each shelf measures 80 cm long by 25 cm high.

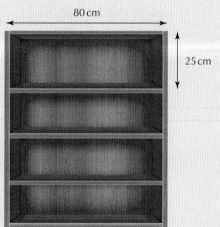

John has identical picture frames he wants to store on the shelves.

Each frame has the measurements shown.

The frames do not have to be stored in a particular way and the shelves are deep enough to fit the frames whichever way they are stacked.

a How many ways could John store the frames? Draw sketches to show the different ways.

b Work out the maximum number of frames John could store on the shelving.

c Explain to John the best way to store the frames so he can get the greatest number on the shelves.

If he stores them horizontally, how many ways are there? If he stores them vertically, how many ways are there?

N4

Using a first-fit algorithm

In Exercise 19A all the items to be packed or stored were the same shape and size. In other situations, you may have to store items of different shapes and sizes. This can make fitting them in more complicated.

An **algorithm** is a process for solving a problem, based on following a sequence of actions.

The **first-fit algorithm** describes a packing method where each item is packed or stored in the first available container or storage space. This may mean putting items in a storage space where items are already packed or allocated.

This method is often used because it is a quick way of packing or storing – you don't have to think about different options. However, it is not always the most efficient way of packing.

Using the first-fit algorithm, you pack or store items in the order you are given. For example, if you are packing a suitcase, you might start by packing your socks first because they are in your top drawer, but this approach might not get the most items in your suitcase.

> ### Example 19.2
>
> A ferry runs between two islands. The ferry has four transport lanes, each 30 m long.
>
> The ferry company allows:
>
> - 4 m for a car
> - 5 m for a van
> - 9 m for a lorry.
>
> On one day, there were 12 cars, 9 vans and 4 lorries.
>
> If they are loaded in this order, is there enough space for the vehicles?
>
>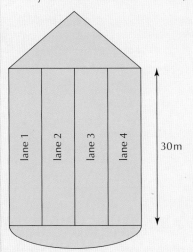
>
> Lane 1: $30 \div 4 = 7.5$ ●────── Divide the space in lane 1 by the length allowed for a car, because cars are loaded first.
>
> So, 7 cars loaded in lane 1. ●────── Round 7.5 down to 7.

(continued)

N4

Lane 2: 12 − 7 = 5 cars remaining

5 × 4 = 20 m

> Calculate the length occupied by the remaining cars.

30 − 20 = 10 m

> Calculate the space left in lane 2.

10 ÷ 5 = 2 vans

> Calculate the number of vans that can fit into this space, remembering that 5 m is allowed for a van.

Lane 3: 9 − 2 = 7 vans remaining

30 ÷ 5 = 6 vans

> Calculate the number of vans that can fit into lane 3.

Lane 4: 7 − 6 = 1 van remaining

1 van occupies 5 m

30 − 5 = 25 m

25 ÷ 9 = 2.7777…

> Calculate the number of lorries that can fit into this space.

So, 2 lorries can fit in lane 4.

No, there is not space for all the vehicles as 2 lorries are left over.

> There are 4 lorries waiting to board but only 2 can fit in lane 4.

Exercise 19B

1 Sarah has a collection of CDs, including some special edition CDs she wants to put into a CD rack. She needs to store the CDs with their spines showing.

The CD rack has 3 shelves and each shelf measures 50 cm by 14 cm.

Regular CDs measure 12.5 cm by 14 cm by 1 cm (spine width) but the special edition CDs have a spine width of 1.5 cm.

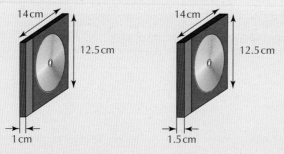

Sarah has 40 special edition CDs. If she stores these first, how many regular CDs can she store:

a **i** vertically

ii horizontally?

b Which is more efficient?

N4

2 Jim runs a guesthouse. At breakfast, he provides three different types of cereal:

- a box of cereal A measures 20 cm (depth) by 27 cm (height) by 4 cm (width)
- a box of cereal B measures 21 cm (depth) by 29 cm (height) by 6 cm (width)
- a box of cereal C measures 20 cm (depth) by 30 cm (height) by 5 cm (width).

Jim buys the cereals in bulk and so often has to store lots of boxes at the same time.

One week he has 14 boxes of cereal A, 8 boxes of cereal B and 7 boxes of cereal C.

In his larder Jim has one shelf measuring 21 cm by 130 cm by 30 cm. He packs them in order, A to C.

a Can he fit all the boxes in if he stores them vertically, as shown? Justify your answer.

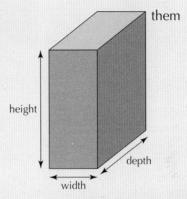

b Can he fit all the boxes if he stores them horizontally, as shown? Justify your answer.

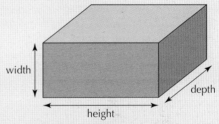

★ 3 A ferry runs between an island and the mainland. The ferry has four transport lanes, each 40 m long.

The ferry company allows:

- 6 m for a van
- 4 m for a car
- 10 m for a lorry.

On one day, there were 10 vans, 12 cars and 5 lorries.

a If they are loaded in this order, is there enough space for all the vehicles?

b If the lorries are loaded first, and then the vans, can you fit all the vehicles on the ferry? Justify your answer.

c What can you conclude about the first-fit algorithm and the size of items to be fitted into a given space?

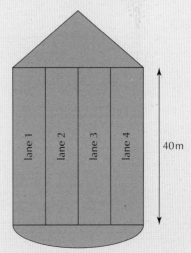

Your answers for parts **a** and **b** should be different.

N4

4 Sam has a collection of DVDs, including some special edition DVDs, he wants to put into a bookcase. He wants to store them with their spines showing.

The bookcase has 3 shelves and each shelf measures 90 cm by 20 cm.

The regular DVDs measure 13.5 cm by 20 cm by 1.5 cm (spine width), but the special edition DVDs have a spine width of 2.5 cm.

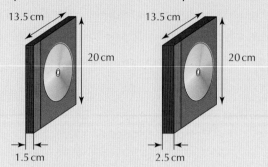

Sam has 25 special edition DVDs. If he stores these first, how many regular DVDs can he store:

a **i** vertically

ii horizontally?

b Which is more efficient?

5 Morag is packing cans into a cardboard box.

Cylindrical cans of soup have a diameter of 8 cm and a height of 10 cm.

Cylindrical cans of tuna have a diameter of 10 cm and a height of 4 cm.

There are 10 cans of soup and 15 cans of tuna.

Morag is packing the cans into a cardboard box with dimensions 35 cm by 20 cm by 25 cm.

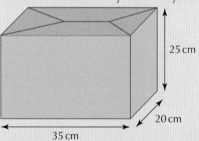

⚠ Storing a cylinder is equivalent to storing a cuboid with length and breadth the same as the diameter.

a If all the cans stay upright, will they all fit into the box?

b If some cans can be placed on their side, can they all fit? Give a reason for your answer.

N4

6 Ms Harris has three different sizes of textbook:

- book A measures 20 cm (depth) by 27 cm (height) by 1.5 cm (spine width)
- book B measures 21 cm (depth) by 25 cm (height) by 2 cm (spine width)
- book C measures 20 cm (depth) by 30 cm (height) by 1 cm (spine width).

There are 15 copies of book A, 17 of book B and 30 of book C.

Ms Harris has one bookshelf measuring 90 cm by 30 cm.

a Can she fit all the books if she stores them vertically? Does the order matter? Justify your answer.

b Can she fit all the books if she stores them horizontally? Does the order matter? Justify your answer.

GO! Activity

1 Look at Exercise 19A Q4. If the boxes do not have to be stacked 'This way up' and can be placed any way:

a how many different ways can you arrange the boxes?

b which way is the most efficient?

2 Look at Exercise 19B Q3. If you can fit the lorries, vans and cars in any possible order, investigate the maximum number of vehicles that can be loaded onto the ferry if there are **at least** three of each vehicle.

> ⚠ Start by investigating the most efficient way to fit lorries, vans and cars into one lane.

Chapter review

1 Mr Marconi has bought a bookshelf for storing his textbooks.

The bookshelf has 4 shelves. Each shelf measures 95 cm long by 27 cm high.

He has identical textbooks he wants to put into the bookcase.

Each book measures 20 cm by 26 cm by 2.5 cm (spine width).

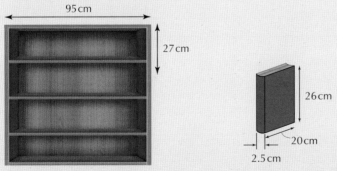

Mr Marconi can either stack the books vertically or horizontally.

a Work out the maximum number of books he can put in the bookcase:

    i vertically   **ii** horizontally.

b Explain to Mr Marconi how he should stack his books so he can get the greatest number into the bookcase.

(continued)

N4

Mr Marconi also wants to put his revision books in the bookcase.
Each revision book measures 20 cm by 27 cm by 1.5 cm (spine width).
He has 30 revision books.

c If he stores the revision books first, how many of the original textbooks can he store:

    i vertically   **ii** horizontally?

d In part **c**, which is more efficient?

2 Sunita makes cuboid-shaped candles with a square base and with the dimensions shown.

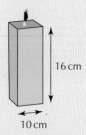

She packs the candles in cardboard boxes when she distributes them to shops. The boxes have dimensions 40 cm by 32 cm by 20 cm.

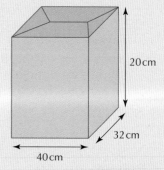

a If Sunita packs the candles upright, how many can she pack in the box?

b If Sunita can pack the candles on their sides, can she pack them more efficiently? Give a reason for your answer.

- I can pack items into a container or storage space.
  ★ Exercise 19A Q1a

- I can find the most efficient packing solution.
  ★ Exercise 19A Q1b

- I can use the first-fit algorithm to carry out container packing. ★ Exercise 19B Q3

20 Gradient of a slope

This chapter will show you how to:

N4

- calculate the gradient of a slope
- use gradient in real-life situations.

You should already know:

- the meaning of the terms slope, horizontal and vertical
- how to convert between metric units.

N4

Gradient

The **gradient** of a slope is a measure of its steepness. To find the gradient, we compare the **vertical height** and **horizontal distance**.

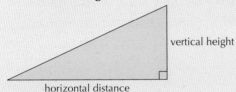

vertical height

horizontal distance

Vertical height is the same as a vertical distance. Steepness or gradient is calculated using this formula:

$$\text{gradient } (m) \ = \ \frac{\textbf{vertical distance}}{\textbf{horizontal distance}}$$

where the symbol m is used to represent gradient.

The sloping line in the diagram below is steeper than in the diagram above – it has a greater gradient. In the diagram below, more height is gained over the same horizontal distance.

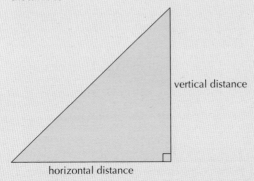

vertical distance

horizontal distance

N4

Example 20.1

Calculate the gradient of this slope.

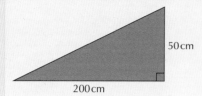

50 cm

200 cm

$m = \dfrac{50}{200}$

$= \dfrac{1}{4}$ ———————————————————————(Simplify your answer.)

Comparing gradients

In real-life situations, the purpose of calculating a gradient is often to compare it to a regulation or requirement. For example, there may be a maximum gradient allowed for a ramp giving disability access, or a minimum gradient permitted for a roof to ensure appropriate drainage. Road signs sometimes give gradients of steep roads in percentages.

When comparing gradients it is better to express the gradients as decimal fractions (or percentages) because it is easier to compare them when they are in the same form.

To convert a fraction into a decimal fraction, divide the numerator by the denominator.

In Example 20.1, the gradient $\frac{1}{4}$ can be converted to the decimal fraction 0.25

Example 20.2

According to government safety regulations, the maximum gradient of a ladder placed against a wall is 4.

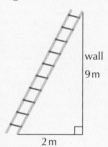

wall
9 m

2 m

If John places his ladder 2 m away from the wall and it reaches a height of 9 m against the wall, does it meet the regulation? Give a reason for your answer.

$m = \dfrac{9}{2}$

$= 4.5$

No, it does not meet the regulation as 4.5 is ——(Remember to give a reason for your answer.)
more than 4; the ladder is too steep.

N4 **Exercise 20A**

★ 1 Calculate the gradient of each slope.

a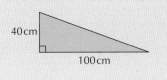

b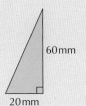

c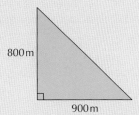

⚙ 2 According to government safety regulations, the maximum gradient a ladder placed against a wall can have is 4. By calculating the gradient of each ladder, decide whether it meets the regulations.

a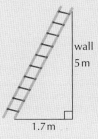

b

c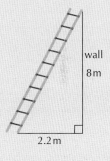

⚙ 3 This ladder is placed against the wall.

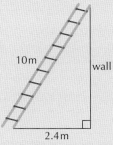

a Find the vertical height the ladder reaches up the wall. Give your answer to 1 decimal place.

b Find the gradient, and state whether it meets the safety regulation described in Question 2.

> Use Pythagoras' theorem $(a^2 + b^2 = c^2)$. See Chapter 21 for more on this. ⚠

N4 ⚙4 Climbs in a cycle race are classified according to their gradient as listed in the table.

Find the gradient of each climb, and classify it according to the table.

Gradient	Classification
0 to 0.08	Easy
0.08 to 0.15	Challenging
More than 0.15	Painful

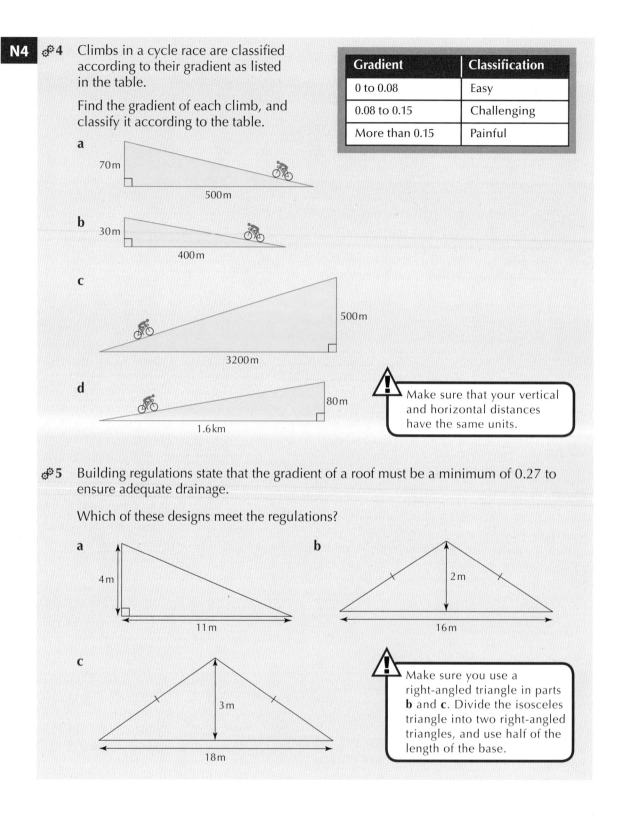

a
70 m
500 m

b
30 m
400 m

c
500 m
3200 m

d
80 m
1.6 km

⚠ Make sure that your vertical and horizontal distances have the same units.

⚙5 Building regulations state that the gradient of a roof must be a minimum of 0.27 to ensure adequate drainage.

Which of these designs meet the regulations?

a
4 m
11 m

b
2 m
16 m

c
3 m
18 m

⚠ Make sure you use a right-angled triangle in parts **b** and **c**. Divide the isosceles triangle into two right-angled triangles, and use half of the length of the base.

N4 ⚙6 For safety reasons, aeroplanes must have a gradient between 0.05 and 0.1 within the first 500 m of take-off.

a During take-off, an aeroplane rose to 30 m above ground over the first 500 m.

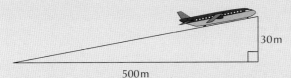

30 m

500 m

Was this take-off within the safety regulations?

When landing, an aeroplane must have a gradient of between 0.021 and 0.025.

b During landing, an aeroplane landed from a vertical height of 100 m above ground over a horizontal distance of 4500 m.

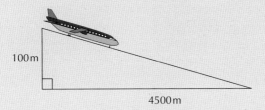

100 m

4500 m

Was this landing within the safety regulations?

c Why are safety regulations different for take-off and landing?

⚙7 For drainage reasons, a tennis court must have a gradient between 0.012 and 0.015.

Which of these tennis courts meets the requirements?

a 0.4 m

35 m

b 0.45 m

37 m

c 29 cm

28 m

Make sure that your vertical and horizontal distances have the same units. ⚠

251

N4 ⚙ **8** For a staircase to pass safety regulations, the 'rake' of each step, or gradient, must be less than 0.9.

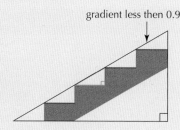

gradient less then 0.9

Do the following steps meet the regulation?

a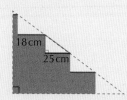

18 cm
25 cm

b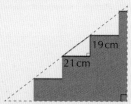

19 cm
21 cm

c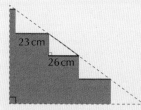

23 cm
26 cm

★ **9** A council states that the maximum gradient
⚙ a wheelchair ramp is allowed to have is 0.07.

Does this ramp meet the council's
regulations? Give a reason for your answer.

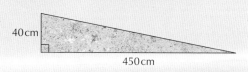

40 cm
450 cm

🟢GO! Activity

1 Conventionally, gradient uses the letter *m*. Research and find at least two theories explaining why *m* is used.

2 The government's document *Protection from Falling, Collision and Impact* specifies that a staircase in a house must follow these regulations:

- the rise of each stair must be between 150 mm and 225 mm

- the run (or tread) of each stair must be between 245 mm and 260 mm

- the gradient must be no more than 0.9.

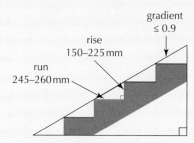

gradient ≤ 0.9

rise
150–225 mm

run
245–260 mm

If you have stairs at home or at school, measure the steps. Do they meet the current regulations? Give a reason for your answer.

3 a Find out the gradient of a horizontal line.

b Find out the gradient of a vertical line.

N4 **Chapter review**

1   Calculate the gradient of this slope.

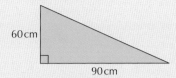

60 cm
90 cm

⚙ 2   Building regulations state that the maximum gradient a long ramp can have is 0.05

Does this ramp meet the requirements? Give a reason for your answer.

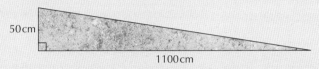

50 cm
1100 cm

⚙ 3   A local council's regulations state that a tractor mower cannot be used if the gradient of the grassy area to be mown is more than 0.7.

Can this grassy area be cut with a tractor mower?

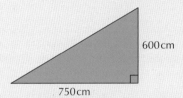

600 cm
750 cm

⚙ 4   This ladder is placed against the wall.

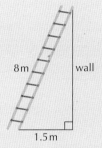

8 m   wall
1.5 m

   a   Find the vertical height the ladder reaches up the wall. Give your answer to 2 decimal places.

According to government regulations, the maximum gradient of a ladder placed against a wall is 4.

   b   Find the gradient of the ladder in part **a** and state whether it meets the government's regulations.

• I can calculate gradient. ★ Exercise 20A Q1

• I can use gradient in real-life situations.
  ★ Exercise 20A Q9

21 Pythagoras' theorem

This chapter will show you how to:

N4

- use Pythagoras' theorem to find the length of the hypotenuse of a right-angled triangle
- use Pythagoras' theorem to find the length of a shorter side of a right-angled triangle
- choose a method for finding the length of any side of a right-angled triangle
- solve problems using Pythagoras' theorem.

You should already know:

- how to find the square and square root of a number
- how to round an answer to a required degree of accuracy.

N4

Right-angled triangles

Pythagoras' theorem gives the relationship between the lengths of the sides in a right-angled triangle.

The relationship has been known since ancient times, and there is evidence that it was known in Babylon, China and Egypt. The builders of the Egyptian pyramids used a rope with 12 equally spaced knots which formed a right-angled triangle.

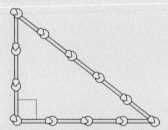

Pythagoras was a Greek mathematician who lived about 580–500 BCE. Although the theorem is named after him, it is not known whether he actually discovered it.

Hypotenuse

The **hypotenuse** of a right-angled triangle is the name given to its longest side.

The longest side is always opposite the right angle.

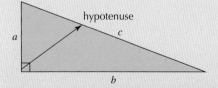

By convention, the hypotenuse is usually labelled c and the shorter sides are labelled a and b (it doesn't matter which shorter side is labelled a and which is labelled b).

N4 **Exercise 21A**

1 **a** Make an accurate copy (to scale) of each triangle shown below.

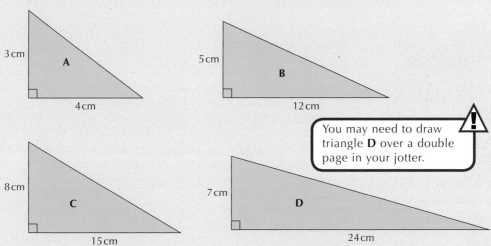

You may need to draw triangle **D** over a double page in your jotter.

b Using your ruler, measure the hypotenuse (longest side) of each triangle.

If you have drawn these accurately, it should give a whole number answer.

c **i** Copy the table below.

Triangle	a	b	c	a^2	b^2	c^2
A	3	4				
B	5	12				
C	8	15				
D	7	24				

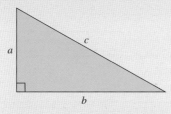

ii Write your answers to part **b** in the table.

iii Square the lengths of all sides in your triangles and complete the columns for a^2, b^2 and c^2.

To 'square' a number, multiply the number by itself. For example, $3^2 = 3 \times 3$.

d For each triangle, look at the values in the columns for a^2, b^2 and c^2.

Write down a connection between them, describing the relationship between the three sides of each triangle.

N4 Pythagoras' theorem

Pythagoras' theorem gives the relationship between the lengths of sides in a right-angled triangle.

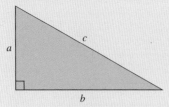

The theorem states:

'In any right-angled triangle, the sum of the squares of the two shorter sides is equal to the square of the hypotenuse.'

When c is the hypotenuse and a and b are the shorter sides, as in the triangle above, Pythagoras' theorem can be written as:

$$a^2 + b^2 = c^2$$

Find the length of the hypotenuse

You can find the length of the hypotenuse of a right-angled triangle if you know the length of the two shorter sides.

Example 21.1

Calculate the length of the side labelled x.

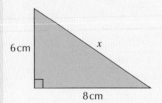

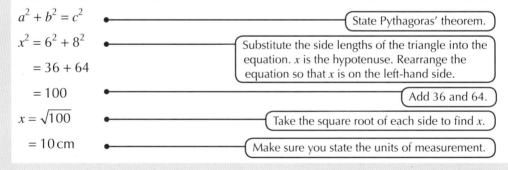

$a^2 + b^2 = c^2$ — State Pythagoras' theorem.

$x^2 = 6^2 + 8^2$ — Substitute the side lengths of the triangle into the equation. x is the hypotenuse. Rearrange the equation so that x is on the left-hand side.

$\quad = 36 + 64$

$\quad = 100$ — Add 36 and 64.

$x = \sqrt{100}$ — Take the square root of each side to find x.

$\quad = 10\,\text{cm}$ — Make sure you state the units of measurement.

N4

Example 21.2

A ramp has a horizontal base of 120 cm and a vertical height of 30 cm

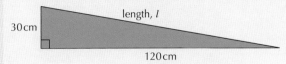

Calculate the length, l, of the ramp.

Give your answer to 1 decimal place.

$a^2 + b^2 = c^2$

$l^2 = 30^2 + 120^2$

$\quad = 900 + 14\,400$

$\quad = 15\,300$

$l = \sqrt{15300}$

$\quad = 123.693...$

$\quad = 123.7\,\text{cm}$ (1 d.p.) ●————

> Round your answer to 1 decimal place as instructed, and state the units of measurement.

Exercise 21B

1 Calculate the length of the hypotenuse in each of the following right-angled triangles.

a

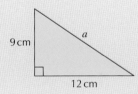

b

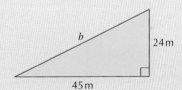

c

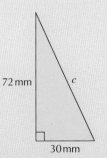

d

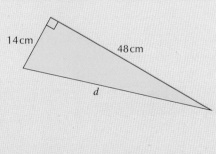

2 Calculate the length of the hypotenuse in each of the following right-angled triangles. Give your answer to 1 decimal place.

a

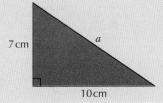

b

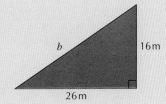

(continued)

N4

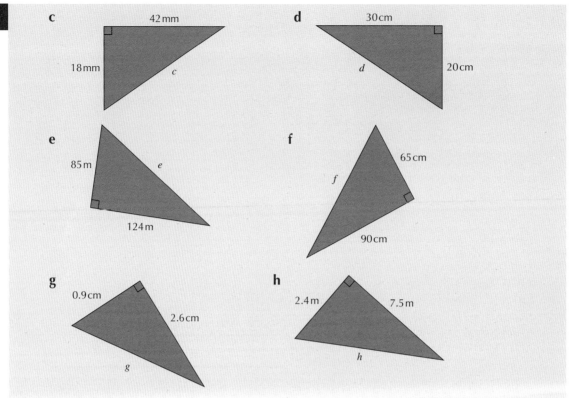

c   42 mm   18 mm   c

d   30 cm   d   20 cm

e   85 m   e   124 m

f   65 cm   f   90 cm

g   0.9 cm   2.6 cm   g

h   2.4 m   7.5 m   h

★ **3**   A slide in a play park has a ladder with vertical height 1.7 m and a horizontal base of 3.2 m.

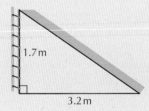

1.7 m

3.2 m

What is the sloping length of the slide? Give your answer to 2 decimal places.

4   Metal brackets to support a shelf are in the shape of a right-angled triangle. The arms measure 50 cm and 33 cm.

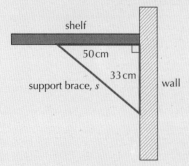

shelf

50 cm

33 cm   wall

support brace, *s*

What is the length of the support brace, *s*? Give your answer to 1 decimal place.

N4

5 A ridge tent needs a guy rope to hold the tent pole in place. The tent pole measures 2.4 m.

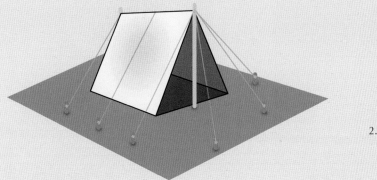

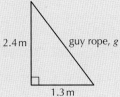

2.4 m   guy rope, g

1.3 m

If the bottom of the guy rope is 1.3 m from the base of the tent pole, what is the length of the guy rope, g? Give your answer to 2 decimal places.

6 This flag is a rectangle. The breadth of the rectangle is 150 cm and the height is 78 cm.

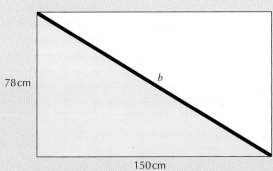

78 cm

b

150 cm

The flag has a diagonal thin, black strip of length b cm. What is the value of b? Give your answer to the nearest centimetre.

Find the length of a shorter side
You can find the length of a shorter side of a right-angled triangle if you know the lengths of the hypotenuse and the other shorter side.

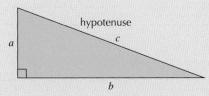

hypotenuse

c

a

b

Pythagoras' theorem states:

$$a^2 + b^2 = c^2$$

By rearranging the equation, you get:

$$a^2 = c^2 - b^2 \quad \text{or} \quad b^2 = c^2 - a^2$$

> The square of one of the shorter sides is equal to the square of the hypotenuse **minus** the square of the other shorter side.

N4

Example 21.3

Calculate the length of the side labelled y.

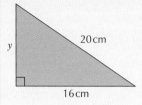

$a^2 + b^2 = c^2$

$y^2 + 16^2 = 20^2$ ●————————————————(Substitute the side lengths into the formula.)

$y^2 = 20^2 - 16^2$ ●————————————————(Rearrange the equation.)

$\quad = 400 - 256$

$\quad = 144$

$y = \sqrt{144}$

$\quad = 12 \text{ cm}$

Example 21.4

A 4-metre ladder is placed against a vertical wall. The bottom of the ladder is 1.5 m from the bottom of the wall.

What height does the ladder reach? Give your answer to 2 decimal places.

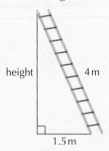

$a^2 + b^2 = c^2$

$h^2 + 1.5^2 = 4^2$ ●————————————(Use a letter to represent the height, e.g. h.)

$h^2 = 4^2 - 1.5^2$

$\quad = 16 - 2.25$

$\quad = 13.75$

$h = \sqrt{13.75}$

$\quad = 3.708...$

$\quad = 3.71 \text{ m (2 d.p.)}$ ●———(Round your answer to 2 decimal places as instructed, and state the units of measurement.)

N4   **Exercise 21C**

1   Calculate the length of the shorter side labelled with a letter in each of the following right-angled triangles.

a
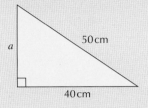

b
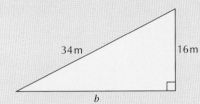

c
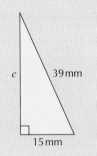

d
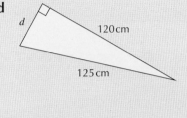

2   Calculate the length of the missing side labelled with a letter in each of the following right-angled triangles. Give your answers to 1 decimal place.

a
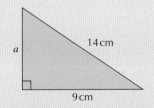

b
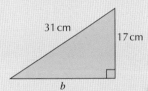

c
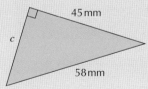

d
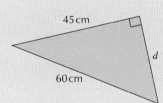

e
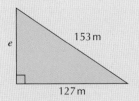

f
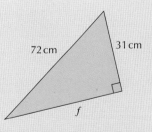

g
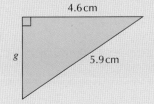

h
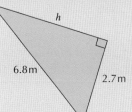

N4 ★ **3** A 14-metre wire is connected from the top of a vertical 12-metre telegraph pole to a point on the ground.

What is the distance, *d*, between the bottom of the wire and the base of the pole?

Give your answer to 1 decimal place.

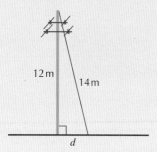

4 The base of a door wedge measures 10 cm and the sloping edge measures 10.5 cm.

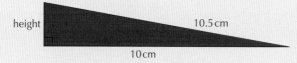

Calculate the height of the door wedge. Give your answer to 1 decimal place.

5 A firework is launched. It travels 35 metres and explodes at a point which is 27 metres horizontally from the point where it was launched.

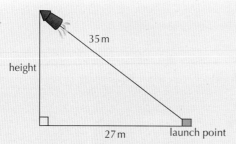

What height did the firework reach when it exploded? Give your answer to 1 decimal place.

6 A 7-metre tree fell in a storm and landed on a nearby office block. The top of the tree hit the top of the office block, and the base of the tree was 2.7 m from the office block.

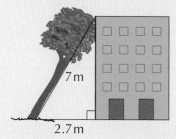

Calculate the height of the office block. Give your answer to 2 decimal places.

N4 ## Choosing the correct method

The missing side might be the hypotenuse or a shorter side in the right-angled triangle. To work out which form of Pythagoras' theorem to use, follow these steps:

- draw an arrow from the right angle to the long side opposite – this is *always* the hypotenuse

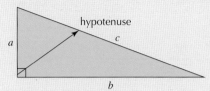

- if the missing side is the hypotenuse, **add** the squares of the two shorter sides and use the formula:
$$a^2 + b^2 = c^2$$

- if the missing side is a shorter side, **subtract** the square of the known shorter side from the square of the hypotenuse and use the formula:
$$a^2 = c^2 - b^2 \quad \text{or} \quad b^2 = c^2 - a^2$$

Once you have decided on the first line of working, you can then solve as before.

Example 21.5

Calculate the length of the side marked x.

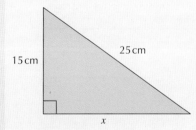

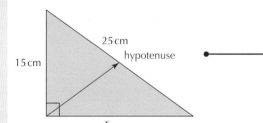

Draw the arrow from the right angle to the hypotenuse opposite. The hypotenuse is the 25 cm side, so the missing side is a shorter side.

$$a^2 = c^2 - b^2$$

Write the formula for finding the shorter side.

$$x^2 = 25^2 - 15^2$$
$$= 625 - 225$$
$$= 400$$
$$x = \sqrt{400}$$
$$= 20 \, \text{cm}$$

N4

Example 21.6

A flagpole is 3 m high. To stabilise it, a wire is connected from the top of the pole to a point on the ground 1.7 m away. What is the length of the wire?

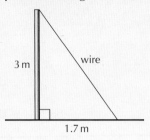

Give your answer to 2 decimal places.

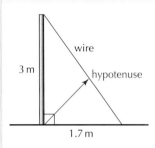

$a^2 + b^2 = c^2$

$3^2 + 1.7^2 = w^2$ ●━━━━━━━━━━ Use a letter to represent the missing side, e.g. w (for wire).

$w^2 = 9 + 2.89$

$\quad = 11.89$

$w = \sqrt{11.89}$

$\quad = 3.45 \, \text{m}$

Exercise 21D

1   Calculate the length of the side labelled with a letter in each of the following right-angled triangles.

a

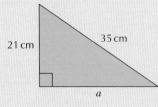

b

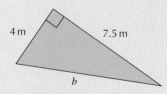

c

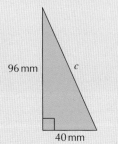

d

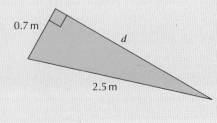

N4

2   Calculate the length of the side labelled with a letter in each of the following right-angled triangles. Give your answers to 1 decimal place.

a   **b**   **c**

16 cm   32 mm   1.5 m   4.2 m

a   *b*

12 cm   59 mm   *c*

d   **e**   **f**

                                                  1.1 m

d   210 m   *e*   2.9 m

                        9.6 cm   *f*

175 m   7.8 cm

★ 3   A taxi has a ramp at the back for disability access. The top of the ramp is at a height of 1.6 m and the ramp rests on the ground 4.7 m from the taxi.

What is the length of the ramp? Give your answer to 2 decimal places.

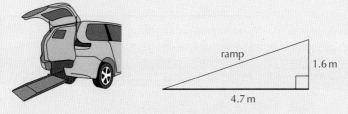

ramp

1.6 m

4.7 m

4   A hot air balloon is fixed to the ground with a rope 80 m long. The wind has blown the balloon to a point 45 metres horizontally from the bottom of the rope.

What height is the balloon above ground? Give your answer correct to the nearest metre.

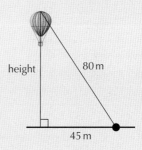

height   80 m

45 m

5   A crate for storing fence posts measures 2.3 m in length and 1.5 m in breadth.

Fence posts must be stored flat so they don't warp.

What is the greatest length of fence post that can be stored in the crate? Give your answer to 1 decimal place.

6   Jessie has a garden in the shape of a right-angled triangle. The longest side is 10 m and one of the shorter sides is 6 m.

a   What is the length of the third side?

Jessie wants to put a fence around her garden.

b   What length of fence does she need?

c   One metre of fence costs £6. How much will the fence cost her?

⚠ Draw a sketch to find a right-angled triangle and label the sides.

N4 **Problem-solving**

Usually you will find questions involving Pythagoras' theorem within a context or story. You have already been dealing with basic problem-solving questions. The same approach can be extended to more complicated shapes or more complex stories. The key to solving such problems is to recognise the right-angled triangle within each question. Sketch the right-angled triangle and solve as before.

Example 21.7

Calculate the height of this isosceles triangle with sides of length 10 cm and 15 cm. Give your answer correct to 1 decimal place.

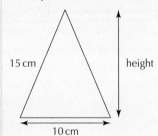

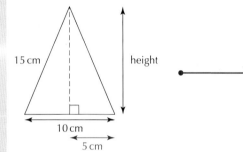

Any isosceles triangle can be split into two identical right-angled triangles. The base of the right-angled triangle is half the base of the original triangle.

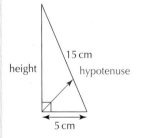

The hypotenuse is the 15 cm side, so the missing side is a shorter side.

$a^2 = c^2 - b^2$

$h^2 = 15^2 - 5^2$

$\quad = 225 - 25$

$\quad = 200$

$h = \sqrt{200}$

$\quad = 14.142... \text{ cm}$

$\quad = 14.1 \text{ cm (1 d.p.)}$

N4

Example 21.8

A helicopter leaves an airport and flies north for 30 km, then changes course and travels 50 km east.

What distance is the helicopter from the airport? Give your answer to the nearest kilometre.

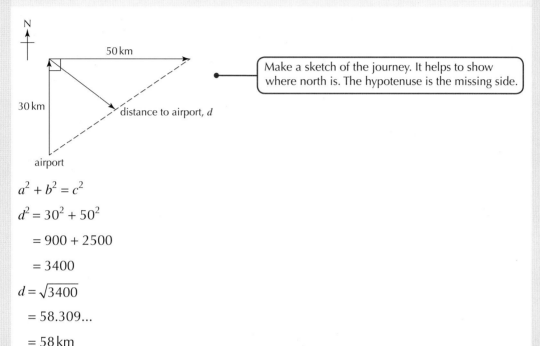

Make a sketch of the journey. It helps to show where north is. The hypotenuse is the missing side.

$a^2 + b^2 = c^2$

$d^2 = 30^2 + 50^2$

$\quad = 900 + 2500$

$\quad = 3400$

$d = \sqrt{3400}$

$\quad = 58.309...$

$\quad = 58 \text{ km}$

Exercise 21E

1   This advertising logo is in the shape of an isosceles triangle. It has a base of 60 cm and each sloping side is 70 cm.

What is the height of the logo? Give your answer correct to 1 decimal place.

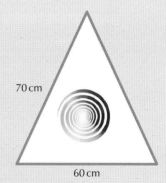

70 cm

60 cm

2   The roof of a house forms an isosceles triangle with a horizontal beam.
The point of the roof is 3 m above the beam and the beam is 15 m long.

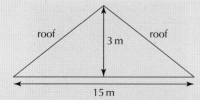

roof   3 m   roof

15 m

What is the length of one side of the roof? Give your answer correct to 1 decimal place.

N4

3 A ship leaves port. It travels 40 km east then changes course and sails 70 km south.

How far is the ship from the port? Give your answer to the nearest kilometre.

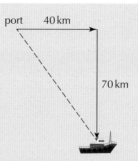

port   40 km

70 km

4 An aeroplane leaves the airport. It travels 100 km south then flies 65 km west.

If the plane flies directly back to the airport, what distance will it have travelled altogether? Give your answer to the nearest kilometre.

Draw a diagram to represent the journey.

5 A rhombus has one diagonal of 8 cm and sides of length 5 cm.

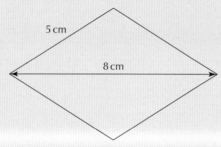

5 cm

8 cm

Redraw the rhombus with both diagonals drawn. Use one of the right-angled triangles to find out the length of the other diagonal.

The formula for calculating the area A of a rhombus is:

$A = \frac{1}{2} d_1 d_2$

Look back at Chapter 15 if you need help.

a Calculate the length of the other diagonal.

b Calculate the area of the rhombus.

★ **6** A garage has a sloping roof as shown in the diagram.

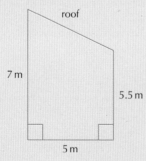

roof

7 m

5.5 m

5 m

Split the shape into a rectangle and a right-angled triangle.

What is the length of the sloping roof? Give your answer to 1 decimal place.

7 A field is the shape of a rectangle.

a What is the length of the diagonal of the field? Give your answer to one decimal place.

b If you walked around the outside of the field instead of walking across the diagonal, how much further would you walk?

20 m

35 m

N4

8 A window is the shape of a symmetrical trapezium as shown in the diagram.

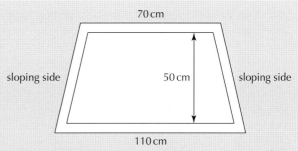

70 cm

50 cm

sloping side · · · sloping side

110 cm

a Find the length of each sloping side. Give your answer to 1 decimal place.

b Find the length of the surrounding window frame.

> ⚠ The trapezium is symmetrical, which means the sloping sides are the same length.

9 A kite has sides of length 30 cm and 70 cm. The short diagonal has a length of 46 cm.

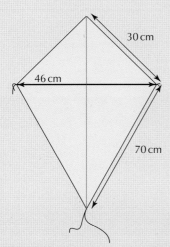

30 cm

46 cm

70 cm

> ⚠ Find the length of the two parts of the diagonal then add them together.

a Find the length of the long diagonal. Give your answer to the nearest centimetre.

b Find the area of the kite.

c Every side and both diagonals make a frame for the kite. Calculate the length of the frame.

10 a The length of the side of a square is 7 cm.
Find the length of its diagonal.
Give your answer correct to 1 decimal place.

b The diagonal of a square is 67 cm.
Find the length, l, of one of its sides.
Give your answer correct to 1 decimal place.

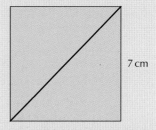

7 cm

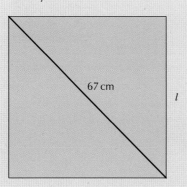

67 cm

l

N4

11 A room is made of a rectangle and right-angled triangle.

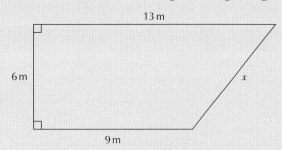

a Calculate the length of the side marked x.
Round your answer to 1 decimal place.

b Carpet grippers are to be placed around the
room. Using your answer to part **a**, calculate
the length of carpet grippers required.

c Carpet grippers costs £0.80 per metre. How much will it cost for the carpet
grippers?

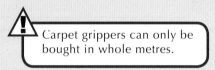

Carpet grippers can only be
bought in whole metres.

GO! Activity

1 Using Pythagoras' theorem, decide whether these triangles are right-angled.

a   **b**

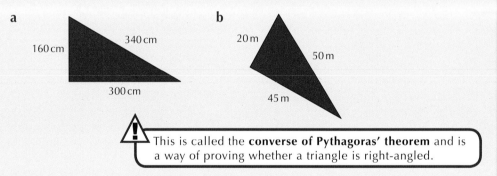

This is called the **converse of Pythagoras' theorem** and is
a way of proving whether a triangle is right-angled.

2 A spiral shape can be created using right-angled
triangles.

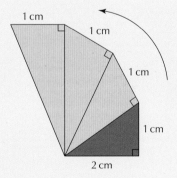

Start with a right-angled triangle with base 2 cm
and height 1 cm (this is the shaded triangle at
the bottom of the diagram).

The second right-angled triangle has the
hypotenuse of the first as its base and also
has a height of 1 cm.

The shape grows by adding right-angled triangles
onto each other.

a Draw this shape as far as you can (as accurately as possible).

b Measure the hypotenuse of the last triangle you have drawn.

c Now use Pythagoras' theorem to calculate the length of the last hypotenuse
drawn. How accurate was your scale drawing?

N4 **Chapter review**

1 Find the length of the hypotenuse of this triangle. Give your answer to
1 decimal place.

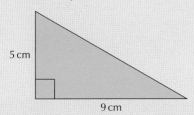

5 cm

9 cm

2 Find the length of the missing shorter side of this triangle. Give your answer to
2 decimal places.

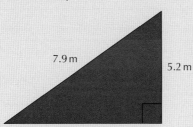

7.9 m

5.2 m

3 Find the missing length on each of these triangles. Give each answer correct to
1 decimal place.

a

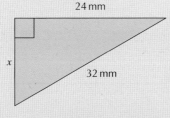

24 mm

x

32 mm

b

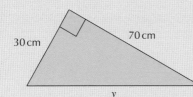

30 cm

70 cm

y

You need to decide first if the missing
length is the hypotenuse or a shorter side.

4 A 100 m zip wire is attached from the top of a vertical cliff to a point on the ground
to enable equipment to be transported. The point on the ground is 85 m from the
cliff.

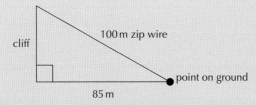

100 m zip wire

cliff

point on ground

85 m

What is the height of the cliff? Give your answer to 1 decimal place.

N4

5 Josh has a garden with the following shape.

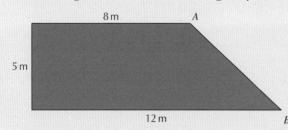

He wants to plant a hedge along edge *AB*. What is the length of hedge to be planted? Give your answer to 1 decimal place.

N4

- I can use Pythagoras' theorem to find the length of the hypotenuse of a right-angled triangle.
  ★ Exercise 21B Q3

- I can use Pythagoras' theorem to find the length of a shorter side of a right-angled triangle.
  ★ Exercise 21C Q3

- I can choose a method for finding the length of any side of a right-angled triangle.
  ★ Exercise 21D Q3

- I can solve problems using Pythagoras' theorem.
  ★ Exercise 21E Q6

N4 Case studies

Stan's garden

> **This case study focuses on the following skills:**
> - working with units of measurement **(Ch. 11)**
> - calculating the area of a 2D shape **(Ch. 15)**.

Stan has a garden which consists of a rectangle and a right-angled triangle.

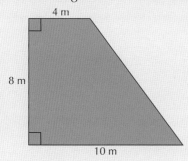

1   **a**   Calculate the area of Stan's garden.

      He would like to plant grass seeds to grow a new lawn. One packet of grass seed costs £3.75 and covers $10\,m^2$.

  b   How many packets does he need to buy?

  c   How much will this cost him?

Children's nursery

> **This case study focuses on the following skills:**
> - using Pythagoras' theorem **(Ch. 21)**
> - working with units of measurement **(Ch. 11)**
> - finding the gradient of a slope **(Ch. 20)**.

Part of a slide in a children's nursery class forms a right-angled triangle.

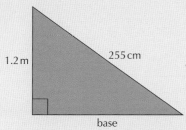

1   Calculate the length of the base of the slide.

2   For the nursery to receive its safety certificate, this type of children's slide must have a gradient of less than 0.4

    Does this slide pass the regulations? Give a reason for your answer.

N4 Orienteering

This case study focuses on the following skills:

- direction and navigation **(Ch. 13)**
- scale drawing **(Ch. 12)**
- scale factor **(Ch. 17).**

Josh is taking part in an orienteering course. He is given these instructions:

- start at checkpoint A
- checkpoint A to checkpoint B: 500 m on a bearing of 130°
- checkpoint B to checkpoint C: 700 m on a bearing of 085°
- checkpoint C to checkpoint D: 900 m on a bearing of 145°
- return to start.

1 a Using a scale of 1 cm to 100 m, make a scale drawing to represent Josh's journey.

   b What is the bearing and distance from checkpoint D back to the start?

2 A new course is designed to be $\frac{3}{5}$ of the size of the course Josh completed. What is the new distance from:

   a checkpoint B to checkpoint C

   b checkpoint D to the start?

Sally's flower shop

This case study focuses on the following skills:

- carrying out container packing **(Ch. 19)**
- speed, distance and time calculations **(Ch. 25)**
- time intervals and time management **(Ch. 10).**

Sally owns a flower shop. She collects the flowers from the flower market in a van. The space for transporting the flowers is in the shape of a cuboid.

The storage space in the van has a length of 150 cm, breadth of 140 cm and a height of 120 cm.

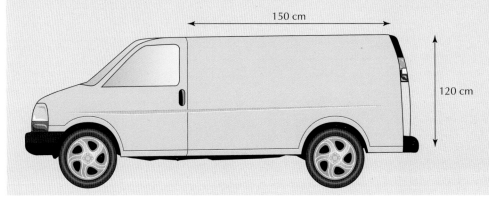

N4 The crates for transporting the flowers have dimensions 50 cm by 35 cm by 30 cm as shown. The crates must stay upright.

50 cm   35 cm   30 cm

1   By considering two different ways of storing the crates, find the maximum number of boxes that can be transported in the van.

Sally's shop is 18 km from the flower market. She travels at an average speed of 54 km/h on this road.

2   How long does it take her to get to the flower market? Give your answer in minutes.

Sally leaves her shop at 5:45 am and travels to the flower market.

She spends 15 minutes selecting and buying the flowers.

After she has bought the flowers, she takes 25 minutes to load the van.

She drives back to the shop at an average speed of 54 km/h.

It takes her 20 minutes to unload the van.

3   At what time does she expect to have unloaded the van?

22 Notation, order of operations, rounding and selecting units

This chapter will show you how to:

- select and use appropriate numerical notation
- use the correct order of operations
- select and use appropriate units
- round to a given degree of accuracy

N4 • round a given number to 1 significant figure.

You should already know:

- how to add and subtract whole numbers without a calculator
- how to multiply and divide by a single digit without a calculator
- how to add, subtract, multiply and divide with a calculator
- how to round to the nearest unit, 10, 100, and 1 and 2 decimal places.

Numerical notation

Most of the problems that you will be asked to solve in maths will involve calculations.

You need to be able to choose the correct process (or operation) and the correct symbol for each calculation.

You will be familiar with most of the symbols already. Many of the symbols have several different words for them.

Symbol	Meaning
+	add
−	subtract
×	multiply
÷	divide
=	equals
<	less than
>	bigger than or greater than
(…)	brackets
%	percentage
:	ratio (e.g. 1 : 3 means one part to three parts)
.	decimal point
/	forward slash (sometimes used for division or to show a fraction, e.g. 3/4 means $\frac{3}{4}$ or three quarters)

Example 22.1

Which of the symbols in the table would you use if you are asked to find the **product** of two numbers?

× •————○ Product means the same as multiply, so you would use the symbol ×.

Example 22.2

Write the sentence '246 is greater than 193' using symbols.

246 > 193 ●————————————

> The symbol > means 'is greater than'. Notice that the point of the symbol points towards the smaller of the two numbers.

Order of operations

When you are given a calculation to do that involves more than one process (or operation), it is important to follow the same rules so that everyone gets the same answer.

Think about the calculation $4 + 6 \times 2$.

Do you add the 4 and 6 and then multiply by 2, or do you multiply 6 by 2 and then add 4?

Is the answer 20 or is it 16?

Mathematicians have decided that the operations should be done in a particular order. The rules are:

First	**B**rackets
Second	Powers/**O**f
Third	**M**ultiplication and **D**ivision (these are of equal importance); when a calculation involves only multiplication and division, you work from left to right
Fourth	**A**ddition and **S**ubtraction (these are of equal importance); when a calculation involves only addition and subtraction, you work from left to right

These rules mean that you have to do any brackets first, then do **all** the multiplying and dividing before you do **any** adding or subtracting.

The rules can be remembered as:

BODMAS   or   **BOMDAS**

Example 22.3

Calculate the answers.

a $20 + 6 \times 3$ **b** $3 \times (8 - 1)$ **c** $30 - 7 \times 3 + 16 \div 2$

a $20 + 6 \times 3$

$= 20 + 18$ ●————

> Work out the multiplication before doing the addition.

$= 38$

b $3 \times (8 - 1)$

$= 3 \times 7$ ●————

> Work out the brackets before doing the multiplication.

$= 21$

c $30 - 7 \times 3 + 16 \div 2$

$= 30 - 21 + 8$ ●————

> Work out both the multiplication and the division before doing the addition and subtraction.

$= 9 + 8$ ●————

$= 17$

> When the calculation **only** contains addition and subtraction or **only** contains multiplication and division, work from left to right to get the answer.

Example 22.4

On Saturday, a bakery shop sold 17 vanilla cupcakes and 23 chocolate cupcakes.

Write the ratio of vanilla cupcakes to chocolate cupcakes using ratio notation.

vanilla cupcakes : chocolate cupcakes

17 : 23

> Write the quantities you are comparing with a ':' between them.

> Write the number of each quantity underneath the quantity. The ratio is read as '17 to 23'.

Exercise 22A

★ 1 List as many different words or phrases as you can for each of these symbols:

    a ×   **b** +   **c** ÷   **d** −   **e** <   **f** >   **g** %

2 Evaluate the following.

    a $3 + 7 \times 5$ **b** $(18 - 14) \times (6 + 7)$ **c** $\frac{1}{2}$ of $(23 + 17)$

    d $18 \div 3 + 14 \times 2$ **e** $21 \times 3 \div 9$ **f** $87 - 21 + 14$

★ 3 Copy these statements and use > or < to make them true.

    a $4 \times 7 \ldots 13 + 14$ **b** $(24 \div 3) + 7 \ldots 13 - 3$

    c $9 - 2 \ldots (16 + 8) \div 2$ **d** $(28 - 4) + 6 \ldots 12 \times 2$

    e $(20 - 5) \times 2 \ldots 31 + 16 - 8$ **f** $6 \times 12 \div 4 \ldots 10 + \frac{1}{4}$ of 24

4 Orange paint is mixed using 1 part of yellow to 3 parts of red.

    Write this mix using the ratio notation.

5 Class 4B has 13 boys and 17 girls in it.

    Write the ratio of boys to girls using ratio notation.

Rounding numbers

You will often be asked to **round** the answer that you get in a calculation.

You should already be able to round to the nearest whole number, nearest 10, 100 or 1000 and to 1 or 2 decimal places.

Example 22.5

Round each of the following to the accuracy given.

a 28 (nearest 10)   **b** 1248 (nearest 100)   **c** 4963 (nearest 1000)

a 28 → 30 to the nearest 10

b 1248 → 1200 to the nearest 100

c 4963 → 5000 to the nearest 1000

Example 22.6

Round each of the following to 2 decimal places (2 d.p.).

a 3.8761   **b** 18.602   **c** 236.995

a 3.87**6**1 → 3.88 to 2 d.p. •——— The highlighted digit **6** is bigger than 5, so the 7 'rounds up' to an 8.

b 18.60**2** → 18.60 to 2 d.p. •——— The highlighted digit **2** is less than 5 and so the 0 in the second decimal place is unchanged. The 0 must be included in the answer to show that you have rounded to 2 d.p. and not 1 d.p.

c 236.99**5** → 237.00 to 2 d.p. •——— The answer must include both zeros after the point to show that you have rounded to 2 d.p.

N4   Rounding to 1 significant figure

When you round a number so that there is only 1 non-zero digit in the answer, it is called rounding to **1 significant figure** or to **1 s.f.**

When you are asked to give your answer to 1 s.f. you need to:

- find the first non-zero digit
- decide which column this digit is in
- round to that column using the usual rules for rounding.

Example 22.7

Round each of these to 1 significant figure:

a 486   **b** 3.965   **c** 19.98   **d** 0.062   **e** 0.37

a 486 → 500 to 1 s.f. •——— The first non-zero digit is the 4 and it is in the **hundreds** column, so round to the nearest 100.

b 3.965 → 4 to 1 s.f. •——— The first non-zero digit is in the **units** column, so round to the nearest whole number. Notice that you do **not** have a decimal point or any digits after it in the answer.

c 19.98 → 20 to 1 s.f. •——— The first non-zero digit is in the **tens** column, so round to the nearest 10. Again there is no decimal point or any digits after it in the answer.

d 0.062 → 0.06 to 1 s.f. •——— The first non-zero digit is 6 in the **hundredths** column, so round to the nearest hundredth, which is the same as rounding to 2 d.p.

e 0.37 → 0.4 to 1 s.f. •——— The first non-zero digit is in the **tenths** column so round to the nearest tenth, which is the same as rounding to 1 d.p.

Exercise 22B

1   Round each number to the nearest 10.

   a 37   **b** 461   **c** 3567   **d** 597

2   Round each number to the nearest 100.

   a 376   **b** 85   **c** 9267   **d** 2961

3   Round each number to the nearest 1000.

   a 3162   **b** 14832   **c** 571   **d** 20169

4   Round each number to 2 decimal places.

   a 4.963   **b** 0.0068 **c** 19.8735 **d** 143.996

N4

5   Round each number to 1 significant figure.

   a 783   **b** 27   **c** 13.76   **d** 0.0573

   e 1.0059 **f** 0.00063 **g** 349   **h** 7192

★ 6   4567 people attended the Ted Shorin concert in Glasgow.

   Round the number of people in the audience to:

   a the nearest 100

N4   **b** 1 significant figure.

★ 7   When Ali and Val went on a round-the-world trip they travelled a total of 37 492 miles.

   Round the number of miles travelled to:

   a the nearest 1000

N4   **b** 1 significant figure.

★ 8   A plant is measured as 16.375 cm tall.

   Round this height to:

   a 1 decimal place   **b** the nearest centimetre.

Selecting and using units

In everyday maths, you need to be very careful that you use the correct units when you communicate.

For example, if you are asked how far it is from your house to your school, if you just say 6, that could mean 6 metres, 6 miles or 6 kilometres.

If you are buying some sweets in a shop and you are told at the till that the cost is 45, does that mean 45p or £45?

You will need to be able to use a variety of units throughout your Applications of Maths course.

You need to be able to choose which unit to use in each question.

Some of the units that you will need to know about are shown in the table.

Money	pence (p) pounds (£)	100p = £1
Length	millimetres (mm) centimetres (cm) metres (m) kilometres (km) miles	100 mm = 1 cm 1000 mm = 100 cm = 1 m 1000 m = 1 km
Area	square millimetres (mm²) square centimetres (cm²) square metres (m²)	100 mm² = 1 cm² 10 000 cm² = 1 m²
Volume/ capacity	millilitres (ml) litres (l) cubic centimetres (cm³) cubic metres (m³)	1000 ml = 1 l 1 ml = 1 cm³ 1000 l = 1 cm³
Weight	grams (g) kilograms (kg) tonnes (t)	1000 g = 1 kg 1000 kg = 1 t
Time	seconds (s) minutes (min) hours (h) days weeks months years	60 s = 1 min 60 min = 1 h 24 h = 1 day 7 days = 1 week 365 days = 1 year 52 weeks = 1 year 12 months = 1 year
Temperature	Celsius (°C) Fahrenheit (°F)	

Example 22.8

Which unit would you use:

a   to weigh a pencil

b   to give the distance from Edinburgh to Glasgow

c   to give the length of time from today until next weekend?

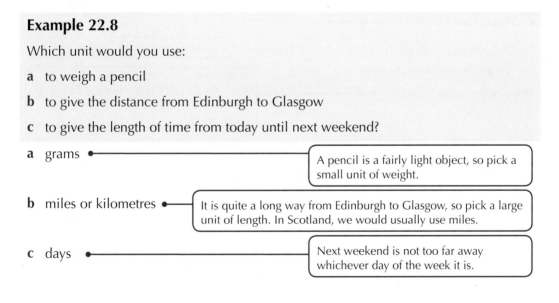

a   grams ●——————— A pencil is a fairly light object, so pick a small unit of weight.

b   miles or kilometres ●——— It is quite a long way from Edinburgh to Glasgow, so pick a large unit of length. In Scotland, we would usually use miles.

c   days ●——————— Next weekend is not too far away whichever day of the week it is.

Example 22.9

A very rough conversion from degrees Celsius (°C) to degrees Fahrenheit (°F) is to double the temperature in °C and then add 30.

The temperature in Nice in the south of France on 5 August was 39 °C.

Use the rule to convert this temperature to °F.

To find the temperature in °F, the rule tells you:

- to double the temperature in °C   (Double means the same as multiply by 2.)

- then add 30.

So the temperature in °F was:

$39 \times 2 + 30$ (Remember to use BODMAS when you work out the answer. That means you must do the multiplying before the adding.)

$= 78 + 30 = 108$

So the temperature in Nice was approximately 108 °F. (Remember to include the units in your answer.)

Example 22.10

A very rough conversion from °F to °C is to subtract 30 from the temperature in °F and then halve the answer.

The temperature at Wick on 5 August was 58 °F.

Use this rule to convert the temperature to °C.

To find the temperature in °C, the rule tells you:

- to subtract 30 from the temperature in °F

- then halve the answer.   (Halve means the same as divide by 2.)

So the temperature in °C was:

$(58 - 30) \div 2$ (Remember to use BODMAS when you work out the answer. Write the subtraction part in a bracket as it must be done before the dividing.)

$= 28 \div 2 = 14$

So the temperature in Wick was approximately 14 °C.

Exercise 22C

1 Use the table on page 281 to decide which units you should use to measure each of the following.

   a the width of the classroom

   b the weight of an aeroplane

   c the amount of water in a swimming pool

   d the weight of a page of this book

   e the temperature in Australia

   f the distance from Inverness to Aberdeen

2 Write down a list of all the subjects that you are studying in school.

   Write down which units might be used in each.

★ **3** Where might you use each of the following units outside school?

  a kilograms   **b** centimetres

  c litres   **d** kilometres

4 A very rough conversion from degrees Celsius (°C) to degrees Fahrenheit (°F) is to double the temperature in °C and then add 30.

Convert each of the following temperatures to °F using this rule.

  a 28 °C   **b** 12 °C   **c** 100 °C   **d** 0 °C

5 A very rough conversion from °F to °C is to subtract 30 from the temperature in °F and then halve the answer.

Use this rule to convert the following temperatures to °C.

  a 46 °F   **b** 126 °F   **c** 200 °F   **d** 180 °F

⚙ **6** The temperature scale on a domestic oven is usually in °C.

Older recipe books will tell you temperatures in °F.

Use the formula in Question 5 to decide what temperature the oven should be set:

  a to bake a cake where the recipe says 325 °F

  b to cook a chicken where the recipe says 375 °F

  c to bake a meringue where the recipe says 230 °F.

GO! Activity

What numerical notation would be used when planning a charity coffee morning?

Think about all the tasks that you might need to do to organise such an event.

Write a summary of these tasks and note what units you have had to use.

Chapter review

1 Evaluate the following.

  a $5 + 20 \div 4$ **b** $19 + 12 - 3 \times 2$ **c** $\frac{1}{3}$ of $(27 + 6)$

  d $3 \times (6 + 2) - 5$ **e** $21 \div 7 \times 4$ **f** $22 - 21 \div 3$

2 Copy these statements and use > or < to make them true.

  a $3 \times 8 \ldots 19 + 7$ **b** $(30 \div 5) + 9 \ldots 4 \times 4 + 3$

  c $23 - 5 + 17 \ldots (16 + 4) \times 2$ **d** $5 \times 8 \div 2 \ldots 8 + \frac{1}{3}$ of 27

3 The junior running club has 22 girls and 19 boys in it.

Write the ratio of girls to boys using ratio notation.

4 12 448 people attended a football match.

Round the number of people who attended the match to:

  a the nearest 10   **b** the nearest 100   **c** the nearest 1000.

5 Round each number to:

  i 1 decimal place   **ii** 2 decimal places.

  a 22.149   **b** 2.055   **c** 0.0549

N4 6 Round each number to 1 significant figure.

    a   362   **b** 29.03   **c** 0.044   **d** 0.682

7 Which units would you use to measure each of the following?

    a   the amount of water in a kettle

    b   the weight of a mouse

    c   the height of a door

    d   the distance from Edinburgh to Oban

    e   the temperature in India

    f   the weight of a car.

8 A very rough conversion from degrees Celsius (°C) to degrees Fahrenheit (°F) is to double the temperature in °C and then add 30.

  The temperature in Rome on 14 August was 28 °C.

  Use the rule to convert this temperature to °F.

• I can select and use numerical notation. ★ Exercise 22A Q1	◯	◯	◯
• I can use the correct order of operations. ★ Exercise 22A Q3	◯	◯	◯
• I can round to a given degree of accuracy. ★ Exercise 22B Q6a, Q7a, Q8	◯	◯	◯
N4 • I can round a given number to 1 significant figure. ★ Exercise 22B Q6b, Q7b	◯	◯	◯
• I can select and use appropriate units. ★ Exercise 22C Q3	◯	◯	◯

23 Decimal calculations and converting units

This chapter will show you how to:

- add and subtract decimal numbers
- multiply and divide decimals by whole numbers up to 10
- multiply and divide by 10, 100 and 1000
- **N4** multiply and divide by multiples of 10, 100 and 1000
- use rounding to estimate answers
- convert between units of measure.

You should already know:

- the multiplication and division facts up to 10×10
- what is meant by a decimal
- how to round to a given degree of accuracy
- the most common units of measurement.

Decimal calculations

You will come across calculations involving decimals throughout Applications of Maths.

One of the main areas is Finance, where you will usually be working to the nearest penny or 2 decimal places.

This section revises adding, subtracting, multiplying and dividing calculations which involve decimals.

This chapter demonstrates non-calculator methods for calculating with decimals. When you have finished each exercise, you should check your answers with a calculator.

Adding and subtracting decimals

The important thing to remember here is that you must **line up the decimal points**. This will ensure that your **values** are in the right **place**.

Example 23.1

Calculate:

> Remember that **calculate** just means 'work out the answer'.

a $3.91 + 16.07$ **b** $156.3 - 2.137$ **c** $27 - 14.36$

a
```
    3.91
+ 16.07
  19.98
```

b
```
  156.300
-   2.137
  154.163
```

> Write in the two extra zeros on the top line so every column has a digit in it.

c
```
  27.00
- 14.36
  12.64
```

Example 23.2

Carol spent £14.95 on a t-shirt, £26.30 on a pair of trousers and £11.55 on a hat.

How much change did she get from £60?

Total spent is

```
  14.95
  26.30
+ 11.55
  52.80
```

> You need to find the **total** that Carol spent by adding up the prices of the three items.

Amount left is

```
  60.00
- 52.80
   7.20
```

> To find the change, you need to subtract the amount she has spent from £60.

Carol got £7.20 change.

Multiplying and dividing decimals by a whole number

When you multiply and divide decimal numbers by a whole number, you need to line up the decimal point in the answer with the decimal point in the question.

Example 23.3

Calculate:

a 43.72 × 8   **b** 21.56 ÷ 7

a
```
    43.72
  ×     8
   349.76
    2 5  1
```

b
```
     3·0 8
  7 | 21·5 ⁵6
```

> It is important to write down the zero in the middle of the answer: 3.08 and 3.8 are different numbers.

Exercise 23A

1 Calculate these sums.

   a 43.61 + 1.972   **b** 3.6 + 150.72   **c** 68.74 + 2.315   **d** 539.8 + 1.27

2 Calculate these differences.

   a 5.32 − 1.07   **b** 396.1 − 23.48   **c** 83.3 − 7.09   **d** 204 − 59.8

3 Work out these products.

   a 37.6 × 5   **b** 60.4 × 9   **c** 187.52 × 3   **d** 8.84 × 7

4 Calculate these divisions.

   a 14.6 ÷ 4   **b** 70.14 ÷ 2   **c** 6.048 ÷ 6   **d** 255 ÷ 8

N4 ★ 5　a　$3 \times 4.93 - 2 \times 6.85$

b　$4(8.71 + 1.29) + 23.9$

c　$8.61 + 5 \times 7.93 - 2.254 \div 7$

> ⚠ $4(8.71 + 1.29)$ is the same as $4 \times (8.71 + 1.29)$

6　Naomi bought 5 boxes of chocolates. Each box cost £5.75.

How much change did she get from £30?

7　Ed and his 3 friends went out for a meal.

The bill for the meal came to £93.80 in total.

They decide to split the bill equally between them.

How much will each person have to pay?

When you have finished the questions in this exercise, check your answers with a calculator.

Multiplying and dividing by multiples of 10, 100 and 1000

When you multiply by 10, 100 and 1000 you move all the digits 1, 2 or 3 places to the left.

When you divide by 10, 100 and 1000, all the digits move to the right.

Example 23.4

Calculate:

a　34×10　　b　6.91×1000　　c　$743 \div 100$　　d　$27.61 \div 1000$

a

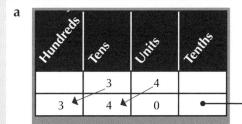

> When you multiply by 10, the digits move 1 place to the left, so the 3 moves to the hundreds column and the 4 to the tens column. Remember to fill in the 'empty' units column with a zero.

$34 \times 10 = 340$

b

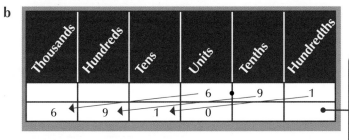

> When you multiply by 1000, the digits move 3 places to the left. The 6 goes into the thousands column, the 9 into the hundreds column, the 1 into the tens column and you write a 0 in the units column.

$6.91 \times 1000 = 6910$

c

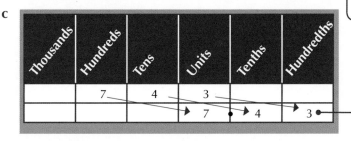

> When you divide by 100, the digits move 2 places to the right. Remember to insert the decimal point between the units and the tenths.

$743 \div 100 = 7.43$

N4

d

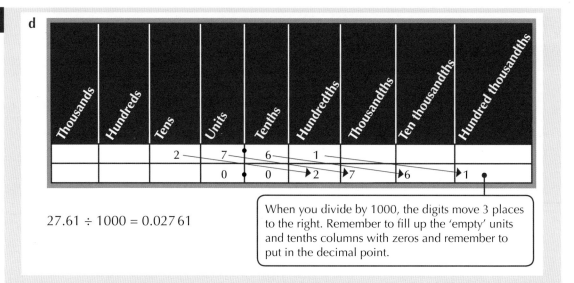

Thousands	Hundreds	Tens	Units	Tenths	Hundredths	Thousandths	Ten thousandths	Hundred thousandths
		2	7	6	1			
			0	0	2	7	6	1

$27.61 \div 1000 = 0.02761$

> When you divide by 1000, the digits move 3 places to the right. Remember to fill up the 'empty' units and tenths columns with zeros and remember to put in the decimal point.

Multiplying and dividing using factors

To multiply by numbers such as 20, 40, or 5000, we can split the number we are multiplying by into **factors**. A factor of a number is a number that divides into the larger number an exact number of times with no remainder.

For example: 20 is split into pairs of factors in several ways:

- $1 \times 20 = 20$
- $2 \times 10 = 20$
- $4 \times 5 = 20$

1, 2, 4, 5, 10 and 20 are all factors of 20.

The pair of factors of 20 that makes multiplying or dividing easiest is 2×10.

40 and 5000 have lots of different combinations of factors. The ones that make the multiplying or dividing calculation easiest are the ones that contain 100 and 1000:

- factors to use for 20 would be 2×10
- factors to use for 400 would be 4×100
- factors to use for 5000 would be 5×1000.

Example 23.5

Calculate:

a 36×20 **b** 41.723×500 **c** 8.61×7000

a $36 \times 20 = 36 \times 2 \times 10$

$= 72 \times 10 = 720$

> 20 is split into its factors 2 and 10. Multiply by 2 and then by 10.

b $41.723 \times 500 = 41.723 \times 5 \times 100$

$= 208.615 \times 100 = 20861.5$

> 500 is split into its factors 5 and 100. Multiply by 5 and then by 100.

c $8.61 \times 7000 = 8.61 \times 7 \times 1000$

$= 60.27 \times 1000 = 60270$

> 7000 is split into its factors 7 and 1000. Multiply by 7 and then by 1000.

N4 The same method is used for dividing using factors. For example, to divide by 30, you need to split 30 into its two factors of 3 and 10, and divide by both factors.

Example 23.6

Evaluate:

a $154.8 \div 30$　　**b** $9240 \div 400$　　**c** $81\,120 \div 6000$

a $154.8 \div 30 = 154.8 \div 3 \div 10$

> 30 is split into its factors 3 and 10. Divide by 3 and then by 10.

$\qquad = 51.6 \div 10$

$\qquad = 5.16$

b $9240 \div 400 = 9240 \div 4 \div 100$

$\qquad = 2310 \div 100$

$\qquad = 23.10$

c $81\,120 \div 6000 = 81\,120 \div 6 \div 1000$

$\qquad = 13\,520 \div 1000$

$\qquad = 13.52$

Example 23.7

Kat earns £8.40 per hour.

She works for 30 hours each week.

How much will her pay be each week before deductions?

$8.40 \times 30 = 8.40 \times 3 \times 10$

> The weekly pay is the rate per hour multiplied by the number of hours worked.

$\qquad = 25.20 \times 10 = 252$

Kat earns £252 each week before deductions.

> Remember to put your answer in context.

Example 23.8

James's car can travel 40 miles on each gallon of fuel.

How much fuel will he need for a journey of 1440 miles?

$1440 \div 40 = 1440 \div 4 \div 10$

> The number of gallons needed will be the total number of miles divided by the number of miles James can travel on 1 gallon.

$\qquad = 360 \div 10 = 36$

James will need 36 gallons of fuel.

Exercise 23B

1 Calculate:

　a 47×300　　　**b** 861×7000　　　**c** 2461×500

2 Calculate:

　a 3.91×40　　　**b** 16.041×200　　　**c** 107.02×6000

3 Work out the answers to these divisions.

　a $1920 \div 60$　　　**b** $18\,900 \div 700$　　　**c** $24\,300 \div 300$

N4

4   Calculate:

    a $1638 \div 200$ **b** $12.6 \div 40$ **c** $13\,696 \div 8000$

★ 5   Calculate:

    a $43 \times 20 + 16 \times 70$ **b** $92 - 1150 \div 50$ **c** $0.82 \times 300 - 1.79 \times 40$

6   Laura is training to run a marathon.

    She runs 16 miles each day for 30 days.

    How many miles has she run in total after the 30 days?

7   William earns a total of £186 a week before deductions.

    He works for 20 hours each week.

    What is his hourly rate of pay?

When you have finished the questions in this exercise, check your answers with a calculator.

Using rounding to estimate answers

Being able to estimate the answer to a calculation is a very important skill to have.

It means that you can have a good idea of what the correct answer should be even before you type the numbers into a calculator. In everyday life, it is useful to be able to estimate answers so you can see quickly if you have enough money for your spending.

Estimates are always made by rounding numbers.

Example 23.9

Find approximate answers to these by first rounding each number to 1 significant figure:

a 56×347 **b** 179×236 **c** 13.7×62 **d** 0.052×38

a $56 \times 347 \approx 60 \times 300$

        $= 6 \times 10 \times 3 \times 100$

        $= 6 \times 3 \times 10 \times 100$

        $= 18\,000$

> Round each number to 1 significant figure before multiplying.

> Split the 60 and 300 into factors in the same way as in Example 23.5.

b $179 \times 236 \approx 200 \times 200$

        $= 2 \times 100 \times 2 \times 100$

        $= 2 \times 2 \times 100 \times 100$

        $= 40\,000$

c $13.7 \times 62 \approx 10 \times 60$ **d** $0.052 \times 38 \approx 0.05 \times 40$

        $= 10 \times 6 \times 10$ $= 0.05 \times 4 \times 10$

        $= 6 \times 10 \times 10$ $= 0.2 \times 10$

        $= 600$ $= 2$

N4

Example 23.10

Find approximate answers to these by first rounding each number to 1 significant figure:

a 821 ÷ 43 **b** 5789 ÷ 527 **c** 73.9 ÷ 6.8 **d** 237 ÷ 431

a 821 ÷ 43 ≈ 800 ÷ 40

= 800 ÷ 4 ÷ 10

= 200 ÷ 10

= 20

Round each number to 1 significant figure before dividing.

Split the 40 into factors in the same way as Example 23.6.

b 5789 ÷ 527 ≈ 6000 ÷ 500

= 6000 ÷ 5 ÷ 100

= 1200 ÷ 100

= 12

c 73.9 ÷ 6.8 ≈ 70 ÷ 7

= 10

d 237 ÷ 431 ≈ 200 ÷ 400

= 200 ÷ 4 ÷ 100

= 50 ÷ 100

= 0.50

Example 23.11

Jo is organising a trip to Dynamic Earth in Edinburgh.

There are 43 children going on the trip.

The price for each child is £8.55.

The children have raised £250 to try to cover the cost of the tickets.

Is this enough to cover the cost of the children's tickets?

8.55 × 43 ≈ 9 × 40

= 360

The total cost of the tickets will be the price per ticket multiplied by 43.

Round each number to 1 significant figure before multiplying.

So the tickets will cost roughly £360.

The amount raised will not cover the cost of the tickets.

N4 **Exercise 23C**

In Question 1 and Question 2, estimate the answers by first rounding each number to 1 significant figure.

1 **a** 29×37 **b** 83×17 **c** 341×72

  d 419×768 **e** 3821×297

2 **a** $83 \div 42$ **b** $8419 \div 235$ **c** $296 \div 64$

  d $7215 \div 468$ **e** $3146 \div 782$

★ **3** By rounding each number to 1 significant figure before multiplying or dividing, decide which of the three suggested answers **A**, **B** or **C** is correct.

a	78×31	**A**	241.8	**B**	2418	**C**	24 180
b	329×46	**A**	15 134	**B**	1513.4	**C**	15 340
c	$828 \div 36$	**A**	230	**B**	2.3	**C**	23
d	$236.88 \div 423$	**A**	56	**B**	0.56	**C**	5.6

When you have finished the questions in this exercise, check your answers with a calculator.

Converting units

When you are working with metric units of length, weight and volume, you sometimes need to convert between units. Because the metric system uses multiples of 10, conversion between units is simply a matter of multiplying or dividing by 10, 100 or 1000.

Length	millimetres (mm) centimetres (cm) metres (m) kilometres (km)	10 mm = 1 cm 1000 mm = 100 cm = 1 m 1000 m = 1 km
Weight	grams (g) kilograms (kg) tonnes (t)	1000 g = 1 kg 1000 kg = 1 t
Volume/ capacity	millilitres (ml) litres (l) cubic centimetres (cm³) cubic metres (m³)	1000 ml = 1 l 1 ml = 1 cm³

If you are converting from a bigger unit to a smaller one, you multiply.

If you are converting from a smaller unit to a bigger one, you divide.

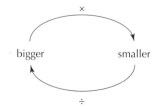

Example 23.12

Convert:

a 43.61 m to cm   **b** 917 g to kg   **c** 346 823 mm to km

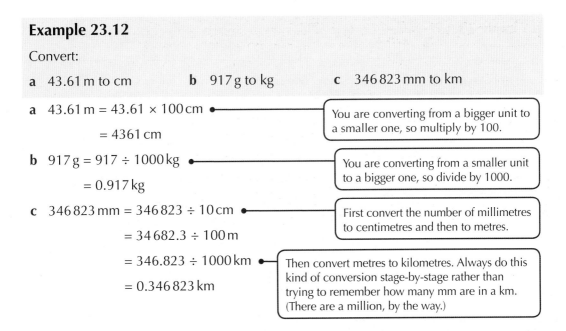

a 43.61 m = 43.61 × 100 cm ●────── You are converting from a bigger unit to a smaller one, so multiply by 100.

= 4361 cm

b 917 g = 917 ÷ 1000 kg ●────── You are converting from a smaller unit to a bigger one, so divide by 1000.

= 0.917 kg

c 346 823 mm = 346 823 ÷ 10 cm ●────── First convert the number of millimetres to centimetres and then to metres.

= 34 682.3 ÷ 100 m

= 346.823 ÷ 1000 km ●────── Then convert metres to kilometres. Always do this kind of conversion stage-by-stage rather than trying to remember how many mm are in a km. (There are a million, by the way.)

= 0.346 823 km

 ## Exercise 23D

In Questions 1–4 convert each measurement to the unit given.

1   **a**   46 mm to cm   **b**   865 cm to m   **c**   1285 m to km

    d   34.16 m to cm   **e**   41.9 km to m

2   **a**   340.6 tonnes to kg   **b**   234 g to kg   **c**   71.3 kg to g

3   **a**   2500 ml to litres   **b**   14 litres to cm^3

★ **4**   **a**   31 m to mm   **b**   2 km to cm   **c**   2.3 tonnes to g

When you have finished the questions in this exercise, check your answers with a calculator.

Choosing the correct calculation

Each time you are given a problem to solve in Applications of Maths, you will need to decide what sort of calculation you are being asked to do. Do you need to add, subtract, multiply or divide?

You may need to do two different types of calculation to get to the final answer. Look back at Chapter 22 to revise the different words that might help you decide what you are being asked to do.

You might need to explain your answer. If you need to do this you must refer back to your working to **justify** the decision that you have made.

Example 23.13

Naomi went on holiday from her home in Biggar to York. Her total journey was 184 miles.

She stopped after 61 miles at Gretna for coffee and then 42 miles later for a comfort break.

How many miles did she still have to go before she reached York?

Distance travelled:

61 + 42 = 103 ●————— You need to find the **total** she has travelled so far, so **add** the two distances.

Distance still to go:

184 − 103 = 81 ●————— To find the distance still to go, you need to subtract the distance covered so far from the complete journey.

She still had 81 miles to go to reach York. ●————— Remember to write a sentence at the end to explain your answer.

 Exercise 23E

1 Joe buys 4 boxes of sweets each costing £4.76.

How much change will he get from £20?

⚙★ **2** Sam buys 64 cakes at 72 pence each to serve at a coffee morning she is organising.

She has £40 to spend.

Will this be enough to pay for the cakes?

3 Anton is organising juice drinks for a children's party.

Each child will get 175 ml of juice.

How many **litres** of juice will he need for 40 children?

⚙★ **4** Imran is baking cakes.

Each cake needs 80 g of flour.

He has 2.7 kg of flour available.

What is the **maximum** number of cakes that Imran can make?

⚙★ **5** Rory is trying to find a new mobile phone deal.

He finds two companies who both offer a 12-month contract.

The table shows information for each deal.

Company 1: Fones R Fun	Company 2: Calls 4 U
12-month contract	12-month contract
Handset only £23	Free handset
£20 per month for unlimited calls, texts and 10Gb data	First 4 months free, then £32 per month for unlimited calls, texts and 10Gb data

Which company should Rory choose? Use your working to justify your answer.

When you have finished the questions in this exercise, check your answers with a calculator.

● Activity

Imagine that you are organising a children's birthday party for 20 eight-year-olds.

You have a budget of £175.

You are going to use the local community hall, which will cost £45 to hire.

Make a list of all the things that you might need for the party.

Don't forget food, drinks, entertainment, prizes for games and party bags.

Work out the total cost of running the party, remembering that you have a maximum budget.

Chapter review

1   Alison's car does 8.04 miles on each litre of fuel.

   How far will she be able to go on 50 litres of fuel?

2   Laura makes 30 scarves.

   She sews ribbon around the edge of each scarf.

   Each scarf needs 254 cm of ribbon.

   Laura has 80 m of the ribbon.

   Is this enough for all 30 scarves?

3   Aneesa buys concert tickets for herself and her 6 friends.

   Each ticket costs £23.50.

   How much will the tickets cost altogether?

4   The local football club held a coffee morning to raise funds for a trip to Canada.

   The cost to hire the hall was £120.

   The total takings for the day are shown below.

   60 cakes sold   @ 65 p each

   raffle ticket sales £83

   beat the goalie £31

   30 packs of homemade cards @ £3.75 each

   50 badges @ £1.25 each

   Calculate the total profit that the football club made at the coffee morning.

5   A school trip is being organised.

   In total, 156 pupils and 18 staff are going on the trip.

   The local bus hire company has two sizes of bus available:

   • 45-seater costs £320

   • 20-seater costs £155

   The school wants to pay the least possible price for the bus hire.

   Work out how many of each size of bus they should hire and how much this will cost.

6   Brendan makes four different shapes of candles.

He counts up how many of each type of candle he has.

The numbers and prices are shown in the table.

Shape	Number	Price
Cylinder	8	£6.50
Sphere	7	£4.75
Cube	9	£5.65
Cone	6	£3.95

He wants to use the money that he raises from selling all of his candles to buy a new bike, which costs £285.

How much **extra** money will he still need to raise after he has sold all of his candles?

When you have finished the questions in this exercise, check your answers with a calculator.

- I can add and subtract decimal numbers. ★ Exercise 23A Q5

- I can multiply and divide decimals by whole numbers up to 10. ★ Exercise 23A Q5

N4
- I can multiply and divide by 10, 100 and 1000 and by multiples of these. ★ Exercise 23B Q5

- I can use rounding to 1 significant figure to estimate answers. ★ Exercise 23C Q3

- I can convert between units of measure. ★ Exercise 23D Q4

- I can choose the correct calculations to solve problems. ★ Exercise 23E Q2, Q4, Q5

24 Fractions and percentages

Working with fractions

Fractions occur all around us in everyday life. You will come across fractions such as $\frac{1}{2}$, $\frac{1}{4}$ and $\frac{1}{3}$ regularly. This section shows you how to find a fraction of an amount.

Finding a fraction of a shape

Example 24.1

Colour in $\frac{1}{2}$ of this rectangle.

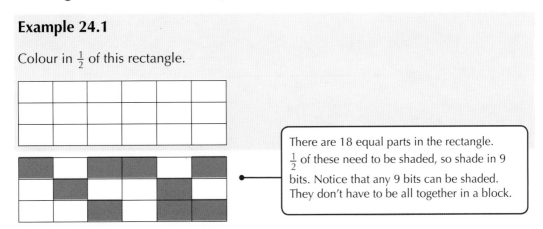

There are 18 equal parts in the rectangle. $\frac{1}{2}$ of these need to be shaded, so shade in 9 bits. Notice that any 9 bits can be shaded. They don't have to be all together in a block.

The important part in Example 24.1 was being able to calculate $\frac{1}{2}$ of 18.

The rule for finding a fraction of any amount is:

- divide the amount by the bottom number of the fraction (the **denominator**)

- multiply your answer by the top number of the fraction (the **numerator**).

Example 24.2

Calculate:

a $\frac{1}{5}$ of 35 m **b** $\frac{1}{3}$ of 96 kg **c** $\frac{3}{8}$ of £60

a 35 ÷ 5 = 7

So $\frac{1}{5}$ of 35 m is 7 m ●————

> When the numerator is 1, you don't actually need to do the multiplication since multiplying by 1 doesn't change the answer.
>
> Remember to include the units in the answer.

b 96 ÷ 3 = 32

So $\frac{1}{3}$ of 96 kg = 32 kg

c 60 ÷ 8 = 7.5

7.5 × 3 = 22.5 ●————

> In this question, you **do** need to multiply by the numerator because it is 3, not 1.

So $\frac{3}{8}$ of £60 is £22.50 ●————

> You need to write a zero at the end because amounts of money must have 2 digits after the decimal point.

Example 24.3

Alan won £480 in a lottery.

He decides to keep $\frac{2}{5}$ of his winnings for himself, give $\frac{1}{4}$ of his winnings to his son and $\frac{1}{3}$ of his winnings to his daughter.

He donates the rest of the money to charity.

How much will he give to charity?

Alan: $\frac{2}{5}$ of £480 ●————

> First work out the amount that Alan will get.

480 ÷ 5 = 96

96 × 2 = 192

Alan gets £192.

Alan's son: $\frac{1}{4}$ of £480 ●————

> Next work out the amount that Alan's son will get.

480 ÷ 4 = 120

Alan's son gets £120.

Alan's daughter: $\frac{1}{3}$ of £480 ●————

> Then work out the amount that Alan's daughter will get.

480 ÷ 3 = 160

Alan's daughter gets £160.

£192 + £120 + £160 = £472 ●————

> Alan, his son and his daughter receive £472 in total.

There is £480 − £472 = £8 left over to go to charity. ●————

> Subtract the total received by Alan, his son and his daughter from the original amount.

Exercise 24A

1   Calculate the following amounts.

    a $\frac{1}{2}$ of £34   **b** $\frac{1}{3}$ of 81 m   **c** $\frac{1}{5}$ of 95 kg

    d $\frac{2}{3}$ of 120 ml   **e** $\frac{3}{7}$ of 147 cm   **f** $\frac{2}{9}$ of £73.80

    g $\frac{7}{20}$ of 19.4 m   **h** $\frac{1}{100}$ of 3.65 km   **i** $\frac{5}{6}$ of 188.4 mm

    j $\frac{3}{4}$ of 0.84 m   **k** $\frac{2}{3}$ of £120.33   **l** $\frac{7}{10}$ of 134.87 kg

2   Calculate the following amounts.

    You can use a calculator for these, but you still need to show your working.

    a $\frac{5}{17}$ of 102 kg   **b** $\frac{3}{22}$ of 180.4 km   **c** $\frac{8}{19}$ of £686.28

    d $\frac{4}{11}$ of 15.07 g   **e** $\frac{7}{15}$ of 0.375 cm   **f** $\frac{11}{13}$ of 13.65 cm^2

    g $\frac{23}{25}$ of 6325 l   **h** $\frac{7}{12}$ of 201.6 ml   **i** $\frac{21}{34}$ of 578 mm

    j $\frac{41}{55}$ of £207.90   **k** $\frac{83}{100}$ of 216 g   **l** $\frac{23}{30}$ of 76.50 m

3   Julian has 80 sweeties. He gives $\frac{1}{4}$ to Sam, $\frac{1}{5}$ to Marcus and keeps the rest for himself.

    How many sweeties does each person get?

★ 4   A clothing shop is holding a sale.

    They are taking $\frac{1}{3}$ off the price of everything they sell.

    a How much will be taken off:

        i a t-shirt that cost £27.99 before the sale

        ii a pair of jeans that cost £45.99 before the sale

        iii a jacket that cost £153.99 before the sale?

    b Calculate the sale price for each of these items.

★ 5   Park House High School has 350 students in the senior school.

    Of these, $\frac{2}{5}$ come to school by bus, $\frac{3}{7}$ walk, $\frac{1}{10}$ cycle and the rest are driven to school by their parents.

    How many students in the senior school are driven to school by their parents?

6 189 tickets were sold in the maths department raffle.

$\frac{2}{7}$ of the tickets will win a pencil, $\frac{4}{9}$ of the tickets will win a ruler and $\frac{1}{27}$ of the tickets will win a calculator.

How many of each prize will need to be bought?

Simplifying fractions

Simplifying fractions is also known as **cancelling fractions** or expressing a fraction in its **lowest terms**.

To simplify a fraction, you need to find a number that is a **factor** of both the numerator (the top line) and the denominator (the bottom line) and then divide both by that factor.

A factor is a number that divides exactly with no remainder. For example:

- 3 is a factor of 12 because $12 \div 3 = 4$

- 7 is not a factor of 12 because $12 \div 7 = 1$ remainder 5

To express a fraction in its lowest terms, you need to divide both numerator and denominator by the greatest common factor (the biggest factor common to both of them).

Example 24.4

Simplify each fraction to its lowest terms.

a $\frac{5}{10}$ **b** $\frac{9}{12}$ **c** $\frac{18}{24}$ **d** $\frac{70}{105}$

a $\frac{5}{10} = \frac{5 \div 5}{10 \div 5}$ The greatest factor for the numerator **and** the denominator is 5, so divide both by 5.

$= \frac{1}{2}$

b $\frac{9}{12} = \frac{9 \div 3}{12 \div 3}$ The greatest common factor is 3.

$= \frac{3}{4}$

c $\frac{18}{24} = \frac{3}{4}$ The greatest common factor is 6.

d $\frac{70}{105} = \frac{70 \div 5}{105 \div 5}$ You can simplify in stages. The numerator and denominator both have 5 as a factor, so first divide both by 5.

$= \frac{14}{21} = \frac{14 \div 7}{21 \div 7}$ You can see that both numerator and denominator have a factor of 7, so divide them both by 7.

$= \frac{2}{3}$ You can't simplify any further, so the fraction is in simplest terms.

N4 **Equivalent fractions**

When you are asked to compare the sizes of two fractions, it is easier if they have the same denominator.

It will usually be necessary to scale one or both of the fractions up (by multiplying) or down (by dividing) to get common denominators.

N4

Example 24.5

For each part:

   i   change the fractions so that they have the same denominator

   ii state which fraction is larger.

a $\frac{1}{2}$ and $\frac{3}{4}$ **b** $\frac{2}{3}$ and $\frac{7}{12}$ **c** $\frac{2}{3}$ and $\frac{3}{4}$ **d** $\frac{3}{5}, \frac{3}{4}$ and $\frac{7}{10}$

---

a **i** $\frac{1}{2} = \frac{1 \times 2}{2 \times 2} = \frac{2}{4}$

      $\frac{3}{4}$ does not need to be changed

> The denominators of the two fractions are 2 and 4. The first number that is a multiple of 2 **and** 4 is 4, so you need to change the $\frac{1}{2}$ to have a denominator of 4 by multiplying both the numerator and the denominator by 2.
> The **multiples** of a number are the numbers in the times table for that number.

  ii $\frac{3}{4}$ is larger than $\frac{2}{4}$

      So $\frac{3}{4}$ is bigger than $\frac{1}{2}$

> $\frac{3}{4}$ is bigger than $\frac{2}{4}$ because its numerator is larger.

b **i** $\frac{2}{3} = \frac{2 \times 4}{3 \times 4} = \frac{8}{12}$

      $\frac{7}{12}$ does not need to be changed

> The first multiple of both 3 and is 12, so the new common denominator needs to be 12.

  ii $\frac{8}{12}$ is larger than $\frac{7}{12}$

      So $\frac{2}{3}$ is larger than $\frac{7}{12}$

> $\frac{8}{12}$ is bigger than $\frac{7}{12}$ because its numerator is larger.

c **i** $\frac{2}{3} = \frac{2 \times 4}{3 \times 4} = \frac{8}{12}$

      $\frac{3}{4} = \frac{3 \times 3}{4 \times 3} = \frac{9}{12}$

> The denominators are 3 and 4. The first multiple of both is 12, so the new common denominator needs to be 12.

  ii $\frac{9}{12}$ is larger than $\frac{8}{12}$

      So $\frac{3}{4}$ is larger than $\frac{2}{3}$

d **i** $\frac{3}{5} = \frac{3 \times 4}{5 \times 4} = \frac{12}{20}$

      $\frac{3}{4} = \frac{3 \times 5}{4 \times 5} = \frac{15}{20}$

      $\frac{7}{10} = \frac{7 \times 2}{10 \times 2} = \frac{14}{20}$

> The denominators are 5, 4 and 10. The first multiple of **all** of these is 20, so the common denominator needs to be 20.

  ii $\frac{15}{20}$ is the largest, then $\frac{14}{20}$, then $\frac{12}{20}$

      So $\frac{3}{4}$ is the largest, then $\frac{7}{10}$, then $\frac{3}{5}$

Exercise 24B

★ **1** Simplify each fraction to its simplest terms.

   a $\dfrac{3}{6}$ b $\dfrac{3}{9}$ c $\dfrac{2}{8}$ d $\dfrac{5}{10}$ e $\dfrac{10}{12}$ f $\dfrac{15}{20}$ g $\dfrac{24}{30}$

   h $\dfrac{45}{54}$ i $\dfrac{24}{32}$ j $\dfrac{54}{72}$ k $\dfrac{105}{120}$ l $\dfrac{120}{160}$ m $\dfrac{120}{360}$ n $\dfrac{162}{270}$

N4

2 Change some or all of the fractions in each set so they have the same denominator. Then write the fractions in each set in order from largest to smallest.

   a $\dfrac{1}{2}$ and $\dfrac{1}{3}$ b $\dfrac{1}{4}$ and $\dfrac{1}{3}$ c $\dfrac{2}{3}$ and $\dfrac{3}{5}$ d $\dfrac{3}{5}$ and $\dfrac{3}{4}$

   e $\dfrac{1}{2}, \dfrac{7}{8}$ and $\dfrac{3}{4}$ f $\dfrac{5}{6}, \dfrac{9}{10}$ and $\dfrac{4}{5}$ g $\dfrac{5}{7}, \dfrac{1}{2}$ and $\dfrac{3}{4}$

★ **3** The Pink Sweetie Shop sells bags of assorted sweets. On Friday morning they weighed out the bags they would need for the weekend.

   On Friday, they sold $\frac{1}{4}$ of the bags, on Saturday they sold $\frac{2}{5}$ of the bags and on

   Sunday they sold $\frac{1}{3}$ of the bags.

   a   On which day did they sell most bags of sweets?

   b   The actual number of bags sold on Sunday was 20.

   How many bags did they have left when the shop closed on Sunday?

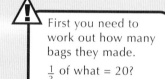

First you need to work out how many bags they made. $\frac{1}{3}$ of what = 20?

Working with percentages

Percentages are just another way of describing a fraction.

Percentages without a calculator

You should already be able to change some percentages into fractions.

The table below shows those you should know.

Percentage	Fraction equivalent	How to work it out	Percentage	Fraction equivalent	How to work it out
1%	$\dfrac{1}{100}$	divide by 100	$33\frac{1}{3}\%$	$\dfrac{1}{3}$	divide by 3
5%	$\dfrac{1}{20}$	divide by 20	50%	$\dfrac{1}{2}$	divide by 2
10%	$\dfrac{1}{10}$	divide by 10	$66\frac{2}{3}\%$	$\dfrac{2}{3}$	divide by 3 then multiply by 2
20%	$\dfrac{1}{5}$	divide by 5	75%	$\dfrac{3}{4}$	divide by 4 then multiply by 3
25%	$\dfrac{1}{4}$	divide by 4	100%	1	

Examples 24.6 and 24.7 show you how to tackle percentage questions when you don't have a calculator.

Example 24.6

Calculate:

a 50% of £64   **b** 75% of 96 kg   **c** $33\frac{1}{3}$% of 126 km

a 64 ÷ 2 = 32

50% of £64 is £32.

> 50% is the same as $\frac{1}{2}$, so find $\frac{1}{2}$ of £64 by dividing by 2.

b 96 ÷ 4 = 24

24 × 3 = 72

75% of 96 kg is 72 kg.

> 75% is the same as $\frac{3}{4}$. First find $\frac{1}{4}$ of 96 kg by dividing by 4.

> Then multiply your answer by 3.

> Remember to include any units in your answer.

c 126 ÷ 3 = 42

$33\frac{1}{3}$% of 126 km is 42 km.

> $33\frac{1}{3}$% is the same as $\frac{1}{3}$, so find $\frac{1}{3}$ of 126 km by dividing by 3.

N4

Example 24.7

Calculate:

a 30% of 48 cm   **b** 8% of 346 m   **c** 15% of £24

a 48 ÷ 10 = 4.8

4.8 × 3 = 14.4

30% of 48 cm is 14.4 cm.

> 30% is the same as 3 lots of 10%. So first find 10% of 48 by dividing by 10.

> Then multiply the answer by 3.

b 346 ÷ 100 = 3.46

3.46 × 8 = 27.68

8% of 346 m is 27.68 m.

> 8% is the same as 8 lots of 1%. So first find 1% of 346 by dividing by 100.

> Then multiply the answer by 8.

c 24 ÷ 10 = 2.4

2.4 ÷ 2 = 1.2

2.4 + 1.2 = 3.6

15% of £24 is £3.60.

> 15% = 10% + 5% so first find 10% of 24.

> Now find 5% by dividing that answer by 2.

> Now add the answers.

> Write your answer to 2 d.p. for money.

Exercise 24C

⚠️ Remember to include the units in your answer.

★ **1** Calculate each of the following amounts.

a 50% of £36	**b** 25% of 84 kg	**c** 20% of 412 km
d 75% of 256 ml	**e** 1% of 43 cm	**f** $33\frac{1}{3}$% of 93 mm
g 5% of 42 g	**h** 10% of 23.5 m	**i** $66\frac{2}{3}$% of £48

N4

2 Calculate:

a 30% of £456	**b** 70% of 65 km	**c** 15% of £125
d 65% of 450 kg	**e** $2\frac{1}{2}$% of 46 l	**f** $17\frac{1}{2}$% of £230

★ **3** All Styles clothes shop is having a sale.

They are taking 25% off everything they sell.

For each of the following items, work out:

    i the discount (the amount of money off)   **ii** the sale price.

    a a shirt originally costing £32

    b a pair of trousers originally costing £52.60

    c a jumper originally costing £22.

★ **4** Jack works in a supermarket. He gets paid £7 per hour.

    He is given a 3% pay rise.

    a What is his new hourly rate of pay?

    b How much will he get paid, before any deductions are made, when he works a 30-hour week?

⚠️ Remember to add the increase to his original rate of pay.

Percentages with a calculator

In many cases, the percentage that needs to be calculated is not straightforward.

In this case, you will need to use your calculator to work out the answer.

You should write down the calculation that you actually entered into the calculator, not only the answer that you get.

Example 24.8

Calculate:

a 43% of £875   **b** 31% of 549 kg   **c** 22.3% of £217.50

a 875 ÷ 100 × 43 = 376.25

So 43% of £875 is £376.25.

> 43% means $\frac{43}{100}$, so divide 875 by 100 and then multiply by 43.

b 549 ÷ 100 × 31 = 170.19

So 31% of 549 kg is 170.19 kg.

> 22.3% means $\frac{22.3}{100}$, so divide by 100 and then multiply by 22.3.

c 217.50 ÷ 100 × 22.3 = 48.5025

So 22.3% of £217.50 is £48.50.

> This question deals with money, so the final answer must be rounded to 2 decimal places.

Notice that in each question in Example 24.8, you need to divide by 100 before multiplying by the number of the percentage involved in the question.

N4

Example 24.9

Sairash bought a car for £8200.

After 1 year, the car had lost 27% of its value.

How much was the car worth after 1 year?

27% of 8200 = 8200 ÷ 100 × 27

= 2214

£8200 − £2214 = £5986 ●————— The car has lost value, so subtract. The new value must be less than the original value.

The new value of the car will be £5986.

Example 24.10

Ronan bought an antique vase for £455.

After 2 years the value of the vase had gone up by 13%.

How much was the vase worth after 2 years?

13% of £455 = 455 ÷ 100 × 13

= 59.15

£455 + £59.15 = £514.15 ●————— The vase has gained value, so add. The new value must be more than the original value.

The vase was worth = £514.15.

Exercise 24D

Remember to show your calculations. ⚠

★1   Calculate the following.

a	31% of 76 kg	**b**	23% of £125	**c**	87% of 34.8 km
d	47% of 653 cm	**e**	18.3% of 871 g	**f**	6.5% of £34
g	9.5% of 12.8 l	**h**	0.6% of 90 ml	**i**	14.7% of 56 m

2   A car bought for £2300 decreases in value by 12%.
    Calculate the new value of the car.

3   Mark earns £21 400 per annum (each year).
    He gets a 2.5% pay rise.
    What is his new annual pay?

N4 ★ 4 Mr and Mrs Khan have been told that their electricity bill is going to rise by 7.6%.
Their current monthly bill is £83.50.
What will their new monthly bill be?
Give your answer to the nearest penny.

5 A computer shop is reducing the prices of all its stock by $12\frac{1}{2}$% in its January sale.

How much will the sale price be of a laptop which cost £160 before the sale?

6 A vet tells Laura that her dog Riley needs to lose some weight.
Riley weighs 40 kg at the start of his diet.
He loses 9.3% of his original bodyweight.
How much does he weigh now?

7 Fuel costs £1.22 per litre.
The cost of fuel is to rise by 3.1%.
What will the new price per litre be?
Give your answer to the nearest penny.

8 A carton of orange juice usually contains 0.75 litres.
As a special offer, the company increases the size of the carton so that it contains
$17\frac{1}{2}$% extra orange juice for no extra cost.
How much does the larger carton hold?
Give your answer to the nearest millilitre.

9 Julie earns £136 each week after deductions.
She spends 18% of this on her rent and 38% on bills.
How much money does she have left?

★ 10 A publisher gives a 13% discount on orders over £500.
Stewartwood High School orders books costing a total of £625 from the publisher.
How much will they need to pay after the discount has been taken off?

Changing a fraction into a percentage

This section of the chapter shows you how to change a fraction into a percentage.

A fraction means 'what part of the whole thing have you got?'

Since a 'whole thing' is the same as 100%, you need to find what fraction of 100% you have.

You find the fraction the same way as before:

- divide 100% by the denominator (the bottom line) of the fraction

- then multiply that answer by the numerator (the top line) of the fraction.

Example 24.11

Change each fraction into a percentage.

N4

a $\dfrac{1}{2}$ **b** $\dfrac{3}{5}$ **c** $\dfrac{3}{4}$

N4

a $\dfrac{1}{2}$ of $100\% = 100 \div 2 \times 1$

$\qquad\qquad\qquad = 50$

$\dfrac{1}{2} = 50\%$

N4

b $\dfrac{3}{5}$ of $100\% = 100 \div 5 \times 3 = 60$

$\dfrac{3}{5} = 60\%$

c $\dfrac{3}{4}$ of $100\% = 100 \div 4 \times 3 = 75$

$\dfrac{3}{4} = 75\%$

In most cases, you won't get an exact answer for the percentage.

When the answer is not exact, round the percentage to 1 decimal place unless you are told otherwise.

Example 24.12

Change each fraction into a percentage.

N4

a $\dfrac{1}{7}$ **b** $\dfrac{2}{9}$ **c** $\dfrac{19}{35}$

a $\dfrac{1}{7}$ of $100\% = 100 \div 7 \times 1 = 14.285\ldots$

> Write down the first 3 decimal places before you round to 1 d.p.

$\qquad\qquad\qquad = 14.3$ (1 d.p.)

$\dfrac{1}{7} = 14.3\%$

N4

b $\dfrac{2}{9}$ of $100\% = 100 \div 9 \times 2 = 22.222\ldots$

$\qquad\qquad\qquad = 22.2$ (1 d.p.)

$\dfrac{2}{9} = 22.2\%$

c $\dfrac{19}{35}$ of $100\% = 100 \div 35 \times 19 = 54.285\ldots$

$\qquad\qquad\qquad = 54.3$ (1 d.p.)

$\dfrac{19}{35} = 54.3\%$

N4 Changing fractions to percentages gives you an alternative way to compare the sizes of fractions as shown in Example 24.13.

Example 24.13

Megan sat three tests in maths.

She scored $\frac{19}{27}$ in the first one, $\frac{32}{45}$ in the second one and $\frac{38}{55}$ in the third one.

In which test did Megan do best?

Test 1:

$\frac{19}{27}$ of 100% = 100 ÷ 27 × 19

$\qquad\qquad = 70.370...$

$\qquad\qquad = 70.4$ (1 d.p.)

She scored 70.4% in her first test.

> For each test, you need to change Megan's score into a percentage.

Test 2:

$\frac{32}{45}$ of 100% = 100 ÷ 45 × 32

$\qquad\qquad = 71.111...$

$\qquad\qquad = 71.1$ (1 d.p.)

She scored 71.1% in her second test.

Test 3:

$\frac{38}{55}$ of 100% = 100 ÷ 55 × 38

$\qquad\qquad = 69.090...$

$\qquad\qquad = 69.1$ (1 d.p.)

She scored 69.1% in her third test.

She did best in her second test.

> Remember to state your conclusion at the end of the question.

Exercise 24E

★ **1** Change each fraction to a percentage.

   a $\frac{1}{5}$ **b** $\frac{1}{8}$ **c** $\frac{1}{9}$ **d** $\frac{1}{11}$ **e** $\frac{1}{61}$

2 Change each fraction to a percentage.

   a $\frac{17}{30}$ **b** $\frac{1}{12}$ **c** $\frac{17}{36}$ **d** $\frac{21}{43}$ **e** $\frac{127}{765}$

3 Adnan collects football programmes.

   He had 85 from Premier League games.

   He sold 32 of them.

   What percentage of his programmes did he sell?

N4

4   James had £23. He spent £16 on a new shirt.

What percentage of his money did he spend?

5   Mhairi had 36 sweets. She gave 19 to her friend Jane.

What percentage of sweets did Mhairi give to Jane?

6   At Abervay High School, 83 out of 124 pupils in S4 walk to school.

What percentage of pupils in S4 at Abervay High School walk to school?

7   There are 64 players in the Edinburgh Concert Band.

One evening only 49 players came to rehearsal.

What percentage of the total number of players came to the rehearsal that evening?

8   A bus company runs three services on a particular route each day.

They use a different size of bus each time as different numbers of passengers use the buses at different times of day.

For the morning service, 31 out of 40 seats were taken. At lunchtime, 16 out of 23 seats were taken. In the evening, 21 out of 35 seats were taken.

Which service had the lowest percentage of seats taken?

★9   Rory scored $\frac{35}{45}$ in his maths test, $\frac{27}{35}$ in his science test and $\frac{39}{55}$ in his geography test.

In which test did Rory do best?

10   Ethan bought a painting for £340 and sold it again for £400.

   a   How much profit did he make when he sold the painting?

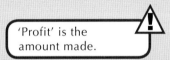

'Profit' is the amount made.

   b   What was his profit as a percentage of the buying price?

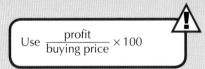

Use $\dfrac{\text{profit}}{\text{buying price}} \times 100$

★11   Changying bought a car for £2700 and sold it for £2100 a year later.

   a   How much of a loss did she make on the car?

   b   What was her loss as a percentage of her buying price?

Converting between a fraction and a decimal fraction

Converting a fraction to a decimal fraction

A fraction is a different way to write down a division calculation. For example, $\frac{1}{8}$ means exactly the same as $1 \div 8$.

To convert a fraction into a decimal fraction, you need to calculate: **numerator ÷ denominator**

This is very straightforward if you have a calculator.

Simply enter '1 ÷ 8 =' and the calculator will display 0.125.

Example 24.14 shows how to convert a fraction into a decimal fraction if you don't have a calculator.

Example 24.14

Change each fraction into a decimal fraction. Give your answer to 2 decimal places.

a $\frac{1}{4}$ **N4**   **b** $\frac{4}{7}$ **c** $\frac{5}{9}$

a $\frac{1}{4} = 1 \div 4$

$$\begin{array}{r} 0.25 \\ 4\overline{\smash{)}1.{}^{1}0{}^{2}0} \end{array}$$

$\frac{1}{4} = 0.25$

> Lay out the division as shown, lining up the decimal point in the answer line above the decimal point after the 1.
>
> Remember that you can write as many zeros as you need after the decimal point.

N4

b $\frac{4}{7} = 4 \div 7$

$$\begin{array}{r} 0.571 \\ 7\overline{\smash{)}4.0{}^{5}0{}^{1}0} \end{array}$$

$\frac{4}{7} = 0.57$ (to 2 d.p.)

> You need to work out the third decimal place so that you can then round the answer to 2 d.p. correctly.

c

$$\begin{array}{r} 0.555 \\ 9\overline{\smash{)}5.0{}^{5}0{}^{5}0} \end{array}$$

$\frac{5}{9} = 0.56$ (to 2 d.p.)

> Again, work out the third decimal place so that you can round the answer to 2 d.p.

N4

Converting a decimal fraction to a fraction

To convert a decimal to a fraction, you need to remember place value column headings:

$$\text{H} \quad \text{T} \quad \text{U} \quad . \quad \frac{1}{10} \quad \frac{1}{100} \quad \frac{1}{1000}$$

Example 24.15

Change each decimal fraction into a fraction in its lowest terms.

a 0.8   b 0.36   c 0.048

a $0.8 = \frac{8}{10}$ ⟶ The 0 is in the units column and the 8 is in the tenths column, so 0.8 is the same as 8 tenths.

$\frac{8}{10} = \frac{4}{5}$ ⟶ $\frac{8}{10}$ can be simplified by dividing both 8 and 10 by their common factor, 2.

$0.8 = \frac{4}{5}$

b $0.36 = \frac{36}{100}$ ⟶ The 0 is in the units column, the 3 is in the tenths column and the 6 is in the hundredths column, so 0.36 is the same as 36 hundredths.

$\frac{36}{100} = \frac{9}{25}$ ⟶ $\frac{36}{100}$ can be simplified by dividing both 36 and 100 by their common factor, 4.

$0.36 = \frac{9}{25}$

c $0.048 = \frac{48}{1000}$

$\frac{48}{1000} = \frac{6}{125}$ ⟶ Simplify.

$0.048 = \frac{6}{125}$

Exercise 24F

★ 1 Change each fraction to a decimal fraction. Round your answer to 2 decimal places where necessary.

     a $\frac{1}{5}$ b $\frac{1}{6}$ c $\frac{1}{3}$ d $\frac{1}{11}$

N4

2 Change each fraction to a decimal fraction. Round your answer to 2 decimal places where necessary.

     a $\frac{3}{7}$ b $\frac{7}{9}$ c $\frac{5}{16}$ d $\frac{21}{25}$ e $\frac{33}{71}$ f $\frac{5}{23}$

3 Change each decimal fraction into a fraction in its lowest terms.

     a 0.3   b 0.6   c 0.12   d 0.84   e 0.06   f 0.234

★ 4 Change each fraction to a decimal fraction and then arrange them in order from smallest to largest.

     $\frac{9}{13}$ $\frac{3}{4}$ $\frac{2}{3}$ $\frac{5}{7}$

GO! Activity

How many different ways are there to fold a strip of paper in half? For example:

Can you think of more ways?

Now try to find different ways of folding a strip into quarters, thirds and fifths without measuring.

Finally, get 10 strips of paper, all the same size, at least 20 cm long.

Try to fold the strips so that you have one that is in halves, one in thirds, one in quarters, one in fifths, all the way to tenths.

Label each strip with its fraction. Line up the strips. What do you notice?

Chapter review

1 Ollie won £850 on the lottery.

   He gave $\frac{1}{4}$ to his mother, $\frac{1}{5}$ to his brother and kept the rest himself.

   How much money did each person get?

2 Murdo's Computer Shop has a sale.

   They are taking $\frac{1}{3}$ off the price of all their stock.

   Calculate the sale price of:

   a a monitor which cost £117 before the sale

   b a laptop which cost £328.50 before the sale.

3 In a school raffle, $\frac{2}{7}$ of the tickets will win a prize.
   How many winning tickets will there be if 196 tickets are sold?

N4

4 Leanne earns £21 500 per annum.
   She is given a 2.8% pay rise.
   Calculate Leanne's new annual pay.

5 A plane was flying at 32 000 feet.
   Due to bad weather, the plane had to reduce its height by 23%.
   What was the new height of the plane?

6 A jacket cost £85.
   The price of the jacket was reduced by 48% in the sale.
   What was the sale price of the jacket?

7 A new vacuum cleaner is advertised for sale at a cash price of £280.

   The vacuum cleaner can be bought using a finance deal. The finance deal consists of:

   • a deposit of 15% of the cash price

   • then 12 monthly payments of £25.

   How much **extra** does the finance deal cost?

   ⚠ Look at Chapter 3 if you need a reminder about working out finance deals.

N4

8 A holiday to Spain is advertised at £345 per adult.

A child pays 70% of the adult price.

How much will this holiday cost for 2 adults and 3 children?

9 The number of absentees in each year group in Strathmuckle Academy was recorded on the first Monday of February last year. The table shows the results.

Year group	Total number in year	Number of absences
S1	125	16
S2	134	24
S3	117	18
S4	109	17
S5	67	12
S6	43	9

Which year group had the lowest percentage of absences?

10 Rosey makes jewellery.

It costs her £12 to make a pair of earrings.

She sells each pair of earrings for £17.50.

Calculate the percentage profit that Rosey makes on each pair of earrings.

11 Marlos invests £2450 in a savings account.

The bank pays 1.3% interest per annum (per year).

Marlos thinks that after 1 year, he will have enough interest to buy a new computer game costing £28.50. Is Marlos correct? Use your working to justify your answer.

- • I can find a fraction of a shape and of a quantity. ★ Exercise 24A Q4, Q5
- • I can simplify fractions. ★ Exercise 24B Q1

N4
- • I can find equivalent fractions. ★ Exercise 24B Q3

- • I can find a percentage of an amount without a calculator. ★ Exercise 24C Q1

N4
- • I can find a percentage of an amount with and without a calculator. ★ Exercise 24C Q3, Q4 ★ Exercise 24D Q1

- • I can calculate a percentage increase and a percentage decrease. ★ Exercise 24D Q4, Q10

- • I can convert between simple fractions, decimal fractions and percentages. ★ Exercise 24E Q1 ★ Exercise 24F Q1

N4
- • I can convert between fractions, decimal fractions and percentages. ★ Exercise 24E Q9, Q11 ★ Exercise 24F Q4

25 Speed, distance and time

This chapter will show you how to:

N4
- calculate distance, speed and time.

You should already know:

N4
- the correct units to use for distance, speed and time.

N4
Calculating distance, speed and time

Speed is a measure of the distance travelled in a set time. Speed is usually measured in metres per second (m/s), kilometres per hour (km/h) or miles per hour (mph).

You will often be asked to solve problems involving journeys. The problems might ask you to calculate:

- the distance covered for a given time and speed
- the average speed to travel a given distance in a given time.
- the time taken for a journey for a given speed and distance.

Speed, distance and time are related. If you know the values of two of them, you will be able to calculate the third one.

$$\text{distance} = \text{speed} \times \text{time} \qquad \text{speed} = \frac{\text{distance}}{\text{time}} \qquad \text{time} = \frac{\text{distance}}{\text{speed}}$$

Calculating the distance for a journey

If you travel at an average speed of 40 mph for 3 hours, you cover 40 miles in the first hour, 40 miles in the second hour and 40 miles in the third hour.

This gives a total of 3 lots of 40 miles. We write this as:

distance = 3 × 40 = 120 miles

So to find the **distance** covered you need to **multiply** the **average speed** and the **time** taken for the journey. This is written as a formula:

distance = speed × time

$d = s \times t$

N4

Example 25.1

Laura travels at an average speed of 35 km/h for 4 hours.

What is the total distance that she covers on her journey?

$d = s \times t$

$= 35 \times 4$ ●————— Substitute the values you have for speed (35) and time (4).

$= 140$ km

Laura covers a total of 140 km. ●————— Remember to put the correct units in the answer. The speed was in **km** per hour, so the distance is in **km**.

Example 25.2

Stevie the snail moves at an average speed of 1.5 cm per second.

How far will he travel after 3 minutes?

3 minutes = $3 \times 60 = 180$ s ●————— The speed is given here in cm per **second** but the time is given in **minutes**. Convert the 3 minutes into seconds before you substitute into the formula.

$d = s \times t$

$= 1.5 \times 180$

$= 270$ cm

Stevie travels 270 cm in 3 minutes. ●————— The units are **cm** this time because the speed was in **cm** per second.

Fractions of hours

Most journeys do not last an exact number of hours. Parts of hours are usually given in minutes. To use these parts of hours, you need to convert the minutes to decimal fractions:

15 minutes = $\frac{1}{4}$ of an hour = 0.25 hours

30 minutes = $\frac{1}{2}$ of an hour = 0.5 hours

45 minutes = $\frac{3}{4}$ of an hour = 0.75 hours

Example 25.3

Ruby travels at an average speed of 30 mph for 4 hours and 30 minutes.

How far does she travel in that time?

$d = s \times t$

$= 30 \times 4.5$ ●————— Change the time to a decimal fraction and substitute into the formula.

$= 135$ m

Ruby travels 135 miles in 4 hours 30 minutes.

N4

Example 25.4

The flight from Carcassonne Airport in the south of France to Glasgow International Airport takes 2 hours 15 minutes.

The aeroplane flies at an average speed of 480 mph.

How far is it from Carcassonne Airport to Glasgow International Airport?

$d = s \times t$

$\quad = 480 \times 2.25$ •————————

$\quad = 1080$ miles

> Change the time to a decimal fraction and substitute into the formula.

It is 1080 miles from Carcassonne Airport to Glasgow International Airport.

Exercise 25A

All the speeds given in Exercise 25A are average speeds.

1 Find the distance travelled in miles if:

    a you walk at 3 mph for 2 hours   **b** you run at 5 mph for 3 hours

    c you cycle at 7 mph for 4 hours   **d** you drive at 42 mph for 6 hours.

2 Calculate the distance travelled by:

    a a bus travelling at 25 mph for 4 hours

    b a car travelling at 55 mph for 3 hours

    c a plane travelling at 450 mph for 5 hours

    d a ship travelling at 15 mph for 8 hours.

3 Kirsty went for a walk with her friend Lucy. They walked at 3 mph for 4 hours. How far did they walk?

4 Robbie drove for 3 hours 30 minutes at 42 mph. How far does he go?

5 Colin drives a lorry. He drives at a speed of 46 km/h for 1 hour 45 minutes. How far does he go?

6 David is an athlete. He runs at 14 km/h for 2 hours 15 minutes. How far does he run?

7 A train leaves Inverness at 1440 and arrives in Glasgow at 1810. The train's speed is 48 mph for the journey. How far is it from Inverness to Glasgow?

★ 8 A ferry leaves Oban at 0740 and arrives at Coll at 1025. The boat travels at a speed of 18 mph. How far is it from Oban to Coll?

N4

Calculating the average speed for a journey

You can calculate the average speed for a journey if you know the distance travelled and the time taken. Average speed cameras are used on sections of the A9, in the Highlands, and other roads around Scotland to check if drivers are driving within the speed limit. The camera system records how long each car takes to travel a set distance and it can calculate the average speed using a formula.

$$\text{speed} = \text{distance} \div \text{time}$$

$$= \frac{\text{distance}}{\text{time}}$$

$$s = \frac{d}{t}$$

Example 25.5

Jacob drove 180 miles in 3 hours.

What was his average speed?

$$s = \frac{d}{t}$$

$$= \frac{180}{3}$$

$$= 60 \text{ miles per hour}$$

> Remember to put the correct units in the answer. The distance was in **miles**, and the time was in **hours**, so the speed will be in **miles per hour**, or **mph**.

So Jacob was travelling at an average speed of 60 mph.

Example 25.6

Sue the slug covered 504 cm in 3 minutes.

What was her speed in cm per second?

$$3 \text{ minutes} = 3 \times 60 \text{ seconds} = 180 \text{ seconds}$$

$$s = d \div t$$

$$= 504 \div 180$$

$$= 2.8 \text{ cm per second}$$

> The time is given here in **minutes** but the question asks for the speed in cm per **second**. You must convert the 3 minutes into seconds before you can substitute into the formula.

Sue was travelling at an average speed of 2.8 cm per second.

Example 25.7

Jean took 2 hours 45 minutes to complete a journey of 121 km.

What was her average speed for the journey?

$$s = d \div t$$

$$= 121 \div 2.75$$

$$= 44 \text{ kilometres per hour}$$

> Change the time to a decimal fraction and substitute into the formula.

Jean's average speed was 44 km/h.

N4 **Exercise 25B**

Remember to give the units in your answer for each question.

1   Find the average speed for each of the following journeys:

   a   24 miles in 3 hours   **b**   224 km in 4 hours

   c   46 metres in 2 minutes   **d**   200 metres in 25 seconds

   e   273 km in 6 hours   **f**   110 miles in 4 hours

   g   216 metres in 5 minutes   **h**   1453.6 miles in 23 hours.

2   Find the average speed for each of these journeys:

   a   36 miles in 1 hour 30 minutes   **b**   15 miles in $\frac{1}{2}$ hour

   c   12 miles in 15 minutes   **d**   67.5 km in 2 hours 15 minutes

   e   207 miles in 5 hours 45 minutes   **f**   18 metres in 45 minutes

   g   407 miles in 9 hours 15 minutes   **h**   234.9 km in 6 hours 45 minutes.

3   Andreas travels from Aberdeen to Brechin, a distance of 40 miles.

   The journey takes him 2 hours 30 minutes.

   What was the average speed for his journey?

4   Michael is on holiday in France.

   He drove from Paris to Marseilles, a distance of 779 km.

   The journey took him 10 hours 15 minutes.

   What was his average speed for his journey?

5   A plane flies from New York to Amsterdam.

   The journey takes 7 hours 15 minutes.

   The distance is 3625 miles.

   Calculate the average speed of the plane.

6   A delivery van left Edinburgh at 0930 and arrived in Bathgate at 1045.

   The distance covered in that time was 26 miles.

   Calculate the average speed for the van's journey.

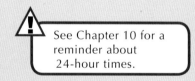

See Chapter 10 for a reminder about 24-hour times.

7   A train left Aberdeen at 1830 and arrived in Glasgow at 2115.

   The distance from Aberdeen to Glasgow is 145.75 miles.

   Calculate the average speed of the train.

★ 8   A ferry leaves Gills Bay in Caithness at 1135 to sail to St Margaret's Hope in Orkney, a distance of 21 miles.

   The ferry arrives at 1305.

   What is the average speed of the ferry?

Calculating the time taken for a journey

To calculate the time taken for a journey you need to know the distance travelled and the average speed of the object that is moving.

$$\text{time} = \text{distance} \div \text{speed} = \frac{\text{distance}}{\text{speed}} \qquad t = \frac{d}{s}$$

N4

Example 25.8

Pauline drove for 150 miles at an average speed of 50 mph.

How long did her journey take her?

$$t = \frac{d}{s} = \frac{150}{50}$$
$$= 3 \text{ hours}$$

Pauline's journey lasted for 3 hours.

Example 25.9

Ben cycled for 35 miles at an average speed of 20 mph.

How long did his journey take? Give your answer in hours and minutes.

$$t = \frac{d}{s} = \frac{35}{20}$$
$$= 1.75 \text{ hours} \bullet$$

> This decimal time needs to be converted into hours and minutes.
> 0.75 hours = 45 minutes

Ben's bike ride took 1 hour 45 minutes.

Example 25.10

Ella lives in Inverness. She has tickets for a concert in Glasgow.

The distance from her house to the venue is 170 miles. She knows that she can travel at an average speed of 40 mph.

She wants to arrive at the venue at 6 pm.

What is the latest time that she can leave Inverness so that she can arrive at the venue at 6 pm?

$$t = \frac{d}{s} = 170 \div 40 \bullet$$

> Start by working out how long Ella's journey will take.

$$= 4.25 \text{ hours} \bullet$$

> Remember that 0.25 hours is the same as 15 minutes.

Ella's journey takes 4 hours 15 minutes.

4 hours before 6 pm is 2 pm.

> You now need to work back from her arrival time of 6 pm to find the latest time that she can leave.

15 minutes before 2 pm is 1:45 pm.

Ella needs to leave Inverness no later than 1:45 pm.

N4 **Exercise 25C**

1   Find the time taken for each of these journeys.

     a   180 miles at 30 mph   b   150 km at 50 km/h

     c   160 miles at 40 mph   d   105 miles at 35 mph

     e   164 km at 41 km/h   f   207 miles at 34.5 mph

     g   800 metres at 25 metres per second   h   260 cm at 13 cm per second

     i   2560 km at 320 km/h   j   149.1 miles at 21.3 mph

2   Find the time taken for each of these journeys.

     Give your answer in hours and minutes.

     a   100 miles at 40 mph   b   137.5 km at 50 km/h

     c   52 miles at 16 mph   d   90 miles at 60 mph

     e   198 km at 36 km/h   f   135 km at 20 km/h

     g   1225 miles at 700 mph   h   40 km at 80 km/h

     i   30 miles at 40 mph   j   17.5 km at 70 km/h

3   Gerry drove from Beauly to Aberdeen at an average speed of 39 mph.

     The distance driven was 117 miles.

     How long did the journey take him?

4   Chris cycled from Perth to Dundee, a distance of 24 miles.

     Chris cycled at an average speed of 12 mph.

     How long did it take him to get from Perth to Dundee?

5   Angela ran 24 km at an average speed of 16 km/h.

     How long did her run take?

6   Pedro lives in Manchester. He is planning to drive to Glasgow to meet his girlfriend Toyah.

     The distance from Manchester to Glasgow is 217 miles and he knows that he can drive at an average speed of 62 mph for this journey.

     He has arranged to meet Toyah at 12:20 pm.

     What is the latest time that Pedro can leave Manchester if he is going to be on time?

7   Meredith is planning a night out in Edinburgh.

     Meredith lives in North Berwick, which is 22.5 miles from Edinburgh.

     She drives at an average speed of 30 mph.

     How long will it take her to drive to Edinburgh?

★ 8   A train from London arrived in Edinburgh at 1610.

     The train travelled at an average speed of 84 mph.

     The distance from London to Edinburgh is 399 miles.

     What time did the train leave London?

N4

Choosing the correct formula

In most questions, the first decision that you will need to make is which of the three formulae you need to use.

You will need to look for the key words in the question.

What you are asked to find	Key words
Distance	How far ...
Speed	How fast ...
Time	How long ...

Use the *SDT* triangle to help remember the formulae.

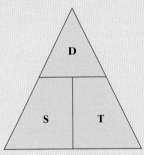

> To use the triangle, place your thumb over the quantity you want to find and look at the relationship between the other two quantities – are they beside each other (multiply) or is one above the other (divide)?

distance = speed × time

$$speed = \frac{distance}{time}$$

$$time = \frac{distance}{speed}$$

Example 25.11

Dev lives in Birmingham.

He travels to Glasgow to go to a football match.

The distance from Birmingham to Glasgow is 288 miles.

Dev takes 4 hours 30 minutes to complete the journey.

How fast was Dev travelling on the journey?

$s = \dfrac{d}{t}$ — The question asks **how fast** Dev was travelling, so you need to work out a **speed** for the journey.

$= 288 \div 4.5$

$= 64$

Dev's average speed was 64 mph. — Remember to change 4 hours 30 minutes into decimal time.

N4

Example 25.12

A plane left Glasgow International Airport at 1125 and landed in Dublin Airport at 1240.

The average speed of the plane was 316 km/h.

How far did the plane fly on this journey?

$d = s \times t$

$= 316 \times 1.25$

$= 395$

This question asks **how far** so you need to work out the **distance** travelled.

Use the departure and arrival times of the plane to work out how long the journey takes. Change the time from 1 hour 15 minutes into decimal time.

The distance from Glasgow International Airport to Dublin Airport is 395 km.

Make sure that you use the correct units. The speed was in **km/h** so the distance will be in **km**.

Example 25.13

Seonaid and Merryn are being driven from Biggar to Glasgow by Merryn's dad to see the indoor cycling championships.

The journey is 51 miles and Merryn's dad reckons that he can go at an average of 34 mph.

Seonaid and Merryn want to arrive at the venue when the doors open at 6 pm.

If they leave Biggar at 1650, will they be at the venue on time?

$t = d \div s$

$= 51 \div 34$

$= 1.5$ hours

$= 1$ hour 30 minutes

This question asks you to find **how long** the journey is going to take. This means that you are finding the **time taken** for the journey.

Add this time to the time they leave Biggar to find when they will arrive in Glasgow.

1650 + 1 hour 30 minutes = 1820 or 6:20 pm.

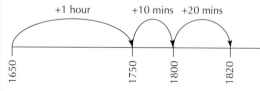

They will arrive 20 minutes after the doors open so, no, they will not be on time.

N4

Exercise 25D

In each question, you will first need to decide which of the three formulae to use.
Remember to look out for the key words that will help you.

1   A police car responding to an emergency call covered 25 miles in 30 minutes.
    What was the average speed of the police car in miles per hour?

2   A hot air balloon flight covered 35 km at an average speed of 14 km/h.
    How long did the balloon flight last?

3   A train left Paris at 1427 and arrived in Amsterdam at 1742.
    The distance from Paris to Amsterdam is 520 km.
    Calculate the average speed of the train.

4   Mick cycled from Land's End to London at an average speed of 12 mph.
    The journey took him 28 hours 45 minutes.
    How far did Mick cycle?

5   Campbell drove from Aberdovey in Wales to Biggar, a distance of 294 miles.
    He can drive at an average speed of 56 mph.
    How long will the journey take him?

6   Harry walks to school from his house each day.
    He leaves home at 8:10 am and arrives at school at 8:40 am.
    He walks at an average speed of 3 mph.
    How far is Harry's school from his house?

7   A bird takes 9.5 days to migrate from South Africa to Scotland.
    The bird can fly at an average speed of 1500 miles per day.
    How far does the bird fly in total?

8   The A9 road has average speed cameras set up to try to stop drivers from breaking
    the speed limit.
    One of the cameras records the length of time taken for a car to cover 21 miles.
    The speed limit on this part of the road is 70 mph.
    a   Emma covers this distance in 15 minutes.
        Is Emma breaking the speed limit?
    b   James covers this distance in 30 minutes.
        Is James breaking the speed limit?

★ 9   Tractor driver Joe leaves his farmhouse at 0730.
    He stops for 1 hour for lunch and also has 2 breaks of 20 minutes each during the day.
    He drives the tractor back to his farm at the end of the day.
    The tractor covers a total distance of 46 km that day.
    The tractor has an average speed of 8 km/h.
    At what time will Joe get back to his farmhouse?

N4

GO! Activity

A TV production company is planning a programme called *Breakout*.

In the programme, contestants have to travel as far as they can from their house in 24 hours.

The contestants can only use public transport. That means that they can only use buses, trains and planes.

The TV company will pay all the travel costs.

Use the internet to see how far you can go from your house in 24 hours.

Chapter review

1   Louise leaves her house at 11:35 am and drives to her friend Rebecca's house.

Rebecca lives 24 km from Louise.

Louise arrives at Rebecca's house at 12:50 pm.

Calculate Louise's average speed for the journey.

2   Brendan runs 10 000-metre road races.

His average speed is 8 km/h.

He thinks that he will complete his next race in under 1 hour 10 minutes if he runs at this speed.

Is he correct?

Use your working to explain your answer.

3   A plane takes 13 hours 45 minutes to fly from Dubai in the United Arab Emirates to Sydney in Australia.

The average speed of the plane is 544 mph.

Calculate how far the plane flew on this journey.

• I can calculate distance, speed and time.
  ★ Exercise 25A Q8 ★ Exercise 25B Q8
  ★ Exercise 25C Q8 ★ Exercise 25D Q9

26 Reading straightforward scales and negative numbers in context

N4

This chapter will show you how to:

- read a straightforward scale which has marked numbered divisions
- read a straightforward scale which has marked unnumbered divisions
- interpret negative numbers in real life contexts
- add and subtract negative numbers in context.

You should already know:

- how to measure a line using a ruler
- how to draw a number line for positive numbers
- how to use a number line to add and subtract numbers.

Reading straightforward scales

There are many occasions in everyday life where you will need to be able to read a scale.

You will already be familiar with rulers and protractors.

If you are cooking you will be using weighing scales to measure out dry ingredients and a measuring jug to measure out liquids.

This section looks at the scales that might be used in these situations.

Example 26.1

The scale on the ruler shown is in centimetres.

What measurement is shown by each of arrows **A**, **B**, **C** and **D**?

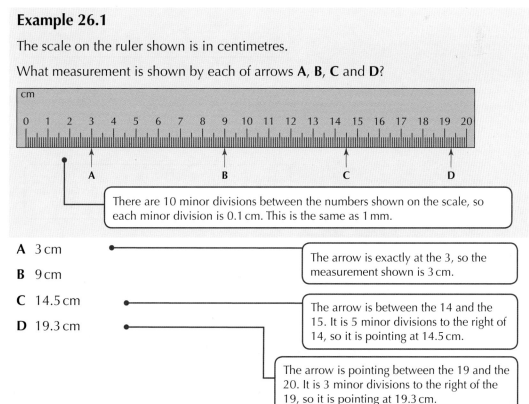

There are 10 minor divisions between the numbers shown on the scale, so each minor division is 0.1 cm. This is the same as 1 mm.

A 3 cm

The arrow is exactly at the 3, so the measurement shown is 3 cm.

B 9 cm

C 14.5 cm

The arrow is between the 14 and the 15. It is 5 minor divisions to the right of 14, so it is pointing at 14.5 cm.

D 19.3 cm

The arrow is pointing between the 19 and the 20. It is 3 minor divisions to the right of the 19, so it is pointing at 19.3 cm.

N4

Example 26.2

What is the size of each angle?

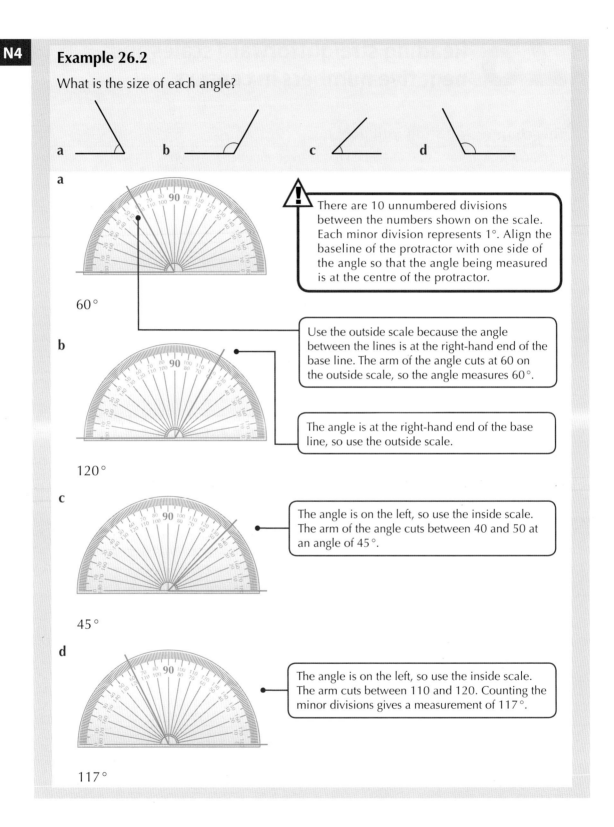

a

60°

> There are 10 unnumbered divisions between the numbers shown on the scale. Each minor division represents 1°. Align the baseline of the protractor with one side of the angle so that the angle being measured is at the centre of the protractor.

b

120°

> Use the outside scale because the angle between the lines is at the right-hand end of the base line. The arm of the angle cuts at 60 on the outside scale, so the angle measures 60°.

> The angle is at the right-hand end of the base line, so use the outside scale.

c

45°

> The angle is on the left, so use the inside scale. The arm of the angle cuts between 40 and 50 at an angle of 45°.

d

117°

> The angle is on the left, so use the inside scale. The arm cuts between 110 and 120. Counting the minor divisions gives a measurement of 117°.

Example 26.3

What is the size of each angle?

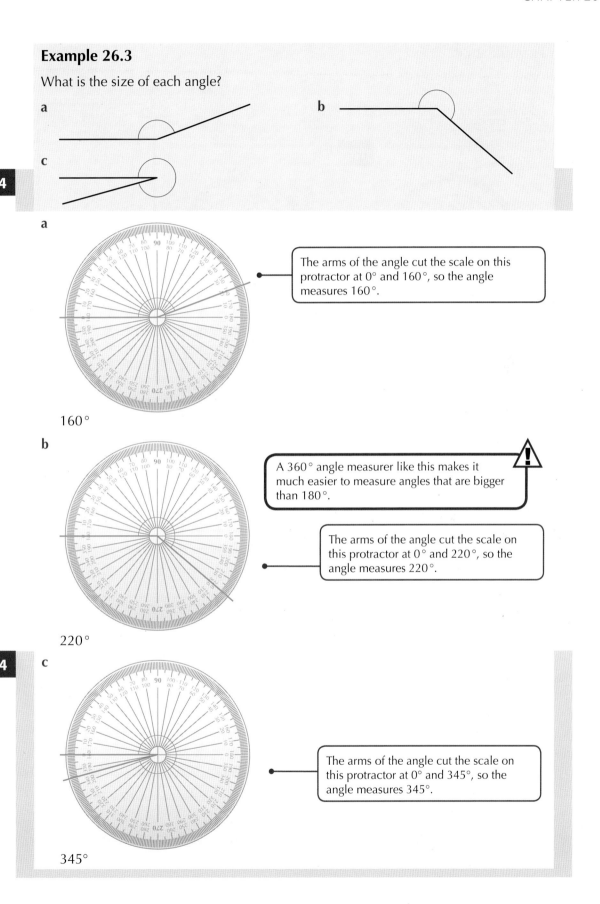

a

The arms of the angle cut the scale on this protractor at 0° and 160°, so the angle measures 160°.

160°

b

A 360° angle measurer like this makes it much easier to measure angles that are bigger than 180°.

The arms of the angle cut the scale on this protractor at 0° and 220°, so the angle measures 220°.

220°

c

The arms of the angle cut the scale on this protractor at 0° and 345°, so the angle measures 345°.

345°

Example 26.4

What is the weight shown in each set of scales?

Give the answers to parts **a** and **b** in kilograms and the answers to **c** and **d** in pounds (lb).

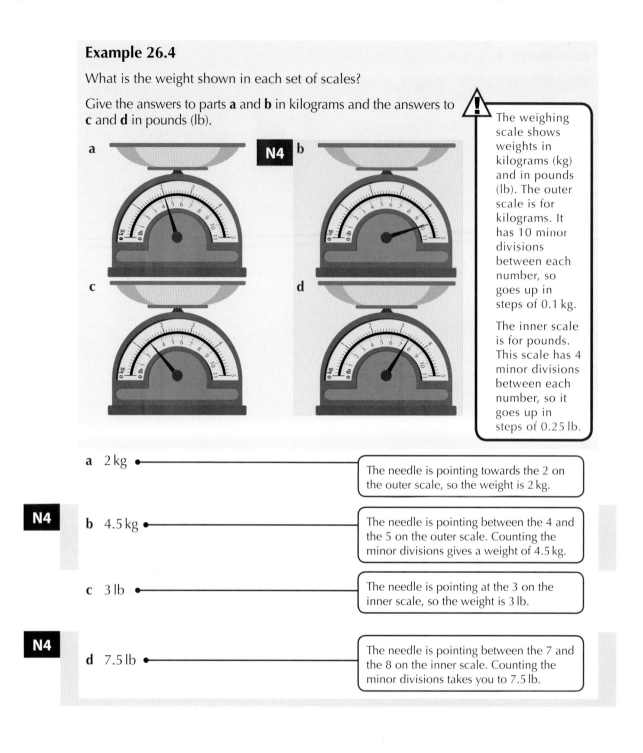

The weighing scale shows weights in kilograms (kg) and in pounds (lb). The outer scale is for kilograms. It has 10 minor divisions between each number, so goes up in steps of 0.1 kg.

The inner scale is for pounds. This scale has 4 minor divisions between each number, so it goes up in steps of 0.25 lb.

a 2 kg ●——————————— The needle is pointing towards the 2 on the outer scale, so the weight is 2 kg.

b 4.5 kg ●——————————— The needle is pointing between the 4 and the 5 on the outer scale. Counting the minor divisions gives a weight of 4.5 kg.

c 3 lb ●——————————— The needle is pointing at the 3 on the inner scale, so the weight is 3 lb.

d 7.5 lb ●——————————— The needle is pointing between the 7 and the 8 on the inner scale. Counting the minor divisions takes you to 7.5 lb.

Example 26.5

What volume of liquid is in each measuring jug?

> Use the scale on the left for millilitres.
>
> Use the scale on the right for fluid ounces.

Give your answer in:

a millilitres (ml)

N4 **b** fluid ounces (fl oz).

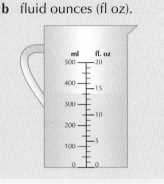

a 350 ml

N4 **b** 14 fl oz

> The liquid is on the 4th division between 10 and 15. There are 5 minor divisions between 10 and 15. The liquid comes up to 14 fl oz.

N4

Example 26.6

Annie is making pancakes.

She needs a total of 450 ml of milk for her recipe.

How much more milk will she need to add to the jug if she is going to make the pancakes?

She needs to add another 220 ml of milk.

> The minor divisions on this scale each represent 10 ml.
>
> There are 230 ml of milk in the jug to start with, so she needs to add another 220 ml to make it up to a total of 450 ml.

Exercise 26A

1   The scale on the ruler shown is in centimetres.

    What measurement is shown by each of arrows **A**, **B** and **C**?

N4

2   The scale on the ruler shown is in centimetres.

    What measurement is shown by each of arrows **A**, **B** and **C**?

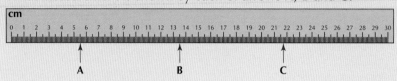

3   What is the size of each angle?

    a   b

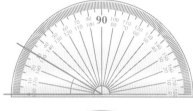   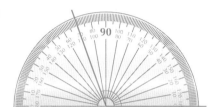

    c

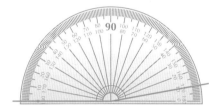

N4

4   What is the size of each angle?

    a   b

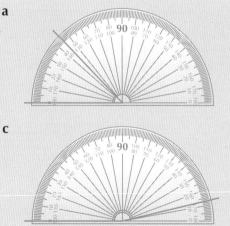   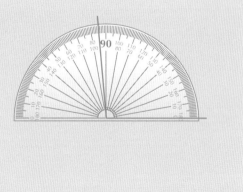

    c

5   What is the size of each angle?

a

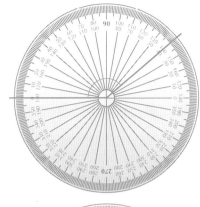

b

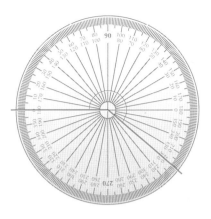

c

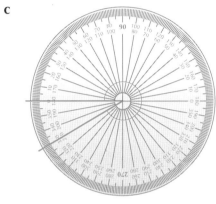

6   What is the size of each angle?

a

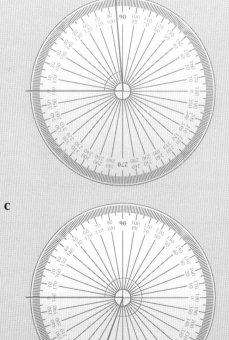

b

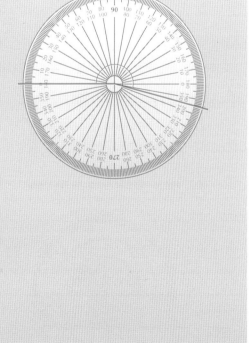

c

★ 7 What is the weight shown in each set of scales?
Give the answers to parts **a** and **b** in kilograms
Give the answers to parts **c** and **d** in pounds.

a

b

c

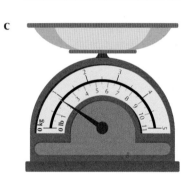

d

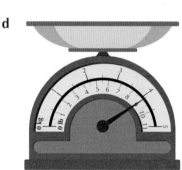

N4 8 What is the weight shown in each set of scales?
★ Give the answers to parts **a** and **b** in kilograms
Give the answers to parts **c** and **d** in pounds.

a

b

c

d

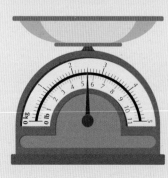

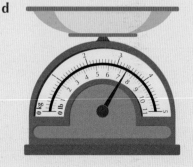

9   What volume of liquid is shown in each of these measuring jugs?

a

b

c

d

N4

10 How much needs to be added to each of these cylinders to give the total volume needed each time?

a   400 ml needed in total   b   300 ml needed in total

c   520 ml needed in total   d   170 ml needed in total

N4 11 Mrs Sheridan went on holiday.

She had three suitcases that she needed to check in at the airport.

She weighed the suitcases at home before she left.

The reading on the weighing scales for each one is shown below.

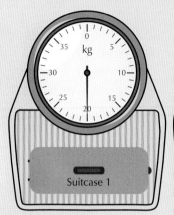 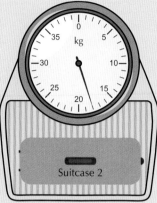 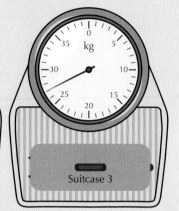

a What was the weight of each suitcase?

At the airport, the weighing scales have a digital display.

The readings on the airport weighing scales are shown for each suitcase.

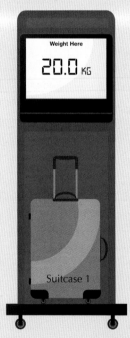  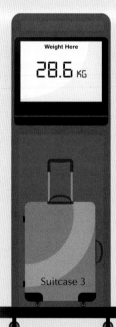

b Did Mrs Sheridan have the correct weight for each suitcase?

N4 ## Negative numbers in real life

Negative numbers occur in a number of everyday situations. The most common one is in weather forecasting, when we see negative temperatures during the winter. Other common situations are bank overdrafts, depths of objects under the sea measured as distances below sea level, and levels in underground car parks.

Reading a scale involving negative numbers

You are most likely to come across negative numbers when you are dealing with temperatures.

Temperatures below freezing point when measured in degrees Celsius are negative.

The weather forecasts on the TV often have negative temperatures displayed during the winter.

Example 26.7

What temperature, in degrees Celsius, is shown on each of the following thermometers?

The thermometer shows two scales. The one on the left is in Celsius (°C) and the one on the right is in Fahrenheit, (°F). There are 10 unmarked minor divisions between the marked numbers of –20, –10, 0, 10, 20 etc. Each minor division represents 1°.

a 20°C

In this question you only need to use the Celsius scale on the left. The red line reaches the 20 on the Celsius scale.

b 14°C

The red line stops between the 10 and the 20. Count the minor divisions to give 14°C.

c –10°C

d –17°C

Negative numbers can also be used on your bank statements. If you are overdrawn at the bank, it means that you have spent money that you don't actually have. You have less than £0 (so you owe money to the bank).

The balance in your account tells you how much money you have.

A positive balance means that you have money to spend.

A negative balance means that you are overdrawn.

N4

Example 26.8

For each balance, explain how much money is in the account.

a Balance +£143.78

b Balance –£34

c Balance –£23.85

a £143.78 available to spend ●——————

b Overdraft of £34 ●——

c Overdraft of £23.85

> This balance is **positive**, so there is £143.78 available to spend.

> This balance is **negative**, so there is an overdraft of £34.

Example 26.9

Tessa's bank balance stands at –£28.

How much does Tessa need to pay into the account to clear her overdraft?

Tessa would need to pay in £28 to clear her overdraft. ●——

> Clearing an overdraft means getting the balance back to £0.

Exercise 26B

1 What temperature, in degrees Celsius, is shown on each of the following thermometers?

a

b

c

d

2 For each balance, explain how much money is in the account.

    a Balance +£65

    b Balance –£19

    c Balance –£41.72

3 Subash's bank balance stood at –£34.98.

    How much will he need to pay into his account to clear his overdraft?

N4 ## Calculations involving negative numbers

You will often need to solve problems that involve adding or subtracting negative numbers.

The easiest way to do this is to use a number line.

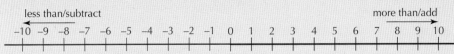

less than/subtract   more than/add
−10 −9 −8 −7 −6 −5 −4 −3 −2 −1 0 1 2 3 4 5 6 7 8 9 10

Example 26.10

Use the number line above to answer the following questions.

What temperature is:

a   8 °C more than −5 °C

b   13 °C more than −7 °C

c   5 °C less than 2 °C

d   10 °C less than 9 °C?

a   −5 + 8 = 3 °C   •——— On the number line start at −5 and count 8 places to the right.

b   −7 + 13 = 6 °C   •——— On the number line start at −7 and count 13 places to the right.

c   2 − 5 = −3 °C   •——— On the number line start at 2 and count 5 places to the left.

d   9 − 10 = −1 °C   •——— On the number line start at 9 and count 10 places to the left.

Example 26.11

The temperature in Sydney, Australia, one day in January was 23 °C.

The temperature in Moscow, Russia, was −9 °C.

What was the difference in temperature between Sydney and Moscow on that day?

Temperature in Sydney = +23 °C

Temperature in Moscow = −9 °C   •———

Difference = 23 − (−9)

= 23 + 9 = 32 °C

The temperature in Moscow was 9 °C below 0 °C, so to find the difference, you can add 23 + 9 = 32 °C.

You can sketch a number line to help.

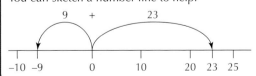

9   +   23

−10 −9   0   10   20 23 25

N4

Example 26.12

Use a number line to find the difference between each pair of temperatures.

a 2 °C and 7 °C

b –7 °C and 10 °C

c –2 °C and 5 °C

d –18 °C and –9 °C

⚠ Finding the difference is the same as subtracting. The easiest way to do this is to use the number line and count the number of spaces between each pair of numbers.

a 7 – 2 = 5 °C •————— There are 5 spaces between 2 and 7, so the difference is 5 °C.

b 10 – –7 = 10 + 7 = 17 °C •————— There are 17 spaces between –7 and 10, so the difference is 17 °C.

c 5 – –2 = 5 + 2 = 7 °C •————— There are 7 spaces between –2 and 5, so the difference is 7 °C.

d –9 – –18 = –9 + 18 = 9 °C •————— There are 9 spaces between –18 and –9, so the difference is 9 °C.

Example 26.13

Martin had £30 in his bank account.

He used his bank card to buy a t-shirt for £10 and a pair of jeans for £40.

How much money does Martin now have in his account?

£10 + £40 = £50 •————— Add the cost of the t-shirt and jeans to find the total amount he spent.

£30 – £50 = –£20 •—————

Martin will have an overdraft of £20. This will show on his statement as a balance of –£20.

The total cost is £20 more than Martin has in his account.

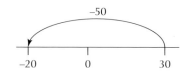

N4

Example 26.14

Barney has £14 in his bank account at the start of May.

He keeps a note of all the transactions on his account for the month of May.

These are shown below:

Date	Transaction	Balance
1 May		+£14
6 May	£24 debit	
10 May	£18 credit	
17 May	£21 debit	
21 May	£34 credit	
30 May	£18 debit	

> Remember that a **credit** is when money is added to the account and a **debit** is when money is subtracted from the account.

What is the balance in Barney's account at the end of May?

Date	Transaction	Balance
1 May		+£14
6 May	£24 debit	£14 – £24 = –£10
10 May	£18 credit	–£10 + £18 = +£8
17 May	£21 debit	£8 – £21 = –£13
21 May	£34 credit	–£13 + £34 = +£21
30 May	£18 debit	£21 – £18 = **+£3**

> Add or subtract each transaction as it occurs.

At the end of May, Barney has a balance of +£3.

Exercise 26C

Use a number line to answer these questions.

1   What temperature is:
   a   5 °C higher than –4 °C
   b   8 °C lower than 1 °C
   c   12 °C higher than –6 °C
   d   4 °C lower than 1 °C
   e   2 °C higher than –6 °C
   f   7 °C lower than –1 °C
   g   15 °C less than 5 °C
   h   3 °C more than –7 °C
   i   34 °C less than 21 °C
   j   40 °C less than 17 °C?

2   What is the difference between these pairs of temperatures?
   a   3 °C and 8 °C
   b   –4 °C and 6 °C
   c   –8 °C and 12 °C
   d   –2 °C and 9 °C
   e   –12 °C and 16 °C
   f   –7 °C and –4 °C
   g   –16 °C and –7 °C
   h   –1 °C and 6 °C
   i   –5 °C and 0 °C
   j   –8 °C and 12 °C

N4

3 The temperature in Glasgow was –8 °C at 7 am on the first Monday in February.

The temperature rose by 10 °C by noon.

What was the temperature at noon?

★ 4 The temperature in Edinburgh on the same day was –4 °C at 7 am.

In Edinburgh, the temperature rose by 12 °C by noon.

What was the temperature at noon in Edinburgh?

5 A helicopter is flying at 500 metres above sea level.

The pilot is in contact with the captain of a submarine that is 300 metres below sea level directly below the helicopter.

How far apart are the helicopter pilot and the submarine captain?

★ 6 A gannet is flying at 200 feet above the sea.

It spots a fish directly below it that is 35 feet below sea level.

How far apart are the gannet and the fish?

7 Rohan had £20 in his account.

He spent £15 on a shirt and £35 on a pair of shoes.

What will his bank balance be now?

8 Jerry has £45 in his bank account.

He wants to buy a new games console for £50 and a new computer game for £25.

His mum paid £15 into his account towards the cost of these.

What will his balance be after he has bought these two items?

★ 9 Copy and complete Barney's bank balance for June.

Date	Transaction	Balance
1 June		+£3
3 June	£28 debit	
9 June	£16 credit	
14 June	£54 credit	
16 June	£12 debit	
19 June	£25 credit	
23 June	£83 debit	

What was Barney's balance at the end of June?

 Activity

In Britain we use a combination of two systems of units.

We use some **imperial** units such as miles and some **metric** units such as metres.

Investigate the origins of the two systems of units.

Find out the names of the different units used in the imperial system and where they came from.

Find out the connection between the units for length, weight and volume for the metric system.

Which system is easier to use?

Chapter review

1   What lengths are shown by the arrows on these rulers?

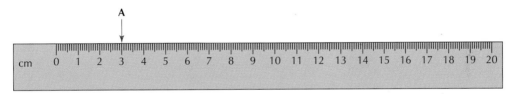

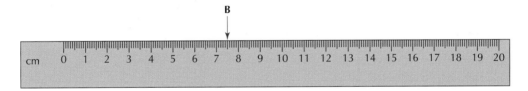

2   What is the size of each angle shown?

a

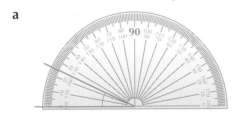

b

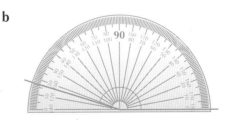

3   In January, the average temperature in Cape Town was 20 °C.

The average temperature in Alaska in January was –13 °C.

What is the difference between these two temperatures?

4 a Copy and complete Cameron's bank balance for February.

Date	Transaction	Balance
1 February		+£34
3 February	£92 debit	
9 February	£43 credit	
15 February	£31 credit	
21 February	£56 debit	
23 February	£15 credit	
28 February	£51 debit	

b Cameron will pay bank charges of 3% of the value of his overdraft plus a fixed fee of £25 if he is overdrawn on the last day of the month.

How much will he have to pay at the end of February?

- I can read a straightforward scale which has marked numbered divisions. ★ Exercise 26A Q7

N4

- I can read a straightforward scale which has marked unnumbered divisions. ★ Exercise 26A Q8

- I can interpret negative numbers in real life contexts. ★ Exercise 26C Q4, Q6

- I can add and subtract negative numbers in context. ★ Exercise 26C Q9

27 Ratio and proportion

This chapter will show you how to:

- find the ratio comparing two or more different quantities
- simplify ratios
- use ratios in calculations
- solve problems involving direct proportion.

You should already know:

- how to simplify a fraction
- how to scale a fraction up
- how to find a fraction of an amount.

Ratio

Ratios are often used in everyday life. Some examples include:

- the ratio of butter to sugar in a cake recipe
- the ratio of sand to cement in a mortar mix
- the ratio of yellow paint to blue paint to make a particular shade of green.

In each case you will be given the ratio for a 'single quantity' of the mixture.

You will then need to scale this up or down if you want to make a larger or smaller amount.

Finding a ratio

A ratio compares one quantity with another quantity. We use the colon **:** as the symbol to show a ratio.

Example 27.1

The picture shows 3 dogs and 4 cats.

What is the ratio of:

a cats to dogs

b dogs to cats?

a The ratio of cats : dogs is:

4 : 3 ●————

> Order is important – always give the ratio in the same order as asked in a question. In this question, the cats came first, so the 4 comes first in the ratio. Note the use of the **:** symbol to show the ratio.

b The ratio of dogs : cats is:

3 : 4 ●————

> This time the dogs came first, so the 3 is in the first part of the ratio.

N4

Example 27.2

Sanjay had 19 sweets, Farida had 14 sweets and Rohida had 13 sweets.

What is the ratio of:

a Sanjay's sweets to Farida's sweets

b Farida's sweets to Sanjay's sweets to Rohida's sweets?

a The ratio is 19:14

b The ratio is 14:19:13 ●────────

> A ratio can compare more than two quantities. Remember to write all the quantities in the order given.

Exercise 27A

1 Liam has a collection of marbles.

He has 18 red marbles, 17 green marbles, 11 yellow marbles and 23 blue marbles.

For Liam's marbles, what is the ratio of:

    a green to blue   **b** red to green   **c** blue to red   **d** green to yellow?

2 The chef in a transport café cooks breakfast.

He cooks 209 sausages, 151 rashers of bacon, 97 slices of black pudding and 350 fried eggs.

What is the ratio of:

    a fried eggs to sausages

    b rashers of bacon to sausages

    c black pudding to rashers of bacon

    d fried eggs to black pudding to rashers of bacon

    e black pudding to sausages to fried eggs?

3 A car park contains 83 cars, 47 vans, 17 lorries and 3 buses.

What is the ratio of:

    a cars to buses   **b** vans to lorries

    c buses to lorries   **d** cars to vans

    e vans to cars to buses   **f** lorries to cars to vans?

4 A lucky dip at a school fair contains 80 prizes in total.

There are 37 pencils, 23 pens, 7 erasers and the rest are sharpeners.

What is the ratio of:

    a pens to pencils

    b pens to sharpeners

    c sharpeners to pencils

    d erasers to sharpeners to pens

    e pens to erasers to pencils?

N4 ★ 5 Will is travelling from London to Edinburgh, a distance of 415 miles.

He drives 138 miles to the Hilton Park Services and stops for a break.

What is the ratio of:

a the distance he has covered to the total distance

b the distance he has covered to the distance he still has to travel?

Simplifying a ratio

In Chapter 24, you learned how to simplify a fraction. You can simplify a ratio in the same way.

You need to find a number that is a factor of all the parts of the ratio and then divide by that number.

To express a ratio in its simplest form (simplify it as far as possible), find the greatest common factor of all the parts.

> Always look for the greatest common factor, but, as with simplifying fractions, you can simplify in two or more steps if you don't spot the greatest factor immediately.

Example 27.3

Simplify each ratio as far as possible.

a 30:40   **b** 16:20   **c** 240:150

a 30:40 ●————— 30 and 40 both have a factor of 10, so divide each of them by 10.

3:4

b 16:20 ●————— 4 is the greatest factor of both 16 and 20, so divide them both by 4.

4:5

c 240:150 ●————— If you can't spot the greatest factor immediately you can simplify in two or more steps. There is a factor of 10, so divide by 10.

24:15

8:5 ●————— There is a common factor of 3, so divide by 3.

N4

Example 27.4

Jimmy, Paul and Mary win some money in a lottery.

Jimmy wins £3300, Paul wins £2400 and Mary wins £1800.

Find each ratio in its simplest form for the money won.

a Jimmy : Paul

b Mary : Jimmy

c Paul : Mary : Jimmy

a Jimmy : Paul

3300 : 2400 ———————————————— Factor of 100.

33 : 24 ———————————————— Factor of 3.

11 : 8

b Mary : Jimmy

1800 : 3300 ———————————————— Factor of 100.

18 : 33 ———————————————— Factor of 3.

6 : 11

c Paul : Mary : Jimmy

2400 : 1800 : 3300 ———————————————— Factor of 100.

24 : 18 : 33 ———————————————— Factor of 3.

8 : 6 : 11 ————————————

You can't simplify any further as there is no common factor for 8, 6 **and** 11.

Exercise 27B

Look for the greatest common factor.

1 Simplify each ratio as far as possible.

a 20:40	**b** 16:24	**c** 14:35	**d** 3:9
e 5:20	**f** 18:8	**g** 36:24	**h** 150:100
i 35:45	**j** 189:315	**k** 36:42	**l** 105:245
m 9:12:15	**n** 40:72:24	**o** 81:195:27	**p** 126:144:102

2 Rosie won £3200 and Freddie won £4600 in a lottery.
Give the ratio of Rosie's winnings to Freddie's winnings in its simplified form.

3 Mr Wilson, Ms Lee and Mr Noon are farmers.
Mr Wilson has 360 acres, 200 cattle and 140 sheep.
Ms Lee has 480 acres, 350 cattle and 120 sheep.
Mr Noon has 120 acres, 150 cattle and 80 sheep.
In its simplest form, find the ratio of:

a Mr Wilson's acres to Ms Lee's acres

b Mr Noon's sheep to Ms Lee's sheep

N4

  c Ms Lee's cattle to Mr Noon's cattle to Mr Wilson's cattle

  d Ms Lee's sheep to Mr Noon's sheep to Mr Wilson's sheep.

4 After school each evening, Catriona does 120 minutes of homework, Harry does 80 minutes of homework and Stevie does 90 minutes of homework.

 What is the ratio, in its simplest form, of:

 Harry's homework to Catriona's homework to Stevie's homework?

5 In 4th year there were a total of 140 students. Of these 86 are girls.

 What is the ratio, in its simplest form, of:

 a number of girls to total number of students

 b number of girls to number of boys?

6 Sue earns £34 000, Jenny earns £40 000 and John earns £24 000 per annum (each year).

 What is the ratio, in its simplest form, of:

 a Sue's earnings to John's earnings

 b Jenny's earnings to Sue's earnings

 c John's earnings to Sue's earnings to Jenny's earnings?

★ **7** A concert venue employs 15 security staff and 20 catering staff for every 1000 audience members.

 Give the ratio, in its simplest form, of:

 a security staff to audience members

 b audience members to catering staff

 c security staff to catering staff to audience members.

★ **8** A rectangle measures 8 cm by 5 cm.

 Give the ratio, in its simplest terms, of its perimeter to its area.

Scaling up a ratio

The method used to scale up a ratio is similar to the method for making equivalent fractions shown in Chapter 24.

You need to multiply **all** the parts of the ratio by the **same** number to get an equivalent ratio.

Example 27.5

The recipe for a sponge cake is given as 1 egg : 60 g sugar : 60 g flour

What weight of sugar and flour are needed for 4 eggs?

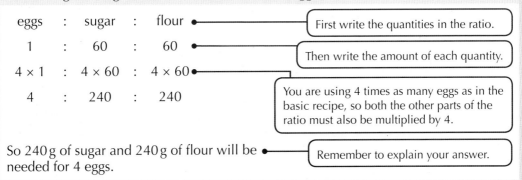

eggs	:	sugar	:	flour
1	:	60	:	60
4 × 1	:	4 × 60	:	4 × 60
4	:	240	:	240

First write the quantities in the ratio.

Then write the amount of each quantity.

You are using 4 times as many eggs as in the basic recipe, so both the other parts of the ratio must also be multiplied by 4.

So 240 g of sugar and 240 g of flour will be needed for 4 eggs.

Remember to explain your answer.

N4

Example 27.6

Orange paint is made by mixing red paint and yellow paint in the ratio 3:5

a How much yellow paint will be needed for 18 litres of red paint?

b How much red paint is needed for 15 litres of yellow paint?

c 56 litres of orange paint are needed in total. How many litres each of red paint and yellow paint are needed to give a total of 56 litres of orange?

a red:yellow

   3:5

   18:? •———————— Write the ratio you are given and express the problem, using ? for the quantity you want to find.

   18 = **6** × 3

   so ? = **6** × 5 = 30•———— 18 = 6 × 3; 6 times as much red is being used this time, so 6 times as much yellow is needed.

   18:30

30 litres of yellow paint are needed.

b red:yellow

   3:5

   ? :15

   15 = **3** × 5

   so ? = **3** × 3 = 9 •———— 3 times as much yellow is used this time, so 3 times as much red is needed.

   9:15

9 litres of red paint are needed.

c 1 'batch' of orange is:

   red:yellow

   3:5 = 8 litres •———— Each 'batch' of paint uses 3 litres of red and 5 litres of yellow, giving 8 litres of orange in total.

   56 ÷ 8 = **7** •———— Calculate how many batches give a total of 56 litres of orange.

   Red: **7** × 3 = 21 litres

   Yellow: **7** × 5 = 35 litres •———— Multiply the amount of red and the amount of yellow needed for 1 batch by the number of batches.

So 21 litres of red paint and 35 litres of yellow paint are needed to make 56 litres of orange paint.   •———— Remember to explain your answer.

N4 **Exercise 27C**

1   Ally is saving up for a new bike.

His dad says that he will give Ally £2 for every £5 that Ally saves.

In March, Ally saved a total of £40.

a   How much will his dad need to give him?

b   How much money will Ally have in total in March?

2   Purple paint is made by mixing red paint and blue paint in the ratio 2:7

a   How much blue paint is needed for 8 litres of red paint?

b   How much red paint is needed for 21 litres of blue paint?

c   How much of each colour is needed to make 45 litres of purple paint?

3   A model of a car is 9 cm long and 3 cm high.

The real car is 450 cm long.

How high is the real car?

4   On a school trip, there needs to be 1 teacher for every 12 pupils.

How many teachers are needed for 132 pupils?

5   In a pet rescue centre, the ratio of pens for cats:dogs is 5:6

When all the pens are being used, there are 75 cats in the centre.

How many dogs are there when all the pens are being used?

6   A flower shop stocks daffodils, tulips and hyacinths in the ratio 10:5:6

a   How many tulips will there be when there are 50 daffodils?

b   How many hyacinths will there be when there are 15 tulips?

c   How many daffodils and tulips will there be when there are 24 hyacinths?

7   The recipe for beef stew mixes beef and vegetables in the ratio 20:5

a   What weight of vegetables will be needed for 440 g of beef?

b   What is the total weight of the stew that can be made with 440 g of beef?

★ 8   The number of men, women and children in the audience of a school show is in the ratio 3:4:2

a   If there were 140 women in the audience, how many men and how many children were there?

b   How many were in the audience altogether?

9   To make pastry, you need 25 g of flour for every 10 g of butter.

Geoffrey wants to use 120 g of butter.

a   How much flour should he use?

b   What weight of pastry will he have if he uses 120 g of butter?

10   The ratio of easy questions to hard questions in a quiz night is 4:7

a   How many hard questions are needed when there are 24 easy ones?

b   How many questions will there be in total when there are 21 hard questions?

N4 **Dividing a quantity in a given ratio**

Sometimes you are given a total amount and you are asked to split that amount into a given ratio of two or three parts.

One way to handle this type of question is to picture dealing out cards, as shown in Examples 27.7–27.9.

Example 27.7

Split £200 between Mark and Sam in the ratio 2:3

Mark:Sam

2:3 •————— If you 'dealt out' the money, you would give £2 to Mark and then £3 to Sam, then another £2 to Mark and another £3 to Sam until you ran out of money.

2 + 3 = 5

£5 is used each time.

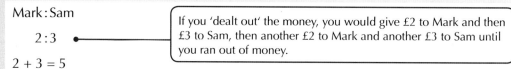

Mark gets $\frac{2}{5} \times 200 = 80$ •————— Mark gets $\frac{2}{5}$ of the money.

Sam gets $\frac{3}{5} \times 200 = 120$ •————— Sam gets $\frac{3}{5}$ of the money.

Mark gets £80 and Sam gets £120.

Check: 80 + 120 = 200 ✓ •————— Check that the individual amounts add up to the total.

Example 27.8

Red paint and blue paint are mixed in the ratio 5:3 to make purple paint.

How many litres of red paint and blue paint are needed to make 320 litres of purple paint?

red:blue

5:3

8 litres is used each time. •————— Each time the paint is mixed, 5 litres + 3 litres = 8 litres is used up.

$\frac{5}{8} \times 320 = 200$ •————— Red makes up $\frac{5}{8}$ of the purple paint.

$\frac{3}{8} \times 320 = 120$ •————— Blue makes up $\frac{3}{8}$ of the purple paint.

There will be 200 litres of red paint and 120 litres of blue paint in 320 litres of purple paint.

Check: 200 + 120 = 320 ✓

N4

Example 27.9

Olivia, Rita and Kieran club together to buy lottery tickets.

Olivia puts in £3, Rita puts in £2 and Kieran puts in £5.

Between them they win £8600.

They split the money in the ratio of the money they put in.

How much will each person get?

Olivia : Rita : Kieran

   3 : 2 : 5

$3 + 2 + 5 = 10$

£10 is used each time.

$\frac{3}{10}$ of 8600 = 2580 •———————— Olivia gets $\frac{3}{10}$ of the money.

$\frac{2}{10}$ of 8600 = 1720 •———————— Rita gets $\frac{2}{10}$ of the money.

$\frac{5}{10}$ of 8600 = 4300 •———————— Kieran gets $\frac{5}{10}$ of the money.

Olivia gets £2580, Rita gets £1720 and Kieran gets £4300.

Check: $2580 + 1720 + 4300 = 8600$ ✓

Exercise 27D

1   Gen and Barry love ice cream. They have a 2000 ml tub of ice cream which they are going to share in the ratio 2 : 3, with Barry getting the bigger share.
     How many millilitres of ice cream will each get?

2   Zoe and Marie have 42 chocolates which they are going to share in the ratio 2 : 5 with Zoe getting the smaller share.
     How many chocolates will each girl get?

3   Give each ratio in the same order as the names in each question part.
    a   Share £1000 between Elijah and Wyatt in the ratio 3 : 7
    b   Share £3200 between Joe and Laura in the ratio 5 : 3
    c   Share £440 between Jan and Sam in the ratio 9 : 2
    d   Share $45 between Alison and Kayden in the ratio 1 : 8
    e   Share $7600 between Seonaid and Kirsty in the ratio 12 : 7
    f   Share €936 (euros) between Angela and David in the ratio 4 : 5
    g   Share €8400 between Campbell, Jamir and Donna in the ratio 2 : 7 : 3
    h   Share £465 000 between Tanisha, Mark and Emily in the ratio 2 : 3 : 10

N4

4   Artur makes jewellery. In one year he made 3400 pieces of jewellery, with gold : silver items in the ratio of 7 : 10
How many gold items and how many silver items did Artur make?

5   Farrah and Bernard set up a company making teddy bears.
Farrah invests £750 and Bernard invests £1250.
They split the profit in the same ratio as their investment.
In the first year the company makes £240 000 profit.
How much will each get?

6   Millie is 10 years old, Meg is 14 years old and Jack is 18 years old.
Their Aunt Kate gives them £15 120 to split between them in the ratio of their ages.
How much will each person get?

★ 7   Anton, Findlay and Rory club together to buy lottery tickets one week.
Anton puts in £4, Findlay puts in £6 and Rory puts in £2.
When the lottery is drawn, the boys find that they have a winning ticket worth £720 000.
They decide to split their winnings in the same ratio as the money they put in.
How much will each of them get?

Solving problems involving direct proportion

There are many quantities in everyday life that are related by **direct proportion**.

Two quantities are in direct proportion if the two quantities increase at the same rate, that is, as one quantity increases, the other increases at the same rate.

Some examples of this include:

*   working out the amount of money you will earn in a given number of hours when you know the hourly rate of pay

*   working out the distance you have travelled when you know the time taken or the average speed.

In each problem you need to:

*   decide the basic connection between the two quantities from the information given

*   divide to find the value of a single item

*   multiply to answer the problem.

Examples 27.10–27.12 show you how to do this.

Example 27.10

A car takes 4 hours to travel 160 miles.

How far did it travel in 3 hours?

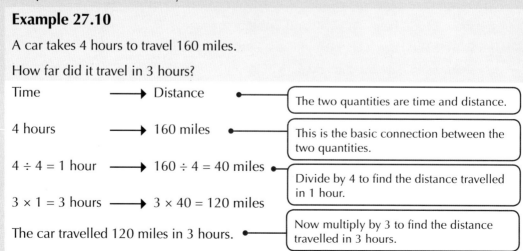

Time $\longrightarrow$ Distance — The two quantities are time and distance.

4 hours $\longrightarrow$ 160 miles — This is the basic connection between the two quantities.

$4 \div 4 = 1$ hour $\longrightarrow$ $160 \div 4 = 40$ miles — Divide by 4 to find the distance travelled in 1 hour.

$3 \times 1 = 3$ hours $\longrightarrow$ $3 \times 40 = 120$ miles

The car travelled 120 miles in 3 hours. — Now multiply by 3 to find the distance travelled in 3 hours.

N4

Example 27.11

When Jed works for 30 hours, he earns £252.

How much will he earn when he works for 42 hours?

Hours		Money earned

Hours $\longrightarrow$ Money earned •——— The two quantities are hours worked and money earned.

30 hours $\longrightarrow$ £252

$30 \div 30 = 1$ hour $\longrightarrow$ £252 $\div 30 = £8.40$ •——— Find how much he earns in 1 hour by dividing by 30.

$42 \times 1 = 42$ hours $\longrightarrow$ $42 \times £8.40 = £352.80$ •——— Multiply the hourly rate by 42 to find the amount earned in 42 hours. Remember to write a zero to express an amount of money.

So Jed will earn £352.80 for 42 hours' work.

Example 27.12

Leona and Kirsten changed their pounds sterling (£) into euros (€) before going on holiday.

Leona got €95 for £80.

a How many euros did Kirsten get for £120?

b What was the rate of exchange for these transactions?

a Pounds $\longrightarrow$ Euros •——— The two quantities are pounds sterling and euros.

£80 $\longrightarrow$ €95

$80 \div 80 = £1$ $\longrightarrow$ $95 \div 80 = €1.1875$ •——— Find how many euros there are for £1.

Do not round until the end of the answer.

$120 \times 1 = £120$ $\longrightarrow$ £120 $\times 1.1875 = €142.50$ •——— Find how many euros there are for £120.

b The rate of exchange is £1 = €1.1875 •——— The rate of exchange is the number of euros that you get for £1.

Exercise 27E

1 A supermarket sells 4 apples for 88 p.

How much will 14 apples cost?

2 Jane takes 5 minutes to type 600 words.

How many words will she type in 42 minutes?

3 A publisher sells 12 copies of a textbook for £179.40.

How much will 30 copies of this textbook cost?

N4

4   It costs £36 to hire 2 bikes for an hour.

How much will it cost to hire 9 bikes for an hour?

5   50 g of sweets cost 75 p.

How much will 140 g of these sweets cost?

6   A car can travel 550 miles on 11 gallons of fuel.

How far can it go on 7 gallons?

★ 7   12 goats need 36 kg of dry feed in a week.

How much will 17 goats need in a week?

8   A track cyclist can cover 200 metres in 12 seconds.

How long will it take her to cover 750 metres?

★ 9   A car travels 175 miles in 3 hours 30 minutes.

How far can it go in 1 hour 15 minutes at the same average speed?

10 Francis and Andrei are going to the USA on holiday.

They change their pounds sterling (£) into US dollars ($) before they go.

When Francis changes £120 he gets $156.

How many US dollars will Andrei get for £94?

🔘 GO! Activity

Rectangle A has length 5 cm and breadth 4 cm. What is its area?

The length and breadth of rectangle B are twice those of rectangle A. What is the area of rectangle B?

What is the ratio of the areas of rectangles A and B?

The length and breadth of rectangle C are twice those of rectangle B. What is the area of rectangle C?

What is the ratio of the areas of rectangles A, B and C?

Can you draw a conclusion about what happens to the area of rectangle when you double its dimensions?

Chapter review

1   A café sells 80 bacon rolls, 110 sausage rolls and 85 egg rolls each week.

Write down the following ratios, giving your answers in their simplest form.

a   sausage rolls : bacon rolls

b   egg rolls : sausage rolls

c   bacon rolls : egg rolls : sausage rolls

2   A flower shop sells bunches of roses and carnations.

They sell bunches of roses and carnations in the ratio 3 : 7

a   How many carnations are needed for 15 bunches of flowers?

b   How many roses will the shop need when they have 42 carnations?

N4

3   In a school exam the ratio of easier questions to harder questions is 5 : 3

　　a   How many harder questions are there when there are 15 easier questions?

　　b   How many questions are there altogether in the exam?

4   6500 hectares of land is to be divided in the ratio 3 : 2 : 5 between grazing animals, crops and forest.

　　How many hectares will be allocated to grazing animals, crops and forest?

5   A painter has 30 litres of red paint and 45 litres of blue paint.

　　He mixes purple paint using the ratio 2 litres of red for every 5 litres of blue.

　　a   What is the maximum volume of purple paint that he can mix using this ratio?

　　b   How much of each colour of paint will he have left?

6   Marcus earns £292.50 for working a 30-hour week.

　　How much will he earn for working a 40-hour week?

7   Clare sells cars. She is paid commission based on her sales.

　　When she sells £34 000 worth of cars, she is paid £1020 in commission.

　　How much will Clare get in commission when she sells £24 000 worth of cars?

8   Mick and Linda are going to Canada on holiday.

　　Mick receives CA$414 (Canadian dollars) when he changes £230.

　　How many Canadian dollars will Linda get for £170?

9   Jade and Belinda work together.

　　Jade works 18 hours each week and Belinda works 24 hours each week.

　　They are going to share a bonus of £315.

　　They will share the bonus in the same ratio as the hours they work.

　　Jade thinks that she will get £120.

　　Is she correct?

10   80 g of flour, as well as other ingredients, are needed to make 9 cupcakes.

　　Ian has 1 kg of flour.

　　What is the maximum number of cupcakes that he can make, assuming he has enough of the other ingredients?

- I can find the ratio comparing two or more quantities. ★ Exercise 27A Q5
- I can simplify ratios. ★ Exercise 27B Q7, Q8
- I can use ratios in calculations. ★ Exercise 27C Q8 ★ Exercise 27D Q7
- I can solve problems using direct proportion. ★ Exercise 27E Q7, Q9

28 Extracting and interpreting data

This chapter will show you how to:

- extract and interpret data in a table

N4
- extract and interpret data in a pie chart

- extract and interpret data in a bar graph and a line graph

N4
- extract and interpret data in a scatter graph
- extract and interpret data in a stem and leaf diagram.

You should already know:

N4
- how to construct a pie chart

- how to construct a bar, line and scatter graph

N4
- how to construct a stem and leaf diagram

- how to read a straightforward scale.

Data presented in a table

There are lots of situations when the information that you need is given in a table.

These might include finance tables where you are working out the cost of a loan, taking out insurance, booking a holiday or reading bus and train timetables when planning a journey.

Examples 28.1 and 28.2 show you how to interpret the information given in a table.

Example 28.1

The table shows the monthly repayments to be made when money is borrowed from a finance company.

Amount borrowed	Monthly repayments		
	2-year term	5-year term	10-year term
£50 000	£2246.78	£1000.76	£592.26
£30 000	£1329.65	£601.43	£342.19
£20 000	£898.13	£405.64	£243.78
£10 000	£452.67	£215.22	£136.98

James borrows £30 000 over 10 years.

a How much will his monthly repayments be?

b How much will he pay back in total?

c How much does this loan actually cost him?

⚠️ The cost of a loan is actually the amount of interest that is charged in total over the term of the loan plus any fees that have to be paid. These are worked out by the loan company and included in the monthly payments.

a James's monthly repayment will be £342.19.

> Read across the row for £30 000 and find where it meets the column for 10 years.

b 120 × 342.19 = 41 062.80

> James needs to pay back £342.19 every month for 10 years, so he will make 120 payments in total.

James will pay back a total of £41 062.80.

> The **cost** of the loan is the difference between the amount borrowed and the amount paid back in total.

c £41 062.80 − £30 000 = £11 062.80

The loan costs James £11 062.80.

N4

Example 28.2

The table shows some travel insurance premiums charged by Supertrip Holidays.

Insurance premium per person				
Number of days	**UK**	**Europe**	**USA**	**Rest of the world**
1–6	£10	£14	£24	£36
7–13	£12	£16	£31	£40
14–20	£15	£21	£38	£43
21 or more	£19	£26	£72	£89
Children aged 0–5 pay 20% of adult rate				
Children aged 6–16 pay 60% of adult rate				

The cost of the premium depends on where you are travelling to and for how long you will be there.

a What will the premium be for 1 adult going to the USA for 12 days?

Mr and Mrs Paterson and their 3 children are going on holiday to Spain for 17 days.

Their children are aged 4, 10 and 15.

b How much will the insurance premium be in total for the Paterson family?

a The premium is £31.

> 12 days is between 7 and 13 days, so use the second row of the table and the column for the USA.

b Mr Paterson will pay a full adult premium: £21

Mrs Paterson will pay a full adult premium: £21

> The Paterson family are going to Spain, which is in Europe, for 17 days. You need to use the third row and the column for Europe.

The 4-year-old will pay 20% of the full adult premium: 20% of £21 = £4.20

> You need to calculate the price for each person travelling and then add them up.

The 10-year-old will pay 60% of the full adult premium: 60% of £21 = £12.60

The 15-year-old will pay 60% of the full adult premium: 60% of £21 = £12.60

£21 + £21 + £4.20 + £12.60 + £12.60 = £71.40

The total premium for the family will be £71.40.

Exercise 28A

1   The table shows the monthly repayments to be made when money is borrowed from a finance company.

Amount borrowed	Monthly repayments		
	5-year term	10-year term	20-year term
£50 000	£1000.76	£592.26	£367.93
£30 000	£601.43	£342.19	£220.76
£20 000	£405.64	£243.78	£162.29
£10 000	£215.22	£136.98	£87.49

Saira borrows £20 000 over 20 years.

a   How much will her monthly repayment be?

b   What is the total amount that she must repay?

c   How much does the loan cost Saira in total?

2   Rory wants to buy a new car.

He will need to borrow £10 000 towards the cost of the car.

His monthly budget is shown in the table below.

Item	Income (£)	Expenditure (£)
Salary	1445	
Rent		350
Council tax		130
Electricity		76
Food		400
Telephone		38
Car running costs		150
Emergencies		30
Total	1445	

a   Copy the table and work out his total expenditure.

b   How much money does Rory have left at the end of each month?

Rory wants to pay off his loan in as short a time as possible.

c   Use the table of monthly repayments in Question 1 to work out how many years he should take out the loan for.

d   What will the cost of the loan be for Rory?

N4 3 Lisa takes part in a diving competition.

The scores awarded by the seven judges for each dive are shown in the table.

Dive	A	B	C	D	E	F	G	Degree of difficulty
1	8.5	8.0	7.5	7.0	8.0	8.0	8.0	2.1
2	9.5	9.5	9.0	8.5	8.5	8.0	8.5	1.7
3	9.0	8.5	8.0	8.0	7.5	7.5	7.5	1.8
4	8.0	8.0	7.5	7.0	8.0	7.0	7.5	2.4

For each dive, the final score awarded to Lisa is calculated as follows:

- ignore the highest and lowest scores
- multiply each judge's score by the degree of difficulty for the dive
- add these scores to find a total
- work out 60% of this answer.

a Calculate the final score awarded to Lisa for each dive.

b Lisa will win the competition if she scores over 194.62 points in total.

Does she win the competition?

★ 4 The table shows the cost in pounds sterling to stay in different hotels at different times of year.

The price shown is for 1 adult, room only.

Children under 2 years pay 15% of the adult price.

Children 2–16 years pay 75% of the adult price.

Hotel	April/May		June		July/August		September	
	Length of stay (number of nights)							
	7	14	7	14	7	14	7	14
Royal	176	301	195	370	245	420	201	385
Imperial	198	375	206	387	261	486	203	387
Victoria	315	599	328	641	387	764	325	629
Calypso	217	403	236	455	265	512	227	445
Flamingo	99	168	123	234	156	299	121	239

Each hotel charges £12.95 per adult and £7.95 per child for breakfast.

Mr and Mrs Sheridan and their two children, aged 4 and 7, decide to stay for 14 nights in the Victoria in August.

They will all have breakfast each day.

How much will the hotel cost in total for the Sheridan family?

5 Mark has saved £3500 and decides to invest all the money in a bank account.

He finds that different banks pay different rates of interest depending on how much money is invested.

These are shown in the table on the next page.

Interest is added on the anniversary of opening the account.

If the money is withdrawn before 1 year, interest will be paid for the proportion of the year for which the money was invested.

(continued)

Bank	Amount invested				
	£1–£499	£500–£1499	£1500–£2999	£3000–£4999	£5000 or more
Bank A	0.2%	0.3%	0.9%	1.01%	1.3%
Bank B	0.1%	0.25%	0.81%	0.94%	1.04%
Bank C	0.21%	0.28%	0.78%	1.02%	1.15%
Bank D	0.16%	0.3%	0.65%	0.88%	0.97%

a Which bank would pay the most interest to Mark?

b How much interest would he get after 1 year with this bank?

Mark decides to invest the money with Bank B as there is a branch near his home.

After 6 months, Mark withdraws all of his money to pay for a new computer.

c How much interest will he have earned after 6 months?

Data presented in a pie chart

Pie charts are a very common way for the results of a survey to be presented.

A pie chart can make complicated data easier to understand.

The size of each section in a pie chart tells you the proportion of the data that it represents, that is, how much of the whole it is.

The size of each individual part of a pie chart can be given as a percentage or a fraction, or as a number of degrees.

Example 28.3

Lucy did a survey of the different colours of cars in the school car park.

The pie chart shows her results.

Lucy counted 150 cars in total.

How many cars of each colour were there?

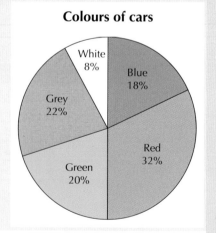

Colours of cars

Blue: 18% of 150 = 150 ÷ 100 × 18 = 27 cars •—— For each colour, you need to find a percentage of 150.

Red: 32% of 150 = 150 ÷ 100 × 32 = 48 cars

Green: 20% of 150 = 150 ÷ 100 × 20 = 30 cars

Grey: 22% of 150 = 150 ÷ 100 × 22 = 33 cars

White: 8% of 150 = 150 ÷ 100 × 8 = 12 cars

Check: 27 + 48 + 30 + 33 + 12 = 150 ✓ •—— It's a good idea to check that the calculated numbers of cars add up to 150.

N4

Example 28.4

The pie chart shows the results of a customer satisfaction survey carried out by Finnie's Fish Restaurant.

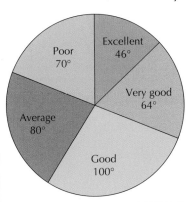

Customer satisfaction survey

A total of 900 customers took part in the survey.

a How many customers said that Finnie's Fish Restaurant was excellent?

Finnie's Fish Restaurant invites **all** the customers who said that they felt that the service was average or poor to an open evening to sample their new menu.

b How many customers do they invite to the open evening?

a Number of customers who said excellent

$$\frac{46}{360} \times 900 = 900 \div 360 \times 46$$
$$= 115$$

115 customers thought the restaurant was excellent.

> The sections in this pie chart are marked in degrees. The number of customers in each section is the fraction of 360° that each angle represents.
>
> Excellent has an angle of 46°, so $\frac{46}{360}$ of the customers thought the restaurant was excellent.

b $80° + 70° = 150°$

> Add the angles for 'average' and 'poor' to find the angle to use.

Number of customers invited

$$\frac{150}{360} \times 900 = 900 \div 360 \times 150$$
$$= 375$$

> Work out $\frac{150}{360}$ of the total number of people in the survey.

The restaurant invites 375 customers to its open evening.

N4 **Exercise 28B**

1 Paul's Pizza Restaurant noted how many of each type of pizza on their menu were sold in one week.

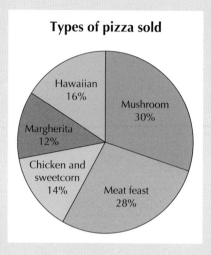

Types of pizza sold

a Which type of pizza did they sell the most?

b What **fraction** of the pizzas sold were 'Meat feast'?

The restaurant sold 150 pizzas that week.

c How many of each type of pizza were sold?

2 180 S4 students were asked to name their favourite school subject.

The pie chart shows the results.

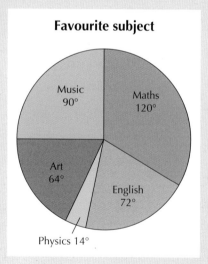

Favourite subject

a What was the least favourite subject?

b What fraction chose Art as their favourite?

c How many students chose each subject as their favourite?

N4 ★ 3 The pie chart shows the number of votes gained by each candidate at a local election in 2005.

A total of 9720 people voted in the election.

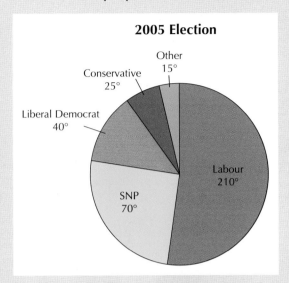

2005 Election

Other 15°
Conservative 25°
Liberal Democrat 40°
Labour 210°
SNP 70°

a Which candidate won the local election?

b How many votes were cast for each candidate?

The next pie chart shows the votes gained by each candidate at the local election in 2008.

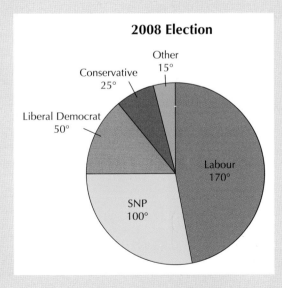

2008 Election

Other 15°
Conservative 25°
Liberal Democrat 50°
Labour 170°
SNP 100°

c Describe the differences in the **share** of the votes received by candidates in the local election in 2008 and the local election in 2005.

Data presented in a graph

There are three sorts of graph that you will regularly see in school, online and in newspapers. These are bar graphs, line graphs and scatter graphs.

These graphs are covered in Chapters 7–9.

Example 28.5

A survey was done of all the S4 pupils to find the most popular sandwich filling.

The bar graph shows the results.

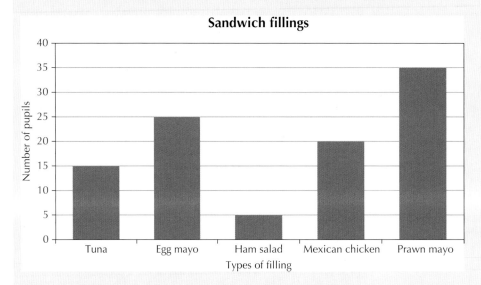

a What was the most popular sandwich filling?

b How many pupils said that egg mayo was their favourite?

c How many pupils were surveyed in total?

d What **fraction** of the pupils said that Mexican chicken was their favourite?

a The most popular filling was prawn mayo. ●——— The bar for prawn mayo is the highest.

b 25 chose egg mayonnaise.

c 15 + 25 + 5 + 20 + 35 = 100 ●——— Add up the number who voted for each filling.

A total of 100 pupils were surveyed.

d $\frac{20}{100} = \frac{1}{5}$ chose Mexican chicken. ●——— Simplify $\frac{20}{100}$

Example 28.6

The temperature was taken in Ms Wallace's maths classroom each hour, starting at 9 am.

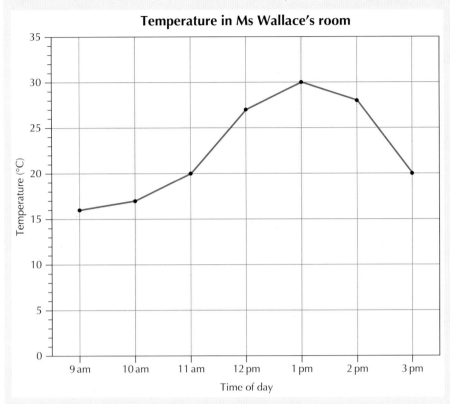

Temperature in Ms Wallace's room

a   At what time was the highest temperature recorded?

b   What was the highest temperature?

c   What was the range of temperatures in the classroom throughout the day?

Ms Wallace has been told that she can take her class to a different room if her room is too cold or too hot.

Her room is too cold when it is less than 20 °C and too hot when it is hotter than 27 °C.

d   Between which times can Ms Wallace ask for a different room?

a   The highest temperature was recorded at 1 pm.

b   The temperature was 30 °C at that time.

> The range of temperatures is found by subtracting the lowest temperature from the highest temperature.

c   Range = 30 − 16 = 14 °C ●

d   Ms Wallace can ask for a different room from 9 am until 11 am, when the room was too cold, and from noon until 2 pm, when the room was too hot.

> Ms Wallace's room was less than 20 °C until 11 am and was more than 27 °C between noon and 2 pm.

N4

Example 28.7

The scattergraph shows the results, as percentages, scored in a maths test and a French test by 10 students.

A line of best fit has been drawn.

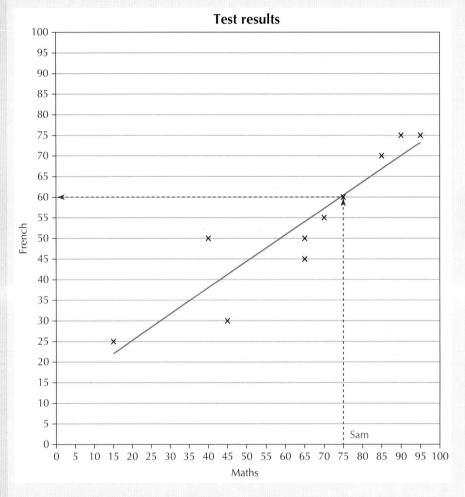

a Describe the trend of the graph.

Sam got 75% in her maths test but was absent for her French test.

b Use the line of best fit to estimate her score in the French test.

a The line of best fit shows that, on the whole, students who are good at maths are also good at French.

b Sam's score in the French test would have been about 60%.

> Draw a vertical line from 75% on the Maths axis to the line of best fit, then draw a horizontal line from that point to the French axis.

Exercise 28C

1   A group of adults were asked what their favourite fruit was.

The bar graph shows the results.

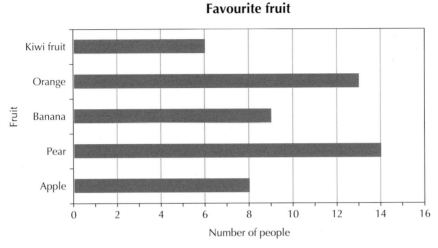

Favourite fruit

a   How many said that their favourite fruit was a pear?

b   How many were asked in total?

c   What **percentage** of the group chose kiwi fruit as their favourite fruit?

★ 2   The bar graph shows the numbers of boys and girls who cycle to school in each of S1 to S4.

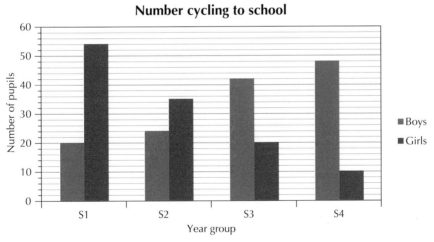

Number cycling to school

a   How many boys cycled to school in S2?

b   In which Year groups did more girls than boys cycle to school?

c   How many pupils cycled to school in total in S1–S4?

d   Compare the numbers of boys and girls who cycle to school across the Year groups.

Describe any trends that you see.

3 The line graph shows the temperatures in °C one day in Madrid in Spain.

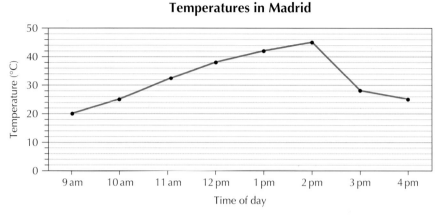

Temperatures in Madrid

a What was the temperature at 11 am?

b What was the difference between the highest temperature and the lowest temperature that day?

The temperature dropped suddenly when it started to rain.

c At what time did it start to rain?

★ **4** The line graph shows the average daily amount spent per visitor each month in the café at the Recreation Centre. The green line shows sales of fruit and the purple line shows sales of sweets.

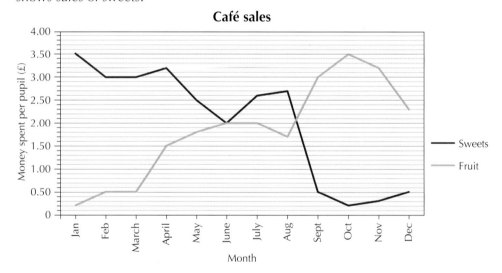

Café sales

a How much was spent each day by each visitor, on average, on sweets in March?

b How much was spent each day by each visitor, on average, on fruit in December?

c During which month was the average daily spend the same on fruit and sweets?

The Recreation Centre ran a healthy eating campaign during one month.

d Which month do you think that was? Give a reason for your answer.

N4

5 The temperature and rainfall were recorded each day at 4 pm during 10 days in November. The scattergraph shows the results.

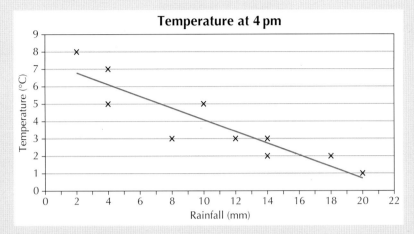

a What was the temperature on the day when there was 18 mm rainfall?

b What was the rainfall on the day when the temperature was 7 °C?

c What was the highest rainfall recorded?

d What was the lowest temperature recorded?

e Use the line of best fit to estimate the temperature on a day that has 13 mm of rainfall.

f Use the line of best fit to estimate the rainfall on a day when the temperature 6 °C.

g Describe the trend of the graph.

★ **6** An ice cream vendor records the number of ice cream cones she sells each day for 10 days during July. The scattergraph shows the results.

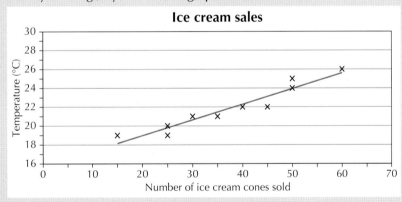

a What was the temperature on the day when 15 ice cream cones were sold?

b How many ice cream cones were sold on days when the temperature was 22°C?

c What was the greatest number of ice cream cones sold in one day?

d What was the lowest temperature recorded during the 10-day period?

e Use the line of best fit to estimate the temperature on a day when 55 ice cream cones are sold.

f Use the line of best fit to estimate the number of ice cream cones sold on a day when the temperature is 23 °C.

g Describe the trend of the graph.

N4 Data presented in a stem and leaf diagram

Another way of presenting data is the **stem and leaf diagram**.

Example 28.8 should remind you how to interpret the data in a stem and leaf diagram.

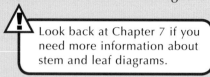

⚠ Look back at Chapter 7 if you need more information about stem and leaf diagrams.

Example 28.8

The ages of the brass section of a community band are shown in the stem and leaf diagram.

Age in years

2	3	4	6		
3	4	5	5	7	
4	0	2	3	3	6	9
5	1	2	2	7	9

$n = 18$ Key: $3 \mid 5 = 35$ years

a How old is the youngest member of the brass section?

b How many members are in their 40s?

c How many members are in the brass section in total?

d What is the range of ages in the brass section?

a The youngest member is 23 years old. ●——— The youngest member is the first entry in the first row.

b 6 members are in their 40s. ●——— There are 6 entries in the row that has a stem of 4.

c There are 18 members in the brass section. ●——— The key tells you that $n = 18$. You could also just count up all the entries in the stem and leaf diagram.

d The age range is $59 - 23 = 36$ years. ●——— The range of ages is the oldest member's age minus the youngest member's age.

N4 Example 28.9 shows a **back-to-back stem and leaf diagram**. You use a back-to-back stem and leaf diagram when you want to compare two sets of data.

Example 28.9

The back-to-back stem and leaf diagram shows the weights in kilograms of a group of boys and a group of girls aged 10 years.

Weights in kg

Boys							Girls					
				9	**1**	3	8					
6	6	4	3		**2**	0	1	3	4	5	6	9
4	3	2	1	0 0	**3**	1	6	7	8	9		
		6	5		**4**	0						

$n = 13$ 　　　　　$n = 15$

Key:　$0 \mid 3$

　　　　$3 \mid 0$ $= 30\,\text{kg}$

a How many boys and how many girls were in the group?

b What is the weight of the lightest boy?

c What is the weight of the heaviest girl?

d What is the range of weights for the boys and for the girls?

e What is the median weight for the boys and for the girls?

f Make a comment comparing the weights of the boys and the girls.

a There were 13 boys and 15 girls in the group. ●——

> The key reads $n = 13$ on the boys' side and $n = 15$ on the girls' side.

b The lightest boy is 19 kg. ●——

> On the boys' side of the diagram, 9 | 1 means 19 not 91.

c The heaviest girl weighs 40 kg.

d Boys: range = 46 − 19 = 27 kg.

Girls: range = 40 − 13 = 27 kg.

e Boys: median is 30 kg.

Girls: median is 26 kg. ●——

> The median is the middle item of data in an ordered list.

f The range of the weights for the boys is the same as for the girls, so the spread of weights is the same for the boys and the girls.

> When you are asked to make a comment comparing statistics, make sure that you mention the context of the question in your answer.

The girls have a lower median weight, so, on average, the girls weigh less than the boys.

> Use the word 'average' when comparing the median and the word 'spread' when comparing the range.

N4   **Exercise 28D**

1   The stem and leaf diagram shows the number of marks scored out of 50 in a maths test.

Scores in maths test

0	2 4 5 5
1	3 4 4
2	5 6 6 7 8 8
3	0 1 2 2 3
4	3 6 7 7 8

$n = 23$ $3\,|\,2 = 32$ marks

a   What was the highest mark scored in the test?

b   What was the range of marks scored in the test?

c   What was the median mark in the test?

2   The stem and leaf diagram shows the distances thrown in a junior shot put competition.

a   What was the longest distance thrown?

b   What was the shortest distance thrown?

c   What was the range of distances thrown?

d   What was the median distance thrown?

Distances thrown

3	4 5 9
4	2 6 7 8
5	1 1 3 4 4 5
6	0 1 5
7	0

$n = 17$ $5\,|\,1 = 5.1$ m

3   The pupils in two S1 classes were asked how much money they spent on sweets in the previous week.

The results for the boys and girls are shown in the back-to-back stem and leaf diagram.

Money spent on sweets

Boys		Girls
	1	0 1 2 2
9 8 8 7	2	0 1 1 3 4 7
5 4 2 2 0	3	1 1 3 5 5 6 6
9 9 8 3 1	4	2 2 3 7
7 6 5 5 3 0	5	1 2
5	6	

$n = 21$ $n = 23$

Key: $7\,|\,2$ = £2.70
      $2\,|\,7$

a   What was the least amount spent by the boys?

b   What was the greatest amount spent by the girls?

c   What is the range of amounts spent by the boys?

d   What is the range of amounts spent by the girls?

e   What is the median amount spent by the boys?

f   What is the median amount spent by the girls?

g   Make two comments comparing the amount spent by the boys and by the girls.

N4

4 The marks scored in a test out of 60 by the pupils in classes 4A3 and 4B3 are shown in the back-to-back stem and leaf diagram.

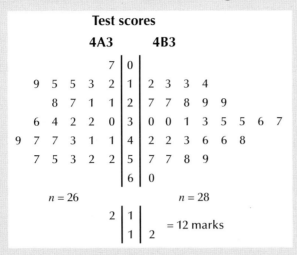

Test scores

		4A3						4B3						
				7	0								
9	5	5	3	2	1	2	3	3	4				
	8	7	1	1	2	7	7	8	9	9			
	6	4	2	2	0	3	0	0	1	3	5	5	6	7
9	7	7	3	1	1	4	2	2	3	6	6	8	
	7	5	3	2	2	5	7	7	8	9			
					6	0							

n = 26   n = 28

2 | 1
1 | 2   = 12 marks

a What was the range of marks for 4A3?

b What was the range of marks for 4B3?

c What was the median mark for class 4A3?

d What was the median mark for class 4B3?

e Make two comments comparing the marks in this test for 4A3 and 4B3.

5 The weekly wages of a group of men and a group of women are shown in the back-to-back stem and leaf diagram.

Weekly wages

Men						Women			
				1	7	8			
	8	7	3	2	1	1	3	4	
7	5	2	2	1	3	0	0	6	7
	4	3	0	0	4	3	4		
			2	1	5				

n = 14   n = 12

3 | 2
2 | 3   = £230

a What is the range of weekly wages for the men?

b What is the range of weekly wages for the women?

c What is the median weekly wage for the men?

d What is the median weekly wage for the women?

e Make two comments comparing the weekly wages of the men and the women.

N4

6 A survey was done of the monthly rental prices for houses in Glasgow and in Inverness.

The results are shown in the stem and leaf diagram.

a Calculate the range of rental prices for houses in Glasgow.

b Calculate the range of rental prices for houses in Inverness.

c What is the median house rental price in Glasgow?

d What is the median house rental price in Inverness?

e Make two comments comparing the house rental prices in Glasgow and Inverness.

House rental prices

Glasgow		Inverness
4 3 2	3	
8 6 4 4 0	4	2 2
8 7 3 2 2 1	5	0 1 6 7
6 5 5 3 2	6	0 3 4 4 7 9
8 5 4	7	4 5 5 6 8
3	8	3 8 8 9

$n = 23$ $n = 21$

1	5	
	5	1

= £510

GO! Activity

Graphs, charts and diagrams are used every day in news reports to explain the information that is being discussed.

They are used a lot in the coverage of general, Scottish Parliament and local elections.

Investigate the way that graphs and charts are used in elections.

Do the graphs and charts always give an accurate description of the data? How can a graph or chart mislead you? Try to find some graphs and charts that do this.

Chapter review

1 The table shows the cost of borrowing £5000 from four different companies.

The prices quoted are the monthly repayments, in pounds (£), with payment protection and without payment protection.

	12 months		24 months		60 months	
	without	with	without	with	without	with
Loans for You	491.67	503.91	276.31	295.42	152.33	158.41
Moonshine Money	520.83	536.83	309.47	316.72	182.36	194.51
Cost Effective Cash	566.67	578.61	356.21	372.33	227.73	239.81
Big Red Loans	466.67	481.32	246.31	270.33	122.56	132.91

Jenny wants to borrow £5000 to buy a new car.

She calculates that she can afford to spend up to £350 per month on the loan.

She has a permanent job, so she decides to take the loan without payment protection.

She wants to pay off the loan as quickly as possible.

a From which company should she take the loan and over how many months?

b How much will the loan actually cost her?

N4

2 A total of 648 adults were asked to choose their favourite hot drink.

The pie chart shows the results.

Favourite drink

a How many adults chose tea as their favourite hot drink?

b How many adults chose coffee (any sort) as their favourite hot drink?

c How many adults did not choose herbal tea as their favourite hot drink?

3 Mr Freeman kept a note of the number of detentions that he issued to each class that he taught last year.

The bar graph shows the results.

Number of detentions

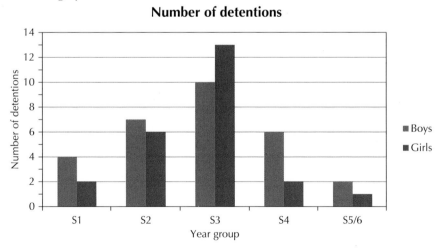

a In which Year group did more girls than boys get a detention?

b How many detentions were given out in total?

c Compare the number of detentions issued to boys and girls across the Year groups. Describe any trend that you see.

4   Lucy runs a café that sells hot and cold drinks.

She notes how much money she takes for the drinks each day for one week.

The line graph shows the results.

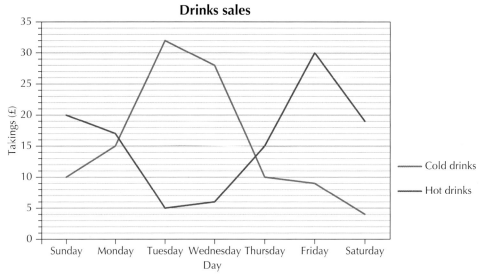

a   How much money did she take for cold drinks on Monday?

b   On which day of the week did she take £15 for hot drink sales?

c   How much money did she take in total for the week in sales of hot and cold drinks?

Lucy notices that she sells more cold drinks on sunny days and more hot drinks on rainy days.

d   During the week that Lucy noted her takings, which days do you think were sunny and which do you think were rainy? Give reasons for your answers.

N4   5   Class 4X1 sat a maths test.

Ms Deans thinks that the number of days a pupil has been absent in the two weeks before the test affects the pupil's result in the test.

She plots a scattergraph of the test results for 15 of her pupils.

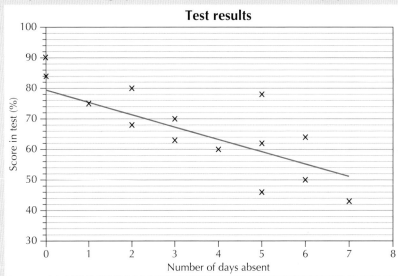

N4

a What percentage did the pupil who was absent for one day in the two weeks before the test score?

b One pupil scored 50% in the test. How many days had that pupil been absent in the two weeks before the test?

c Use the line of best fit to predict the score in the test for a pupil who was absent for 4 days in the two weeks before the test.

d One pupil whose marks are not shown in the scattergraph scored 66% in the test. Use the line of best fit to estimate how many days that pupil had been absent in the two weeks before the test.

e Use the graph to describe the relationship between the number of days a pupil is absent from school in the two weeks before a test and the score they get in the test.

6 The stem and leaf diagram shows the ages of the players in two hockey teams.

Ages of players in years

	Team 1						Team 2					
			9	8	1						
7	6	4	4	3	2	4	5	5	6	7	
7	6	5	2	1	1	3	1	3	3	5	9	9
					4	0	1				

$n = 13$ $n = 13$

| | 4 | 2 | | |
| | | 2 | 4 = 24 years |

a What is the range of ages in Team 1?

b What is the range of ages in Team 2?

c What is the median age in Team 1?

d What is the median age in Team 2?

e Make two comments comparing the ages of the two teams.

- I can extract and interpret data in a table.
  ★ Exercise 28A Q4   ◯ ◯ ⬭

N4
- I can extract and interpret data in a pie chart.
  ★ Exercise 28B Q3   ◯ ◯ ⬭

- I can extract and interpret data in a bar graph and a line graph. ★ Exercise 28C Q2, Q4   ◯ ◯ ⬭

N4
- I can extract and interpret data in a scattergraph.
  ★ Exercise 28C Q6   ◯ ◯ ⬭

- I can extract and interpret data in a stem and leaf diagram. ★ Exercise 28D Q6   ◯ ◯ ⬭

29 Probability

This chapter will show you how to:

- calculate the probability of an event
- compare probabilities
- use relative frequencies to predict the number of times an event will happen.

You should already know:

- how to simplify fractions
- how to compare fractions by finding a common denominator.

Calculating the probability of an event

You will often come across situations where you need to consider the chance of something happening.

If you are playing a board game, what is the chance that you will roll a 6 on the dice?

When you toss a coin, what is the chance that you will get a head?

When you are planning to go out for a walk, what is the chance that it will rain?

Sometimes the chance of something happening is easy to predict mathematically.

This prediction is called the **probability** of the event happening.

The probability of an event is a measure of how likely it is that the event will occur.

An event that is **impossible** has a probability of **0**.

An event that is **certain to happen** has a probability of **1**.

Every other event has a probability somewhere between 0 and 1.

A **probability scale** is a line numbered from 0 to 1 which represents all probabilities.

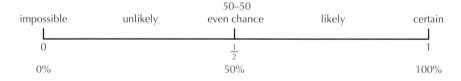

Example 29.1

Use the probability line above to decide the probability of the following happening.

a A man will live to be 654 years old.

b It will rain most days somewhere in Scotland in November.

c If I put my bare hand in a bowl of water, my hand will get wet.

d If I fall out of a first floor window I will not hurt myself.

a The probability is 0. ●————————————

> It is impossible for a man to live to be 654 years old.

b The probability is between $\frac{1}{2}$ and 1. ●———

> The weather in Scotland in November is usually quite wet, so it is likely that it will rain somewhere in Scotland on most of the days.

c The probability is 1. ●————————

> If I put my bare hand into water it is certain it will get wet.

d The probability is between 0 and $\frac{1}{2}$. ●———

> It is unlikely that I will not hurt myself if I fall out of a first floor window, but there is a small chance that I will be unhurt.

It is usually more useful to be able to put an actual value on the probability of an event occurring, rather than just knowing if it is less than $\frac{1}{2}$ or more than $\frac{1}{2}$.

When you are working out the probability of something happening you need to:

- work out the total number of possible outcomes
- work out the number of these outcomes that would be successful. 'Successful' means the number of outcomes that would be a result that you would want.

The probability of an event is found using this formula:

$$\textbf{Probability of an event} = \frac{\textbf{number of successful outcomes}}{\textbf{total possible number of outcomes}}$$

For example, when you toss a coin and need a head to win:

- there are 2 possible outcomes, a head or a tail
- only 1 of these outcomes would be a success for you – the head.

So the probability of getting a head is:

$$\text{Probability} = \frac{\text{number of ways the coin can land heads up}}{\text{total number of ways the coin can land}} = \frac{1}{2}$$

This is written as P(head) = $\frac{1}{2}$

Example 29.2

When a coin is tossed, what is the probability that it will land tails up?

$$\text{Probability} = \frac{\text{number of ways the coin can land tails up}}{\text{total number of ways the coin can land}} = \frac{1}{2}$$

P(tail) = $\frac{1}{2}$

Example 29.3

A bag contains 8 red sweets, 5 yellow sweets and 7 green sweets.

What is the probability that a sweet picked at random will be yellow?

Give your answer as a fraction in its simplest form.

Total number of sweets is 8 + 5 + 7 = 20 •——— You need to find the total number of sweets in the bag. The number of sweets is the total possible number of outcomes.

$$\text{Probability} = \frac{\text{number of yellow sweets}}{\text{total number of sweets}}$$

$$= \frac{5}{20} = \frac{1}{4}$$ •——— Remember to simplify the fraction.

$$P(\text{yellow}) = \frac{1}{4}$$ •——— A successful outcome in this question is to pick a yellow sweet.

Example 29.4

When using an ordinary dice, what is the probability that the number rolled will be a 4 or a 5?

Give your answer as a fraction in its simplest form.

Total number of outcomes = 6 •——— There are 6 different numbers on an ordinary dice so the total number of possible outcomes is 6.

Total number of successful outcomes = 2 •——— A successful outcome is a 4 or a 5, so there are 2 successful outcomes

$$\text{Probability} = \frac{\text{number of successful outcomes}}{\text{total number of ways a dice can land}} = \frac{2}{6}$$

$$P(4 \text{ or } 5) = \frac{2}{6} = \frac{1}{3}$$ •——— Always simplify the fraction.

Exercise 29A

1   An ordinary dice numbered 1 to 6 is rolled.

What is the change that it will show:
   a a 6   **b** a 3   **c** an even number   **d** a number bigger than 4?

2   The rules for a new mathematical board game need you to roll a prime number to start.
   What is the chance that you will be able to start on the first roll of the dice?

3   A nine-sided spinner is marked with the letters A to I.

What is the probability that the spinner will land on:
   a the letter C   **b** a vowel   **c** a consonant?

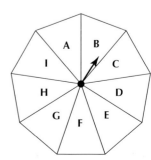

4 An ordinary pack of cards contains 52 cards.

It is shuffled and a card is drawn at random.

   a What is the probability that the card drawn is a Heart?

   b What is the probability that the card drawn is a Queen?

   c What is the probability that the card drawn is a red?

   d What is the probability that the card drawn has a value from 7 to 10?

   e What is the probability that the card drawn is the Ace of Spades?

★ **5** At a school fundraising event, one of the stalls is a 'treasure hunt'.

Lose	Win 50p	Lose	Lose	Win 25p
Win 25p	Lose	Lose	Win 25p	Lose
Lose	Win £1	Lose	Lose	Win 50p
Lose	Lose	Win 25p	Lose	Win 25p
Win 50p	Lose	Lose	Win 50p	Lose

Every square is all covered so that the customer doesn't see what prize they might win.

People pay 50p to choose a square from the board.

   a What is the probability that you will win £1?

   b What is the probability that you will win 25p?

   c What is the probability that you will lose?

How many squares are there in total?

The stall holder sells all 25 tickets and pays out all the prizes.

   d How much profit did they make?

★ **6** A bag contains 30 red counters, 15 blue counters, 10 green counters and 25 yellow counters.

A counter is drawn at random and is then replaced in the bag.

   a What is the probability that the counter drawn is red?

   b What is the probability that the counter drawn is blue?

   c What is the probability that the counter drawn is green?

   d What is the probability that the counter drawn is yellow?

   e What is the probability that the counter drawn is either red or green?

   f What is the probability that the counter drawn is **not** blue?

Comparing probabilities

One of the main reasons that we work with probabilities is to compare the chances of different events occurring.

Probabilities are compared in the same way as fractions.

You will need to:

- change all the fractions so that they have a common denominator, or
- change all the fractions into decimal fractions, or
- change all the fractions into percentages.

Once all the probabilities have been changed to the same format, it is easy to see which is the highest and therefore the most likely to happen.

Example 29.5

There are three classes in fourth year at Kilmore High School.

- in 4A1 there are 12 girls and 16 boys
- in 4A2 there are 14 girls and 16 boys
- in 4A3 there are 10 girls and 12 boys.

A pupil is to be chosen at random from each of the three classes.

a For each class, calculate the probability that the pupil chosen is a girl.

b Which class has the highest probability that the chosen pupil will be a girl?

a The probability that a girl will be chosen is:

for 4A1 this is $\frac{12}{28} = \frac{3}{7}$

for 4A2 this is $\frac{14}{30} = \frac{7}{15}$

for 4A3 this is $\frac{10}{22} = \frac{5}{11}$

> The probability that a girl is chosen is $\frac{\text{total number of girls in the class}}{\text{total number of pupils in the class}}$

b **Method 1   Common denominators**

4A1: $\frac{3}{7} = \frac{495}{1155}$

4A2: $\frac{7}{15} = \frac{539}{1155}$

4A3: $\frac{5}{11} = \frac{525}{1155}$

The class with the highest probability of a girl being chosen is 4A2.

> To compare the fractions, they need to be changed so that they have a common denominator
>
> The lowest common denominator here is $7 \times 15 \times 11 = 1155$.

> The numerator is highest for 4A2, so the chance of picking a girl is highest in that class.

Method 2   Changing the fractions to decimals

4A1: $3 \div 7 = 0.429$

4A2: $7 \div 15 = 0.467$

4A3: $5 \div 11 = 0.455$

The class with the highest probability of a girl being chosen is 4A2.

> To change a fraction to a decimal fraction you need to calculate numerator ÷ denominator.
>
> Round your answers to 3 decimal places so that you can make an accurate comparison.

> The answer for 4A2 is highest.

Method 3 Changing the fractions to percentages

> Remember that to change a fraction to a percentage, you need to multiply it by 100%.

4A1: $\frac{3}{7} = \frac{3}{7} \times 100\% = 100 \div 7 \times 3 = 42.9\%$

4A2: $\frac{7}{15} = \frac{7}{15} \times 100\% = 100 \div 15 \times 7 = 46.7\%$

4A3: $\frac{5}{11} = \frac{5}{11} \times 100\% = 100 \div 11 \times 5 = 45.5\%$

The class with the highest probability of a girl being chosen is 4A2.

> The percentage for class 4A2 is highest.

You can choose which of these three methods you use.

Exercise 29B

1   Parkview Academy has three classes in S4.

A survey is done to find out how many pupils in each class walk to school each day.

The results are shown in the table.

Class	Total number in class	Number in class who walk
4M1	27	14
4M2	28	15
4M3	30	17

a   What is the probability that a pupil chosen at random in each class walks to school?

b   Which class has the highest probability that a pupil will walk to school?

> ⚠ Work out the decimal fraction or percentage.

2   A football club holds two raffles to raise funds.

The club sells 125 red tickets at 50 p each and 90 blue tickets at £1 each.

There are 25 prizes for the red tickets and 20 prizes for the blue tickets.

Bert buys 1 red ticket and 1 blue ticket.

a   Find the probability that Bert wins a prize in the red raffle.

b   Find the probability that Bert wins a prize in the blue raffle.

c   Which raffle gives Bert a better chance of winning a prize?

The club spends a total of £60 on all the prizes for the two raffles.

d   How much money do they raise with these two raffles?

★ 3   A television quiz show offers the winning player a choice in the 'end game'.

The player can either:

● pick 1 card from 25 cards available, or

● spin an octagonal spinner once.

There are 6 winning cards and 2 winning numbers on the spinner.

a   What is the probability that the player will win a prize if they pick a card?

b   What is the probability that the player will win a prize if they spin the spinner?

c   Which should the player choose?

4 The table shows the number of hours of sunshine each day for one week in June in Benidorm.

Day	Sunday	Monday	Tuesday	Wednesday	Thursday	Friday	Saturday
Hours	7	8	8	10	11	12	12

What is the chance that there were 10 or more hours of sunshine on a day chosen at random?

N4 Relative frequencies

Another name for probability is **relative frequency**.

The relative frequency can be used to predict how often an event will happen.

Example 29.6

The relative frequency of a coin landing heads up is 0.5.

Calculate the number of heads that would be expected when a coin is tossed 50 times.

$50 \times 0.5 = 25$ ● —— The number of heads expected is the number of times the coin is tossed multiplied by the relative frequency of landing heads up.

Example 29.7

The relative frequency of rolling a 3 on an ordinary fair dice is $\frac{1}{6}$.

How many 3s would you expect if the dice is rolled 432 times?

$432 \times \dfrac{1}{6} = 72$

You would expect 72 3s.

Example 29.8

Naomi carries out a survey of the makes of cars she sees passing her house.

Her results are shown in the table.

Make of car	Number
Ford	16
Kia	9
Renault	11
Mercedes	5
Land Rover	3
Other	6

The local multi-storey car park, which has space for 1600 cars, is full.

How many of each make of car would she expect to find in the car park, based on her survey?

N4

You need to add a column for **relative frequency** to the table. For each make you need to divide the number of that make by the total number of cars that Naomi saw.

Make of car	Number	Relative frequency	Expected number
Ford	16	$\frac{16}{50} = 0.32$	$0.32 \times 1600 = 512$
Kia	9	$\frac{9}{50} = 0.18$	$0.18 \times 1600 = 288$
Renault	11	$\frac{11}{50} = 0.22$	$0.22 \times 1600 = 352$
Mercedes	5	$\frac{5}{50} = 0.10$	$0.1 \times 1600 = 160$
Land Rover	3	$\frac{3}{50} = 0.06$	$0.06 \times 1600 = 96$
Other	6	$\frac{6}{50} = 0.12$	$0.12 \times 1600 = 192$
Total	**50**	**1.00**	**1600**

The **expected number** of each make is the relative frequency of that make multiplied by the total number of cars in the car park.

Exercise 29C

1 In a game show, the contestant wins a prize if they draw a King from a pack of playing cards.

   After each contestant draws a card, it is replaced in the pack ready for the next contestant.

   The relative frequency of picking a King from a pack of playing cards is $\frac{1}{13}$.

   A total of 91 contestants take part in the game show.

   How many prizes would you expect to be won?

2 Ed carries out a survey of the colour of cars in the school car park.

   His results are shown in the table.

Colour	Number
Red	23
Black	12
Silver	19
White	6
Green	11
Blue	9

   a Copy the table and add a column to show the relative frequency of each colour.

   b Based on his survey, how many cars of each colour would he expect to find in the local car park containing 1440 cars?

N4 ★ **3** A dice is rolled 45 times.

The results are shown in the table.

Result	Number of times
1	6
2	10
3	7
4	8
5	6
6	8

a Calculate the relative frequency of each result.

b Use the relative frequencies to predict how many of each result you would expect if you rolled the dice 1000 times.

c Do you think the dice is fair?

Use your working to explain your answer.

GO! Activity

A number of lotteries are run in Britain.

These include Lotto (the National Lottery), the Postcode Lottery, the Scottish Children's Lottery and Euromillions.

In Lotto, you need to choose 6 numbers out of a total of 59 numbers available.

The probability of winning the jackpot prize is 1 in 45 057 474, that is, about 1 in 45 million.

Investigate the probability of winning the jackpot prize in other lotteries in Britain.

Which one do you think is the best one to play?

You should consider how many numbers you get to choose from, how many numbers you have to pick and the cost of a single ticket.

Some lotteries only offer a jackpot prize whereas others offer smaller prizes as well.

Does this affect which lottery game you think is best?

Chapter review

1 Jess has a bag containing 13 red sweets, 21 green sweets, 10 blue sweets and 16 yellow sweets.

a When Jess picks a sweet at random from the bag, what is the probability that it will be green?

Give your answer as a fraction in its lowest terms.

Jess doesn't like the taste of the blue sweets but likes all the others.

b What is the probability that she will pick a sweet at random that she likes?

2   To start a maths board game, a player has to roll an even number less than 6 on an ordinary dice.

What is the probability that a player will be able to start on her next roll of the dice?

3   In a television game show, a contestant must roll 2 ordinary dice.

A contestant will win the top prize if they roll a 'double 6'.

a   What is the probability that a contestant will win the top prize?

A contestant will win a lower-value prize if the **total** on the two dice is 4 or less.

b   What is the probability that they will win a lower-value prize?

4   Cowglen High School conducts a survey to find out the probability of a child in S1 walking to school.

In class 1A, 8 out of 26 pupils walk, in class 1B, 6 out of 21 walk and in class 1C, 9 out of 24 walk.

In which class is there the highest probability that a pupil chosen at random walks to school?

N4

5   In football a player will sometimes have to take a penalty kick.

The player places the ball on a spot 11 metres from the goal line and then kicks the ball towards the goal mouth.

The player kicking the ball will aim at a particular area of the goal mouth.

Research has shown that the relative frequencies of each area of the goal mouth being targeted are as shown in the table.

Area of the goal mouth targeted	Relative frequency
Top left	0.24
Top right	0.2
Bottom left	0.4
Bottom right	0.16

In one season 125 penalties were taken in the Scottish First Division.

a   How many would you expect to be aimed at each area of the goal mouth?

b   Why do you think more kicks are aimed at the bottom left than any other area of the goal mouth?

- I can calculate the probability of an event.
  ★ Exercise 29A Q5, Q6

- I can compare probabilities. ★ Exercise 29B Q3

N4
- I can use relative frequencies to predict the number of times an event will happen. ★ Exercise 29C Q3

Unit 3 Case study

Egg production

> **This case study focuses on the following skills:**
>
> - comparing data **(Ch. 8)**
> - calculating with decimal numbers **(Ch. 23)**
> - finding a percentage of an amount **(Ch. 24)**
> - extracting and interpreting data in a table and in a back-to-back stem and leaf diagram **(Ch. 28)**.

A sample of 25 eggs was taken from each of two hen houses.

The eggs were weighed in grams.

The weights are shown in the stem and leaf diagram.

Weights of eggs in grams

```
        House 1                           House 2

                        3 | 1  1  3  5
        4  4  3  2  1  0 | 4 | 4  4  5  6  7
  8  7  7  6  3  0  0  | 5 | 0  0  1  2  7  8  8
           5  3  2  1  1 | 6 | 0  0  1  2  2  2  2  3
              2  1  1  0  0 | 7 | 0
                    1  0 | 8 |

        n = 25                    n = 25

                        0 | 5
                                   = 50 g
                        5 | 0
```

1   What is the median weight in:

    a   House 1   **b**   House 2?

2   What is the range of weights in:

    a   House 1   **b**   House 2?

3   Make two comments comparing the weights of eggs in House 1 and House 2.

Eggs are graded according to their weight. The producer charges different amounts per egg depending on the grading.

The table shows the different grades.

Weight	Size	Price per egg
73 g or more	Very Large	21 p
63 g to 72.9 g	Large	17 p
53 g to 62.9 g	Medium	15 p
43 g to 52.9 g	Small	12 p
less than 43 g	Ungraded	5 p

N4

4 How many eggs in the sample from House 1 would be graded as Large?

5 How many eggs in the sample from House 2 would be Ungraded?

The egg producer assumes that the samples taken from the two houses are typical of all the eggs produced by the houses.

He collects a total of 700 eggs from House 1 and 500 eggs from House 2.

6 How many of each grade of egg will he get from each house?

8% of the eggs collected can't be sold because they are dirty or damaged.

The producer sells all the remaining eggs.

7 Calculate the total amount of money that he will get when he sells all of the eggs.